BRUNEL UNIVERSITY LIBRARY

Bannerman Centre,
Uxbridge, Middlesex,
UB8 3PH

Renewals: www.brunel.ac.uk/renew
OR
01895 266141

LONG LOAN

WITHDRAWN

W. L. I. H. E.

GORDON HOUSE LIBRARY

300 St

Twicke

081 891 0121

D1428565

WL 0132306

IMPERATIVES, BEHAVIORS,
AND
IDENTITIES

Essays in Early American

Cultural History

Jack P. Greene

UNIVERSITY PRESS OF VIRGINIA

Charlottesville and London

THE UNIVERSITY PRESS OF VIRGINIA

Copyright © 1992 by the Rector and Visitors
of the University of Virginia

First published 1992

Library of Congress Cataloging-in-Publication Data
Greene, Jack P.
    Imperatives, behaviors, and identities : essays in early American
cultural history / Jack P. Greene.
    p. cm.
    Includes bibliographical references and index.
    ISBN 0-8139-1406-X (cloth).—ISBN 0-8139-1408-6 (paper)
    1. United States—Civilization—To 1783.   I. Title.
E163.G74   1993
973—dc20   92-15422
                                                              CIP

Printed in the United States of America

E
173
G74

WLIHE | LOC. GH
CONTROL No. 0 813 914 06x
BAR CODE No. 0132306?
CLASS No. 973 GRE

MARIA GREY
LIBRARY
W. L. I. H. E.

Contents

Preface

ALTHOUGH scholars have used the concept *culture* for only a little more than a century and a half, they have endowed it with a wide variety of meanings.[1] Early generations of early American historians often used the older concept *civilization*[2] or the more general term *life*, as in Arthur M. Schlesinger and Dixon Ryan Fox's A History of American Life series, to cover what anthropologists were already referring to as culture. When, starting in the late 1930s, a few early American historians, the most prolific of whom were Louis B. Wright, Perry Miller, and Carl Bridenbaugh, began to devote more systematic and sophisticated attention to aspects of cultural history, they generally used the term *culture* to apply mostly to the intellectual, religious, literary, and artistic activities of the cultivated segments of colonial society and to the social and material expressions of those activities.

Published in 1957 as a volume in The New American Nation Series, Wright's *The Cultural Life of the American Colonies, 1607–1763*[3] is representative of this approach. Beginning with a chapter on social structure and elite development, it proceeds through a series of subjects that the author and his contemporaries considered to be the appropriate components of cul-

---

[1] See the extensive discussion in A. L. Kroeber and Clyde Kluckholm, *Culture: A Critical Review of Concepts and Definitions* (Cambridge, Mass., 1952).

[2] For instance, Edward Eggleston, *The Transit of Civilization from England to America in the Seventeenth Century* (New York, 1901).

[3] Louis B. Wright, *The Cultural Life of the American Colonies, 1607–1763* (New York, 1957).

ture: social values, ethnic divisions among the European settler population, religion, education, books and libraries, literary productions, drama and music, architecture and the decorative arts, scientific activities, and the press and communications. According to this conception, culture served as a kind of grand residual category that included all subjects that did not obviously fall within the realms of economics and politics.

Gradually, however, starting in the late 1960s and early 1970s, culture began to acquire a more central place in early American historical studies. This development was both expressed and stimulated by the massive outpouring of studies on the religious and intellectual development of colonial New England,[4] the innovative studies of early American education by Bernard Bailyn and Lawrence Cremin,[5] the sophisticated analyses of late eighteenth-century American political ideology by Bailyn, Gordon S. Wood, J. G. A. Pocock, Joyce Appleby, and others,[6] and the powerful dissection of white Anglo-American racial attitudes by Winthrop D. Jordan.[7] The notion of culture implicit in these works did not, however, directly challenge older conceptions of culture as fundamentally the expression of ideas and practices of elites and other privileged social groups.

But the new attention and emphasis upon cultural history also grew logically out of the even more powerful turn toward social and community studies that emerged at the same time. As scholars more and more came to sense the need for a more explicit notion of what made a community a community, a society a society, or a region a region, they increasingly came to employ a more inclusive conception of culture of the sort long used by anthropologists. By this conception, culture connotes not just the extrapolitical and

---

[4] David D. Hall, "Religion and Society: Problems and Reconsiderations," in Jack P. Greene and J. R. Pole, eds., *Colonial British America: Essays in the New History of the Early Modern Era* (Baltimore, 1984), 317–44, provides an excellent analysis of this literature. See also Jack P. Greene, "Recent Developments in the Historiography of Colonial New England," *Acadiensis* 18 (1988): 143–77.

[5] Bernard Bailyn, *Education and the Forming of American Society: Needs and Opportunities for Study* (Chapel Hill, N.C., 1960); Lawrence A. Cremin, *American Education: The Colonial Experience 1607–1763* (New York, 1970).

[6] Principally, Bernard Bailyn, *The Ideological Origins of the American Revolution* (Cambridge, Mass., 1967); Gordon S. Wood, *The Creation of the American Republic, 1776–1787* (Chapel Hill, N.C., 1969); J. G. A. Pocock, *The Machiavellian Moment: Florentine Political Thought and the Atlantic Republican Tradition* (Princeton, N.J., 1975); Joyce Appleby, *Capitalism and the New Social Order: The Republican Vision of the 1790s* (New York, 1984).

[7] Winthrop D. Jordan, *White over Black: American Attitudes toward the Negro, 1550–1812* (Chapel Hill, N.C., 1968).

extraeconomic activities of the socially dominant but the entire range of values, practices, behaviors, and character traits that identify all the people of specific places, times, or social groupings as distinctive and make them, as both collectivities and individuals, in many respects more similar to each other than to peoples of other times, places, or social groupings. Consisting of those learned patterns of behavior and social interaction that characterize those populations, the socially approved material and social expressions of those behaviors, and the symbolic representations that those populations construct to endow their behaviors and experiences with larger meanings and comprehensibility, culture, in this expanded conception, has been slowly acquiring a central place in recent historical studies.

Works reflecting this new emphasis include many of the best studies published in early American studies over the past fifteen years. Philip Greven's subtle evocation of the emergence of two contrasting styles of child rearing and religious orientation,[8] Rhys Isaac's reconstruction of two competing mental and social worlds in late eighteenth-century Virginia,[9] and Mechal Sobel's suggestive discussion of selected aspects of the process of cultural exchange between Europeans and Africans in the formation of the culture of eighteenth-century Virginia[10] are three of the more imaginative and prominent of many recent monographs with a strong cultural dimension. On a more general level, Richard L. Bushman's effort to erect a framework for a comprehensive cultural history of early America around the tensions between genteel and vernacular styles,[11] the development by historical geographers of the concept of the culture hearth as a device to comprehend the process by which in new societies, in D. W. Meinig's words, "new basic cultural systems and configurations are developed and nurtured before spreading vigorously outward to alter the character of much larger areas,"[12]

---

[8] Philip Greven, *The Protestant Temperament: Patterns of Child-Rearing, Religious Experience, and the Self in Early America* (New York, 1977).

[9] Rhys Isaac, *The Transformation of Virginia, 1740–1790* (Chapel Hill, N.C., 1982).

[10] Mechal Sobel, *The World They Made Together: Black and White Values in Eighteenth-Century Virginia* (Princeton, N.J., 1989).

[11] Richard L. Bushman, "American High-Style and Vernacular Cultures," in Greene and Pole, *Colonial British America*, 345–83.

[12] Robert D. Mitchell, "The Formation of Early American Cultural Regions: An Interpretation," in James R. Gibson, ed., *European Settlement and Development in North America: Essays on Geographical Change in Honour and Memory of Andrew Hill Clark* (Toronto, 1978), 66–90; Terry G. Jordan and Matti Kaups, *The American Backwoods Frontier: An Ethnic and Ecological Interpretation* (Baltimore, 1989); and D. W. Meinig, *Atlantic America, 1492–1800* (New Haven, 1986), 52.

and David Hackett Fischer's extended effort to illustrate the importance of
the English cultural inheritance by tracing the transfer and persistence of
specific English folkways in four American regions[13] are also worthy of note.

This volume is a collection of sixteen essays on selected themes in this rich
area of analysis. Fifteen of them have been published previously in widely
scattered places, seven as chapters in books, five as journal articles, one as a
newspaper essay, one as a separate booklet, and one as the introduction to a
book. Of these, all but four have appeared since 1984 and all but one after
1975. They may thus seem to represent a relatively recent engagement with
cultural themes in early America. But my interest in this area is much older,
going back to my earliest research as a young Fulbright student in London
in 1953–54.

My primary project during that year was to investigate the development
of the legislatures of the southern continental colonies during the eighteenth
century, and that ambitious undertaking required me to spend most of my
time diligently working through the vast collections of official records and
papers of prominent public officials, most of which were at the Public Record Office. For the times when that institution was closed, early in the morning and on Saturday afternoons, I set myself the task of reading in the British Museum (now the British Library) as much as I could find of
the contemporary published descriptive and historical literature on the
broader early modern British Empire in America. Beginning with works
about the empire as a whole and the four colonies on which my dissertation
focused, I soon moved on to other colonies farther north and in the West
Indies. My immediate purpose was to develop at least a rudimentary sense
of how contemporaries viewed some of the political and constitutional developments that I was investigating and to get some comparative perspective on
those developments.

As I read through this literature, however, I slowly came to realize that,
while it did indeed contain some useful material for that purpose, it spoke
far more directly and sometimes eloquently to the even more fundamental
subject of how contemporaries defined and represented the still relatively
new societies that were being created under British auspices in America,
societies whose character, history, and inhabitants they sought to describe.
Out of these materials I began to draw questions that have never ceased to
fascinate me, questions about what the settlers of those societies thought they

---

[13] David Hackett Fischer, *Albion's Seed: Four British Folkways in America* (New York, 1989).
Among several other similiar, if more limited efforts, David Grayson Allen, *In English Ways:
The Movement of Societies and the Transferral of English Local Law and Custom to Massachusetts
Bay in the Seventeenth Century* (Chapel Hill, N.C., 1981) is especially important.

had done and were doing in America, how they represented themselves to the outside world and especially to the significant other world of Britain that had spawned them, and how, in turn, these American creations appeared to outsiders.

But many years passed before I found time and occasion to pursue more systematically my interest in these and other questions about early American cultural history. My research interests during the late 1950s and early 1960s, like those of many historians of my generation in this field, were firmly fixed upon the political history of the late colonial and Revolutionary eras, and I did not make a serious foray into cultural history until the mid–1960s while I was finishing up my edition of the diary of the Richmond County, Virginia, planter Landon Carter. After considering a variety of possible introductions to that extraordinarily rich text, I opted to write a character study that would analyze Carter in terms of both his personal values and the social imperatives of the gentry group of which he was a conspicuous member.[14] During the next decade, I also wrote several related pieces on aspects of colonial and Revolutionary Virginia political culture,[15] a more general essay on the ways in which inherited ideology and the circumstances of political life combined to shape legislative behavior all over colonial British America,[16] and a few early pieces more directly in the field of cultural history.[17] For the most part, however, I pursued my interest in this area primarily by encouraging graduate students whose own sensibilities led them in that direction to write dissertations in cultural history and by myself formulating but never finding time to pursue ambitious projects to study such subjects as changing styles of life and patterns of consumption and material

[14] This work was separately published as *Landon Carter: An Inquiry into the Personal Values and Social Imperatives of the Eighteenth-Century Virginia Gentry* (Charlottesville, Va., 1967).

[15] For example, "Society, Ideology, and Politics: An Analysis of the Political Culture of Mid-Eighteenth-Century Virginia," in Richard M. Jellison, ed., *Society, Freedom, and Conscience: The Coming of the Revolution in Virginia, Massachusetts, and New York* (New York, 1976), 14–76, 191–200; " 'Virtus et Libertas': Political Culture, Social Change, and the Origins of the American Revolution in Virginia," in Jeffrey Crow, ed., *The Southern Experience in the American Revolution* (Chapel Hill, N.C., 1978), 55–102; and "Character, Persona, and Authority: A Study in Alternative Styles of Political Leadership in Revolutionary Virginia," in W. Robert Higgins, ed., *The Revolutionary War in the South: Essays in Honor of John Richard Alden* (Durham, N.C., 1979), 3–42.

[16] "Political Mimesis: A Consideration of the Historical and Cultural Roots of Legislative Behavior in the British Colonies in the Eighteenth Century," *American Historical Review* 75 (1969): 337–67.

[17] The most important of these are included in this volume as chapters six, seven, ten, and eleven.

culture through probate records or collective social priorities through an analysis of public spending.

Only during the late 1970s did I move into this area in a more serious and sustained way. At that time, I began to try to utilize materials from contemporary descriptions, histories, travel accounts, and other discursive writings of the kind that I had first encountered in London a quarter century earlier as a basis for a study of the changing corporate identities of the colonies and inhabitants of Virginia, Barbados, Jamaica, and South Carolina—Britain's four most valued colonies—between the late sixteenth and the early nineteenth centuries.[18] This project has turned out to be far less tractable than I ever imagined and remains incomplete. However, my thinking about the problem of identity formation in new societies, along with my recent effort, *Pursuits of Happiness*, to situate the roots of American culture in the dominant social and individual aspirations of successive generations of settlers as they worked themselves out and were reinforced by the social circumstances and social histories of the several distinctive cultural regions of colonial America,[19] has forced me to confront anew a number of problems about colonial and Revolutionary culture that I have endeavored to explore in the essays published in this volume.

The volume begins with a general essay, "Mastery and the Definition of Cultural Space in Early America: A Perspective." This chapter considers the extent to which an implicit idea of mastery has been central to definitions of America since the Columbian encounter and attempts to articulate a perspective for looking at early America as an agglomeration of contested cultural spaces defined by a process of negotiation between mastering and mastered groups.

The next four chapters analyze aspects of the definition of three of those cultural spaces in the West Indies and the Lower South. Chapter two, "Changing Identity in the British West Indies in the Early Modern Era: Barbados as a Case Study," traces the changing representations of that colony from its first settlement through the late eighteenth century. Chapter three, "Colonial South Carolina and the Caribbean Connection," considers South Carolina's Caribbean roots, its continuing connection with the West Indian colonies during the colonial period, and the developmental parallels and contrasts between it and the island colonies that also emerged out of the Barbadian culture hearth. Chapter four, "Early South Carolina and the Psy-

---

[18] The current working title of this volume is *Paradise Defined: Studies in the Formation and Changing Character of Corporate Identities in Early Modern Plantation America, 1585 to 1820*.

[19] Jack P. Greene, *Pursuits of Happiness: The Social Development of Early Modern British Colonies and the Formation of American Culture* (Chapel Hill, N.C., 1988).

chology of British Colonization," uses South Carolina promotional literature to illuminate the individual and social goals that drew immigrants to that colony. Chapter five, "Travails of an Infant Colony: The Search for Viability, Coherence, and Identity in Colonial Georgia," explores the changing identity of Britain's newest continental colony from its founding until the outbreak of the American Revolution.

Chapters six through eight return to general themes involving eighteenth-century colonial and post-colonial cultural development. Chapter six, "Search for Identity: An Interpretation of the Meaning of Selected Patterns of Social Response in Eighteenth-Century America," explores how the collective self-conceptions of colonial British Americans were affected by their perceived failure to live up to the standards of either the earliest generations of settlers or contemporary metropolitan norms between roughly 1700 and 1775. Chapter seven, "Independence and Dependence: The Psychology of the Colonial Relationship on the Eve of the American Revolution," briefly considers the conditions that fostered both an imperative of independence and a yearning for dependence among free colonial British Americans and the ways in which the tension between those two impulses affected colonial attitudes toward their connection with Britain. Chapter eight, "Independence, Improvement, and Authority: Toward a Framework for Understanding the Histories of the Southern Backcountry during the Era of the Revolution," tries to show how well-developed notions about independence, improvement, and authority operated to shape the individual and social goals of new areas of settlement in the southern backcountry and to make those societies as much a reflection of the older colonial British-American world as a prefigurement of a new American order.

Chapters nine through eleven involve additional considerations of the sources and meaning of political language in mid and late eighteenth-century America. Chapter nine, "The Concept of Virtue in Late Colonial British America," analyzes American usage of the concept of virtue as a basis for exploring the profound divergence between that usage and the ideology of civic virtue expounded by country ideologists in contemporary Britain. By contrast, Chapter ten, "All Men Are Created Equal: Some Reflections on the Character of the American Revolution," shows how, reinforced by conditions in America, traditional British ideas about civic competence, manhood, and independence affected American ideas about the franchise during the American Revolution and functioned to limit the social thrust of the Revolution. Chapter eleven, " 'Slavery or Independence': Some Reflections on the Relationship among Liberty, Black Bondage, and Equality in Revolutionary South Carolina," considers the ways in which local social conditions, specifically the experience with chattel slavery and a highly stratified free society, affected the conceptions of liberty and equality in South Carolina during the Revolution.

Chapters twelve through fifteen examine other aspects of American cultural development during the Revolutionary era. An effort to put the appearance of American nationalism in its broadest social context, chapter twelve, "A Fortuitous Convergence: Culture, Circumstance, and Contingency in the Emergence of the American Nation," stresses both the problematic and the contingent character of American nationalism during the era of the Revolution. Chapter thirteen, "The Pursuit of Happiness, the Private Realm, and the Movement for a Stronger National Government," briefly considers the ways in which the private orientation of American society affected the movement for a new constitution during the late 1780s. Chapter fourteen, "'An Instructive Monitor': Experience and the Fabrication of the Federal Constitution," analyzes the diverse ways in which those who wrote, argued for, and ratified the Federal Constitution used the concept of experience and the extraordinary importance they attached to their own immediate experience in trying to govern themselves beginning in 1776. Chapter fifteen, "The Constitution of 1787 and the Question of Southern Distinctiveness," reexamines older questions about the extent to which the southern states constituted a distinctive entity with a coherent regional consciousness at the time of the ratifying of the Constitution.

The volume concludes with another general piece. Chapter sixteen, "America and the Creation of the Revolutionary Intellectual World of the Enlightenment," traces in broad outline the changing meaning of America for Europeans from the Columbian encounter until the French Revolution and explores the influence of the conception of America as an unformed space upon traditional European social and political thought.

Written one by one at various times over two decades, many by invitation or in response to some contemporary historiographical issue, and many also originally appearing in limited publications that are now inaccessible, these essays range over such a wide variety of topics that at first glance they may seem to lack internal coherence. However, except for chapter sixteen, they mostly deal with one or the other of two closely connected subjects: first, the formation of the new English or, after 1707, British cultural spaces in America and their special character as dependent and derivative entities on the far periphery of an established core culture, each of them having its own distinctive physical space and socioeconomic and political situation; and, second, the bearing of experience and social circumstances upon the priorities of American cultures before and during the American Revolution.

By metropolitan standards, the cultures created by Europeans and their offspring in America were in most ways peculiar. Animated by a powerful urge to re-create an English or British world in the new, colonial settlers nonetheless everywhere created societies and cultures that diverged sharply from those they had left behind and to which they long remained attached. These do not fall neatly into any of the categories into which historians have classified European societies—feudal, court, old regime, corporate. If, in many ways, including their devotion to private property and their sanctioning of labor exploitation of marginal groups, these American entities remained European, their newness, their differing physical contexts, and many of their social attributes, including the broad scope for private endeavor, the widespread achievement of independence by free men, the deep empowering process to which that achievement testified, the absence of legally privileged social orders, the comparative weakness of authority structures, and the shallowness of elite culture, all operated to produce distinctive colonial societies and cultures that need to be understood and analyzed in their own terms.

Among the most important of a cluster of interrelated themes addressed in these essays, eight are especially prominent: 1) how the aspirations that immigrants brought with them from the Old World or from older parts of the New World shaped their behavior and social objectives in new settlements and provided standards for the social evaluation of those settlements (chapters one, four, and eight); 2) the extent to which social practices developed in an older American cultural hearth were or were not reproduced in new places and why (chapters three and eight); 3) how the collective identities of political entities were formed and changed and were bounded by considerations of place, time, and social organization (chapters two and five); 4) how social and behavorial standards inherited from the Old World and from earlier times affected evaluations of self and society (chapter six); 5) how tensions between the imperatives of independence and mastery and the yearning for dependence affected colonial relations with Britain (chapter seven); 6) how social circumstances and experience in America changed or reinforced the meaning of inherited terms of political analysis (chapters nine, ten, eleven, and fourteen); 7) how the broad scope of the private sphere affected activities and attitudes toward the public sphere (chapter thirteen); and 8) how local loyalties and social and political experience operated to facilitate or to inhibit the formation of larger regional and national consciousness during the Revolutionary era (chapters twelve and fifteen).

In preparing this volume for publication, I have been careful to make no substantive changes in the fifteen republished pieces. For that reason, the volume contains some minor repetitions of central themes. I have, however, made a few small editorial changes; standardized form, spelling, and citations; and added at the end of each chapter a short paragraph recounting its history and giving the place of original publication.

Several people helped in putting this volume together. Peter S. Onuf read through a large number of pieces and offered excellent advice about selection and organization. Amy Turner Bushnell made a number of valuable editorial suggestions. Sarah Springer retyped older essays that were not already on computer disks and, going way beyond the normal role of secretary, helped to put the text and notes into a standardized form. Steven Sarson and Karin Wulf did a splendid job reading proofs. Jacqueline Megan Greene did the index. The University of California, Irvine, and The Johns Hopkins University provided financial assistance.

IMPERATIVES, BEHAVIORS, AND IDENTITIES

Essays in Early American Cultural History

ONE

Mastery and the Definition of Cultural Space in Early America: *A Perspective*

DURING THE ERA OF the American Revolution, the dominant populations of the thirteen colonies appropriated the term *America* to desig-
nate primarily the physical spaces that became part of the United States and
the noun *American* almost exclusively to refer to themselves and their progenitors. This usage has proven extraordinarily durable, even among the
most sophisticated elements of the scholarly community. Thus, for most of
its forty-eight-year history as a magazine of "Early American History and
Culture" the *William and Mary Quarterly*, leading journal of the early phases
of "American" history, has effectively reserved the name of *American* for the
settlers of mostly European ancestry who populated the mainland colonies of
English or, after 1707, British America and their progeny.

In vain have residents of the many other Americas to the north and the
south of the United States and students of those other areas of European
occupation that subsequently became part of the United States, including the
Spanish Borderlands and French Louisiana, protested the exclusion of their
areas and populations. Indeed, only during the last twenty years have historians come to recognize Afro-Americans, Amerindians, and other less stra-
tegically well-situated groups who resided in the area that would become the
United States as significant actors within "American" history and thereby to
accord them and their descendants an acknowledged status as full Americans.
The success of these efforts has produced a fundamental challenge to older
conceptions of America and Americans and has generated a demand that we
both make explicit how America has been defined and reconsider the question of how it should be.[1]

---

[1] Implicit in this enterprise is a series of even larger—and quite fundamental—questions
about how historians define and frame what they do, how they establish priorities among the

This chapter represents a preliminary attempt to come to terms with these problems. For that purpose, it employs two central concepts, cultural space and mastery. By the term *cultural space* I mean to refer to a physical or social space defined by a set of behaviors and a mode of life associated with the particular group or groups occupying that space. Implying dominance and capacity, the concept of *mastery* was central to the definition of political and social relations during the early modern era. Mastery meant dominion, rule, superiority, or preeminence. To master meant, first, to rule or govern or to conquer or overpower. A master was a director or governor, an owner or proprietor "with the idea of governing," a lord or ruler, a chief or head, a "Possessor," "One uncontrouled," one who had servants.[2]

This chapter calls attention to the extent to which an implicit notion of mastery has always been fundamental to conceptions of America and argues that mastery or some equivalent concept remains a useful tool in helping us to comprehend and describe the complex process of cultural change and reformulation set in motion by the Columbian encounter. Without acknowledging that they were doing so, older approaches defined America almost exclusively in terms set by the population that would eventually dominate it and thereby effectively ignored the contributions of other groups. The approach advocated here suggests that by making the concept of mastery explicit, we can at once acknowledge the dominance of mastering groups in defining cultural space and recognize that mastery has almost never been uncontested and has rarely been either absolute or enduring. In turn, such recognition enables us to comprehend that the forms, behaviors, and representations by which almost any given space is defined are usually the products not of simple imposition by those groups who would eventually succeed in asserting their control over that space but of a process of negotiation between those groups and other contesting groups whom they were trying to bring— and to keep—under their domination.

When we use the term *America* we are of course referring to the vast and enormously varied physical entity to which shortly after the Columbian en-

subjects they study, how they assign value, what they regard as data, how they organize and attribute meaning to those data. To raise these questions is of course to direct attention to the problem of what kinds of mental frameworks historians have or ought to have in their heads when they go about the business of doing history, specifically, in the case at hand, the history of colonial British America.

[2] These definitions come from Samuel Johnson, *A Dictionary of the English Language*, 8th ed., 2 vols. (London, 1799).

counter people gave the name America, a physical entity that includes two large continents and many adjacent islands of various sizes. But America also refers to an equally differentiated agglomeration of cultural spaces into which the human beings who for some length of time have occupied—that is, contested for and established their mastery over—portions of that physical entity have organized it.

A series of adjectives can be used to identify and distinguish among those cultural spaces. At the most general level, we can distinguish between Aboriginal America and European America. Aboriginal America subsumes an enormously rich, varied, often contested, and interrelated series of cultural spaces. Defined by the ethnicity, folkways, economic activities, and patterns of social and gender relations of the particular populations that occupied them, these cultural spaces ranged from the simple and sparsely peopled fishing cultures of the Alaskan and Patagonian coasts, to the demographically more dense and agricultural forest cultures of eastern North America and the Amazon Basin, to the complex and highly populated imperial cultures of Mexico and Peru. The identification of one of these cultural spaces as Maya or Iroquois or Sioux implicitly acknowledges that one or more groups of people called by those names had, at least for the time of designation, established their mastery over those cultural spaces. This Aboriginal America, or perhaps we should say, these Aboriginal Americas, existed both before and after the Columbian encounter.

But that encounter began the process by which a new America, European America, came into being. As that process proceeded from contact to trade to conquest to colonization and settlement, the many existing Aboriginal Americas had to contest, leave, or share portions—as it turned out, ever increasing portions—of the physical spaces of America with Europeans, people from another continent. As Europeans established small beachheads, including trading enclaves, forts, and missions, their activities and the native resistance they encountered created new arenas of conflict in which the adversaries struggled for physical control over territory and, in some cases, for mastery over still other peoples in that territory. For Europeans the stakes in this contest were nothing less than the capacity to create and define new cultural spaces—insofar as they could manage it, European cultural spaces. To understand this process, it may be worthwhile to look at it, in as neutral a way as possible, as a contest for mastery over physical space and the power to define it as cultural space.

Of course, a term like *European America* is analytically useful only when juxtaposed to an equally crude and general term like *Aboriginal America*. For Europeans contested territory and prospective cultural space not only with Amerindians but also among themselves, and no refined understanding of the meaning of the term *European America* can be achieved without breaking it down into its many constituent parts. The European penetrators of America acted not as Europeans but as members of loose cultural coalitions, very often with authorization and much less often with money from the governments of the new national and maritime states of Spain, Portugal, England, the Netherlands, France, Sweden, and, eventually, Denmark and Russia.

Whatever the degree of their sponsorship by these states, European adventurers in America acted as agents in creating new cultural spaces under the nominal control of the states they represented and, with considerably less success, in the images of the Old World cultural spaces over which those states presided. As a result of their efforts, a whole new series of Americas—a Spanish America, a Portuguese America, a British America, a Dutch America, a French America, etc.—all new cultural spaces of varying sizes and complexity, gradually, beginning in the sixteenth century, took shape, solidified, and expanded. In the process of creating these new cultural spaces, these European invaders sought to obliterate, displace, or incorporate the aboriginal cultural spaces that stood in their way.

Contests in America over the power to define cultural space were not European imports. Groups of Amerindians had been fighting and negotiating over dominance of territory and cultural space since time immemorial. At least some of them, the Incas and the Aztecs being two prominent examples during the era of the Columbian encounter, had been highly and successfully imperial, extending their hegemony over large territories and groups of people and, as an essential feature of their efforts, expropriating and redefining the cultural spaces of the groups they conquered or reduced to tributary relationship.

What was new about the imperial efforts of the Europeans was their scale and comprehensiveness. As maritime peoples, Europeans rather quickly, within little more than a century, acquired at least a general sense of the whole of the Americas and, encouraged by their early successes, aspired to bring it all under their domination. By the late seventeenth century, of course, these aspirations had come to be played out within or along the contested margins of rather well demarcated spheres of activity claimed by rival European national groups.

The details of the ways by which Europeans sought to create new cultural spaces in America varied from one national entity to another and from one place and time to another within each of those national entities, but everywhere in America the general process—the process of establishing mastery—was much the same. Europeans gave names to particular places, drew maps on which they recorded those names, divided up territory into large political units and gave them names (often but not always European names), began to contest local inhabitants for and then to occupy those territories, and then, once they had achieved a secure foothold, inaugurated the long work of transforming those territories into European cultural spaces, each of which would be divided—along European lines—into numerous administrative or religious subunits and private properties with carefully designated boundaries and names that were also recorded on maps as a signification that they too had been mastered by the new European population.

But the creation of European cultural spaces in America involved far more than assigning names and boundaries. It also required the transformation of existing social landscapes as well as the organization and modes of cultural interaction that went on in those landscapes. As Europeans and their descendants imprinted upon their new physical spaces European patterns of land occupation; land and resource use; economic, social, and political organization; gender, class, and race relations; and a variety of imported practices ranging from law to housing to diet and institutions—as they did all these things, they produced new cultural spaces that, in almost all cases, eventually could be easily distinguished from the aboriginal cultural spaces that preceded them in the same physical spaces or that still existed in adjacent physical spaces.

Of course, Europeans never had an entirely free hand in this process. That is, the degree to which they could Europeanize a cultural space was always limited by the extent of their borrowings from and the continuing influences of Amerindian cultures, the deep and pervasive influence of the large number of non-Europeans, specifically Africans, whom they imported for labor, and a variety of environmental and economic constraints. Once they had established their mastery over an area, however, they always exercised the dominant defining role, one result of which was that, although there were more and less heavily Africanized European Americas and even Africanized Aboriginal Americas, there was never, except for small Maroon communities and until the St. Domingue revolt, an African America in the same sense that there was an Aboriginal America or a European America.

People in every European metropolis valued some of the new European Americas their agents had created over others, their evaluations usually being based largely on perceptions of how much wealth a particular space brought to the metropolitan society to which it was connected. But only in Hispanic America is it possible to conceive of a hierarchy of cultural spaces, the complex cultural spaces represented by Spanish Peru and Mexico, spaces generating enormous wealth and filled with large populations of Amerindians and Iberians, being significantly different from the many less richly endowed and fully peopled areas the Spanish brought under their hegemony during the sixteenth and seventeenth centuries. For other areas of European

America, it does not seem particularly useful to think in terms of such a hierarchy.

To make this observation, however, raises the very significant question of how, if not in terms of hierarchies, we should think about, that is, organize our knowledge about, classify, and understand these many new European cultural spaces, the spaces, for instance, to which we refer when we use the term *colonial British America*, the specific cultural area that is the subject of this volume. It may be useful to think about each of these spaces as divided into three broad zones: an ecumene or mastered area; an intermediate sphere of European penetration characterized by trade or warfare in which either European traders, resource gatherers, missionaries, and other boundary crossers served as the advance agents of European mastery or Europeans were in active contest with Amerindians over control of territory; and a more distant zone over which its European claimants had nothing more than an unenforceable title.[3] Only within the ecumene did Europeans have the power, the mastery, necessary to create a new European cultural space. Like other areas of European America, British America was most fully epitomized by and, at any given time, effectively limited to its ecumenes, or areas over which settlers of British origin or those of other European origins who had joined them had successfully asserted their mastery and that comprised the foundations and effective limits of each developing cultural space. Thus, when we invoke the construct colonial British America it is to these core spaces, these ecumenes, that we primarily refer.

When we examine those core spaces more closely, we see immediately that they can be categorized—and understood—in relation to each other. We see that these core spaces were divided into political units known as colonies, politically defined collectivities that immediately began to develop histories peculiar to them and identities represented by those histories. But we can also see that we can distinguish among groups of colonies or cultural spaces in terms of broad—and necessarily crude—divisions between plantation areas and farm areas, places that made heavy use of bound labor and those that relied primarily on family and free labor, those that had large numbers of inhabitants of African descent and those that did not, those of relatively greater or lesser wealth or of greater or lesser social stratification. Also, we can see that, notwithstanding their incorporation into separate political entities, adjacent cultural spaces frequently manifested so many similarities that it makes sense to think of them in regional terms as cultural spaces that

---

[3] Amy Turner Bushnell, *Situado and Sabana: Spain's Support System for the Presidio and Mission Provinces of Florida* (New York, 1993).

spilled across political boundaries. Finally, an even closer inspection reveals that each of those regional spaces was subdivided into two or more variants.

In short, however we look at the mastered cultural spaces that evolved in the extensive area that constituted colonial British America, or, for that matter, any other colonial European America, we cannot possibly fail to be impressed by the variety among them, and what is true for us has generally been true for previous generations. Except possibly for the first generation of historians who were trying to emphasize the unities among the new American states, historians of colonial British America have always been most impressed and given most emphasis to the extraordinarily visible differences among colonies, among regions, and among subregions. One might approach the problem of how to think about colonial British America primarily as an exercise in specifying this luxuriant variety, and, indeed, recent historians have done just that, identifying six regions, six large cultural spaces, that took shape between the first successful English settlements at the beginning of the seventeenth century and the American Revolution in the Chesapeake, New England, Middle Colonies, Lower South, West Indies, and Atlantic islands.[4]

Yet, in analyzing and thinking about colonial British America and the cultural spaces it included, it is also necessary to take a broader perspective. Impressed with the variety in the cultural spaces created on the North American continent by British and associated peoples and knowing that most of those spaces later would amalgamate to form the United States, most previous historians have employed what might be called a little America framework. That is, they have evaluated the impressive differences among colonial British-American cultural spaces in terms of how they seemed to fit with what would become or what they wanted to believe had become the predominant elements in the cultural spaces that subsequently comprised independent republican America, the United States.

As many scholars have suggested, however, an alternative and preferable approach is to put more emphasis upon the word *British* in the concept of colonial British America and to consider in what ways the colonies were British, and, in deciding what was and was not important, to situate ourselves in contemporary Britain rather than in nineteenth-century or even Revolutionary America. This approach produces a number of advantages

---

[4] The powerful movement toward the definition of colonial British America in terms of its regional components is discussed in Jack P. Greene, "Interpretive Frameworks: The Quest for Intellectual Order in Early American History," *William and Mary Quarterly*, 3d ser., 48 (1991): 515–30.

other than the mere avoidance of anachronism. It encourages us to look at British-American cultural spaces not only as fields of action for individuals seeking lives different from those they had in the Old World but also as instruments of British imperial designs, as outlets for British enterprise and investment, and, what is perhaps most relevant to the kind of questions explored in this volume, as outposts of British authority and culture. It enables us to see those spaces as part of a broad transatlantic Anglophone cultural space, a greater Great Britain, which included, in addition to the island of Great Britain itself, Ireland and on the western side of the Atlantic stretched from Barbados north to Newfoundland and from Bermuda west to the Allegheny Mountains and Jamaica. It helps us not only to develop a fuller appreciation of the interconnectedness and extraordinary variety in that vast British cultural space but also to identify the ways in which the many different cultural spaces created in America by British and associated peoples were British and to call attention to the broad unities that tied them all into a common entity and distinguished them from Aboriginal and other European Americas.

Before we can even begin to identify these unities, of course, we have to confront the further questions of what we mean when we use the words *English* or *British*. Like America, England/Britain was a complex cultural space with some ethnic and several regional variations and very sharp contrasts between rural areas and burgeoning urban centers, especially London. England was also an area that in the two centuries beginning with the reign of Elizabeth I underwent rapid and deep social, economic, and political changes as a result of growing commercialization and its attendant effects. It was emphatically not that golden "world we have lost," a world of ordered stability, intergenerational warmth, and communal familiarity, a world defined by hardy, independent, and self-sufficient yeomen, a world that provided many of its inhabitants with a secure sense of place and well-being, though it may very well have had pockets that could be so characterized. It was not, in short, the kind of static world that so many historians like to use as a device to provide themselves with a stable background against which they can mark the changes they wish to describe.

Rather, it was a dynamic, changing, insecure, and, notwithstanding its hierarchical organization, in many respects highly disordered world, a harsh and unwelcoming world with much population mobility, much social displacement, and deep social divisions between a small population of independent mastering people on the one hand and a massive number of dependent mastered people on the other. It was a world that provided meagerly for many of its inhabitants, a world in which vast numbers had no secure place, a world in which unfortunates, social dependents, and all kinds of laborers were treated callously, a world with few openings to the elusive independence that it regarded as essential to personal and family security or to the mastery over property and people it considered necessary for elevation to higher statuses; it was a world that, at least within itself, did not have nearly enough openings even to keep younger sons of independent people from falling into dependency or to enable all those whose ambitions had been stimulated by economic expansion to realize them.

By deromanticizing this English world, by seeing it for the uncertain, unequal, exploitative, restless, and, in many respects, chaotic world that it was, we can better understand why the allegedly wide-open, uncultivated, and free physical spaces of America exerted such a wide appeal for English people. We can see the wide range of individual and social behaviors in colonial British America not as aberrations from the world we have lost but as well within the parameters—and logical extensions—of English behaviors. We can understand the many new cultural spaces those English people created in America as the products of the quest for independence and for mastery, mastery over real and personal property, over dependents, over family, and over self by the English individuals who populated them. We can understand the willingness—the eagerness—of those individuals who were successful in that quest to expropriate the labor of others and to reduce them to dependency as thoroughly English and British American. We can view the institutions of Amerindian and black slavery as occupying the most extreme point on a spectrum of exploitative English labor systems. We can better understand both how fundamental and how normative the psychology of exploitation was in colonial British America and the symbiotic relationship between independence and dependence. And we can better comprehend that any place in which dependency was not widespread would have been quite exceptional in the early modern Anglophone world.

But it is also necessary to understand that early modern England was a world that aspired to better itself. First, like the rest of early modern Europe, it was deeply caught up in what the German sociologist Norbert Elias has called the civilizing process, a drive for civility that, he argues, was intensifying and expanding through the early modern period and (although Elias, with typical European myopia, does not consider the possibility) may have been given much additional impetus by the new and contemporary associations with the allegedly savage—and uncivil—native peoples of Africa and America, peoples against whom Europeans defined themselves as civilized.[5]

Second, and perhaps even more fully than other Old World places, En-

---

[5] Norbert Elias, *The Civilizing Process: The History of Manners* (New York, 1978).

gland was also caught up in a related drive for what was called improvement. Stimulated by commercialization, the new learning, and the scientific revolution, this drive looked forward not to Progress but to many incremental changes and discoveries that would gradually better the condition of humanity and make society more productive, more orderly and coherent, perhaps more benign, and certainly more conducive to human mastery.[6]

Third, contact with the supposedly savage peoples of the New World and Africa stimulated Europeans to try to explain cultural differences and to absorb patently different "others" into their own conceptual universe by developing the concept of cultural evolution in which people—and their cultural spaces—could be classified according to their supposed membership in one or another of a hierarchy of developing stages. The Spanish religious José Acosta, who spent much time in America, was the first to develop such a scheme at the end of the seventeenth century. In the British world this effort was most fully developed during the eighteenth century by the Scottish conjectural historians, who saw human development as proceeding through four stages: hunting, grazing, agriculture, and commerce.[7]

By providing European settlers and their descendants with coherent explanations and justifications for their efforts to establish their mastery over existing American populations, these three phenomena—the civilizing process, the concept of improvement, and the emerging notion of cultural evolution—functioned as powerful instruments of imperial domination. But these same phenomena also entailed upon peoples of European descent in the far peripheries of European civilization in America both a set of standards for the cultural spaces they were creating and a conceptual device, what I have elsewhere called a developmental model,[8] to explain how those spaces were supposed to develop through time into more civilized, more improved, more commercialized spaces. In the larger sense, the drive for mastery over American physical spaces would not be complete until those spaces had, in addition to being split into a series of mastered particles or plots, been transformed—and elevated—into civilized, improved, commercialized, that is, fully European, cultural spaces, spaces that were emphatically not aboriginal. The same set of concepts also supplied the basis for distinguishing among areas within a given American cultural space according to the extent

---

[6] In the absence of a comprehensive history of the concept of *improvement* in early modern English thought, see Joan Thirsk, *Economic Policy and Projects: The Development of a Consumer Society in Early Modern Europe* (Oxford, 1978).

[7] Ronald L. Meek, *Social Science and the Ignoble Savage* (Cambridge, 1978).

[8] Jack P. Greene, *Pursuits of Happiness: The Social Development of Early Modern British Colonies and the Formation of American Culture* (Chapel Hill, N.C., 1988).

of their development and carried the promise—the expectation and the demand—that undeveloped segments of those spaces would eventually be transformed into developed ones. Developed worlds, it need hardly be said, were not worlds without dependency.

In particular cultural spaces, the power of this Europeanizing or, in colonial British America, anglicizing impulse was, of course, limited, reshaped, or both, by several important variables. These certainly included the proportion of population that was non-British or non-European, the amount of wealth, and, after—and I stress the word *after*—the conversion of strategic segments of the population of Britain to antislavery during the last half of the eighteenth century, the presence or absence of racial slavery.

Whatever the different social results produced by these variables—and they should not be minimized—the anglicizing impulse operated throughout the colonial period to provide the inhabitants of the several distinctive cultural spaces of British America with a common framework for what they were doing and a set of shared aspirations for those spaces. Along with the common experiences and psychologies that emerged from several generations of people, as individuals and as collectivities, endeavoring with considerable success to establish their mastery over their cultural spaces, that common British framework and those shared aspirations increasingly enabled the people who inhabited these several distinctive cultural spaces to perceive the unities among them as more important than the diversities. And that perception goes a long way toward facilitating an understanding of why people in those spaces ever thought that they could come together to form a single political entity, how they could possibly think that they might eventually form a single—an American—social entity, and why they took so long to develop an appreciation that differing labor systems were dividing them into two separate and incompatible social systems, a division that provided the basis for a profound struggle over who—what regions and groups— would ultimately have the power to define—and thereby establish their mastery over—the new cultural space represented by the republican United States.

The contention of this chapter is that the concept of mastery is a useful device for understanding the process of cultural change and reformulation that occurred in America during the three centuries following the Columbian encounter. Throughout this long period, the drive for mastery was central to European colonizing activities. The force of that drive was a principal element in enabling European settlers and their descendants to take control over, reshape, and redefine larger and larger segments of the physical spaces of America. Their achievements in this regard make it necessary for us to continue to acknowledge their dominant role in the creation of new American cultural spaces. At the same time, however, we must also recognize that those achievements were rarely uncontested and invariably involved concessions to or borrowings from antagonists. As either individual or social objective, mastery always aims for more than the urge it represents can either deliver or sustain.

This chapter is a revised version of a paper presented at a session entitled *"Pursuits of Happiness*: A Reconsideration" at the Fifty-seventh Annual Meeting of the Southern Historical Association in Fort Worth, Texas, Nov. 15, 1991.

—Two—

Changing Identity in the British West Indies in the Early Modern Era: *Barbados as a Case Study*

Dimensions of Identity

STUDENTS OF THE EUROPEAN colonizing experience have long insisted that one of the most attractive aspects of their subject is the opportunity to observe the development of the new social entities they study from their very beginnings. In contrast to the European societies from which they emanated, the origins of which are no longer recoverable, early modern colonies in America and elsewhere all have identifiable beginnings, about which, in many cases, the documentary record is sufficiently detailed to permit a reconstruction of the basic processes of social formation. Especially in recent years, considerable attention has been devoted to the economic, social, and cultural institutions and structures created by colonists in this process. With the notable exception of Puritan New England,[1] however, much less consideration has been given to the ways in which those colonists acquired coherent identities as peoples and societies knit together by a series of common aspirations and experiences in particular places.

Each time a group of Europeans occupied a new segment of America, they encountered what was for them "a strange Country,"[2] but it is important to recognize that in no instance was the region encountered a tabula rasa. Not only was it a physical entity with its own distinctive ecosystem, topography, animal and vegetable life, and climate, but, in most cases, the physi-

---

[1] In particular, Sacvan Bercovitch, *The Puritan Origins of the American Self* (New Haven, 1975), and Michael Zuckermann, "The Fabrication of Identity in Early America," *William and Mary Quarterly*, 3d ser., 34 (1977): 183–214.

[2] The quotation is from Richard Ligon, *A True & Exact History of the Island of Barbadoes* (London, 1673), 121.

cal landscape also already had been organized into an articulated social and cultural landscape inhabited by one or more particular groups of people. By determining to an important degree what could and could not be done there by its new occupants, by both presenting them with certain opportunities and depriving them of others, these preexisting physical and social attributes of place constituted one of the most important ingredients in defining the identities of the new societies that would be constructed in them. At the same time that they were coming to terms with their new spaces, learning both how to manipulate them for their own survival and material advantage and how to describe them in terms that would enable them and others to comprehend them, European settlers also became active agents in changing them, in creating new social landscapes.

The shape and content of these new landscapes as well as of the identities that they sustained were determined not just by characteristics of place. Three additional sets of variables also had a powerful influence. First were the short-term and long-term social and economic goals that had initially drawn and, as revised in the light of local potentialities, would continue to draw European settlers to specific places. Second were the standards of what a civilized society should be and how its members should behave. These standards had initially been brought by the earliest settlers from their metropolis, but they were subsequently revised or updated through a process of continuous cultural interaction with that metropolis. Third were the collective experience—the history—that successive generations of inhabitants shared in their particular place.

Out of the interaction among these four sets of variables—attributes of place, goals, standards, and history—the inhabitants of each new society in the early modern colonial world gradually acquired a well-articulated definition of themselves and the entities they were creating. This definition involved the settlers in considering themselves as belonging to a corporate unit and in viewing themselves as a collection of people who shared not just common membership in a given social order in a particular place but also a set of commonly held values and orientations. These latter provided the inhabitants with a shared basis for approved social behavior and equipped them to interpret both contemporary events and developments and the social meaning of their own individual lives. Only as this definition of the collective self was, little by little, first articulated and refined by both the inhabitants and those who observed them from the outside and then internalized by the inhabitants did those inhabitants come to some clear understanding of what they and their society were about. Finally, through that understanding and the reputation that comprised its external face, the inhabitants achieved a coherent corporate identity; that is, a well-defined sense of themselves and their society and a distinctive reputation by which they were known to the outside world.

This corporate identity was necessarily stereotypical, but it is nonetheless worthy of analysis because it constitutes the only coherent expression of what a particular collectivity of people thought of itself and how it wished to be regarded by outsiders. To this extent, each colony's corporate sense of self provides a key to the contemporary meaning of its inhabitants' collective experiences in founding and developing the new society in which they lived. At the same time, no collective identity is static, and an analysis of its changing content reveals, perhaps as well as can the study of any other single phenomenon, the character of a given colony's responses to the successive social, economic, cultural, and political transformations it underwent. Based upon reflection on some of the voluminous published contemporary descriptions, analyses, and histories, this essay seeks to describe and to explain the changing identity and reputation of colonial Barbados and Barbadians from the colony's first founding during the second quarter of the seventeenth century through the first eight decades of the eighteenth century.

No doubt it would be possible to work on a more general level and to explicate a British West Indian, British plantation colony, British-American, or even pan-British identity during the period considered in this essay. Indeed, some preliminary effort will be made to relate the Barbadian experience to that of other British plantation colonies in the West Indies and on the mainland. But one of the central assumptions underlying this essay is that, notwithstanding certain manifest similarities, the emerging identity of each new early modern American society was powerfully shaped by a distinctive set of place-specific and time-specific experiences that gave it a content unique to the place, society, and people it had been constructed to describe.

This assumption has been confirmed by a much more ambitious, though as yet unfinished, study of the same subject for the same period in three other British-American plantation societies, those of Virginia, Jamaica, and South Carolina,[3] as well as by a shorter analysis of colonial Georgia.[4] The corollary of this assumption is, of course, that a more general understanding of the formation and acquisition of identity in these early plantation societies, of the common elements of what might be designated as a plantation self in

---

[3] The tentative title of this study, which is still in progress, is *Paradise Defined: Studies in the Formation and Changing Character of Corporate Identities in Early Modern Plantation America, 1585 to 1820.*

[4] Jack P. Greene, "Travails of an Infant Colony: Searching for Viability, Coherence, and Identity in Colonial Georgia," in Harvey H. Jackson and Phinizy Spalding, eds., *Forty Years of Diversity: Essays on Colonial Georgia* (Athens, Ga., 1984), 278–309 [chap. 5 below].

early modern colonial British America, can best be undertaken on the basis of careful reconstructions of the identities of specific societies.

"By All the Sweet Negotiation [s] of Sugar"

A small island of only 166 square miles (106,000 acres), Barbados had been ignored by Iberian colonizing powers for more than 125 years before its occupation by the English in 1627. Even then, it was settled without any of the fanfare that had characterized the establishment of Virginia two decades earlier or would accompany the founding of Massachusetts Bay a few years later or the settlements of Jamaica, Carolina, and Pennsylvania following the Restoration. With Jamaica, which was captured from the Spanish in 1656, and the four Leeward Islands of Antigua, Montserrat, Nevis, and St. Christopher (St. Kitts), Barbados was one of the six permanent English colonies settled in the West Indies during the seventeenth century. Though its claim to be the first English West Indian colony has been challenged by both St. Kitts and Nevis, its early success as a staple colony made Barbados a model for all subsequent English settlements in the region, albeit a model that was never fully imitated by any other colony.

During its first decade and a half, Barbados quietly attracted from England a substantial population of yeomen farmers and servants who managed both to raise enough provisions to feed themselves and to develop a modestly lucrative export trade in tobacco, cotton, and ginger.[5] During the 1640s its inhabitants began to raise sugarcane, and within fifteen years they were producing large quantities of sugar for export. With this sugar revolution came more settlers—adventurers in search of their fortunes, white servants from the home country, and black slaves from the coast of Africa—and, among English colonies up to that time, unparalleled wealth. By the 1660s Barbados was probably the most densely populated and intensely cultivated agricultural area in the English-speaking world, and it had acquired a widespread fame as a place of abundance and riches—at least for its free inhabitants.[6]

By 1670, however, Barbados was losing its position as England's leading sugar-producing colony to Jamaica. More than twenty-six times as large as Barbados, with soils not previously subjected to intensive sugar cultivation, Jamaica offered its free inhabitants greater opportunities for acquiring even

---

[5] See F. C. Innes, "The Pre-Sugar Era of European Settlement in Barbados," *Journal of Caribbean History* 1 (1970): 1–22.

[6] Richard S. Dunn, *Sugar and Slaves: The Rise of the Planter Class in the English West Indies, 1624–1713* (Chapel Hill, N.C., 1972), 46–116.

more substantial fortunes as well as for constructing a richer and more extensive social and cultural life. With similarly "new" soils, even smaller islands (including both the four Leeward Islands, the four new Windward Island colonies—Dominica, Grenada, St. Vincent, and Tobago—acquired by the British in the 1760s, and the still newer colonies of Trinidad and St. Lucia conquered during the Napoleonic wars) enjoyed a comparative economic advantage over Barbados during their early decades of settlement, yielding both more sugar per acre and higher rates of profit.[7]

Notwithstanding its relative decline in relation to these newer sugar colonies, Barbados continued to be an important sugar producer throughout the early modern period, producing in its much smaller area between a fifth to a third of the quantity of sugar produced in Jamaica. Perhaps more important, it also continued to be the most densely settled and most intensively cultivated colony in British colonial America and to have a much higher ratio of whites to blacks and, in all probability, a higher proportion of creoles (native born) among both its white and black inhabitants than any other British West Indian colony. Though we lack detailed studies of the social and political development of Barbados during the late eighteenth and early nineteenth centuries, it also seems to have retained vigorous political and social institutions and an active white creole elite population and, in comparison with other British plantation colonies at comparable stages in their development, to have enjoyed a rich cultural life.

Elsewhere in colonial British plantation America, the process of identity formation seems to have involved three sequential, if not always sharply distinguishable, phases. During the first phase, characteristics of place usually assumed primacy. That is, settlers and their sponsors tended to identify their society in terms of the nature and potentialities of the place in which they lived. During a second phase, they tended to define themselves more in terms of how they were actually organizing their social and cultural landscapes and the extent to which those landscapes did—or did not—conform to inherited notions and standards of how such landscapes should be organized. Finally, during a third phase, they gave increasing emphasis to their predominant characteristics as people and to the common experiences shared by themselves and their ancestors.

Because it neither attracted widespread attention in England nor achieved a visible identity until it had already become a thriving concern, Barbados seems largely to have skipped the first phase in this process. In marked

---

[7] Richard B. Sheridan, *Sugar and Slavery: An Economic History of the British West Indies, 1623–1775* (Baltimore, 1974), 30–35, 97–147. See also Richard Pares, *Merchants and Planters* (London, 1960), 14–25.

contrast to the experience of most other early modern colonies in colonial British plantation America, the observers and interpreters who first began to characterize Barbados for themselves and the outside world emphasized less its special attributes as a physical entity than its most prominent features as a sugar-producing society. Through its first eight decades, the predominant image of Barbados as it was set forth in a large variety of reports, descriptions, and travelers' accounts[8] as well as in extended histories by Richard Ligon[9] and John Oldmixon[10] was that of a rich, populous, and flourishing settlement, whose enormous economic value to England and extraordinarily rapid development had almost entirely been accomplished through what Ligon referred to as "the sweet Negotiation[s] of Sugar."[11]

This is not to suggest that either earlier or later writers on Barbados ignored its tropical character. Indeed, although the island's comparatively gentle terrain was reminiscent of home, they could scarcely fail to note the sharp contrasts with England in climate, animal and insect life, and vegetation. Like northern Europeans elsewhere in the tropics, new settlers found the unrelieved and "torrid heat of the Sun," which "scorch't up" the island "from morning till night," especially debilitating, and they complained about the excessive humidity that seemed to produce instant rust on metal tools and implements, the annoying attacks of the numerous populations of mosquitoes and chiggers, the extensiveness of the heavy forests that covered the island, and the fecundity of both animal and vegetable life. In the spring ugly land crabs were so thick upon the ground that it was impossible to walk without stepping on them, while vicious withes grew so fast that they would cover a ten-foot clearing overnight and could be kept from invading cultivated ground only by enormous labor and diligence.[12]

---

[8] These works, citations to which will be found in the notes below, are listed in Jerome S. Handler's excellent *A Guide to Source Materials for the Study of Barbados History, 1627–1834* (Carbondale, Ill., 1971), and in Handler and Samuel J. Hough, "Addenda to *A Guide to Source Materials for the Study of Barbados History, 1627–1834*," published in four parts in the *Journal of the Barbados Museum and Historical Society* 36 (1980–82): 172–77, 279–85, 385–97, 37 (1983): 82–92, 296–307, 38 (1987): 107–16.

[9] Ligon's extensive work was first published in London in 1657 and republished there in 1673 (see note 2 above). All citations to this work in this essay are to the second edition.

[10] John Oldmixon, *The British Empire in America*, 2 vols. (London, 1708), 2:1–196. Devoting far more space to the history of Barbados than to any other colony, Oldmixon's account, updated in a second edition published in London in 1741 (2:1–171), was the most extensive history of the colony published before the early nineteenth century.

[11] Ligon, *True & Exact History*, 96.

[12] Ibid., 24, 27, 62, 66, 97, 102, 106, 110, 117; Alexander Gunkel and Jerome S. Handler, eds. and trans., "A Swiss Medical Doctor's Description of Barbados in 1661: The

For all its fruitfulness, moreover, Barbados was not well suited to produce many of the foods to which Englishmen were accustomed. It wanted the "English man[']s grasse," complained one writer in 1648, "and so the English man[']s Beef, Mutton, Milk, Butter and Cheese." Having no wheat for bread, they had to make do with flour made from cassava roots, "whose juice is poyson, so [that] the negligence of a servant or slave in the right making of it may cost the whole family a poysoning." Though infrequent, hurricanes, such as that which struck the island on August 31, 1675, brought "Pestilential Blasts" of an intensity and duration unknown in England. Finally, although Barbados was thought to be both the "healthfullest in all the westerne islands" and far less lethal than Virginia during its early decades, its illnesses, as Ligon lamented, were "more grievous, and mortality greater by far than in *England*, and these diseases many times contagious." All newcomers lived in dread of the "*Contrey Diseas*," probably yellow fever, while dysentery, malaria, various fevers, and other "dire Disease[s]" killed hundreds and in some years even thousands. "Black Ribbon for mourning," wrote Ligon, "is much worn there."[13]

For all of "Old Nature's Crimes" in Barbados, however, for all of the island's physical dissimilarity from England, its new inhabitants displayed a ready appreciation of its virtues as a tropical paradise. Never cold, it seemed to be "perpetual[ly] springing."

> Whilst the Sun in Northern Clime
> Posts, as if he grudg'd his Time,
> Robbing all of Life's Delights,
> In Short Days and tedious Nights,

one local poet declared in celebratory rhyme early in the eighteenth century, Barbadians were

> Curst with no Cold Winter here,
> Nature shines Serene and Clear,

Account of Felix Christian Spörri," *Journal of the Barbados Museum and Historical Society* 33 (1969): 5; Samuel Clarke, *A True, and Faithful Account of the Four Cheifest Plantations of the English in America* (London, 1670), 58.

[13] Ligon, *True & Exact History*, 21, 23, 25, 29–30, 33–34, 110, 117; Spörri, "Account," 5–6; Beauchamp Plantagenet, *A Description of the Province of New Albion* ([London], 1648), 5; Thomas Verney to Sir Edmund Verney, Feb. 10, 1638, *Letters and Papers of the Verney Family Down to the End of the Year 1639*, ed. John Bruce (London, 1853), 193; *An Ode Pindarick on Barbados* [London, 1710], 1; Neville Connell, "Father Labat's Visit to Barbados in 1700," *Journal of the Barbados Museum and Historical Society* 24 (1957): 164, 171.

Fresh Spring and Summer smiling
all the Year.

Not only, in happy contrast to England, was Barbados always warm and always green, it had also been endowed by the "great Gardiner of the World" with a rich variety of exotic and glorious flowers, fruits, and trees. There was "not a more Royal or Magnificent tree growing on earth, for beauty and largeness," Ligon noted, than the royal palm, and the pineapple, which rarely failed to captivate palates of Europeans wherever they encountered it, contained "all that" was "excellent in a superlative degree, for beauty and taste."[14]

Indeed, by West Indian standards, proponents of Barbados rarely failed to point out, Barbados had a temperate climate, the usual heat of the tropics being tempered by a constant breeze from the gentle trade winds that flowed across the island. Together with these cooling breezes, sweet fruits, fragrant blossoms, verdant prospects, and brilliant night skies contributed to make Barbados an "extremely beautiful" and "Pleasant Place." Notwithstanding the many, for newcomers, unpleasant, even malignant, qualities of the island's climate, Barbados thus came to be routinely depicted by residents and visitors alike as an appealing habitation, a place that was so "happy" in its physical characteristics that its inhabitants might live in ease and comfort in a setting that was more fruitful and more inviting than any that could be found in the more temperate regions of Albion.[15]

If, as one resident avowed shortly after the Restoration, God had "made our Island Habitable and Fruitfull," its new European inhabitants brought the sugarcane that made it rich. From the beginning of settlement, people had come to Barbados for the principal purpose of improving their economic situations. Independent adventurers, like young Thomas Verney, expected to raise large "fortunes in a few years," and impecunious servants hoped to escape the desperate circumstances in which they found themselves in England. To these ends, Barbados early attracted a considerable population. By

---

[14] *Ode Pindarick*, 1–2; Ligon, *True & Exact History*, 75, 80, 82, 84–85; Verney to Verney, Feb. 10, 1638, *Verney Family Papers*, 194.

[15] Ligon, *True & Exact History*, 20–21, 106; Clarke, *True, and Faithful Account*, 59–60; Jerome S. Handler, "Father Antoine Biet's Visit to Barbados in 1654," *Journal of the Barbados Museum and Historical Society* 32 (1967): 64; Verney to Verney, Feb. 10, 1638, *Verney Family Papers*, 194; N. Darnell Davis, ed., "An Early Impression of Barbados," *West India Committee Circular* 28, no. 395 (1913): 539; Peter Heylyn, *Cosmography in Four Books* (London, 1703), 1118; John Speed, *A Prospect of the Most Famous Parts of the World* (London, 1676), 48; Dr. Thomas Towns, "Observations made at Barbadoes," [1676], *Philosophical Transactions of the Royal Society of London, 1672–1683*, 2 vols. (London, 1809), 2: 228–29.

the mid–1640s it was said, almost certainly with exaggeration, that the island had 20,000 European inhabitants. Yet few Barbadian proprietors became wealthy until after they discovered in the late 1640s that "nothing . . . succeed[ed] better than sugar." When he arrived in Barbados in September 1647, Ligon reported, the "great work of Sugar-making" was "but in its infancy, and but faintly understood." By the time he left, just three years later, sugar was being produced "to a high perfection." As it became increasingly clear that sugar would be "the main Plant, to improve the value of the whole Island," Barbadian landholders "bent all their endeavours to . . . planting, and making Sugar," which rapidly became the "soul of Trade" for the island.[16]

Once its landholders had "learned the Art of making Sugar," Barbados "in a short time . . . grew very considerable," increasing dramatically in both "Reputation and Wealth." Though some of them had begun with small investments, many planters had, as a result of the sugar boom, acquired "very great and vast estates." With large work forces of servants and, increasingly, African slaves purchased from their substantial sugar profits, they were able to establish sturdy foundations for the economic security of their posterities while themselves living in ease and affluence without the excessive toil that had been the lot of the first settlers. The most "Industrious and painful" among the planters, men who, like James Drax and Thomas Modiford, had the most "percing sights, and profound judgments," had been able to raise their "fortune[s] to such a height" that they "lived like little princes" and could confidently expect in just "a few years" to have enough money to purchase an English estate valued with an income of £10,000 per annum.[17]

Vast and sudden fortunes for the most successful proprietors were not, however, the only by-products of the sugar revolution in Barbados. Most commentators who had been to the island agreed that its great wealth was being built on the cruel exploitation of its burgeoning labor force. Even among the free population, Ligon observed, "long and tedious hard labour, sleight feeding, and ill lodging" often depressed the spirits of "the meaner

---

[16] Davis, "Early Impression of Barbados," 539: Verney to Verney, Feb. 10, 1638, *Verney Family Papers*, 192; Handler, "Father Biet's Visit," 66, 69; Ligon, *True & Exact History*, 24, 85–86; J. Davies, trans., *The History of Barbados, St. Christophers, Mevis, . . . and the Rest of the Caribby-Islands* (London, 1666), 8–9; John Ogilby, *America: Being the Latest and Most Accurate Description of the New World* (London, 1671), 377.

[17] Handler, "Father Biet's Visit," 64, 66, 69; R[ichard] B[urton], *The English Empire in America, or A Prospect of His Majesties Dominions in the West Indies* (London, 1685), 199; Heylyn, *Cosmography*, 1118; Plantagenet, *Description*, 5; Ligon, *True & Exact History*, 34, 43, 86, 96; Spörri, "Account," 7; Speed, *Prospect*, 48.

sort of Planters" and gradually brought them "to a declining and yielding condition." The unfree seem to have fared much worse. White servants and black slaves alike were reportedly subjected to "very hard labour," fed as little as possible, housed in conditions scarcely fit for animals, and treated with "a great deal of severity." "Truly," wrote Ligon, "I have seen such cruelty there done to Servants, as I did not think one Christian could have done to another." "All are very badly treated," agreed a French visitor. "When they work the overseers, who act like those in charge of galley slaves, are always close by with a stick with which they often prod them when they do not work as fast as is desired."[18]

Ligon claimed that "as discreeter and better natur'd men" had gradually "come to rule" in Barbados as a result of the sugar revolution, the lives of servants had "been much bettered." But the experiences of Marcellus Rivers and Oxenbridge Foyle, two men accused of royalism and rebellion and shipped to Barbados for sale as servants in the mid–1650s, seemed to render Ligon's claim little more than a naive and as yet unfulfilled hope. Along with many other political prisoners, they complained to the English reading public in 1659, they had fallen into the hands of the "most inhuman and barbarous persons," who worked them hard, fed them meagerly, and in general reduced them to the "most deplorable, and (as to Englishmen) . . . unparalleled condition" in which they were "bought and sold . . . from one planter to another, or attached as horses and beasts for the debts of their masters, . . . whipped at the whipping-posts (as rogues) for their masters' pleasure," forced to sleep "in sties worse than hogs in England, and [in] many other ways made miserable, beyond expression or Christian imagination."[19]

If Christians met with such "extream ill usage," the African slaves who year by year after 1650 came to comprise a larger share of the island's labor force and total population had to endure even worse. Because their permanent enslavement gave their masters a strong material incentive to keep them alive and well enough to work, Ligon thought that slaves were "kept and preserv'd with greater care"; a later writer even argued in the early 1670s that they were "well contented with their Conditions." But most other contemporary testimony pointed to the contrary. Even those, like Ligon, who appreciated the intellectual capacities of blacks and advocated their conver-

---

[18] Ligon, *True & Exact History*, 41, 43–44, 91; Handler, "Father Biet's Visit," 66–67; Spörri, "Account," 7; Speed, *Prospect*, 48.

[19] Ligon, *True & Exact History*, 44; Marcellus Rivers and Oxenbridge Foyle, *England's Slavery, or Barbados Merchandize* (London, 1659), 1–7.

sion to Christianity, still considered them to be "as near beasts as may be." Furthermore, blacks were said to have been worked harder and provided with less food, clothing, and shelter even than white servants. Indeed, to blacks it appeared, as one slave was said to have declared, that *"The Devel was in the English-man, that he makes every thing work; he makes the Negro work, the Horse work, the Ass work, the Wood work, the Water work, and the Winde work."* This remark underlines how thoroughly exploitative Barbadian free society was. The fact that it was reputedly "much quoted by the [white] Inhabitants" powerfully suggests that they took considerable pride in their exploitative abilities.[20]

For slaves as well as for servants Barbados was thus not a bountiful mine of white gold but a "place of torment." For them, its true character was symbolized less by the wealth of the great planters than by the story of Yarico, an Indian woman from the mainland. Having fallen in love with and saved a young Englishman from death by her own people, she was repaid for her act of love by being brought to Barbados and there sold into slavery. First recounted by Ligon, this story was subsequently repeated and embroidered by many writers over the following century and a half. A seemingly telling commentary on the willingness of Englishmen in Barbados and elsewhere in the tropics to sacrifice all human feelings in the pursuit of their own avarice, the story of Yarico became for the outside world an emblem of the cruelty and inhumanity that was almost as strong an element in the emerging public reputation of Barbados as was its rapid rise to affluence.[21]

The harsh conditions suffered by the island's numerous laboring population inevitably translated into fear for white proprietors. They liked to think that the spirits of slaves and servants were kept in such awe and subjection as to prevent any effort at combination against their masters. No doubt, as one visitor noted in the early 1650s, many slaves and servants were sufficiently terrified as to "tremble when they speak." But the prevalence of military titles among plantation owners and the character of their houses testified to their underlying fear of "being murthered by" their own "unhappy" laborers. The houses, according to Ligon, were mostly "built in [the] manner of Fortifications, and have Lines, Bulwarks, and Bastions to defend them-

---

[20] Ligon, *True & Exact History*, 43, 45, 47; Richard Blome, *A Description of the Island of Jamaica; with the Other Isles and Terretories in America, to Which the English Are Related, viz. Barbados, St. Christopher, Nievis* (London, 1672), 84–85; *Great Newes from the Barbadoes* (London, 1676), 6–7.

[21] Rivers and Foyle, *England's Slavery*, 1–7; Ligon, *True & Exact History*, 55. On the frequent repetition and popularity of the Yarico story, see Wylie Sypher, *Guinea's Captive Kings* (Chapel Hill, N.C., 1942), 122–37.

selves, in case there should be any uproar of commotion in the Island, either by the Christian servants or *Negro* slaves." That the planters were justified in taking such precautions was borne out by the frequent occurrence of flight, desperate acts of resistance and reprisal, and conspiracies of several shapes and sizes among both slaves and servants on the island. No less than the flammable canes in their fields, labor conditions in Barbados made the colony highly "combustible, and apt to take fire" at any moment.[22]

Fear of the wrath of their maltreated laborers and scorn from the outside world for the severity of their labor system were not the only problems confronting the free inhabitants of Barbados. As Ligon explained to his English readers early in the sugar revolution, sugar, no less than any other agricultural product, was a high-risk crop. Fire, drought, death of livestock or of laborers, and losses at sea were only the most important of many misfortunes that could wipe out a man's assets, destroy his credit, and bring him to an "inevitable ruine" from which, "if he be not well friended, he never can entertain a hope to rise again." Additionally, the high mortality in Barbados meant that planters put their lives as well as their fortunes at risk. Thus, notwithstanding the possibilities offered by sugar for the rapid accumulation of fortunes, the many hazards involved made it a venture fit only for those reckless and competitive men who, having always been "will[ing to] sell their lives at such a rate, as none shall out-bid them," had grown so accustomed to risk as to become "more valiant then other men." Barbados, Ligon warned, was obviously not a place for the faint of heart or for those who preferred to "live in a quiet security."[23]

According to Ligon and other early commentators, even those who succeeded in the sugar lottery faced lives in the colony that by conventional English standards contained few attractions. To be sure, they could afford anything money could buy. Visitors were invariably struck by their great extravagance. "They economize on nothing," declared one Frenchman during the early years of the sugar revolution. They paid outrageous sums for clothes, furnished their houses "sumptuously," went "well mounted on very handsome horses . . . covered with rich saddle-cloths," enjoyed abundant tables, and served "the best wines from more than six areas in Europe, brandy, Rossolis, and many artificial drinks." So high was the demand for

---

[22] Ligon, *True & Exact History*, 29, 45–46; Blome, *Description*, 91; Handler, "Father Biet's Visit," 66–67, 69; Plantagenet, *Description*, 5; *Great Newes from Barbadoes*, 9–13. For a modern analysis of the prevalence of slave discontent in seventeenth-century Barbados, see Jerome S. Handler, "Slave Revolts and Conspiracies in Seventeenth-Century Barbados," *Nieuwe West-Indische Gids* 56 (1982): 5–42.

[23] Ligon, *True & Exact History*, 117–21.

luxury goods that virtually all of the "finest" products of England and Europe were available in the island.[24]

Yet if successful planters enjoyed "exceeding[ly] profuse and costly" material lives, in almost all other respects during these early years of sugar, their lives and their society were, from the perspective of metropolitan England, impoverished and crude. Their almost total concentration on sugar meant that they gave very little attention to any other kinds of husbandry, and their "ill Husbandry" with regard to food crops and livestock was matched by the irregular and contingent character of the social landscapes they were creating. Thus Bridgetown, the chief town in the colony, was built incrementally, house by house, without plan and with no regard either to the healthiness of its situation or to any other consideration—except the convenience of trade. A similar "improvidence, or inconsideration" was revealed in the colony's architecture. Mostly crude wooden structures built without regard for the peculiarities of the climate, their houses, Ligon complained, largely consisted of poorly ventilated "low roofed rooms" that in the heat of the day were more "like Stoves, or heated Ovens" than human habitations. Barbados had stone for better and more permanent buildings. By the early 1650s, moreover, it also had carpenters and masons who were "very great Masters in their Art" and fully competent to "draw a plot, and pursue the design they framed with great diligence, and beautifie the tops of their Doors, Windows, and Chimney-peeces, very prettily." However, "though the Planters talk[ed] of building houses, and wish[ed] them up, yet when they weigh the want of those hands in their sugar work, that must be employed in their building," Ligon lamented, "they fall back, and put on their considering caps."[25]

Nor, for the same reason, did wealthy Barbadians invest much time or energy in creating the cultural amentities enjoyed by their counterparts in urban England. The concerns of most people, Ligon observed, "were so fixt upon, and so rivited to the earth, and the profit that arise out of it, as their souls were lifted no higher." Thus, although Ligon met a few people who "had musical minds," most men, he reported, thought, as some had "been heard to say, that three whip-sawes, going all at once in a Frame or Pit, is the best and sweetest musick that can enter their ears; and to hear a Cow of their own low, or an Assinigo bray, no sound can please them better."[26]

Conventional English moral standards were also reputedly little regarded

---

[24] Handler, "Father Biet's Visit," 67–68.

[25] Blome, *Description,* 89; Ligon, *True & Exact History,* 25, 34, 40, 42, 102; *Great Newes from Barbadoes,* 4.

[26] Ligon, *True & Exact History,* 107.

in Barbados. Drunkenness was so common that it seemed to be the very "custom of the country." Lewdness, fornication, adultery, and incest were common, and fist fighting appeared to be the primary vehicle for settling disputes. Nor, according to many commentators, was such behavior much mitigated by either law or religion. Laws against immorality were "rarely put in execution," and, in any case, the legal system was said to be both loose and mutable, with justices making "laws one court, and break[ing] them the next." Although there were ministers in every parish, "very few people" came to hear them, and the tolerance some Catholic visitors found on this nominally Protestant island was, they thought, largely the product of religious indifference. "To tell the truth," one of them declared, "they have almost no religion."[27]

So deep had "the sins of *Sodom*" penetrated into the island's life that some Quakers and others feared for the future of the colony. That the islanders were guilty of excessive wickedness, "Lewdness, and [other] Abominations," extending even to their refusal to confer "the benefit and blessing of being Christians" upon their slaves, was undeniable. Reminding Barbadians that they had only recently been very "little in thine owne eyes, and in the eyes of all that knew thee," these critics both attributed the island's rapid rise to wealth to God and predicted that without a speedy reformation in their behavior He would sooner or later repay their ingratitude and rebellion against Him by "Blast[ing] their Endeavors, . . . bring[ing] them into Contempt," and "Otherwise . . . bring[ing] Our fruitful Island [once again] into a Wilderness."[28]

Thus did the early image makers of Barbados endow it with an ambivalent identity. At the same time that they were celebrating its great natural beauty and fecundity and its remarkable capacity for generating wealth through sugar, they were depicting an ugly human environment in which mortality and risks of economic failure were high and the vast labor force was cruelly exploited. They also portrayed the society created by the winners in the sugar lottery as extravagant, loose, morally and culturally debased, and riddled with fears of social revolt. Although one writer claimed that the "most considerable inhabitants" thought "themselves so well[-situated in Barbados], that [they] . . . seldom . . . ever remove[d] thence," their behavior as de-

[27] Verney to Verney, Feb. 10, 1638, *Verney Family Papers*, 193–95; Handler, "Father Biet's Visit," 61–62, 68–69; Spörri, "Account," 6; Ligon, *True & Exact History*, 101.

[28] Richard Pinder, *A Loving Invitation (to Repentance and Amendment to Life) unto All the Inhabitants of the Island of Barbados* (London, 1660), 3–5; Davis, "Early Impression of Barbados," 539; Ligon, *True & Exact History*, 82.

scribed by the vast majority of commentators bespoke the contrary. The contingent character of the towns and houses, the planters' heedless spending of labor in the quest for immediate profits, and their evident disinterest in investing in social and cultural amenities strongly suggested that they regarded Barbados as only a temporary abode to be escaped as soon as they had made their fortunes. According to Ligon, there were few "whose minds" were "not over-ballanc'd with avarice and lucre" who did not "hanker after their own Country" and did not intend, as soon as they had enough wealth and could sell their estates, "to settle themselves quietly in England."[29]

During the 1660s and 1670s, however, observers began to put more and more emphasis upon the colony's achievements in many areas, and Barbados gradually began to acquire a more positive image. Sugar, they stressed, had brought the island not only a severe labor system and substantial wealth for a great many of its proprietors but also a surging population. In less than a decade following the introduction of the crop, the white population was thought to have increased by 150 percent from 20,000 to 50,000, and the latter figure became the standard estimate offered in contemporary accounts of the island for most of the rest of the seventeenth century. At the same time, the number of black slaves was said to have jumped to 100,000 by the early 1670s. Although these figures, especially those for whites, were certainly much too generous, Barbados, as one visitor remarked, had become "so heavily populated in such a short time" that virtually no contemporary commentator failed to stress the density of its population in comparison with all other English colonies in America.[30]

At a time when competition among European powers in the West Indies was intense, such a large population made Barbados unusually strong; more important, it gave the island a settled character that, in terms of both its extent and the rapidity with which it had been achieved, was unparalleled among contemporary Anglo-American settlements. In the late 1640s it still had a lot of uncleared forests, but by the mid–1650s a substantial portion of the island had been brought under sugar cultivation. By the mid–1660s it was so intensively planted that from the sea it could be taken, in the words of one writer, "for one great City." By the mid–1670s it had been "so taken up in Plantations, that there" was "no wast ground to be found," the "whole

---

[29] Davies, *History*, 8–9; Ligon, *True & Exact History*, 22, 117.

[30] Ligon, *True & Exact History*, 43; Handler, "Father Biet's Visit," 69; Spörri, "Account," 10; Davies, *History*, 8–9; Ogilby, *America*, 377; Blome, *Description*, 84; Heylyn, *Cosmography*, 1118; *Great Newes from Barbadoes*, 13–14; B[urton], *English Empire in America*, 199.

Isle for these many years" having had, as one earlier observer noted, such "a supernumerary glut of inhabitants" as to make it clear that Barbados was "too small a hive for such a swarm of people."[31]

Acknowledgment of this extraordinary progress in population as well as wealth was reflected in virtually every contemporary assessment of the colony's worth to England. Not only was it "one of the chief of our Plantations" and the "most considerable Colony the *English* hath amongst that Frye of *Isles* called the *Caribbee*[s]," it was also "certainly the most flourishing, and best peopled of all" the colonies "possest by the *English*," a plantation, almost every commentator agreed, that was "worth all the rest which are made by the English"—perhaps even, in the words of one of its most ardent champions, "the finest and worthiest Island in the World." With "not more than five and twenty thousand white Inhabitant," Dalby Thomas pointed out in 1690 in *An Historical Account of the Rise and Growth of the West India Collonies*, the small island of Barbados had "produced in Commodities above thirty Millions *Sterling*" and had "pay'd in Duties to support the [English] Government at a modest Computation, above ¾ of a Million" which, he remarked, must "seem incredible to those that have not Employ'd thoughts on it." To the extent that, as another advocate of Barbados argued just a few years later, it was "the Planters and Settlers of our *America*[*n*] Plantations, to whom *England* owes its greatest Riches and Prosperity," Barbados had contributed a greatly disproportionate share.[32]

Thus, through the agency of sugar, the unpromising island of Barbados had become "very famous in all parts" and had been transformed from a formidable wilderness into a "Spatious and profitable Garden." Ligon and his contemporaries at midcentury had depicted Barbados as a place of great natural beauty in which the industrious newcomer could make a fortune during the first phases of the sugar lottery. By the 1670s Ligon's successors could no longer herald the island as a place of wide-open opportunity in which even industrious and intelligent servants had a chance "to get Estates." By that time, the English West Indian frontier had shifted to the Leeward

---

[31] Ligon, *True & Exact History*, 24, 106; Handler, "Father Biet's Visit," 65–66; Edmund Hickeringill, *Jamaica Viewed* (London, 1661), 16–17; Davis, "Early Impression of Barbados," 539; Davies, *History*, 8–9; Ogilby, *America*, 379; Blome, *Description*, 79; Speed, *Prospect*, 48.

[32] Ogilby, *America*, 378; Blome, *Description*, 65; Heylyn, *Cosmography*, 1118; Speed, *Prospect*, 48; *Great Newes from Barbadoes*, 3, 13–14; B[urton], *English Empire in America*, 198; Dalby Thomas, *An Historical Account of the Rise and Growth of the West India Collonies* (London, 1690), 37; *A State of the Present Condition of the Island of Barbadoes* (London, [1696]), 3.

Islands and Jamaica. They still emphasized the island's astonishing capacity to generate wealth through the production of sugar, even to the point of giving it preeminence in any depiction of the colony. But they now gave almost equal weight to its settled character. They suggested through the increasing use of the term *garden* to describe the colony, that Barbados, unlike England's other colonies both in the islands and on the mainland, had rapidly become a place not just of natural but of cultivated—that is, improved—beauty.[33]

People came to the new societies of colonial British America not merely to better their economic situation but also with the complementary hope of transforming those new places into improved ones. The language of improvement was ubiquitous in the early modern British world. In England and Scotland it referred primarily to schemes, devices, or projects through which the economic position of the country might be advanced, the estates or fortunes of individuals bettered, or existing resources made more productive. In the new societies of colonial British America, the term carried similar connotations. Settlers sought to "improve" their situations by securing the necessary capital and labor to develop their lands and fortunes; towns that would facilitate trade; roads, bridges, and ferries that would provide them with better access to markets.

But the term also acquired a much wider meaning: it was used to describe a state of society that was far removed from the savagery thought to be characteristic of most of America's original inhabitants, one that was not wild, barbaric, irregular, rustic, or crude, but, like England itself, was settled, cultivated, civilized, orderly, developed, and polite. The concept of improvement thus enabled settlers in colonial British America to think of the societies they were creating in developmental terms. Their hope was that the simplifications of traditional social forms that were so obvious during the first phases of settlement would sooner or later be followed by a process of social articulation that would in turn lead ultimately in the direction of an ever greater assimilation to traditional paradigms derived from the socioeconomic, cultural, and political order of the world they had left behind.

By the 1670s the proud boast of Barbados was that it was considerably further into this process of social articulation and replication than any other English colony in America. Fully subdivided into fourteen parishes, each with its own church or chapel already built, it contained several urban settle-

---

[33] Davies, *History*, 8–9; *Great Newes from Barbadoes*, 13; Towns, "Observations," 229; Ligon, *True & Exact History*, 22, 86, 116–17; Handler, "Father Biet's Visit," 60, 64, 67; Thomas, *Historical Account*, 27.

ments. Bridgetown, its capital and "principal *Emporium*," was, despite two devastating fires, a "flourishing City" with "many fair, long, and spatious Streets, furnish'd with a great number of noble Structures." The author of *Great Newes from Barbados*, published in 1676, was conscious that the social condition of the island in his generation contrasted favorably with that which had confronted Ligon, who, writing a mere twenty years earlier, had found little to praise in Barbados other than "that much Celebrated perpetual Verdure that Adorns the Native Trees of that warm World." Now, in 1676, the author described how both the towns and the countryside were full of "Houses which could boast a Grandeur much more considerable than those" of which "most of our [English] Villages are composed of." Furthermore, according to the proud announcement of another writer, virtually every plantation on the island was "delightfully situated" with "pleasant Prospects to the Sea and Land." Each one, "small and great," had "Sugar-works . . . with fair and large Buildings made of Stone and Brick" and "covered with tiles or slate." Together with the dwelling house, many of which were also made of stone and roofed with tiles, this large collection of sturdy and permanent buildings made each plantation look "like a handsome town." To grind its cane, Barbados had about 400 windmills, "whose flying Sailes, besides the Profit they bring the Owner[s]," provided a "Remarkably pleasant . . . first Prospect from the Sea."[34]

Better and more permanent buildings and more intensive urbanization were accompanied by other improvements. In the 1650s Barbadian planters had been so preoccupied with producing sugar that they were content to drink contaminated water from ponds and to rely on the island's many superb natural fruits. By the mid–1670s, however, one correspondent told the Royal Society in London, "almost every sugar-plantation has a well that yields very good water," while some planters had enjoyed "Prodigious Success . . . in the Improvement of several newly introduced Fruits." During the closing decades of the seventeenth century, the extension of sugar cultivation to more recently settled islands with newer and richer soils put Barbados at a serious competitive disadvantage in the race for sugar profits. As contemporaries appreciated, however, this development also had the beneficial effect of forcing Barbadians to become careful husbandmen. More and more after 1680, they had "to dung and improve their Plantations [until they were] like so many Gardens." In the process, Barbados became the

---

[34] *Great Newes from Barbadoes*, 4, 9–13; Davies, *History*, 8–9; Ogilby, *America*, 379; Speed, *Prospect*, 48; Handler, "Father Biet's Visit," 63, 65; Spörri, "Account," 5; Blome, *Description*, 79–80; B[urton], *English Empire in America*, 202; Towns, "Observations," 229; Oldmixon, *British Empire*, 1st ed., 2:116.

colony in the English West Indies noted for having "the greatest Husbandry and Skill."[35]

At the same time, Barbadians had developed a network of roads that, in comparison with those elsewhere in the West Indies, were "undoubtedly very fine." These roads linked the rural inhabitants closely to the towns, where shops and warehouses were "filled with all one could wish from all parts of the world" and where all manner of artisans, including even goldsmiths, jewelers, and clockmakers, provided many of the same specialized services enjoyed by the inhabitants of the largest English towns. Furthermore, in contrast to the simple yet relatively undifferentiated societies of England's other American colonies, Barbados had by the third quarter of the seventeenth century a fully articulated social structure. Like England itself, it had an enormous number of dependent laborers presided over by a small number of independent property owners, the wealthiest of whom, "Masters, Merchants, and Planters, live[d] each like little Sovereigns in their Plantations" in a manner "equal to many of our Nobility and Gentry, of the first Rank in *England*."[36]

At midcentury Ligon had presented Barbados as a place where it was possible for people to grow rich and live a quiet, simple retired life in beautiful tropical surroundings. But he had strongly advised those who loved "the pleasures of *Europe* . . . (or particularly of *England*) and the great variety of those . . . never [to] come there." The society was too crude, the climate too hot, and the landscape too dissimilar, he suggested, to permit the inhabitants to engage in many characteristic English activities. Well before the close of the seventeenth century, however, one reporter after another emphasized that the simplicity of the 1650s had given way to a rich social and cultural life. Barbados was not yet itself a genuinely new England. But especially in comparison with other American colonies, these writers suggested, it was becoming in more and more ways recognizably English.[37]

This was particularly true in relation to the life-styles of the wealthy. "Being *English*, and [by the 1670s and 1680s] having all their commerce from England," members of the island's white elite were always imitating "the Customes, and Fashions of *England*, both as to Apparell, household-Furniture, Eating and Drinking, &c." Their clothes were "fashionable and courtly," their diet "the same with ours in *England*," their "Equipages . . .

[35] Towns, "Observations," 229; *Great Newes from Barbadoes*, 7–8; [William Cleland], *The Present State of the Sugar Plantations Consider'd* (London, 1713), 20.

[36] Connell, "Father Labat's Visit," 163, 173; Oldmixon, *British Empire*, 1st ed., 2:111–14; Ligon, *True & Exact History*, 43; Blome, *Description*, 83–84.

[37] Ligon, *True & Exact History*, 58, 104–6.

rich, their Liveries fine, their Coaches and Horses answerable; their Chairs, Chaises, and all the Conveniences for their travelling, magnificent." Though the heat obliged the islanders to be content for the most part with "sedentary Diversions more than active," the wealthy reportedly enjoyed a perpetual round of "Balls and Consorts," frequently employed their own "Pleasure-Boats, to make the *Tour* of the Island," and provided an avid audience when an English puppet theater company visited the island. Notwithstanding Ligon's prediction that the turf was neither "fine enough, nor the Ground soft enough to make a Bowling Green in Barbadoes," the island boasted two of them by the early eighteenth century.[38]

As Barbados had become more settled and more improved in all these ways, its independent proprietors reputedly had shown increased attention to both comfort and beauty in their lives. If houses in Bridgetown were mostly "well built in the English style with many glass windows" and "magnificently furnished," "houses on the plantations" were "better built [even] than those of the towns," one visitor observing that they were "large with good fenestration completely glazed; the arrangements of the rooms . . . commodious and comfort . . . well understood." Nor did Barbadians apply their vaunted agricultural skills strictly to sugar. All over the island, it was reported, proprietors took pride in the "Excellency" of their kitchen gardens and paid considerable attention to landscape. By 1700, according to one visitor from a nearby French island, this effort had resulted in a "beautiful countryside" in which "Nearly all" plantations exhibited "fine avenues of tamarinds, or, of . . . large orange trees . . ., or of other trees which give shade and make the houses very attractive." This attention to aesthetics reached even to the quarters of the slaves, whose habitations were "well laid out in lines and uniform."[39]

The growing civility of the Barbados elite and achievement of a more cultivated landscape were not the only evidence that Barbados was assimilating ever more closely to the English model of an improved society during the closing years of the seventeenth century and the opening decades of the eighteenth. By the 1670s it already seems to have been characterized by a more settled family life. Following the shift to black slavery as the predominant form of labor between 1650 and 1660, white servant immigration tended to decline. The result was that over the next several decades the white population became less disproportionately male, with marriage more the norm and population replacement more the result of natural increase. By the

---

[38] Thomas, *Historical Account*, 53; Oldmixon, *British Empire*, 1st ed., 2:114–15, 126–27; Blome, *Description*, 88.

[39] Connell, "Father Labat's Visit," 163, 171, 173; *Great Newes from Barbadoes*, 7–8.

end of the century, "everyone" among the white population was married, and, because the women were so "very prolific," there were "swarms of children."[40]

If the social, cultural, and family life of Barbados was looking more and more like that of England, so were the island's public institutions. During the first decades of settlement, the political and legal systems had been unsettled. By the 1650s, however, Barbadians were taking pride in the fact that their government bore "a very near correspondence" with that of England. They had regular courts, were governed for the most part by the "Lawes of *England*, for all Criminal, Civil, Martial, Ecclesiastical, and Maritime affairs," and they had their own local legislature "in nature of the Parliament of *England*" to make additional laws to fit whatever conditions were "peculiar to the place." By 1700 judges, officials, and legislators were often creoles with an English education as well as considerable local expertise. "Of late Years," one writer claimed in 1713, even the legal profession was composed largely of "Men brought up at the Universities, and Inns of Court" in England. One native son, the younger Christopher Coddrington, had so distinguished himself as a classical scholar at Christ Church, Oxford, as to attract the attention and admiration of metropolitan intellectuals and to be appointed royal governor of the nearby Leeward Islands. Upon his death in 1710, he bequeathed £40,000 to establish a college in Barbados. A fitting capstone to the island's increasingly rich cultural life, this institution promised both to make it unnecessary for Barbadian youths to travel to England for advanced education and in general to "produce good Effects upon the Inhabitants, both with respect to Religion and good Manners; and so by consequence [with respect to] the good Government of the Place."[41]

As they increasingly came to emphasize the extent to which Barbados had become an improved society, the colony's interpreters also painted a generally flattering portrait of the "natures and dispositions" of its wealthy proprietors. To be sure, they retained a reputation for extravagance. As one English merchant trading to the island remarked in 1695, "no People in the World have been more remarkable for a Luxuriant way of Living." The English economic and political writer Charles Davenant thought that the "rich soil, easy acquisition of wealth, and . . . warm climate" had "infected" all the English West Indian colonies with "excess and luxury." Thus, not-

---

[40] Davis, "Early Impression of Barbados," 539; Connell, "Father Labat's Visit," 163–64.

[41] Ligon, *True & Exact History*, 50, 100–101; Spörri, "Account," 7; Ogilby, *America*, 380; Blome, *Description*, 94–96; Speed, *Prospect*, 48; [Cleland], *Present State*, 5, 12; William Gordon, *A Sermon Preach'd at the Funeral of the Honourable Colonel Christopher Codrington* (London, 1710), 22.

withstanding a less favorable economic situation produced by declining soil fertility and increased competition from newer sugar settlements, the generation of Barbadians at the turn of the seventeenth century had not, "in any measure, retrench'd those Extravagant Excesses that were wont to abound amongst them, or have yet learn'd what Providence . . . is." If, however, later generations of wealthy Barbadians continued like their ancestors to live "at the height of Pleasure," they now did so, in contrast to their forebears, with considerably more "good taste," discrimination, and politeness.[42]

Besides, this profuse life-style, as several writers noted, seemed to be closely associated with what they regarded as an admirable sociability and liberality. "Very sociable," they reportedly received both friends and strangers "with extraordinary expressions of civility." Nor, apparently, was this "good Hospitality" confined to the wealthy. Rather, according to one writer, it reached down from "those of the better rank to the meanest Inhabitants, who think it a great want of civility to dismiss any one from their houses, before they have presented them with somewhat to eat and drink." Ligon and later writers traced this "Loving, friendly, and hospitable" strain in the Barbadian character to the heterogeneity of the early settlers. Precisely because they were "of several Perswasions," Ligon suggested, they had found it necessary to bury their differences in the quest for sugar profits. Thus, during the English Civil War, they "made a Law amongst themselves, that whosoever nam'd the word *Roundhead* or *Cavalier*, should give to all those that heard him, a Shot and a Turky, to be eaten at his house that made the forfeiture; which," Ligon reported, "sometimes was done purposely, that they might enjoy the company of one another." "So frank, so loving, and so good natur'd were these Gentlemen one to another" that with only a few interruptions, the historian John Oldmixon averred during the first years of the eighteenth century, public affairs in the colony were remarkable for their concord and rarely "troubled with Factions and Parties." Barbadians, it seemed, vied with one another over nothing of any greater moment than the magnificence of their "Liberal Entertainment[s]," which, as one champion of the colony proclaimed, could "not be Exceeded by this their Mother Kingdome itself."[43]

But their commitment to good living did not mean, writers were careful

---

[42] Ligon, *True & Exact History*, 57; A Merchant, *A Discourse of the Duties on Merchandize, More Particularly of That on Sugars* (London, 1695), 11; Charles D'Avenant, *The Political and Commercial Works*, 5 vols. (London, 1771), 2:21–22; Blome, *Description*, 84–89; Connell, "Father Labat's Visit," 163, 171–72.

[43] Oldmixon, *British Empire*, 1st ed., 2:114, 126–27; Davies, *History*, 198–99; Ligon, *True & Exact History*, 57; *Great Newes from Barbadoes*, 7–8, 13–14; Speed, *Prospect*, 48; Handler, "Father Biet's Visit," 62, 68; Connell, "Father Labat's Visit," 167.

to emphasize, that wealthy Barbadians were either soft or lazy. As their spirited help to other islands during the two major intercolonial wars between 1689 and 1713 seemed to demonstrate, Barbadian *"Creoleans* [were] . . . as brave Men as any in the World," and they prided themselves on their industry. Ligon had early stressed the extent to which "sluggard[s were] detested in a Countrey, where Industry and Activity" yielded such high premiums, and the vast estates still enjoyed by later generations stood "as glorious Proofs [both] of the Industry . . . of their Ancestors" and of their own continued diligence in a situation in which declining fertility forced them to triple their efforts to secure the same level of profits achieved by these same ancestors.[44]

During the half century beginning around 1660, Barbados thus gradually had acquired an identity as an improved and settled society in which, in the words of Oldmixon, "Wealth and Pleasure, which are generally Strangers, . . . dwell[ed] . . . together." Full of people who were rich, "civil, generous, hospitable, and very sociable," Barbados was rapidly achieving a reputation, in the words of a French visitor in 1700, as a "congenial society" whose "inhabitants were everywhere esteemed."[45]

Underneath all the surface glitter, however, at least some of the problems that had helped to tarnish Barbados's early image remained. In his extensive treatment of Barbados in his *British Empire in America*, Oldmixon defended the island's planters against the old charges of cruelty toward servants and slaves. Because it contained little meat, the diets of servants, he admitted, were "not so good, as those who have been us'd to rich Farmers['] Tables in *England*." But in all other respects, he contended, their lives were "not very hard," their labor being "much less than our Day-Labourers in *England*, and their Encouragement much more; for if they are good for any thing when they come out of their Times, there are enough [who] will employ them on their own Terms."[46]

Similarly, Oldmixon dismissed the "Stories . . . told of . . . Severities" against slaves as gross exaggerations. He did not deny that their large numbers, their "frequent attempts to get the mastery," and what whites perceived as laziness, carelessness, and dissembling forced masters "to carry a strict Hand over them." He also admitted that slave treatment varied according to

[44] Oldmixon, *British Empire*, 1st ed., 2:111, 113; Ligon, *True & Exact History*, 57, 108; Davis, "Early Impression of Barbadoes," 539; [Cleland], *Present State*, 20; Thomas Tryon, *England's Grandeur, and Way to Get Wealth* (London, 1699), 11–13.

[45] Oldmixon, *British Empire*, 1st ed., 2:111–12, 114; Connell, "Father Labat's Visit," 163, 167.

[46] Oldmixon, *British Empire*, 1st ed., 2:116.

the "Nature or Understanding of the Masters." But he insisted that "few English have been barbarous, as they are all represented to be, by the Enemies of the Plantations." "Their Whipping them with Thongs, till they are all a-gore of Blood; their tying them up by their Hands or Feet, to endure such Stripes, and the pickling afterwards with Brine" were all, he declared, nothing more than mere "Bugbears to frighten Children with, like Tales of *Raw-head, and Bloody-bones*." More commonly, he wrote, planters provided well for their slaves, seeing to it that they had good housing, adequate food and clothing, and family garden plots and that they were dealt with "humanely and prudently" by their overseers. Nor were the planters primarily responsible for the failure of the slaves to become Christians. The truth was, Oldmixon asserted, that slaves were "so fond of their own Idolatry" that few of them showed "any disposition to hearken to the Doctrine of the Christians." [47]

In this extended apology for the Barbadian planter class, Oldmixon also suggested that the gradual articulation of Barbados society and the creolization of the slave population were affecting the character of life on the island in ways that were beneficial to both masters and slaves. As slaves had grown more numerous and the economic and social demands of the free population more elaborate, new opportunities had opened up for the more able and assimilated slaves, who could now rise out of field labor into high-status skilled activities. These included key roles in sugar processing, all the major artisanal trades, and domestic service. Furthermore, according to Oldmixon, the "*Creolian* Negroes," who had been taught by the example of the whites to despise recently arrived "*saltwater* negroes," began both to "value themselves much on being born in *Barbadoes*" and to assimilate more fully to white culture. Thus, for example, did native slaves slowly move away from the "Diabolical Religion" of the "Foreign Slaves" toward that of the English. The implication in Oldmixon's analysis was that these social and demographic developments and the distinctions they had created within the slave population were rendering slavery less onerous, leading to the more complete adjustment of the slaves to slavery and enabling whites both to treat slaves more leniently and to enjoy more secure lives. [48]

But the testimony of other contemporary observers powerfully suggested that Oldmixon was far too sanguine in his accounts of relations between masters and their servants and slaves. A young French missionary, Father Jean-Baptiste Labat, visited Barbados in 1700 and drew a generally favor-

---

[47] Ibid., 115, 118–20.

[48] Ibid., 117, 121–24.

able picture of life in the colony, which he subsequently published in France. Having served since 1694 in the French sugar islands of Martinique and Guadeloupe, Labat fully appreciated that conditions inherent in slavery "often compelled" the "inhabitants of islands of whatever nationality . . . to exceed the limits of moderation in the punishment of their slaves so as to intimidate" them. These measures, he believed, were necessary because the blacks, who outnumbered the whites by the ratio of 10 to 1, were "always ready to rebel and attempt to commit the most terrible crimes to regain their freedom."[49]

Nevertheless, Labat was virtually unstinting in his condemnation of the ways in which Barbadians treated their laborers. White servants, he reported, "groan[ed] under a harsh servitude of 7 or, at least 5 years, when they are compelled to begin a fresh term on pretexts which their masters always have ready, certain that they can do so because the judges never decide against them," and he predicted that in case of invasion, servants would "without fail . . . join with the invading force." And the condition of slaves was even worse. According to Labat, Barbadian whites yet regarded slaves "pretty nearly as beasts to whom every licence" was "allowed, provided that they perform[ed] their work satisfactorily." Uninstructed in the precepts of Christianity, they were "permitted to have several wives and to leave them as they please, provided that they produce[d] a large number of children, . . . work[ed] well and" did "not become ill." But such laxity was accompanied by the most severe labor discipline. It seemed to Labat that overseers appeared "to care less for the life of a negro than that of a horse," and he further charged them with working slaves "beyond measure and [with beating] them mercilessly for the least fault." Neither such rigorous punishment nor the knowledge that torture and death were the certain ends of unsuccessful rebellion prevented slaves from rising up against "their drunken, unreasonable and savage overseers." Those who were subsequently captured, Labat reported, were "burnt alive or exposed in iron cages in which they" were "attached to the branch of a tree, or . . . left to die of hunger and thirst." This last practice, according to Labat, was known in Barbados as "putting a man to dry." Such harsh measures, the witness of Oldmixon notwithstanding, reveal that Barbadian whites still believed themselves to have everything "to fear from their negroes."[50]

In the very same year that Labat visited Barbados, Thomas Tryon, a London merchant who had earlier resided in the colony, published a series

---

[49] Connell, "Father Labat's Visit," 168–69.

[50] Ibid.

of letters in which he condemned sugar production as inherently "violent, I may say cruel." Predicting that Barbados could not long "thrive by such Oppressive Methods and Severities," he publicly urged Barbadian proprietors to "consider with your slaves, that the Groaning of him that suffereth Pain, is the beginning of the Trouble and Misery of them that laid it on." With this precept in mind, Tryon called upon Barbadians to abandon sugar for cotton, to stop mistreating their slaves, and to "begin a reformation in your selves, and cure the looseness and extravagancies of your Youth" before they felt the "Vindicative Hand of the Divine Power."[51]

If, as Tryon also remarked, such wickedness was "a sure Indication of Calamity and Misery to any Country," there were many signs during the three decades beginning in the early 1680s that Barbados was already suffering from divine retribution. Throughout these years, Barbados was beset by a variety of economic and demographic problems. Four to five decades of intense sugar cultivation had left some properties so "extremely barren, dry, and worn out" that their owners had to replant canes at least every other year in order to obtain satisfactory profits. They used so much manure on their lands that some planters began to specialize wholly in providing it to sugar producers. At the same time, lack of land for sugar expansion and consolidation of small estates into larger ones resulted in declining opportunity and considerable out-migration to newer colonies. Finally, a major epidemic of yellow fever broke out in 1691. Continuing intermittently for well over a decade, Oldmixon recounted, it indiscriminately "swept away . . . many . . . Masters, Servants, and Slaves." There had been a steady stream of some of the more successful planters back to England since the early days of the sugar revolution, and this persisting epidemic considerably accelerated this process as some of the colony's "most eminent" planter families migrated to escape the "fatal Disease." The result of all these developments, according to Oldmixon and other observers, was a significant depopulation of the island. The numbers of both whites and blacks fell, perhaps by as much as 25 percent, to 25,000 and 60,000 respectively.[52]

Oldmixon predicted that with the abatement of the epidemic, the population would recover in just a few years, provided Barbadians were "not too much discourag'd from Home." His qualification derived from a widespread feeling in Barbados that, notwithstanding the great wealth it had brought to Britain and the alacrity with which it had contributed to the

---

[51] Thomas Tryon, *Tryon's Letters, Domestick and Foreign* (London, 1700), 183–200.

[52] Ibid., 200; Connell, "Father Labat's Visit," 170; Oldmixon, *British Empire*, 1st ed., 2:111–13; Thomas, *Historical Account*, 53; *A Discourse*, 11–12.

defense of the other West Indian colonies during the intercolonial wars of 1689–1713, the island had indeed already suffered substantial discouragement from England in the decades after the Restoration. This feeling derived from three principal sources. First, in 1663, at the crown's insistence, the Barbados legislature had voted a 4½ percent duty on the export of all dead commodities from the colony to serve as a permanent revenue to cover the colony's civil and military expenses. Over the next twenty years, however, the crown diverted much of this revenue to other uses and thus forced the legislature to raise additional money to support the internal administration of the island. Second, at a time when Barbados was already finding it difficult to compete with newer sugar colonies, Parliament imposed a series of new duties on sugar products in addition to those it had previously levied in 1661. Finally, during the quarter century following the Glorious Revolution, Barbadians complained that they were suffering under a string of oppressive royal governors, who, animated by "Avarice and Love of Power" and supported by the metropolitan government, seemed to be "intent upon nothing but their own private Gain." By promoting parties, engaging in a variety of arbitrary practices, and systematically ignoring the public welfare of the island, these men, defenders of the colony charged, were rapidly destroying its customary public tranquillity.[53]

The many "great discouragement[s]" from England evoked deep resentments within Barbados. Not only did they threaten to bring social and economic ruin upon the colony, but, equally disturbing, they also indicated that metropolitan officials regarded Barbados less as a distant society of kindred English people than as a source of immediate revenue and exploitation. By such measures, Edward Littleton, a Barbadian planter who had recently settled in England, charged in 1689, Barbadians were being "*commanded as Subjects, and . . . crusht as Aliens*." Despite their manifest loyalty, what Littleton referred to as their "Obsequious Devotion to our dear and native . . . Mother Country," they were being treated, he complained, as if they had no claim to the traditional rights, privileges, and benefits of Englishmen and could therefore be used as "miserable Drudges and Beggers" for the profit and pleasure of those who stayed at home. As he pointed out to his English readers, however, Barbadians believed that they had "as good English Bloud in our Veins, as . . . those that we left behind us. How came we to lose our

---

[53] Oldmixon, *British Empire*, 1st ed., 2:113; Thomas, *Historical Account*, 42–43; [Cleland], *Present State*, 8, 18–19; [Edward Littleton], *The Groans of the Plantations; or A True Account of Their Grevious and Extreme Sufferings by the Heavy Impositions upon Sugar and Other Hardships Relating More Particularly to the Island of Barbados* (London, 1689), 1–17.

Countrey, and the Priviledges of it?" he asked. "Why will you cast us out?" Barbadians, another writer similarly declared in 1698, were "no other but *English* Men: They are your Countrey-Men, your Kindred and Relations, and they ought not to be thus Barbarously used."[54]

As these quotations suggest, "barbarous usage" by metropolitan officials not only stirred deep resentment within Barbados, it also touched a particularly sensitive nerve. Like colonists in other overseas territories, seventeenth- and early eighteenth-century Barbadians long had worried lest "the obscurity of their Origine, . . . the harshness of their Language, . . . the barbarisme of the Manners, . . . their strange course of Life, . . . the cruelty of their Wars, . . . their ancient Poverty, [or] . . . the unconstancy of their Fortune" should prevent their "favourable Reception" in England. Aspiring to parity of status with English people who had remained in England and thus already thinking of themselves and fearing that they would be thought of in England as "poor *Caribbeans*," Barbadians were deeply wounded by any suggestion that they were in any way inferior Englishmen. Yet, the common opinion within England during the late seventeenth century seems to have been, in the words of the economic writer Josiah Child, that both *"Virginia* and *Barbados* were first peopled by a Sort of loose vagrant People, vicious and destitute of Means to live at Home (being either unfit for Labour, or such as could find none to employ themselves about, or had so misbehav'd themselves by Whoring, Thieving, or other Debauchery, that none would set them on work)."[55]

In endeavoring to counter this negative image, West Indians and their supporters in England admitted "that, in peopling those Plantations, many persons of obscure Births and very indifferent Characters went, or were, from time to time, sent and transported thither, as Occasion required." But they adamantly denied that the early settlers "consist[ed] only of a sort of Vagabonds and persons of mean condition, as some fondly imagine[d]" in England. Rather, they maintained that "some thousands of Persons of very creditable Families, good Education, and loyal Principles, went thither likewise; some through Narrowness of their Circumstances; some to avoid the Miseries of the Civil War at home; and others to improve such paternal or

---

[54] Thomas, *Historical Account*, iii, 42; [Littleton], *Groans of the Plantations*, 1–2, 15–17, 20–23; *State of the Present Condition*, 3; *The Case of the Inhabitants and Planters in the Island of Jamaica* (London, [1714]), v.

[55] Davies, *History*, dedication pages; Josiah Child, "A Discourse concerning Plantations," in Trevor R. Reese, ed., *The Most Delightful Country of the Universe: Promotional Literature of the Colony of Georgia, 1717–1734* (Savannah, Ga., 1972), 106–7.

acquired Fortunes and Estates, as they thought convenient to carry along with them, at the time." Certainly from the beginning of the sugar revolution, Barbados in particular had "tempted [many] Gentlemen of good Families and moderate Estates." "Whoever will look over the Map of *Barbadoes*," Oldmixon told his readers, would find the names of "Families . . . of the most ancient and honourable in England." To the further credit of Barbados, thirteen of its inhabitants had been knighted by the crown following the Restoration, "more . . . than . . . all the rest of *English* Plantations in *America*" combined. Thus, whatever might have been the case with other colonies, the "common Reflection made upon the Plantations, as to the Meanness of the Planters['] Origins," Oldmixon asserted, was "groundless as to the *Barbadoes*, where," despite the emigration of several of them to England, there were still "as many good Families as . . . in any of the Counties of *England*."[56]

As well as the fact that so many of them derived from prominent English families, the evident significance of their accomplishment in creating—with very little help from home—such an enormously valuable addition to the English world seemed to Barbadians to support their claims for an equal status with and the favorable opinion of metropolitan Englishmen, and their craving for metropolitan acceptance and for a status in the cultural and political center of the Anglophone world commensurate with their wealth and importance was driven by the failure of metropolitan Englishmen to appreciate the laudatory, even the heroic, character of their achievements. Too many people in England, complained the Quaker William Loddington in 1682, had "a sly . . . slighting way of Reflecting upon those that [had] Transplant[ed] themselves and [their] Interest[s] into America, as men of unsetled brains, wandering minds, [who were] void of Solidity and Gravity, &c." But he reminded his readers that "*England* was once as rough and rugged as *America*, and the Inhabitants as blind and barbarous as the *Indians*" and asked them to "consider what a Country *England* it self had now been . . . if our *English* Ancestors had been so solid and staid as to keep in their own Countries." "If their brains had not been thus unsetled," he contended, the "grave" stay-at-homes in contemporary England would never have "had such pleasant and profitable setlements as they" then had. "Every Day, Age, or Generation," Loddington asserted, "hath some peculiar piece of Service to be carried on," which he called "*Generation Work*." Because colonization

---

[56] Davies, *History*, dedication pages, 198–99; *The Groans of Jamaica Express'd in a Letter from a Gentleman Residing There, to His Friend in London* (London, 1714), v; Oldmixon, *British Empire*, 1st ed., 2:110–12.

was "an eminent part of the Generation Work of our Day," it and the people who engaged in it deserved not the scorn but the respect and admiration of the people who stayed behind.[57]

As a result of all their achievements during the first eight decades following the founding of Barbados, its inhabitants had gradually learned to value themselves and their new country. Given their heavy reliance upon their old country for standards of what a civilized—an improved—society should be, however, they could never hope to achieve a fully satisfying sense of themselves and their colony until they had won the approval of the metropolis itself. So poignantly revealed in the writing of Littleton and others of his contemporaries, this deep need for metropolitan approval was, perhaps, no less important than sugar, slavery, or the island's extensive wealth and population in the early stages of the formation of a Barbadian identity.

"Prudence [Is] . . . the Prevailing Principle"

During the seven decades beginning in 1710, a substantial literature on Barbados recorded the changing identity of the island and its dominant white inhabitants. Continuities abounded with the images that had characterized the colony's first eight decades. But there were many subtle yet powerful changes. Before 1740 these changes were mostly in a negative direction. As the colony's old economic difficulties became more severe, it was also beset by serious political discontents. After 1740, however, Barbados slowly began to exhibit a more positive self-image. An expanding local literature explored the inhabitants' collective experiences over time and tried to define their character as both a society and a people. Increasingly, this literature emphasized not the vices but the virtues of Barbadians and not the problems but the achievements of their society.

This change in emphasis seems to have been closely associated with the establishment of the island's first press by the printer Samuel Keimer in 1731. By providing an outlet for local literary productions, many of which he brought together and published in the two-volume collection *Caribbeana* in 1741,[58] Keimer seems to have helped awaken local pride and interest in the island on the part of its native and long-resident inhabitants. In previous decades local literary output had been confined to a few ephemeral and largely polemical pieces published in London. But the next four decades

---

[57] [William Loddington], *Plantation Work the Work of This Generation* (London, 1682), 3, 5–6.

[58] [Samuel Keimer], *Caribbeana: Containing Letters and Dissertations, Together with Political Essays, on Various Subjects and Occasions*, 2 vols. (London, 1741).

witnessed an outpouring of substantial works in other genres, including four short histories,[59] one natural history,[60] two book-length descriptive poems,[61] an agricultural treatise,[62] and a second volume of newspaper contributions.[63] Along with the number of polemical tracts and a growing volume of comment by outsiders, including especially the several general descriptions and histories of the British overseas empire that appeared after 1758,[64] these local productions provide a rich base from which to reconstruct the changing character of Barbadian identity during these years.

Before 1740 Barbados retained the reputation it had developed during the closing decades of the seventeenth century as an unhealthy place in serious economic decline. The malignant fever that had first visited the island in 1691 continued up to midcentury to be especially "fatal to new Comers" and occasionally even to carry off "a great many" oldtimers as well. Barbadians were also thought to age more quickly and to die earlier than people in England. "All the Infirmities of Threescore here," one commentator noted in 1732, were "frequently to be found upon one of five and forty there," while a person of "fifty or fifty four Years" was "a rarer Spectacle in *Barbadoes*, than one of sixty among the like Number of People . . . in *England*."

---

[59] [William Duke], *Some Memoirs of the First Settlement of the Island of Barbados, and Other of the Carribee Islands* . . . (Barbados, 1741); Richard Hall, *A General Account of the First Settlement and of the Trade and Constitution of the Island of Barbados, Written in the Year 1755* (Barbados, 1924); [Henry Frere], *A Short History of Barbados from Its First Discovery and Settlement to the End of the Year 1767* (London, 1768); [Sir John Gay Alleyne], *Remarks upon a Book, Intitled A Short History of Barbados* . . . (Barbados, 1768).

[60] Griffith Hughes, *The Natural History of Barbados* (London, 1750).

[61] [Nathaniel] Weekes, *Barbadoes: A Poem* (London, 1754); John Singleton, *A General Description of the West Indian Islands* . . . *from Barbados to Saint Croix* (Barbados, 1767).

[62] William Belgrove, *A Treatise upon Husbandry or Planting* (Boston, 1755).

[63] [John Orderson?], Extracts from the *Barbados Mercury*, 1772–73 [Barbados, ca. 1773–74]. The apparently only surviving copy of this work lacks a title page and is in the New York Historical Society.

[64] Oldmixon, *British Empire*, 2d ed., 2:1–171; John Harris, *Navigantium atque Itinerantium Bibliotheca*, 2 vols. (London, 1748; rept. 1764), 2:253–57; [Edmund Burke], *An Account of the European Settlements in America*, 2 vols. (London, 1757), 2:81–91; *The Modern Part of an Universal History*, 65 vols. (London, 1747–66), 41:130–211; Daniel Fenning et al., *A New System of Geography: or A General Description of the World*, 2 vols. (London, 1765–66), 1:697–702; William Doyle, *Some Account of the British Dominions Beyond the Atlantic* (London, 1770), 37–39; John Huddleston Wynne, *A General History of the British Empire in America* . . . , 2 vols. (London, 1770), 2:500–505; John Entick et al., *The Present State of the British Empire* . . . , 4 vols. (London, 1774), 4:480–84; Thomas Jeffreys, *The West-India Atlas; or a Compendious Description of the West Indies* (London, 1775; rept. 1794), 20; *American Husbandry*, 2 vols. (London, 1775), 2:151–62.

The many risks that had always been associated with sugar production in Barbados were thus not all economic. Too often, one writer lamented in the early 1740s, new immigrants both "waste[d] their Health" and forfeited their lives in that "distant and scorching Climate."[65]

Barbados was thought to be not only unhealthy but also, in the words of the metropolitan political economist Joshua Gee, "very much worn out" and no longer capable of producing the same "Quantity of Sugars as heretofore." With "every Inch of the Land having been long laboured to the Height" and the soil under constant cultivation for six to ten decades, the colony's planters had to employ "a vast Number of Slaves" and take infinitely greater care to secure profits that, even "in a fruitful Year," were "not above half of what they used to be." Whereas during the seventeenth century sugar had produced such extravagant wealth as to enable the island's planters either to support a luxurious life-style in Barbados or to settle in England, by the 1730s, "the Bulk" of the colony's sugar planters were "considerably in Debt," and it was questionable whether "*Barbadoes*, with all her boasted Wealth," would much longer be "able to support herself in the Perfection to which she is arriv'd." By the mid–1750s, reported William Belgrove, a "regular bred and long experienc'd Planter of the Island," many plantations had "proved not worth holding, and there" were "dismal Prospects of ruinous Buildings in the Island, that were at first very Commodious, which have by various Accidents been destroyed, and only the Land [was any longer] . . . regarded as of Value by joining [it] to other Estates."[66]

In addition to its "drooping [economic] Pow'r" and its malignant disease environment, the Barbadian social environment also helped to tarnish the colony's reputation. Within the island, the institution of chattel slavery was sacrosanct.[67] The successful suppression of a general slave uprising in the early 1690s and the gradual creolization of the slave population during the early years of the eighteenth century seemed to have allayed those white fears of servile revolt that had been nourished by the frequency of slave rebellions during the seventeenth century. Nevertheless, Barbadians realized that "the constant Behaviour of the Negro-Slaves in *America*" left no doubt that they

[65] [Duke], *Some Memoirs*, 61; Hughes, *Natural History*, 37; [Robert Robertson], *A Detection of the State of the Present Sugar Planters, of Barbadoes and the Leeward Islands . . .* (London, 1732), 23, 26; [Jonathan Blenman], *Remarks on Several Acts of Parliament Relating More Especially to the Colonies Abroad . . .* (London, 1742), 124–25; Weekes, *Barbadoes*, 61; Belgrove, *Treatise*, 45.

[66] Joshua Gee, *The Trade and Navigation of Great-Britain Considered* (London, 1729), 45; [Robertson], *Detection*, 15, 25, 81, 88; [Keimer], *Caribbeana* 2:119; Belgrove, *Treatise*, 45.

[67] Weekes, *Barbadoes*, 14.

would try to escape slavery whenever and wherever there was "the least Opening for them." Although some Barbadians warned that those who were tyrants in this world would themselves be condemned to chains in the next and urged more lenient treatment, this consideration seems to have been outweighed by lingering fears of slave revolt. Such fears in turn seemed sufficient to justify both the perpetuation of a harsh labor discipline and a continuing reluctance to provide slaves with the opportunity to become Christians. Englishmen at home might wonder how those in Barbados could "brook to live with so many Slaves as" were "necessary for carrying on a Sugar Plantation." They might lament how descendants of true-born Englishmen could rationalize "bringing our Fellow-Creatures, *who never did us any harm*, into a Condition so justly odious to ourselves." But the omnipresent possibilities of slave revolt prevented white Barbadians from changing their ways. Nonetheless, casual references to what was obviously a brisk sexual commerce between masters and slave women and complaints that continuing association with blacks was producing an Africanization of white language provided evidence of powerful cultural influence of blacks upon whites and illustrated the extent to which white Britons in Barbados were coming to terms with slavery and with the black majority among whom they lived.[68]

Yet another unflattering component of the changing identity of Barbados was its growing fame as a place of discord and contention. During its early generations, the colony had been noted for the tranquillity of its public life. During the last decades of the seventeenth century, however, it gradually had become a scene of "perpetual Struggle and Contention." Throughout most of the early decades of the eighteenth century, it was "miserably divided into Factions," until by the 1730s it was so "full of Discord and Dissensions, perplexed with Parties and Animosities, and involved in such Difficulties of various Kinds" as to bring the island to its "lowest Ebb." Indeed, "the Good People of Barbados" seemed to have grown so accustomed to "venting Fals[e]hoods, Scandals, Absurdities, Scurrilities and Contradictions" in public life as to cause some of the more sober inhabitants to despair that the island would ever again learn "to treat *Public Business* with Decency and Temper" and to conclude that the island's "perpetual Round of Inconsistency

---

[68] [Keimer], *Caribbeana* 1:56, 58, 61–62, 2:5, 105–16; Oldmixon, *British Empire*, 2d ed., 2:53–54; [Robertson], *Detection*, 25–27, 80; Weekes, *Barbadoes*, 33, 56; William Smith, *A Natural History of Nevis, and the Rest of the English Leeward Charibee Islands in America* (Cambridge, 1745), 230–33; William Douglass, *Summary, Historical and Political, of the First Planting, Progressive Improvements, and Present State of the British Settlements in North America*, 2 vols. (Boston, 1749–53), 1:119; [Orderson], Extracts from *Barbadoes Mercury*, 157.

and Tumult" must be attributable "to the Sallies of a warm Imagination in this Climate." But others denied that this "ill State" of affairs was a product of a defect in the Barbadian character. Rather, they blamed it upon the oppression and evil machinations of a long succession of corrupt, greedy, and inept royal governors. As proof of their contention, they cited the brief administration of Viscount Howe, whose generous, liberal, wise, open, and disinterested behavior in 1733–35 had "soon lull'd asleep our jarring Factions" and produced "a general Calm . . . throughout" the "whole Government." Howe's success, Barbadians claimed, gave the lie to "the many Reproaches we have long suffered as a People whom no Governour could please" and showed that when they were "govern'd with Justice" they were peaceful and obedient subjects.[69]

Under Howe's immediate successors, however, the same "tedious Story of the Old Follies of *Barbados* [were] acted over again," and recurring dissensions once more made Barbadians "miserable within ourselves, and ridiculed by the rest of Mankind." The "intestine Divisions among the Inhabitants," lamented Henry Duke, clerk of the assembly in the early 1740s, not only had produced "the greatest Mischiefs" but also had at "several Times" nearly effected "the utter Ruin" of the colony, and he undertook his brief history of the early years of Barbados specifically with the hope of recovering those "true Notions of the right Constitution of this Island" and the principles of social interaction that had enabled the early settlers to live in harmony without discord and partisanship.[70]

Many observers, including some Barbadians, traced all of these problems at least in part to the emerging character of the Barbadians themselves. Their early wealth had led them into luxury, "that Bane of States, . . . Great Foe of Health, and Source of ev'ry Ill." By the 1730s "the receiv'd Notion" throughout the English-speaking world was that Barbadians, along with other West Indians, were "*the most opulent, most splendid, and gayest People of all His Majesty's Dominions,*" a people who, in the words of Joshua Gee, always lived "in great Splendor, and at Vast Expence." Their wealth had led them not only into an extravagant life-style but also into indolence and "a certain Species of Vanity not uncommon among those who[,] subsist[ing] much on Credit and Reputation," desired "to be thought wealthier than they

[69] [Robertson], *Detection*, 28; Oldmixon, *British Empire*, 2d ed., 2:64–65, 73–76; *A Pattern for Governours: Exemplify'd in the Character of Scroop Late Lord Viscount Howe, Baron of Clonawly; and Governour of Barbados* (London, 1735), 3–5, 7; [Keimer], *Caribbeana* 1:35, 219, 2:45, 200.

[70] Thomas Baxter, *A Letter from a Gentleman at Barbadoes* . . . (London, 1740), 2; [Keimer], *Caribbeana* 1:219; [Duke], *Some Memoirs*, i, 64–65, 70.

are." In turn, "this expensive Vanity of the Barbadians" drove them into ostentatious display, wantonness, improvidence, "willful Heedlessness," and unjustified optimism about the future. Reinforcing this unflattering list of qualities were the volatility and imprudence that also seemed to be deeply engraved upon the Barbadian character. Writers disagreed over whether this remarkable warmth of temper was traceable to the climate, as most people seem to have believed, or, as Edmund Burke claimed, to the "fiery, restless tempers" of the original settlers, who "put[ing] no median between being great and being undone" and loving "risk and hazard," found in the West Indies "a fair and ample field" for the expression of their hot, rash, and visionary dispositions. But no one disputed that Barbadians were "of a more volatile and lively Disposition, and more irascible in general" than "*Phlegmatick Londoners*" or inhabitants of other areas "in the Northern Part of the World." Nor did they deny that this disposition discouraged application, persistence, self-discipline, and industry and encouraged "the many rash passionate Actions [that were so common] amongst the *Creols*."[71]

Resentful that they were not "well spoken of, and esteem'd by others," Barbadians agreed that there were and had "been in *Barbadoes*, as in all other Countries, lazy, improvident, and expensive Men." But they argued both that it was unfair to take the "general Character of a People . . . from that of a few Particulars" and that the island's declining economy had long since driven all but the "more unthinking sort" to lead more sober, industrious, and frugal lives. Even the island's more resolute defenders had to admit, however, that the burden of ostensible evidence seemed to weigh heavily against them. They could not deny that Barbadians continued to import from Britain far more goods than they could afford; that some of them annually expended extravagant sums of £200 to £500 to keep their children in Britain, where "*most of them*" proved to be "Beaus *of the first Rate*" who only distinguished "*themselves by the Gaity of their Dress and Equipage*"; or that no less than a hundred Barbadian families had moved to Britain where they were "observed to live" much "more expensively than their Neighbours." From Oldmixon, Britons at home and in North America learned that in 1721 the Barbadians, with their typical penchant for "Parade and Shew," had seized upon the occasion of a visit by the duke and duchess of Portland as an excuse for a profuse celebration to which the inhabitants came "*more*

---

[71] [Keimer], *Caribbeana* 1:35, 2:119; [Robertson], *Detection*, 2–3, 16–17, 19, 29, 55; Weekes, *Barbadoes*, 50, 63; Gee, *Trade and Navigation*, 45; [Orderson], Extracts from *Barbados Mercury*, 47, 97; Oldmixon, *British Empire*, 2d ed., 2:75; Burke, *Account of European Settlements* 2:128, 130, 133; Hughes, *Natural History*, 9–11; Douglass, *Summary, Historical and Political* 1:120.

richly habited" than could be seen at similar events even in Britain itself. Such behaviors as these left observers with little doubt that the Barbadians' inability to quit the vain, extravagant, and improvident habits they had acquired during the days of their great wealth was a principal reason why they could not compete with the frugal and industrious planters in the French sugar islands. These appearances also persuaded metropolitans and North Americans alike that West Indian demands during the 1720s and 1730s for the suppression of British trade with the French islands were at bottom a last-ditch attempt to force the rest of the British world to pay for their own degenerate life-styles and deficiencies in character.[72]

Between 1720 and 1750 the fundamental question about Barbados thus seemed to be whether, despite all their early accomplishments, Barbadians had not already undone themselves by their own excessive behavior. To most outsiders and to some Barbadians, it appeared that their intemperance in drinking and eating was shortening their lives while their extravagance and vanity were bringing them into debt and the island to economic and social ruin. In their desperate efforts to keep up profits so they could maintain their luxurious living, they were importing far more slaves than was either safe or, from the point of view of the white inhabitants, congenial, and the volatility of whites not only made them contentious in public life but also contributed to make island society loose and permissive. Throughout the 1730s contributors to the *Barbados Gazette* complained that respect for authority was slight, public disorder in the towns was rampant, thievery and commerce in stolen goods among slaves were both open and flourishing, gambling was widespread, and murder had become such a "truly heroick Diversion" that it was "oftener committed on this little Spot than in any other Part of the World amongst the like Number of Inhabitants" and had "too frequently gone unpunished." Barbadians, in short, seemed to have become a *"foolish, ridiculous, inconsistent, scurrilous, absurd, malicious,* and *impudent"* people who, in their "extravagant Passion for Riches" and pleasure, made inadequate provision for education and other social amenities in their own island and wholly neglected all civilized moral standards, including "Honor and Probity, Modesty and Chastity." For a people thus interested in "nothing but the Gratification of their own Passions," one local writer lamented in 1732, the future contained nothing but social ruin. Without wholesale changes in behavior, he warned, it was "impossible [that] the Publick Good

---

[72] [Keimer], *Caribbeana* 1:64, 2:119; [John Ashley], *The British Empire in America Considered* (London, 1732), 26; [Robertson], *Detection*, 3, 6–7, 13, 16–17, 24–25; [Blenman], *Remarks on Several Acts of Parliament*, 124–25; Baxter, *Letter from a Gentleman at Barbadoes*, 3; Oldmixon, *British Empire*, 2d ed., 2:75–76; Gee, *Trade and Navigation*, 45.

should [ever] be promoted, Industry encourag'd, or true Virtue establish'd amongst us."[73]

With so many problems with both Barbados and Barbadians, it was no wonder that some of the colony's white inhabitants wanted to flee from their once flourishing but now "degen'rate Isle" to Britain or to other colonies to the northward. In conjunction with the decline in the number of wealthy white proprietors living in the island, moreover, the number of plantations reportedly fell, the number of abandoned buildings rose, the quality of public leadership and expertise in both politics and the law dropped sharply, and Barbados increasingly came to be regarded by whites as only a place of transitory sojourn rather than one of "settled Residence." Unless these trends were reversed, unless Barbadians learned, like New Englanders and other North American colonists, to shun luxury and vice and, by cultivating industry, parsimony, and strict self-discipline, endeavored to make the island a more attractice place to live, various commentators predicted, Barbados would soon consist of "a few valetudenary white Men" and a numerous and "disaffected . . . herd of African slaves."[74]

Along with their economic travails, the slowly declining proportion of whites to blacks gave Barbadians a powerful sense of their own internal weakness. In their "declining State," their many long-standing complaints against the way they were treated by the metropolis seemed ever more grievous. Intermittently, throughout the first half of the eighteenth century, Barbadians continued to protest metropolitan duties and restrictions on the sugar trade, the misapplication of the 4½ percent duty "in Pensions to Courtiers," and their own systematic exclusion from all offices of trust in the colony in favor of "hungrey" British deputies with "no Interest in the Welfare or Quiet of *Barbadoes.*" They called for a return to the free and open trade that had contributed to the island's early economic successes and the elimination of political abuses. But they recognized that they were "under so constant, unalterable, and absolute a Dependence" upon Britain "in all Things," from food and credit to protection against their own slaves, that they had little leverage. If the metropolitan government would not redress their grievances, they had no choice but to endure them. Thus acutely aware that, as

---

[73] [Keimer], *Caribbeana* 1:10, 64, 86, 289, 353, 2:119, 123–24, 154, 195, 199–200, 289–91; [Robertson], *Detection*, 6, 14, 53; Weekes, *Barbadoes*, 36, 50; [Orderson], Extracts from *Barbados Mercury*, 95–97; [Duke], *Some Memoirs*, Appendix, 3; Burke, *Account of European Settlements* 2:90.

[74] [Robertson], *Detection*, 6, 31, 91–92; [Blenman], *Remarks on Several Acts of Parliament*, 125; Hall, *General Account*, 8–9; Belgrove, *Treatise*, 45; [Keimer], *Caribbeana* 1:123–24; Weekes, *Barbadoes*, 14; Douglass, *Summary, Historical and Political* 1:119; Burke, *Account of European Settlements* 2:141–42.

one anonymous writer put it in 1734, "our Situation" rendered any forceful course of action wholly "impracticable," islanders worried that Barbados was becoming a place where traditional British liberties were no longer "*well understood*" and "*not fully enjoyed*" and that Barbadians had themselves become little more than sycophants and dependents who were entirely reliant upon metropolitan pleasure for the preservation of their lives, liberties, and property. In view of their growing impotence, only Britain could any longer protect Barbados

> From Foes at Home, and Enemies Abroad,
>   Protect her still! Her sacred Rights defend;
> Her Laws preserve; and save her from the Fate,
>   Which PATRIOTS dread, and LIBERTY abhors.[75]

In their anguished efforts to comprehend and explain the reasons for their seemingly endemic political conflict and deep economic problems and in their pleas for metropolitan help to arrest the process of economic decline, Barbadians were themselves in large part responsible for their island's increasingly negative image between 1720 and 1740. Yet the burden of argument emanating from the island during these years was that this portrait had been considerably overdrawn by those who envied "and therefore hate[d] and slander[ed] the *British* Sugar Planter." Of all of its American colonies, they reminded people in the metropolis (and reassured themselves) the sugar colonies were the "most beneficial to *England*," and Barbados, "the Mother-Colony" of the British West Indies, had "the Honour to stand foremost in the Sugar-Trade (as the first Founder of it)." Taking pride in the achievements of their predecessors, Barbadians stressed the colony's rapid rise in population and wealth during the seventeenth century and emphasized the remarkable extent of its contribution to British wealth, which they estimated as at least £24 million sterling, or an annual average of £240,000 during the century between 1660 and 1760. But their contention was not only that Barbados had once been, but that it was "still, a good *Milch-cow*, or . . . a *Golden-Mine* to *England*" that "still Yearly yield[ed]" mighty sums. "No County sure, / However large, in all Britannia's Realm, / Can rival Thee in Worth," declared the poet Nathaniel Weekes in the early 1730s. "Great is thy Trade, / And by thy Produce still increasing more." "Those who prize[d] Britannia's Welfare," he added, obviously had to "prize this little

---

[75] [Keimer], *Caribbeana* 1:70, 75, 2:32–37, 219; Harris, *Navigantium atque Intinerantium* 2:254; [Robertson], *Detection*, 29–30; [Ashley], *British Empire*, 27; Weekes, *Barbadoes*, 63.

Isle." Barbados might have lost much of its old opulence. But even at its lowest economic ebb in the 1730s, its partisans insisted, it still had many inhabitants "possessed of affluent Fortunes." In terms of those "great Estates . . . whose yearly Profits exceed[ed] their Expences by many Hundreds, or rather some Thousands of Pounds," Barbados reportedly had three times as many as did all four Leeward Island colonies combined. Total capital improvements in Barbados, according to one estimate in 1732, amounted to £5.5 million, exclusive of dwelling houses and town buildings.[76]

But Barbados's claim that it was still "the most considerable . . . of the Charribee Islands" was not primarily based on its continuing productivity and wealth. Rather it depended on the assertion, boldly advanced by Barbadians and widely endorsed by outsiders, that Barbados, as a British Board of Trade report announced in 1734, was yet more fully improved and settled "than any other of his Majesty's Territories in *America*." By the mid-eighteenth century it had long been cultivated "as far as any Part of it can be cultivated," was fully stocked with slaves, and had three times as many plantations as it had had in the 1670s. Moreover, despite a precipitous decline in the number of white servants, most of whose places had been taken by blacks, and a slight drop in the total number of black slaves, Barbados was still, contemporaries like to boast, "the best peopled . . . Spot of Ground, not in *America* only, but in the whole known World." Contemporaries in the 1750s put the number of whites at between 25,000 and 30,000, about half of the inflated estimates of the 1660s and 1670s. Though this number was also doubtless somewhat exaggerated, it was proportionately much greater than in any other sugar colony, none of which in ratio to its size had more shipping, more imports, or so large a population capable of bearing arms. "Whoever takes a full prospect of this place, views the number of plantations and small tenements, sees how near they are to one another, and how little land is uncultivated throughout the Island, and considers at the same time how well peopled the principal towns are," reported the native historian Richard Hall in 1755, "must suppose Barbados to be as fully settled and inhabited now as it ever was." In terms of both cultivation and population, then, Barbados was obviously both "at a *Ne plus ultra*, and the very best improved Sugar Plantation . . . to be met with any where." Neither Jamaica nor any of the Leeward Islands, declared one writer in the early 1730s,

---

[76] [Ashley], *British Empire*, 26–27; [Robertson], *Detection*, 14–15, 31–32; Harris, *Navigantium atque Itinerantium* 2:253, 255–57; [Keimer], *Caribbeana* 2:iv, vii, 33–34; Hall, *General Account*, 13; Oldmixon, *British Empire*, 2d ed., 2:166; [Dr. John Campbell], *Candid and Impartial Considerations on the Nature of the Sugar Trade . . .* (London, 1763), 26–27; Weekes, *Barbadoes*, 15, 61; [Blenman], *Remarks on Several Acts of Parliament*, 124–25.

could possibly "for many Years to come be improved . . . to the Height Barbados is at present, or that it was fifty or sixty Years ago."[77]

But the message of mid-eighteenth century Barbadians was that the improved state of their island extended considerably beyond the amount of its cultivated land, population, labor force, and capital improvements in mills, buildings, utensils, animals, roads, and bridges accessory to sugar production. Built for "Convenience more than Magnificance," the rural houses of the planters might not have been "so stately as one would [have] expect[ed] from the Riches of the Planters." But they were said to be "generally neat, and fit for the Habitations of Gentlemen." With tiled roofs, they were often three or four stories high and had rooms "as lofty as in England." "Sown thickly on every part of the island," these houses were, moreover, surrounded by gardens, "adorned with Variety of Orange-Walks, Citron Groves, Water-works, and all the lovely and pleasant Fruits and Flowers of that delicious Country, as well as the most curious of" England itself. Though its streets were irregular and narrow, Bridgetown by the mid–1750s had "about 1200 dwellinghouses and Stores." "Mostly built of brick or stone" with glazed windows and sashes, these buildings were constructed in the same substantial style and manner as those in the country. Another "120 small wooden shingled tenements" housed the "lower class of the inhabitants." The annual amount of rents for these structures in 1755 was £37,000. About a quarter as large, Speightstown had about 300 houses that were every bit "as well built" as those in Bridgetown. Besides these private buildings in both country and town, the Anglican churches in each parish were "all handsom, regular Buildings of Stone" with cedar pews and pulpits and "Ornaments as decent as any where in the *British* Empire." The Bridgetown church, one visitor noted in 1741, even had "a fine Set of Organs and Chime of Bells" with a high steeple that commanded "a fine prospect of the town, the Bay, and the country."[78]

Not just its architecture and its social landscape but its cultural life also seemed to be improving. Education, Barbadians had to confess, was inadequate, the college that had been so "well endowed" by Christopher Coddrington early in the century having remained unfinished. But the establish-

---

[77] Hall, *General Account*, 1, 7–9, 23–24; [Keimer], *Caribbeana* 2:62; Hughes, *Natural History*, 22; Harris, *Navigantium atque Itinerantium* 2:253; Weekes, *Barbadoes*, 45; [Robertson], *Detection*, 82; Henry J. Cadbury, ed., "An Account of Barbados 200 Years Ago," *Journal of the Barbados Museum and Historical Society* 9 (1941–42): 83; *American Husbandry* 2:436.

[78] [Ashley], *British Empire*, 26–27; Oldmixon, *British Empire*, 2d ed., 2:103, 105; Burke, *Account of European Settlements* 2:90–91; Hall, *General Account*, 6–7; Cadbury, "Account of Barbados," 82–83; Hughes, *Natural History*, 1.

ment in Barbados of the first press and the first newspaper in the British West Indies in 1731 stimulated Barbadians to develop their literary talents. Their literary productions fostered local pride and, in terms of both quantity and quality, compared favorably with those of other British colonies south of New England. Moreover, though West Indians in general were notorious for living "without the least sense of religion," Barbadians, as earlier, continued to "provide very handsomely for their clergy" and to attend church in considerable numbers. Though one writer reported in 1770 that he "heard many of the inhabitants say, [that] they went [to church] more to see and be seen, than out of devotion," such "public assemblies," he thought, had "contribute[d] much to civilize the people" in Barbados beyond those of other British West Indian colonies. At the same time Barbados was becoming more civilized, it was also, according to many writers after 1740, becoming far less deadly. With virtually all of its trees felled and its bogs and marshes drained, the natural historian Griffith Hughes reported in 1750, the trade winds that blew constantly over the island purified the air and made the colony so "very healthy" that many "natives enjoy[ed] good health, and frequently live[d] to a very old age." Hurricanes were also said to be "much less frequent" than in earlier years or in other islands. If, as a result of all these developments, Barbados was not yet, as its earliest printer suggested in 1741, "Great Britain *itself in Miniature*," it was certainly more "regularly settled" and had "in general an appearance of something more of order and decency, and of a settled people, than in any other colony in the West-Indies." "In point of numbers of people, cultivations of the soil, and those elegancies and conveniences which result from both," Burke declared in the late 1750s, there clearly was "no place in the West-Indies comparable to Barbadoes."[79]

This growing emphasis upon the positive aspects of Barbadian society through the middle decades of the eighteenth century was associated with an expanded awareness of the remarkable achievements of the early generations of English settlers. Widely evident in the literature of the last decades of the seventeenth century, such an awareness had rarely been manifest while the colony was sinking into ever greater economic and political troubles during the first quarter of the eighteenth century. As natives and metropolitans began after 1730 to pay more and more attention to the history of Barbados, however, Barbadians once again began to exhibit a powerful admiration for

---

[79] [Duke], *Some Memoirs*, Appendix, 3; [Keimer], *Caribbeana* 1:iv, ix, 2:iv, 63; Weekes, *Barbadoes*, 16, 20–21; Oldmixon, *British Empire*, 2d ed., 2:98; William Doyle, *Account of the British Dominions*, 37, 39; Hughes, *Natural History*, 3, 29, 32; [Frere], *Short History*, 114, 128–30; Burke, *Account of European Settlements* 2:90–91, 144; *American Husbandry* 2:435.

their island's rapid "progress to power and opulence." In the process, they began to appreciate ever more fully that this extraordinary development could only have been the work of men of great ability, industry, and ingenuity. Barbados might have been first settled by "very indifferent Hands," but the men who were actually responsible for the sugar revolution and the transformation of the island from a wilderness into a golden mine were obviously of quite "another sort," men of "antient and opulent" English families who, having been displaced or impoverished by the vicissitudes of the Civil War, came to Barbados to find a "safe retreat" or to retrieve their lost fortunes.[80]

Although they did not deny, as so many of the island's critics charged, that warm temperatures, wealth, and slavery had combined to produce "a great Deal of Indolence" and to weaken "that enterprising spirit" that had characterized those earlier generations, mid-eighteenth-century defenders of Barbados stressed the extent to which, notwithstanding widespread allegations to the contrary, most contemporary Barbadians were genuine heirs of these early giants. Productive and profitable sugar estates, they emphasized, could only be maintained by "incessant Industry"—on the part of planters as well as slaves. And, they contended, "their Sugar Works, built with so much Strength, Neatness, and Convenience, and every way fitted for the Uses intended; their Highways carry'd over Morasses, and cut thro Mountains; their Bridges [built] over Swamps and Gullies; and their indefatigable Labour in the Culture of their Plantations" all revealed a degree of industry that could "not . . . be match'd, perhaps, by any other Planters upon Earth" and rendered ludicrous all attempts to "charge them with Idleness." Certainly, in comparison with Britain's other West Indian colonies, Barbados was an "industrious . . . Isle."[81]

Mid-eighteenth-century Barbadians argued that they had become not only an industrious but also a prudent people. For generations, they had taken pride in their reputations for hospitality and generosity. They liked to believe that the "hospitable and generous Spirit of most Sugar Planters" in the island exceeded that of "Persons of like Estate or Wealth in *Europe*" and boasted that "no People on Earth" were "more hospitable to Strangers, kinder to their Friends and Neighbours, and more helpful to the Distressed." No doubt, the manifest liberality expressed through this generosity had in earlier and more prosperous times often led them into excesses, which

---

[80] [Frere], *Short History*, iv, 2–11; [Robertson], *Detection*, 90.

[81] Burke, *Account of European Settlements* 2:141; [Blenman], *Remarks on Several Acts of Parliament*, 124; [Ashley], *British Empire*, 26; Weekes, *Barbadoes*, 13; [Orderson], Extracts from *Barbados Mercury*, 47.

along with the "*luxurious dissipation*" of the few proprietors wealthy enough
to live in Britain, had fastened upon the entire island its undeserved reputation for extravagance and prodigality. In the less flush times of the mid-
eighteenth century, however, such excesses, they explained, were "almost
quite over." No longer able to live in "Splendour and Magnificence," Barbadians had made prudence "the prevailing Principle" of their lives, and the
island's advocates praised Barbadian women for their "prudent Behaviour
and Oeconomy" and even held them up as a positive counterimage to their
frivolous and luxury-loving counterparts in Britain. As further proof that
Barbadians were showing a heightened concern for "Frugality and good
Oeconomy," the island's proponents cited the diligence and ingenuity of the
planters in adapting to continuing declines in soil fertility. With more careful and intensive cultivation, they had been able through the decades from
1740 to 1780 not merely to keep sugar profits respectable in the face of ever
growing competition from new sugar areas but also to economize further by
producing an ever "large[r] portion" of their island's food requirements. In
contrast to contemporary Britain, which was widely believed to be fast slid-
ing into an all-consuming luxury, Barbados seemed to be moving in precisely the opposite direction, its inhabitants rapidly coming to terms with the
island's economic limitations in ways that, they were persuaded, earned them
both credit and reputation.[82]

Barbadians also associated a new emphasis upon self-control and moderation with this increased attention to industry and prudence. They acknowledged that they were "of a more volatile and lively Disposition" than Englishmen who remained at home, a phenomenon they attributed to climate
and culture. At the same time that the warm temperatures of the island put
their "Animal Spirits . . . in a high Flow," patterns of child rearing put few
inhibitions upon the will. In particular, as Griffith Hughes explained, "Children, in these *West-India* Islands, are, from their Infancy, waited upon by
Numbers of Slaves, who . . . are obliged to pay them unlimited Obedience;
and . . . when they have thus their favourite Passions nourished with such
indulgent Care, it is no Wonder, that by degrees, they acquire . . . an over-
fond and self-sufficient Opinion of their own Abilities, and so become impatient, as well as regardless, of the Advice of others." By the 1750s, however, Barbadians were suggesting that their traditional volatility had been

---

[82] Hughes, *Natural History*, 9; [Robertson], *Detection*, 3, 53; Weekes, *Barbadoes*, 16–19,
50; [Blenman], *Remarks on Several Acts of Parliament*, 125; [Frere], *Short History*, 60, 112–
13, 116–17; [Alleyne], *Remarks upon a Book*, 15, 33; Belgrove, *Treatise*, 45; Samuel Martin, *An Essay on Plantership*, 6th ed. (Antigua, 1767), ix–xi; *American Husbandry* 2:439–41;
[Orderson], Extracts from *Barbados Mercury*, 126.

transformed into a wholly benign and "cultivated Levity." Whatever might be the case in Britain's other West Indian colonies, the "Liveliness and Activity" usually found among people resident in warm climates had gradually come to be expressed in Barbados through a warm and relaxed sociability, "a great Deal of good Nature," and a degree of self-control that enabled people, blacks as well as whites, to exhibit "most excellent Fronts" even in the most trying circumstances. Notwithstanding their straitened economic conditions, these admirable qualities in turn enabled Barbadians to preserve "that antient British hospitality, for which Great Britain [itself] was once so deservedly famed."[83]

Indeed, the message emanating from Barbados during the third quarter of the eighteenth century was that the colony had finally become what Ligon, a century earlier, had urged: a place where people "of middle earth" could "find moderate delights, with moderate labour." They had not become passively servile or cowardly. Their frequent battles with royal governors during the first half of the century had demonstrated that they could behave "with the honest Freedom" of Englishmen. Even more so, their behavior during the Seven Years' War, when "Barbadians bore no inconsiderable share in the glorious events which [then] distinguished the British arms," showed that they would, "like good Subjects . . . and Men of Honor," act with "Bravery and Gallantry in Defense of their Properties and Liberties" whenever it became necessary to do so. That they were, however, a fundamentally quiet people who eschewed contention and whose earlier public dissensions had been primarily the result of the malicious behavior of "oppressive rapacious governors" seemed to be fully proved by the "revival of unanimity and public spirit" in the mid–1730s under Lord Howe and again for a quarter century beginning in 1747 under a succession of "quiet, easy governor[s]." By pursuing a "disinterested and truly patriotic Conduct" and behaving with "*Prudence* and *Uprightness*," Henry Grenville, Charles Pinfold, and William Spry each went "through his Office without a Murmur" as the colony "continued in great tranquillity."[84]

---

[83] Hughes, *Natural History*, 9–13; Weekes, *Barbadoes*, 22, 43–44, 47, 50; [Orderson], Extracts from the *Barbados Mercury*, 18, 47; [Frere], *Short History*, 113; Singleton, *General Description*, 5, 19, 124; *The Life and Adventures of James Ramble*, 2 vols. (London, 1770), 2:217.

[84] Ligon, *True & Exact History*, 108; Burke, *Account of European Settlements* 2:133, 143; Singleton, *General Description*, 158; [Keimer], *Caribbeana* 1:69, 2:90–91, 155, 176; [Frere], *Short History*, 20–26, 59–74; Hughes, *Natural History*, 9; Weekes, *Barbadoes*, 16; [Duke], *Some Memoirs*, Appendix, 15; [Orderson], Extracts from the *Barbados Mercury*, 94; *Universal History* 41:116, 181, 206; [Alleyne], *Remarks upon a Book*, 7, 9–10, 23–30, 55, 76.

As part of their increasingly positive identity, Barbadians also began to stress the extent to which their "little Spot" was "not without Capacities that would bid fair for the highest Rewards even in *England*." To be sure, they had produced only one Christopher Coddrington, who remained by "far the richest production and most shining ornament Barbadoes ever had." They also lamented that too many of their young had misspent educations that left them "[in]capable of serving their Country or themselves to purpose" and that Coddrington College had never, even as late as the 1770s, fulfilled the intentions of its founder. Yet as proof of the contention that "few of the Youth of other Countries" responded to disciplined educational training "better than our *Creoles*," Barbadians cited many of their offspring in Britain who served "with great Applause in several Posts and Offices of the Government" and made "as good a Figure in the Regiment, on the Bench, at the Bar, and in the Practice of Physick, as any . . . that were born and bred in *England*" itself. Moreover, despite this early drain of talent, Barbados still had many men "with no small Share of Useful Learning, and Knowledge in Trade" and politics. "For near a century and a half," they pointed out, the island had always had "as able and honest representatives" and other local public officials "as . . . any [British] colony could afford."[85]

To some extent, this affirmative self-image was mitigated by continuing awareness that Barbados was still one of the "remote Parts of the *British* Dominions," an essentially "dull Part of the World" where there were such limited opportunities to excel that fame could but rarely acquire "the power of conferring dignity, or of sounding her golden trumpet." But if, for Barbadians, the theater of "GLORY, VIRTUE [and] FAME" remained in Britain, they more and more after 1750 began to depict Barbados as a rural Arcadia, "a second Paradise" whose "Happy inhabitants" lived retired lives in "peace and harmony," affluence, and "social joy," without either the fickle prospects of fame or the "Debauch[ery], lewd riot, and disorder" to be found in Britain. Never before had Barbadians revealed so "warm and Partial an attachment" to "*this dear little Spot of our Nativity*." Not since the very first generations had they manifested such a fulsome appreciation of their island's beauty, which, they emphasized, was a combination of art as well as nature. If Barbados had initially been nature's "darling spot," its polite and industrious proprietors had managed, by art, to turn it into a cultivated garden. Comparable to certain "celebrated" places in the Mediterranean, they announced, it presented the traveler with "most inviting prospect[s]," in which "the Plantations[, themselves] . . . amazingly beautiful, [were] inter-

---

[85] [Keimer], *Caribbeana* 2:93; *American Husbandry* 2:451; [Robertson], *Detection*, 53–54; Hughes, *Natural History*, 9; [Frere], *Short History*, 86; *Universal History* 41:201.

spersed at little distances from each other, and adorned with Fruits of various Colours; some [being] spread out in fine and open Lawns, in others the waving Canes bowed gently to the Wind from hanging Mountains, while the continual motion of the Sugar-Mills dispersed in every part, and working as it were in Concert, enliven the engaging scene." An island thus abounding "in culture and surety," Barbadians asserted proudly, certainly had to be "a Likeness of what *Eden* was." In the process of turning Barbados into "another Paradise," the "lovely Eden of the western isles," its generous and polite proprietors had also boosted it to "the first rank among the best regulated colonies" and made it "a model for" Britain's "other islands."[86]

In thus depicting Barbados as a cultivated British overseas society and as a place of blissful retirement, Barbadians largely glossed over the fact that from two-thirds to four-fifths of their society was composed of black slaves. Indeed, perhaps because they were far more numerous, Barbadian whites, in pointed contrast to their counterparts in Jamaica, displayed in their literature comparatively little interest in the black population of their island. Griffith Hughes, who provided the most systematic and sympathetic account of "the Manners and Customs of these Negroes," even apologized to his readers for the "Digression." But the spread of antislavery sentiment in Britain after 1750 forced white Barbadians to realize that a "state of slavery naturally" filled "an European mind with ideas of pity and detestation" and provided "a plausible objection against those countries that[, like Barbados,] admit it." Contending that "the notions which generally prevail in *Europe*" about slaves were "very erroneous," they asserted, in what would become a conventional proslavery argument, that the institution actually represented "a redemption of them" from a far more barbaric form of slavery "in their own country" to "a milder and more comfortable state of life" in America. "Regularly" fed, clothed, housed, doctored, and allowed time and space to cultivate their own fruits and vegetables and raise their own small animals, slaves in Barbados, according to their masters, not only lived with less care and "in much less indigence" than "the poor inhabitants of many European countries," including even Ireland, but also were able to accumulate some property of their own.

At the same time, apologists for Barbadian slavery suggested that labor discipline among slaves was "not . . . so severe" as that exerted over British

---

[86] [Keimer], *Caribbeana* 1:62, 346, 2:94, 199; Samuel Martin, *An Essay on Plantership*, 6th ed. (Antigua, 1767), vi-vii; Wynne, *General History* 2:505; Weekes, *Barbadoes*, 13–14, 21, 55, 59, 61, 63; Singleton, *General Description*, 16–18, 123–29; Hughes, *Natural History*, 1, 23; Richard Gardiner, *An Account of the Expedition to the West Indies . . .* (London, 1759), 9; Jeffreys, *West-India Atlas*, 20; *Universal History* 41:201–11; [Orderson], Extracts from *Barbados Mercury*, 79.

seamen and soldiers and that the slaves' ignorance of European ideas of liberty "in a great measure" both alleviated "their unhappiness" and added "to their content." One measure of the mildness of Barbadian slavery, they thought, was the wide latitude enjoyed by slaves in the continued practice of African religion and culture. Although Barbadian whites admitted that the early settlers had opposed Quaker efforts to Christianize the slaves, they argued that by the mid-eighteenth century baptism was available to all those who wanted it. That more slaves had not converted, they explained, was attributable to their continued attachment to their own religion, an attachment that was so strong that some thought "it would be impossible [ever] to convert them." Indeed, as Hughes pointed out, they were so "tenaciously addicted" not just to the religion but to all "the Rites, Ceremonies, and Superstitions of their own Countries, particularly in their Plays, Dances, Music, Marriages, and Burials," that even creole slaves could not "be intirely weaned from these Customs."[87]

Notwithstanding the persistence of such Africanisms among slaves, a further argument of white Barbadians was that over time their slaves had become far better adjusted to slavery. Already by 1740, nearly two-thirds of the slaves were creoles and "as much *Barbadians* as the Descendants of the first Planters." "Now . . . habituated to the intercourse of Europeans," white Barbadians suggested, slaves no longer "need[ed] such a strict Hand to be held over them as their Ancestors did." That Barbados was "not so subject now, as formerly, to the insurrections of negroes" could only be explained by the fact that so "many of them" had been "born upon the island, and [were, therefore,] entirely reconciled to their state." One observer in 1755 even thought that in the event of enemy "invasion[,] 10 to 12,000 able negroes" could be safely armed and would willingly join in the defense of the colony. Already all of the drummers and trumpeters in the militia, numbering one hundred in all, were blacks. Hughes even suggested that as a result of prolonged contact the whites were developing a greater appreciation for the capacities of blacks, many of the most able of whom had been elevated to positions as artisans or domestic servants, and were recognizing that the blacks' alleged lack of aptitude in some areas was the result not of a "Want of natural Ability" but of a "Depression of their Spirits by Slavery" itself.[88]

---

[87] Hughes, *Natural History*, 15, 17; [Frere], *Short History*, 31, 124–25; *Universal History* 41:207–9; Samuel Martin, *A Short Treatise on the Slavery of Negroes, in the British Colonies* (Antigua, 1775), 3–8.

[88] Oldmixon, *British Empire*, 2d ed., 2:12; Hughes, *Natural History*, 8, 14–16; [Frere], *Short History*, 11; *Universal History* 41:207; Hall, *General Account*, 23–24; [Alleyne], *Remarks upon a Book*, 52–53.

Ultimately, however, Barbadians could not deny that even in Barbados slavery often tended to brutalize human nature. This was all the more obvious because, as Hughes remarked, the "great Lenity" extended to slaves by those masters who were "influenced by the Principles of Humanity, and the Fear of God," soon wore "the Edge of Savageness away" and rendered the lives of slaves more bearable and the slaves themselves more docile. But Hughes had to admit that too many masters were so "unpolished in their Manners, and insatiable for Riches" as to make the lot of their slaves extremely onerous. Indeed, as he affirmed, "hard Labour, and often the Want of Necessaries" annually "destroy[ed] a greater Number" of slaves than were "bred up" in the island, an outcome that Edmund Burke denounced as an "annual murder of several thousands." Too many masters, as Burke complained, still thought of their slaves as "a sort of beasts, and without souls." To improve the lot of slaves and their own reputation as a people, several Barbadians exhorted all masters to pattern themselves after those benign patriarchs among them who always treated their slaves with "Justice, temperance, patience, and fortitude."[89]

The contention that slavery in Barbados was becoming an ever more benign and acceptable institution was, of course, at once both a plea for exemption from the moral reproach implicit in the emerging antislavery movement and an expression of the uneasy hope that the island no longer had reason to fear destruction at the hands of its servants. These hopes to the contrary notwithstanding, however, the numerical predominance of blacks over whites and the continuing degradations of slavery prevented Barbadians from ever putting entirely to rest their long-standing fears of servile revolt, and those fears became strikingly obvious whenever the colony's white proprietors felt exposed. Slavery might have been one of the primary sources of economic power and prosperity in Barbados and other British sugar colonies; as Burke pointed out, however, the exaggerated alarms precipitated by the "news of any petty armament in the West Indies" was "demonstrative proof" that it also made those colonies unusually weak. In the case of Barbados, this weakness deeply affected its relationship with Britain. During the 1760s and 1770s, when they first began to fear that the metropolitan government might respond to the growing antislavery movement by abolishing slavery in the colonies, Barbadians were outraged at the very thought of a course of action that was so heedless of their property and safety. But their resentment was

---

[89] Hughes, *Natural History*, 14, 16–18; Burke, *Account of European Settlements* 2:148–49, 152–54; Weekes, *Barbadoes*, 33, 56–58; Hall, *General Account*, 64–65; Singleton, *General Description*, 153–54; Martin, *Essay on Plantership*, xv-xvi.

mitigated by an acute awareness of their dependence upon the metropolis for protection against their own slaves. Through the middle decades of the eighteenth century this growing sense of dependence found an outlet in profuse professions of loyalty that emphasized the extent to which Barbadians had "always preserved a uniform and steady attachment to Great Britain."[90]

Whether its vaunted loyalty was merely a cloak for passivity and weakness was a question that, much to the island's embarrassment, was powerfully raised by its behavior during the crisis over the Stamp Act in 1765–66. While almost all of the other colonies were actively resisting that measure, the Barbadian assembly, alone among the legislatures of the older British-American colonies, contented itself with entering a "dutiful representation" against the act in a letter from its committee of correspondence to the island's agent in London. Although the committee complained of the act as a "deprivation of our *old and valuable rights*," it emphasized that the island had "submitted, with all obedience, to the act of Parliament" out of "a *principle of loyalty* to our King and Mother Country," condemned the "violent spirit raised in the North American colonies against this act," and characterized North American behavior as "*REBELLIOUS opposition . . . to authority*." Although the committee subsequently decided to omit the word "rebellious" from the version that was actually sent to London, the initial draft found its way to North America, where reaction was swift and negative. In *An Address to the Committee of Correspondence of Barbados*, the Pennsylvania lawyer John Dickinson both denounced Barbadians for having at once "cast a most high and unprovoked censure on a gallant, generous, loyal people" and raised questions about the legitimacy of Barbadian claims to an identity as men and Englishmen. By submitting to the detestable Stamp Act, Dickinson charged, the Barbadians had reduced themselves "to the miserable dilemma of making a choice between two of the meanest characters—of those who *would be slaves* from *inclination*, tho they pretend to love liberty—and of those who *are dutiful* from fear, tho they pretend to love submission." Refusing to believe that any people would actually choose to be slaves, Dickinson concluded that Barbadians were "*loyal* and *obedient*, as you call yourselves, *because you apprehend you can't safely be otherwise*." By suggesting that this preference for safety over liberty could only be the product of frightened "dreams of submission," Dickinson associated Barbadian behavior with that which was conventionally regarded as more appropriate to women than to men. Such "un-

---

[90] Burke, *Account of European Settlements* 2:155–57; [Frere], *Short History*, iv, 35, 124–25; Weekes, *Barbadoes*, 16; Hughes, *Natural History*, 9; [Orderson], Extracts from the *Barbados Mercury*, 5, 10, 97; Martin, *Short Treatise*, 10–12.

manly timidity," he declared, belonged "not to *Britons*, or [to] their true sons."[91]

For "Gentlemen, and the Descendants of Britons" to be thus "painted as *slaves prostrate* in the Dirt" was unbearable, and Barbadian leaders rushed to defend themselves in three separate pamphlets, including one written by the Speaker of the assembly, John Gay Alleyne. Though one of the authors criticized the committee for the "doubting, pausing, and hesitating" tone of its protest and admitted that Dickinson had written to some extent with "the Voice of Truth," the contention of these works was that the Barbadian response to the Stamp Act by no means deserved to be "branded . . . as slavish and detestable." Indeed, so far from constituting "a *voluntary* and timid Submission to Slavery," it had, according to Alleyne, been "founded on the wisest Policy, without being in the least open to any Kind of Censure for an unmanly Fear." Yet Alleyne admitted that the character of the Barbadian response had been determined by the island's weakness. Whereas "North America, boundless in its Extent of Territory, and formidable in its Numbers," had sufficient "Resources of Empire within itself" to be "*fearless* of the Consequences of Resistance," Barbados was only "a small Island, containing only a Handful of [free] Men." In "struggling for the Liberties she demanded," the former "might possibly have arrived at a State of Independence." But Barbados, "a well cleared . . . little Spot" with "no Woods, no Back-settlements to retreat to," Alleyne declared, "could only . . . have *suffered* by a Revolt." Highly vulnerable to naval attack and dependent on the outside world for the supply of food, clothing, and the slave labor necessary to produce its principal export, Barbados "could not so much as exist without the constant Protection and Support of some superior State." Thus condemned "ever to be dependent," Barbadians could expect nothing from a more spirited resistance than the loss of the liberties they already enjoyed and "the Horror of an *unavoidable Subjection*." Though Alleyne hinted darkly at "other Considerations . . . arising out of Circumstances of Distress and Hazard from within" that tempered Barbadian opposition, he left it to the Reverend Kenneth Morrison, rector of St. James Parish, to make an explicit connection between the moderate character of that opposition and the Barbadians' long-standing fears of servile revolt.[92]

---

[91] "A Letter from the Committee of Correspondence in Barbados, to Their Agent in London," [April 1766], in *The Writings of John Dickinson*, ed. Paul Leicester Ford (Philadelphia, 1895), 254–56; Dickinson, *An Address to the Committee of Correspondence in Barbados* (Philadelphia, 1766), ibid., 259, 265–68, 275–76.

[92] [John Gay Alleyne], *A Letter to the North American, on Occasion of His Address to the Committee of Correspondence in Barbados* (Barbados, 1766), 9–12, 15, 23, 27, 39, 46; A Native of Barbados, *Candid Observations on Two Pamphlets Lately Published* . . . (Barbados,

"To resist *one* Evil, with not only the Hazard, but the Certainty, of bring-ing down *more* and *greater* Evils on our Heads," Barbados's defenders thus argued, was "both absurd and frantick." They agreed that the Stamp Act was oppressive. But they could not, they insisted, permit oppression to rob them "of their Senses, because if it had, *that* must have exposed them to be robbed of every Thing else." "Too weak to succeed by any Thing but pacific Argu-ments," Barbadians in resisting the Stamp Act thus had to eschew "an *active Courage*" and gain "by *Policy* what we wanted in *Strength*." For "a small and helpless Colony" to express its objections "with some Reserve and Modesty" was only a testimony to the "*good Sense* and *just Discernment*" of its repre-sentatives. If such measures had failed, Alleyne assured his readers, "some other Means should then have been resolved upon for our Relief." "Rash, fool-hardy" conduct was no longer consistent with the Barbadian character. "Common *prudence*" and persuasion, not violence, was the Barbadian way. Contending that the "English Nation" had "long been celebrated" not only for its "Love of Justice, and . . . Love of Liberty" but also for its "Moder-ation" and insisting that the "Sons of the Parent have a Right to imitate [*all*] her Virtues," the defenders of Barbados denied that "a dutiful Submission to lawful Authority" could ever be "thought . . . to indicate any Inclination to Slavery." In direct challenge to Dickinson's suggestion that they had become slavish through fear, they praised themselves as exhibiting "two of the most *virtuous* Characters,—of those who are unwilling to part with any of their civil Rights, though they will not easily be prevailed upon to throw off their Allegiance,—and of those who can shew themselves to be dutiful on Prin-ciple, though they will not yield, without a proper Remonstrance, to Oppression."[93]

By thus turning their defenses of Barbadian behavior during the Stamp Act crisis from an apology for their own timidity to a celebration of their own prudence and realism, Barbadians adroitly used this episode both to sharpen and to reinforce the deepening image of themselves as a people among whom moderation was "the Prevailing Principle." Disdaining "the Rashness of the Mob, and all unlawful Opposition to legal Authority," they told themselves that, in marked contrast to colonists on the American conti-nent, they understood that genuine British liberty, like true virtue, was "found as far from an unbridled Freedom, as from downright Slavery," and interpreted their steady attachment to Britain as an example of this middle

---

1766), 6, 11; [Kenneth Morrison], *An Essay towards the Vindication of the Committee of Correspondence in Barbados* (Barbados, 1766), 4, 10, 18.

[93] [Alleyne], *Letter to the North American*, 10–11, 13, 22, 27, 30–31, 41–42; [Morrison], *Essay towards the Vindication*, 9, 18, 20, 26; *Candid Observations*, 36.

way. Indeed, in retrospect their wisdom in contenting themselves with "remonstrating against" the Stamp Act while "trusting to the equity of the British legislature" to repeal it as soon as "its pernicious tendency" had been pointed out seemed both obvious and appropriate. Yet some Barbadians found it difficult to accept this reading of the incident. Pointing out that the even smaller Leeward Islands, which were in no better "Condition to resist" than Barbados, had "sent home spirited Remonstrances" against the Stamp Act, they felt ashamed that "Barbados alone bore the Tyranny with Patience, and Resignation, and without Complaint" and that when its legislature finally did object, it did so in an "abject whining Letter to the Agent" rather than in a "manly and becoming Remonstrance" to the king.[94]

During the 1770s Barbadians continued to explain their failure to follow the lead of the rebellious North American colonies in terms of their prudence, a prudence arising both out of a recognition of their weakness and dependence upon Britain and out of their acceptance of their obligation to "submit without Contention to every legal Ordinance of our Mother Country." Precisely because they had to be thus "content to look tamely on" while patriots elsewhere had "gloriously struggled for and saved the Liberty of America," Barbadians, from the Stamp Act crisis through the end of the American Revolution, remained peculiarly sensitive to any suggestion that they were less than fully devoted to British liberty. In view of their claims to be true sons of Britain, they could scarcely have done otherwise. Thus, in the late 1760s when Henry Frere, a member of the Barbados council, seemed in his *Short History* to be seizing every opportunity to throw "cold Water . . . upon the bright Flame of . . . [Barbadian] Patriotism" by denigrating "every effort of Liberty" by the "Representatives of the People" against the colony's many "*venal, arbitrary*, and *oppressive*" governors, John Gay Alleyne felt compelled to denounce his work as an inaccurate and misleading effort to associate Barbadians with "a Doctrine of the most abject and undistinguishing Submission to our Governors" and as a rank "Apology" for power. In his own counterhistory, Alleyne gave special attention to those many "great Patriot[s]" in Barbados history epitomized by Speaker Samuel Farmer, who during the Restoration had suffered imprisonment in both Barbados and London for "no other" than urging "the Rights of an Englishman in his Country's Cause." If they could not follow the lead of the continental colonies in the late 1770s and early 1780s, however, Barbadians could—and did—engage in a spirited resistance to what they took to be a series of efforts by metropolitan officials to abridge the island's long tradi-

---

[94] *Candid Observations*, 36; [Alleyne], *Letter to the North American*, 32, 47; [Frere], *Short History*, 75–76; [Orderson], Extracts from the *Barbados Mercury*, 49, 65–66, 90.

tions of self-government, and this renewal of the contention that had characterized the island for virtually all of the first half of the eighteenth century helped to assure its inhabitants that they could still mount a "manly" defense of liberty.[95]

"Little England"

During its first eight decades, Barbados had acquired fame as a colony that in proportion to its size exceeded all others in terms of its population, sugar production, and wealth. Despite a malignant disease environment, the hardness of its servile labor system, and the frequency of slave revolts, its inhabitants, many of whom derived from established English families, acquired a reputation for being a civilized, generous, and tranquil people who gloried in the status of Barbados as England's most valuable colony and wanted nothing more than metropolitan recognition of their own Englishness. After 1710, as the Barbadian economy became less robust in comparison with those of newer sugar colonies and the island had to endure a series of what it regarded as rapacious royal governors and other officials, its inhabitants developed a reputation as a passionate and contentious people who, incapable of adjusting to the new economic realities in which they found themselves, continued to live in idle luxury and extravagance heedless of both their own and their island's welfare.

By 1740, however, this negative identity had already begun to improve. Increasingly, between 1740 and 1780, Barbados came to be seen as a settled society whose members, whites and blacks, had come to terms with themselves and their environment with extremely positive results. No longer extravagant and idle, whites had retained their good-natured sociability and liberality at the same time that they had also learned to become more frugal, industrious, and moderate in their behavior, while the black population, heavily creole, reportedly had become both far less restless and more acculturated to white society. With both population groups enjoying better health, Barbados contrasted sharply with Britain's other West Indian colonies in terms of its proportionately greater white population, the comparative mildness of its slave system, and, increasingly after 1750, the tranquillity of its public life. Proud of their own civilized life-style and the cultivated beauty of their social landscape, white Barbadians both celebrated their strong attachment to Britain and exhibited a deeper appreciation for the society they

---

[95] [Orderson], Extracts from the *Barbados Mercury*, 49, 78–79; [Alleyne], *Remarks upon a Book*, 7, 8–10, 15, 17, 76; S. H. H. Carrington, "West Indian Opposition to British Policy: Barbadian Politics, 1774–82," *Journal of Caribbean History* 17 (1982): 26–49.

and their ancestors had created in this "Eternal Summer Country." Alone among Britain's West Indian colonies, Barbados seemed to be overcoming the dehumanizing and deanglicizing effects of the tropics. To be sure, the rise of antislavery in England, with its prescriptive denigration of all slave societies as un-English and the colony's passive response to the Stamp Act raised profound questions about the Barbadians' devotion to liberty, that essential attribute of true sons of Britain. At the same time, however, those developments also pushed Barbadians to focus more and more upon moderation as their principal defining characteristic as a people.[96]

In the decades after 1780, Barbados entered a new era that pushed its inhabitants even further in these same directions. The diminution of contact with the continental colonies in the wake of their independence and the intensification of antislavery in Britain further emphasized Barbadian vulnerability and dependence upon the metropolis and drove the colony to an ever greater emphasis upon moderation as the central ingredient of its identity. Not that Barbadians, like other Britons, could not be "high-spirited" in defense of liberty whenever such behavior was required. But Barbadians took greatest pride in their cautious and disciplined moderation. Some Britons, for whom Barbados represented their first encounter with the West Indies, were impressed by the disheveled appearance of the island, the indolence, profligacy, and provinciality of its inhabitants, and the looseness of its society, and as the end of slavery approached, Barbadians themselves worried about the sudden decline in the size of the island's white population, which during the first three decades of the nineteenth century began to fall substantially for the first time since the late seventeenth century.

In their favor, however, Barbadians had long since adjusted to their less abundant economic circumstances. If other larger and more recently settled sugar colonies were "more prolific," they alone could emphasize their island's standing as the "most ancient" British West Indian colony, in the words of the British traveler George Pinckard, "the venerable and decrepit parent of the race." From the antiquity of Barbados, Pinckard reported, Barbadians "assume[d] a consequence," a "sense of distinction," that was "strongly manifested in the sentiment conveyed by the vulgar expression so common in the island—'neither Charib, nor Creole, but true Barbadian.'" That sentiment, according to Pinckard, was shared "even by the slaves, who proudly arrogate a superiority above the negroes of the other islands! Ask one of them if he was imported, or is a Creole, and he immediately replies—'*Me neder Chrab, nor Creole, Massa!—me troo Barbadian born*.'"

---

[96] Joshua Steele to Mr. More, May 24, 1785, in D. G. C. Allan, "Joshua Steele and the Royal Society of Arts," *Journal of the Barbados Museum and Historical Society* 22 (1955): 95.

The positive sense of being a Barbadian implied in this expression derived from the feeling that, in comparison with other British West Indian colonies, Barbados was a place of settled regularity and its inhabitants a people distinguished by "the natural mildness and benignity of their tempers." This last quality was said by contemporaries to be manifest in many areas of Barbadian behavior: in the growing gentleness of Barbadian society and the perpetuation of the liberal hospitality and easy sociability of Barbadians of all races, in the relative lenity of the Barbadian slave system, and in the continuing warmth of the Barbadian attachment to Great Britain. "Adorned with many" people "of worth and humanity," Barbados seemed to be remarkable for both its gardenlike appearance and its "general confidence between the whites and the blacks." Extolling the status of their island as "the most ancient, humane and polished West Indian colony ever possessed by the freest nation upon earth," Barbadians had begun by the first years of the nineteenth century to refer to the colony as "Little England." The use of this particular phrase as the one that best encapsulated the identity Barbadians had achieved after almost two centuries of colonization would have been enormously pleasing to all generations of white Barbadians that had gone before.[97]

This essay was written for the collection in which it initially appeared and is reprinted with permission and minor corrections and changes from Nicholas Canny and Anthony Pagden, eds., *The Formation of Colonial Identities* (Princeton, N.J.: Princeton University Press, 1987), 213–66. Shortened versions of it were given as lectures at the University of Guyana, Georgetown, Guyana, on Apr. 4, 1984; the University of the West Indies, Cave Hill, Barbados, on Apr. 10, 1984; a panel on "The Cultural Definition of Frontiers in Comparative Perspective," at the Seventh Conference of Mexican and United States Historians in Oaxaca, Mexico, on Oct. 24, 1985; and a seminar in the Department of History at Duke University on Apr. 8, 1987.

[97] John Poyer, *The History of Barbados* . . . (London, 1808), 136, 216; William Dickson, *Letters on Slavery* . . . (London, 1789), v, 93, 145, and *Mitigation of Slavery in Two Parts* (London, 1814), 441; Daniel McKinnen, *A Tour through the British West Indies, in the Years 1802 and 1803* . . . (London, 1804), 23; Henry Nelson Coleridge, *Six Months in the West Indies in 1825* (London, 1826), 135; George Pinckard, *Notes on the West Indies* . . . , 3 vols. (London, 1806), 2:75–76. McKinnen seems to have been the first person to report the use of the phrase "Little England" to refer to Barbados.

—THREE—

Colonial South Carolina and the Caribbean Connection

WITHIN THE LEAVINGS of the Hispanic and Portuguese American empires during the first half of the seventeenth century, English adventurers established viable settlements in four separate areas: the Chesapeake, Bermuda, New England, and Barbados. Notwithstanding the fact that they all shared a common English heritage, no two of the new societies that emerged out of these settlements were alike, and three of them—those in the Chesapeake, New England, and Barbados—became what some cultural geographers refer to as culture hearths. That is, they became sites for the creation of powerful local cultures, including social institutions and ways of manipulating a particular kind of environment, that proved to be remarkably capable of re-creation and, with appropriate modifications, transferable to other areas in the Anglo-American world.

Historians have long been familiar with the processes by which the tobacco and mixed-farming culture of Virginia spread north into Maryland, Delaware, and parts of Pennsylvania and south into North Carolina and by which the mixed-farming and fishing culture of Puritan Massachusetts Bay extended itself into offshoot societies in Connecticut, Rhode Island, New Haven, New Hampshire, Long Island, New Jersey, and Maine. Until recently, they have paid far less attention to the equally fecund staple agricultural culture of Barbados.

During the last half of the seventeenth century, the culture first articulated in Barbados slowly spread to the nearby Leeward Islands in the eastern Caribbean and, after its capture from the Spaniards in 1655, to the large island of Jamaica in the central Caribbean. After 1750 a variant strain of that culture—developed within the English-speaking world, in the Leeward

Island colonies of St. Kitts, Antigua, Nevis, and Montserrat—found a congenial setting in the new British West Indian island colonies of the Virgin Islands, Grenada, St. Vincent, Dominica, and Tobago.

As most South Carolinians familiar with their early history will know, however, the extension of Barbadian culture went beyond the West Indies to the North American mainland. Established in 1670 with some small settlements near the confluence of the Ashley and Cooper rivers, South Carolina and the Lower South culture that developed out of those small beginnings and gradually spread north to the Cape Fear region of North Carolina and south into Georgia and East and West Florida were as much the offspring of Barbados as was Jamaica or the other English West Indian colonies.

Although scholars have long appreciated the role of Barbados in the origins of the Lower South, the sudden and artificial separation of the North American continental colonies from the West Indian colonies as a result of the American Revolution and the simultaneous incorporation of South Carolina and Georgia into the larger American culture of the United States have tended to draw attention away from the continuing vibrancy of South Carolina's Caribbean connection throughout the colonial period. The same developments have also tended to obscure the related fact that, for much of its colonial existence, South Carolina exhibited socioeconomic and cultural patterns that, in many important respects, corresponded more closely to those in the Caribbean colonies than to those in the mainland colonies to the north. Though it is still far from complete, new work over the past fifteen years on the social history of Britain's early modern colonies now makes it more possible than ever before to analyze the developmental parallels and contrasts among the several colonies that trace their origins in some major part to the Barbados culture hearth.

This essay will explore three themes: first, South Carolina's West Indian roots; second, its continuing connection with the West Indian colonies during the colonial period; and third, the developmental parallels between it and the other colonies—the Leeward Islands and Jamaica—that emerged out of the Barbadian culture hearth during the seventeenth and early eighteenth centuries.

Why Barbados became a base and a prototype for the establishment of so many other colonies in the West Indies and in the Lower South can only be explained by an examination of its early history. For ten years after its initial settlement in 1627, Barbados, like earlier English colonies in Virginia and Bermuda, concentrated very largely on tobacco culture, though it also began producing considerable quantities of cotton and indigo during the late 1630s. From the beginning, Barbados was a reasonably successful producer of staples for the English market, and this success drew large numbers of English immigrants to it and set off a feverish rush for land that, within a decade, had resulted in the occupation of virtually all of the arable land both in Barbados, which covered an area of only 166 square miles, and in the nearby Leeward Islands, all four of which covered an area of only 251 square miles.[1]

As had been the case in early Virginia, the entire society was organized for profit. A few people from English gentry and commercial families, mostly younger sons, came to make their fortunes, but most immigrants were single, male, dependent indentured servants imported to labor in the cultivation and processing of tobacco, cotton, and indigo. Every bit as competitive, exploitative, and materialistic as early Virginia, Barbados experienced a rapid concentration of wealth, as the society polarized into small groups of proprietors and a mass of dependent indentured servants or mobile free laborers. Paying but scant attention to religion or other social and cultural institutions, Barbados and the Leeward Islands were notorious for their riotous and abandoned styles of life, while high mortality among new immigrants and the imbalance of the sex ratio in the population contributed to the slow process of family development.[2]

Most of these early tendencies were even further enhanced by the gradual substitution of sugar for minor staple cultivation beginning in Barbados in the mid-1640s and gradually extending to the Leeward Islands and Jamaica in subsequent decades. This capital- and labor-intensive crop led to the further concentration of property into the hands of the few people who could command the capital to purchase the labor and equipment necessary to produce sugar competitively. At the same time that they were amassing larger and larger estates for themselves, these plantation owners were replacing white servants and free white laborers with African slaves, who seem to have been both a more economical and a more reliable source of labor. Like their

---

[1] F. C. Innes, "The Pre-Sugar Era of European Settlement in Barbados," *Journal of Caribbean History* I (1970): 1–22; Richard S. Dunn, *Sugar and Slaves: The Rise of the Planter Class in the English West Indies, 1624–1713* (Chapel Hill, N.C., 1972), 46–59, and "Experiments Holy and Unholy, 1630–1," in K. R. Andrews, N. P. Canny, and P. E. H. Hair, eds., *The Westward Enterprise: English Activities in Ireland, the Atlantic, and America, 1480–1650* (Detroit, 1979), 272–75; Richard B. Sheridan, *Sugar and Slavery: Economic History of the British West Indies, 1623–1775* (Baltimore, 1974), 75–96, 123; Richard Pares, *Merchants and Planters* (Cambridge, 1960), 1–25.

[2] Dunn, *Sugar and Slaves*, 263–334; Babette M. Levy, "Early Puritanism in the Southern and Island Colonies," American Antiquarian Society *Proceedings* 70 (1961): 278–307.

counterparts in Virginia, Barbadian planters had, from the beginning of settlement, shown no reluctance to treat white servant labor as a disposable commodity, and the wholesale importation of African slaves into Barbados and the Leeward Islands represented both a logical extension of that impulse and the first large-scale use of slavery and non-European labor in any of the English colonies.

By the early 1650s, as a result of the sugar revolution, Barbados had achieved a population density greater than that of any comparable area in the English-speaking world except London. But the introduction of black slaves into Barbados contributed to a rapid decline of the white population, as many whites migrated to other colonies where there were greater opportunities to acquire land or returned to England. From a high of about 30,000 in 1650, the number of whites fell to about 20,000 in 1680 and 15,500 in 1700. Despite the drop in the numbers of white settlers, Barbados in 1670 was certainly, as Richard S. Dunn has written, "the richest, most highly developed, most populous, and most congested English colony in America, with a thriving sugar industry and 50,000 inhabitants, including 30,000 Negroes."

As Barbados and its neighboring colonies in the Leeward Islands became more black and the concentration on sugar production became ever more intensive, profits soared and wealth accumulation among the possessing classes was phenomenal. By 1660 the wealth of Barbados, the earliest and best-developed of the island colonies, exceeded that of any other contemporary English overseas possession. But the rapid rise of a wealthy and conspicuous elite did not immediately give either cohesion or stability to Barbadian society. Indeed, many of those few wealthy proprietors who could afford it began to flee the tropical sugar factories they had established for the more settled and, especially after 1680, healthier world of England.[3]

That the socioeconomic model first successfully articulated in Barbados with its exploitative and materialistic orientation, concentration on sugar production, slave-powered plantation system, highly stratified social struc-

---

[3] Carl and Roberta Bridenbaugh, *No Peace beyond the Line: The English in the Caribbean, 1624–1690* (New York, 1972), 165–305; Dunn, *Sugar and Slaves,* 59–83, 117–26, 188–264, "Experiments Holy and Unholy," 285–89, and "The English Sugar Islands and the Founding of South Carolina," *South Carolina Historical Magazine* 72 (1971): 82; Sheridan, *Sugar and Slavery,* 128–40; Hilary Beckles, "Rebels and Reactionaries: The Political Response of White Labourers to Planter-Class Hegemony in Seventeenth-Century Barbados," *Journal of Caribbean History* 15 (1981): 1–19, and "The Economic Origins of Black Slavery in the British West Indies, 1640–1680: A Tentative Analysis of the Barbados Model," ibid., 16 (1982): 36–56; John J. McCusker and Russell R. Menard, *The Economy of British America, 1607–1789* (Chapel Hill, N.C., 1985), 151–53.

ture, great disparities in wealth and styles of life, high ratio of blacks to whites, little attention to the development of family life and other traditional social institutions and cultural amenities, high levels of absenteeism among the wealthy, rapid turnover among the elite, and heavy mortality—that this Barbadian cultural system also came to characterize the four neighboring Leeward Island colonies is scarcely surprising. In part because of the concentration of capital and labor in Barbados and in part because rivalries with the Dutch and French prevented English settlers from securing uncontested control over most of them until 1713, the Leeward Island colonies developed far more slowly than did Barbados and never attracted such a large white immigration. By the 1720s and 1730s, however, they had successfully emulated the experience of Barbados in the previous century.[4]

The Barbadian model also proved capable of transfer beyond the Lesser Antilles in the eastern Caribbean to the much larger physical entities of Jamaica and South Carolina. Settled by the English in the second half of the seventeenth century, these two colonies, like the Leeward Islands, also developed far more slowly than Barbados. But they eventually became highly successful plantation colonies on the Barbadian model. Indeed, by the mid-eighteenth century they had become two of the three wealthiest and economically most important British-American colonies, with only Virginia—and not even Barbados—approaching them in this regard.

Continuously occupied by Spaniards since the early sixteenth century, Jamaica, before the English conquest in 1655, had been primarily a producer of livestock and minor staples, especially cocoa, and had never been an important part of the Hispanic-American empire. With 4,411 square miles of territory, more than twenty-six and a half times that of Barbados and approximately the same size as the area that would later comprise the South Carolina lowcountry, Jamaica was first settled by disbanded English soldiers and the flow of excess population from England's eastern Caribbean colonies. This flow included many planters who, having made considerable fortunes in Barbados or the Leeward Islands, migrated with their slaves to Jamaica, where they hoped to establish a new, and infinitely more expandable, sugar colony that would have land enough to enable them to provide for their younger sons. This migration began in earnest in 1664 when one of Jamaica's first governors, Sir Thomas Modiford, and some 700 other Barbadian planters arrived in the colony with their slaves.

Jamaica soon rivaled Barbados in riches. But in the early decades its wealth came more from the activities of its freebooting buccaneers, who used its strategic position in the central Caribbean to tap the vast wealth of the

---

[4] Sheridan, *Sugar and Slavery*, 148–207.

Hispanic-American empire. Through a combination of trade and raids, they converted their Jamaica base at Port Royal into the richest spot in English America. Primarily because it did not for many decades have access to a plentiful slave supply, however, Jamaica was slow to develop as a sugar-producing staple colony. Following the example of the Spaniards, all of whom had fled the colony within three or four years after the English conquest, leaving their large stocks of cattle behind, many of Jamaica's new proprietors raised cattle and other livestock for food consumption in Jamaica and elsewhere in the Caribbean, while others produced minor staples, including cocoa, indigo, and provisions. Not until the beginning of the eighteenth century did Jamaica export as much sugar as tiny Barbados.[5]

No less than the Leeward Islands and Jamaica, South Carolina also represented a successful extension of the Barbados culture hearth. As more and more of its arable land was converted to sugar, and foodstuffs and other supplies had to be imported from elsewhere, Barbadian leaders began to look to the unoccupied portions of the southeastern mainland of North America as a potential site for new settlements that would be able to supply the provisions and other necessities required to sustain the island's sugar economy. With approval of the Lords Proprietors to whom, following his Restoration to the English throne in 1660, Charles II had granted authority to colonize Carolina and the Bahamas, a group of Barbadians, including the same Sir Thomas Modiford who settled in Jamaica in 1664, had unsuccessfully sought to establish settlements at Cape Fear and Port Royal in the mid–1660s.

As several historians have recently emphasized, Barbadians also played an extensive role in the first successful settlement in 1670. Almost half of the whites and considerably more than half of the blacks who came to the new settlement during the first two years were from Barbados, and this distribution continued for at least two decades. The most thorough and authoritative study we have of the origins of the 1,343 white settlers who immigrated to South Carolina between 1670 and 1690 indicates that more than 54 percent were probably from Barbados. They included people from all social classes. The great majority were from the small planter and freeman classes of families, a small planter owning at least ten acres but fewer than twenty slaves and a freeman owning less than ten acres. Some of these simply sold out and used the proceeds to transport themselves and their families and slaves to Carolina, while others came as indentured servants.

---

[5] Dunn, *Sugar and Slaves*, 149–87; Sheridan, *Sugar and Slavery*, 92–96, 208–16; Orlando Patterson, *The Sociology of Slavery: An Analysis of the Origins, Development, and Structure of Negro Slave Society in Jamaica* (Rutherford, N.J., 1969), 15–69.

But South Carolina's Barbadian immigrants also included a few members of the island's elite. According to Richard S. Dunn, representatives of 18 of those 175 big Barbadian sugar-planting families which had at least sixty slaves apiece, "held the best land, sold the most sugar, and monopolized the chief offices on the island" obtained land in South Carolina. Not all of these families actually settled in the colony, but a significant number, including, among the earlier immigrants, Edward and Arthur Middleton, James Colleton, and Robert and Thomas Gibbes, did. Further research by Richard Waterhouse has shown that, in addition, "representatives of as many as thirty-three 'middling' [Barbadian] planter families settled in Carolina between 1670 and 1690," middling planters being those who owned between twenty and fifty-nine slaves. Finally, a number of Barbadian merchants acquired land in South Carolina. Although many of them used agents to manage their plantations, several, including John Ladson, Benjamin Quelch, and Bernard Schenckingh, actually moved to the colony.

Not only did these Barbadians bring "energy, experience, and wealth" to South Carolina, they also brought the social and cultural system that had been so fully articulated in the island over the previous four decades. The only mainland English colony that began its existence with a preference for African slave labor and a significant number of African slaves among its original settlers, South Carolina early revealed that strong commercial, materialistic, and exploitative mentality that had found such a ready field for action in the West Indies. For at least a generation, the colony functioned effectively as its West Indian proponents had initially intended, as an adjunct to the Barbadian economy. South Carolina developed a vigorous grazing economy that in size rivaled that of Jamaica, and, in return for sugar products and black slaves, it sent large quantities of beef, pork, corn, lumber, naval stores, and Indian slaves to Barbados, the Leeward Islands, and Jamaica.

Even in its earliest days, however, the South Carolina economy was never wholly dependent on trade to the West Indies. Provisioning privateers and pirates and, even more important, trading with the large number of Indians residing in the southeastern part of the North American continent for great quantities of deerskins for export to England were also lucrative activities. No less than early Barbadians, however, early South Carolinians were avid in their search for a profitable agricultural staple that would do for their colony what sugar had done for Barbados. Early experiments with tobacco and indigo were reasonably successful, but it was not until the successful experimentation with rice in the 1690s that the colony's planters found a staple that was sufficiently profitable to provide the basis for a viable plantation system on the Barbadian model. Over the next three decades, rice, naval stores, provisions, and deerskins brought in the capital necessary to acquire the almost wholly African slave labor force that helped to give South Carolina such a close resemblance to its West Indian progenitors. Already by 1710 there were more blacks than whites in South Carolina. By 1720 blacks outnumbered whites by almost two to one, a far higher ratio than would ever be exhibited by any other English mainland colony.[6]

If, especially in recent decades, historians have tended to emphasize the extent to which, "more than any [other] mainland colony," South Carolina's "roots and early commercial ties stretched toward Barbados and other islands of the English Caribbean," they have paid far less attention to the continuing vitality of that connection. Within the early modern British Empire, such connections were maintained through flows of people, goods, and ideas along the major arteries of trade. Of these various flows, that of people probably dropped to quite low levels during the eighteenth century. A small number of wealthy planters and merchants fled the island colonies throughout the eighteenth century. Though most of them went to Britain or to one of the more northerly colonies, especially Rhode Island and New York, a few came to South Carolina. The families of Rawlins Lowndes, which came from St. Kitts in 1730, and Eliza Lucas Pinckney, which came from Antigua in 1738, are conspicuous examples.[7]

But the fact was that few of the island colonies had an exportable population in the eighteenth century. Neither the Leeward Island colonies nor Jamaica ever seem to have had more than a few whites to spare, while Barbados experienced a reversal in its long-term decline of white population only after

[6] South Carolina's early development, including its relations with Barbados and the Leeward Islands, may be followed in John P. Thomas, Jr., "The Barbadians in Early South Carolina," *South Carolina Historical Magazine* 31 (1930): 75–92; M. Eugene Sirmans, *Colonial South Carolina, 1663–1763* (Chapel Hill, N.C., 1966), 1–100; Dunn, "English Sugar Islands and the Founding of South Carolina," 81–93; Richard Waterhouse, "England, the Caribbean, and the Settlement of Carolina," *Journal of American Studies* 9 (1975): 259–81; Converse D. Clowse, *Economic Beginnings in Colonial South Carolina* (Columbia, S.C., 1971); Peter H. Wood, *Black Majority: Negroes in Colonial South Carolina from 1670 through the Stono Rebellion* (New York, 1974), 3–194; Clarence L. Ver Steeg, *Origins of a Southern Mosaic: Studies of Early Carolina and Georgia* (Athens, Ga., 1975), 103–32; Philip M. Brown, "Early Indian Trade in the Development of South Carolina: Politics, Economics, and Social Mobility during the Proprietary Period, 1670–1719," *South Carolina Historical Magazine* 76 (1975): 118–28.

[7] Wood, *Black Majority*, 55; Elise Pinckney, ed., *The Letterbook of Eliza Lucas Pinckney, 1739–1762* (Chapel Hill, N.C., 1972), xv–xxvi.

1710. Perhaps the result of improving health conditions, the number of whites in Barbados rose by almost 50 percent from a low of 13,000 in 1710 to around 18,500 in 1773. Although it had a rising, rather than a falling, white population, Barbados probably sent few of its whites to other colonies after 1710. With regard to the black population, all of the West Indian colonies, including Barbados, experienced high slave mortality of from 2 percent to 6 percent annually throughout the eighteenth century and had to maintain imports at that level just to keep the slave population from declining in absolute numbers.[8]

Although the stream of immigrants from the West Indies to South Carolina all but dried up in the eighteenth century, the flow of goods remained strong. In addition to small quantities of wine, limes, lime juice, cocoa, coffee, and sugar, South Carolina imported directly from the West Indies between 70 percent and 85 percent of the roughly 1,000 hogsheads each of sugar and molasses and 4,000 hogsheads of rum it consumed each year. Down through the 1730s Barbados was the primary source of these sugar products, but both the Leeward Islands and Jamaica surpassed Barbados in the 1750s and 1760s.

In return, South Carolina shipped a variety of products to all of the West Indian colonies. Exports of naval stores were high early in the century but diminished over time; beef and pork, corn and peas, and leather remained fairly steady over the whole period, with Jamaica, Barbados, and the Leeward Islands continuing to be the leading importers of each down into the 1760s. Exports of lumber, barrel staves, and shingles increased dramatically after 1750, with Jamaica usually taking the largest quantities, followed by Barbados, Antigua, and St. Kitts. To the West Indies, as to Europe, South Carolina's leading export was rice. The island colonies took about 10 percent of South Carolina's total rice exports in 1717–20 and around 20 percent in the 1760s. Barbados was the largest market through the 1730s but fell to third place behind Jamaica and the Leeward Islands by the late 1750s.

Altogether, in most years during the eighteenth century, about a fourth to a third of the total tonnage entering Charleston came from or via the West Indies, while between 15 percent and 25 percent of the ships cleared from Charleston traded to the West Indies. This disparity can be partly explained by contemporary shipping routes. Prevailing wind patterns dictated that many vessels from Britain came via the West Indies, while return voyages

---

[8] McCusker and Menard, *Economy of British America*, 153–54; Sheridan, *Sugar and Slavery*, 123, 502–6; Robert V. Wells, *The Population of the British Colonies in America before 1776: A Survey of Census Data* (Princeton, N.J., 1975), 194–251.

usually proceeded directly back to Britain. Although more ships entered Charleston from the West Indies than returned, by the 1760s, nearly forty ships based in the West Indies annually cleared the port of Charleston with return cargoes of rice and other commodities for Jamaica, Barbados, the Leeward Islands, and the Bahamas.[9]

This steady flow of goods back and forth between South Carolina and the West Indies brought news, ideas, even architectural innovations. The published business correspondence of Robert Pringle and Henry Laurens contains frequent correspondence with trading partners in Bridgetown, Barbados, and elsewhere in the West Indies, and the *South Carolina Gazette* often reprinted items from island newspapers, and vice versa. Especially interesting to South Carolina readers was news of the frequent slave uprisings in Jamaica and other sugar islands. As a recent architectural historian has shown, the verandah or front porch, first developed in the West Indies, appeared almost simultaneously about 1735 in most of the North American colonies engaged in the West Indian trade, including South Carolina.

For South Carolina, these continuing connections were made more palpable by the obvious similarities between its own social development and that of the major West Indian colonies of Barbados, the Leeward Islands, and Jamaica. During the eighteenth century, however, no two of these products of the Barbados culture hearth followed precisely the same course.

As declining soil fertility and higher processing costs required more and more capital and labor to yield ever diminishing rates of return, Barbados continued its inexorable movement toward "a capital-intensive, power-intensive system of agriculture conducted on a sustain-yield basis." But the drive toward intensive sugar monoculture and many of the tendencies associated with that drive either lost vigor or changed in character between 1700 and 1775. By the 1730s Barbados exhibited an actual turning away from sugar to livestock, and the movement toward property consolidation had leveled off by 1750, with roughly a third of the proprietors owning somewhat more than half of the estates and sugar mills. By midcentury the colony, once again exhibiting a spirit of innovation of the kind it had demonstrated a century earlier during the sugar revolution, was responding to its increasingly unfavorable place in the Atlantic sugar market by successfully devel-

---

[9] The figures are derived from Converse D. Clowse, *Measuring Charleston's Overseas Commerce, 1717–1767: Statistics from the Port's Naval Lists* (Washington, D.C., 1981).

oping methods to produce more sugar by-products, methods that yielded almost 50 percent more rum than the British West Indian average.

Despite these innovations, neither the size of estates nor the rate of profit was high enough to support much absenteeism among the large planter families, who exhibited a persistence and a commitment to the colony that defied the stereotype of early modern West Indian planter society. Nor were more than 20 percent to 25 percent of the island's whites members of the large-estate-owning class. About a quarter belonged to an intermediate class of officeholders, small merchants, professionals, estate managers, and small estate owners who produced cotton and foodstuffs on less than one hundred acres. The rest consisted of a numerous class of poor whites, families with ten acres or less who lived largely on the margins of the plantation system, many in considerable poverty. After 1710 all classes of whites in Barbados enjoyed more favorable health conditions than did settlers elsewhere in the West Indies, on the southern North American mainland, or even in continental cities such as Boston and Philadelphia.

Along with the steady growth in white population between 1710 and 1775, the slave population continued to rise, increasing by nearly three-fourths over the same period to over 68,500. Slave imports remained fairly high, but they accounted for a declining proportion of the slave population. With falling profits, planters found it more economical to provide better diets and health care in an effort to breed slaves locally and so save the costs of high annual replacements. Better living conditions and a growing ratio of seasoned creoles to the total number of slaves combined to lower annual mortality rates among Barbadian slaves from about 6 percent during the first quarter of the century to 3.8 percent during the third quarter. The ratio of blacks to whites leveled off at around 4 to 1 between 1750 and 1780.[10]

By contrast, the Leeward Islands showed no tendency to turn away from the drive toward sugar monoculture and no reversal in the decline of white settlers. In Nevis and Montserrat, the smallest of those islands, there was a steady loss of whites from the 1670s to a low point in 1745, followed by a slight rise over the next decade and a continuing downward trend thereafter. In St. Kitts and Antigua, which developed later, white population continued to climb into the 1720s and then dropped slowly thereafter.

---

[10] Sheridan, *Sugar and Slavery*, 124–47; McCusker and Menard, *Economy of British America*, 165–66; Karl Watson, *The Civilised Island Barbados: A Social History, 1750–1816* (Bridgetown, Barbados, 1979), 30–125; Wells, *Population of the British Colonies*, 236–51; Gary A. Puckrein, *Little England: Plantation Society and Anglo-Barbadian Politics, 1627–1700* (New York, 1984), 181–94; Hilary Beckles, *Black Rebellion in Barbados: The Struggle against Slavery, 1627–1838* (Bridgetown, Barbados, 1984), 52–85.

Because the black populations tripled in all four islands between 1710 and 1780 and a substantial number of proprietors were absentees, perhaps as many as half in St. Kitts, the ratio of blacks to whites was much higher than in Barbados—15 to 1 in Antigua, 12 to 1 in St. Kitts, 11 to 1 in Nevis, and 7.5 to 1 in Montserrat. The result was that all four of the Leeward Islands were little more than a congeries of sugar factories with large concentrations of black slaves and quite small white populations that consisted of little more than a handful of white settler families, a few plantation managers, and a small intermediate class of merchants, lawyers, and doctors. The Leeward Islands thus represented an extreme version of the Barbadian model that perhaps more closely resembled a nineteenth-century industrial enterprise than the settler societies developing elsewhere in British America. Far more than Barbados, they were being transformed by the 1770s from colonies of settlement to colonies of exploitation with the impoverished cultural and political life usually associated with colonies of that category. The new colonies begun by the British in the West Indies after 1750 all tended to follow the Leeward Island example.[11]

Despite many similarities, Jamaica diverged considerably from the patterns exhibited by the smaller islands. Its sugar industry continued to grow slowly during the first four decades of the eighteenth century because of a variety of factors, including the secular decline of the British sugar market, the engrossment of some of the best sugar lands by large landholders who did not have the labor to exploit them, an inadequate slave supply, and the fierce opposition of the Maroons, bands of runaway slaves who lived in the inaccessible interior and terrorized outlying areas of the colony, especially between 1725 and 1739.

After the cessation of hostilities with the Maroons in 1739 and in response to a rising sugar market, Jamaica experienced spectacular economic growth from 1740 to 1775. The number of slaves and sugar estates doubled. By 1775 Jamaica was exporting ten times as many sugar products as Barbados and had three times as many slaves. Over the same period, the aggregate value of the colony's economy increased almost five times, from just over £3.5 to over £15.1 million. It was far and away Britain's most valuable American colony. Its net worth per free white person was an astonishing £1,200 in 1775, more than nine times that found in the richest continental colonies in the Upper and Lower South.

---

[11] Sheridan, *Sugar and Slavery*, 148–207; Wells, *Population of the British Colonies*, 207–36; Margaret Deane Rouse-Jones, "St. Kitts, 1713–1763: A Study of the Development of a Plantation Society" (Ph.D. diss., Johns Hopkins University, 1977).

But this rapid expansion produced significantly different results from those arising from the similar development of Barbados a century earlier or of the Leeward Islands a half century before. Jamaica never approached becoming a sugar monoculture. Four out of ten slaves were in nonsugar production, and more than half of the plantations were devoted to livestock, provisions, and minor staples. Also, slave mortality was considerably lower than in the Leeward Islands, ranging from 4 percent down to 2 percent annually, probably the result of better dietary standards deriving from the local custom of allowing each slave a small plot of provision ground and one and a half days per week for his or her own activities. From the produce grown on these provision grounds, Jamaica slaves developed a vigorous internal marketing system. The growing size of the free black and colored population, which exceeded that of Barbados by 10 to 1, suggests that the slave system in the island, though it was both harsh and given to frequent revolts, was more easily escaped than elsewhere in the British West Indies. Finally, there was much uncultivated land and considerable land wastage in Jamaica, where the plantation economy was more land-intensive and less labor- and capital-intensive.

Nor did Jamaica experience a loss of white population. Notwithstanding the facts that as high as 30 percent of the sugar plantations may have belonged to absentees by the mid-eighteenth century and that the ratio of blacks to whites climbed steadily from about 6.5 to 1 in 1703 to slightly more than 11 to 1 in 1775, white population increased slowly but steadily from 7,000 in 1703 to 18,000 in 1774. In contrast to that of the Leeward Islands, this population was not limited to a handful of resident managers of large sugar estates and a few professionals and local factors of London merchants. As in Barbados, as many as a fifth of island whites were from large landholding or wealthy and substantial mercantile or professional families, and there were many small planters, estate managers, urban artisans, clerks, and shopkeepers, many of whom lived in Kingston or Spanish Town, respectively Jamaica's chief port and capital. In the mid–1770s Kingston, by far the largest urban place in the British West Indies, numbered over 11,000 inhabitants, including 5,000 whites, 1,200 free blacks and mulattoes, and 5,000 slaves.

Unlike the Leeward Islands but like Barbados, Jamaica managed, despite some absenteeism, to sustain a "self-conscious, articulate, cohesive social class of proprietor-administrators" well into the later eighteenth century. Like the large estate owners in Barbados, these were "committed settlers" who, especially after 1750, constructed grand houses in an emergent Jamaican vernacular style; supported an active press; built churches, schools, and hospitals; and exerted political and social control through dynamic and self-conscious local political institutions.[12]

In many ways, South Carolina's eighteenth-century development paralleled that of Jamaica. Its economic welfare also was closely tied to the fortunes of an external market for its principal staple. What sugar was for the West Indian colonies, rice became for South Carolina. Following its emergence in the 1690s, rice production as measured by exports grew steadily during the first three decades of the eighteenth century from 1.5 million pounds in 1710 to nearly 20 million by 1730. By the 1720s rice had become South Carolina's most valuable export, a position it held throughout the colonial period. Between 1730 and 1750 the rice market was erratic, and exports increased slowly, except for a brief period in the late 1730s. But starting in the early 1750s, exports once again began to surge steadily upward. In terms of total value, rice, by the early 1770s, ranked fourth among exports from Britain's American colonies behind sugar, tobacco, and wheat.[13]

Like Jamaica, South Carolina never became monocultural, however. Throughout the colonial period it continued to export most of its earliest products: deerskins, naval stores, lumber and barrel staves, grains, and meat. Beginning in the 1740s, the reintroduction of indigo by Eliza Lucas Pinckney and others and its successful production provided South Carolina with a second highly profitable staple, albeit one whose quality was not sufficiently high to sustain it following the withdrawal of a British bounty after the American Revolution. Around 1770, rice accounted for about 55 percent of the value of all exports, indigo for 20 percent, deerskins, naval stores, and lumber products each for between 5 percent and 7 percent, and grain and meat products each for about 2 percent. The diversity of the South Carolina economy is illustrated by Robert M. Weir's calculation that the record rice crop of 1770 was grown by less than 50 percent of the slave population on no more than 3 percent of the land in private hands, while the

[12] Sheridan, *Sugar and Slavery*, 208–33; McCusker and Menard, *Economy of British America*, 61; Wells, *Population of the British Colonies*, 194–207; Edward Brathwaite, *The Development of Creole Society in Jamaica, 1770–1820* (Oxford, 1971), xiv, 8–175; Edward Long, *The History of Jamaica*, 3 vols. (London, 1774), 2:103.

[13] McCusker and Menard, *Economy of British America*, 175–80, 186–87; Daniel C. Littlefield, *Rice and Slaves: Ethnicity and the Slave Trade in Colonial South Carolina* (Baton Rouge, La., 1981), 74–114; James M. Clifton, "The Rice Industry in Colonial America," *Agricultural History* 55 (1981): 266–83; Henry C. Dethloff, "The Colonial Rice Trade," ibid., 56 (1982): 231–43; Peter A. Coclanis, "Rice Prices in the 1720s and the Evolution of the South Carolina Economy," *Journal of Southern History* 48 (1982): 531–44.

largest harvest of indigo was grown by only about 13 percent of the slaves on less than 0.5 percent of such land.[14]

Also like Jamaica, staple agriculture brought South Carolina masses of black slaves, a precarious racial balance in the population, and enormous wealth. The black population rose dramatically from about 2,500 in 1700 to 20,000 in 1710, 39,000 in 1730, and 75,000 in 1770. Before 1720, South Carolina's black population seems to have been able to generate a natural increase. But with the intensification of staple agriculture in the 1720s and 1730s and, probably much more important, the importation of large numbers of new slaves from Africa, it began, like its counterparts in the West Indian colonies, to experience a net annual decrease. Though the slave population seems to have again become self-sustaining after 1750, most of the enormous increase in slaves was, throughout the colonial period, the result of imports, which, except for the decade of the 1740s, remained high.[15]

Though it was greater by far than those of any other contemporary British continental colony, the ratio of blacks to whites for South Carolina as a whole never approached that in the West Indian colonies. For most of the period after 1720, it seems to have remained roughly at 2 to 2.5 to 1. But these figures are deceptive. In some lowcountry parishes, the importation of blacks and the emigration of whites, by the 1750s, had raised the ratio as high as 9 to 1, a figure well beyond that found in Barbados and only slightly below that of Jamaica. Such a racial distribution indeed made those parts of the lowcountry seem, in the words of one contemporary, "more like a Negro country" than a settlement of people of European descent.[16]

Because of the proximity of the Spanish in Florida, the French in Louisiana, and many powerful Indian tribes, South Carolina, like the West Indian colonies, already lived in persistent danger of external attack, and the large disproportion of blacks in the rural rice-growing areas gave the colony, again like those in the West Indies, a potentially powerful domestic enemy. Based on that of Barbados, South Carolina's slave code was the most dracon-

---

[14] G. Terry Sharrer, "The Indigo Bonanza in South Carolina, 1740–1790," *Technology and Culture* 12 (1971): 447–55, and "Indigo in Carolina, 1671–1796," *South Carolina Historical Magazine* 72 (1971): 94–103; David L. Coon, "Eliza Pinckney and the Reintroduction of Indigo Culture in South Carolina," ibid., 80 (1979): 61–76; McCusker and Menard, *Economy of British America*, 174; Robert M. Weir, *Colonial South Carolina: A History* (Millwood, N.Y., 1983), 172.

[15] Wood, *Black Majority*, 131–66; "Estimated Population of the American Colonies, 1610–1780," in Jack P. Greene, ed., *Settlements to Society, 1584–1763: A Documentary History of the American Colonies* (New York, 1966), 238–39.

[16] Wood, *Black Majority*, 131–66.

ian on the continent, though some of the harshness that characterized Jamaican slavery may have been mitigated in South Carolina by the task system. Most South Carolina slaves worked not in gangs, like the sugar slaves of the West Indies or the tobacco slaves of the Chesapeake, but by tasks, an arrangement that permitted the more industrious to grow their own produce and raise their own animals for sale to whites in a domestic marketing system that in its extent and economic importance probably approached that of Jamaica. For whatever reasons, South Carolina, in contrast to seventeenth-century Barbados and to Jamaica throughout the colonial period, both of which were riven by slave revolts, had only one major slave uprising, the Stono Rebellion of 1739. But the specter of slave revolt always lurked in the background. Also like the situation in the West Indian colonies, South Carolina seems to have had a higher incidence of interracial sexual unions than any other English colony on the continent.[17]

If staple agriculture and slavery brought South Carolina danger for whites and degradation for blacks, it also, by the middle of the eighteenth century, brought whites wealth that, while considerably less than that enjoyed by their counterparts in Jamaica, far exceeded that of any other settler population in British North America. Per capita wealth in the Charleston district of South Carolina in 1774 was an astonishing £2,337.7, more than four times that of people living in the tobacco areas of the Chesapeake and nearly six times greater than that of people living in the towns of New York and Philadelphia.

This wealth enabled South Carolina's richest planters and merchants to live a luxurious life-style comparable to that of similar groups in seventeenth-century Barbados and eighteenth-century Jamaica. Beginning in the 1740s, members of this group built, usually in the English style but sometimes with some West Indian modifications, several expensive public buildings and many sumptuous private houses. Most wealthy rice planters chose Charleston as the site for their most elegant residences, and, with this large absentee planter class resident for much of the year, Charleston, a city of

---

[17] M. Eugene Sirmans, "The Legal Status of the Slave in South Carolina, 1670–1740," *Journal of Southern History* 28 (1962): 462–73; Philip D. Morgan, "Work and Culture: The Task System and the World of Lowcountry Blacks, 1700 to 1880," *William and Mary Quarterly*, 3d ser., 39 (1982): 563–99; Michael Craton, *Testing the Chains: Resistance to Slavery in the British West Indies* (Ithaca, N.Y., 1982), 67–96, 105–79; David Barry Gaspar, *Bondmen and Rebels: A Study of Master-Slave Relations in Antigua with Implications of Colonial British America* (Baltimore, 1985); Beckles, *Black Rebellion in Barbados*, 25–51; Wood, *Black Majority*, 308–26; Winthrop D. Jordan, "American Chiaroscuro: The Status and Definition of Mulattoes in the British Colonies," *William and Mary Quarterly*, 3d ser., 19 (1962): 183–200.

11,000 by the 1770s, was a lively cultural center with a library company, concerts, theater, horse races, and a variety of benevolent organizations, fraternal groups, and social clubs. By the 1770s some South Carolina families had become sufficiently wealthy that they were even following the example of the West Indians and abandoning the colony altogether. In the early 1770s as many as fifty absentee South Carolina proprietors were living in London.[18]

An important reason why England appealed to both West Indians and South Carolinians was the appalling health conditions that obtained in their home colonies. Life expectancy in South Carolina seems to have been slightly better than that in either Jamaica or the Leeward Islands, both of which were notorious for their high mortality among both whites and blacks. But both Charleston and rural lowcountry South Carolina suffered from a disease environment that was far more malignant than that of any other British continental colony. Crude death rates recently calculated for Charleston in the 1720s show that they were almost twice as high as those in contemporary Philadelphia or England and Wales.[19]

South Carolina had begun in the late seventeenth century as an offshoot of the prolific Barbadian culture hearth; although it lagged somewhat behind, in its subsequent demographic, socioeconomic, and cultural development it closely paralleled Jamaica, Barbados's other principal seventeenth-century colony. Both South Carolina and Jamaica were heavily involved in the production of agricultural staples, and both imported extraordinarily high numbers of African slaves that resulted in a population in which the numerical preponderance of blacks was overwhelming. As a result, both had a harsh system of labor discipline and lived in fear of slave revolt. Elites in both

---

[18] Alice Hanson Jones, *Wealth of a Nation to Be: The American Colonies on the Eve of the Revolution* (New York, 1980), 357; Richard Waterhouse, "The Development of Elite Culture in the Colonial American South: A Study of Charles Town, 1670–1770," *Australian Journal of Politics and History* 28 (1982): 391–404; Lewis P. Frisch, "The Fraternal and Charitable Societies of Colonial South Carolina" (B.A. thesis, Johns Hopkins University, 1969); Diane Sydenham, "'Going Home': South Carolinians in England, 1745–1775" (seminar paper, Johns Hopkins University, 1975).

[19] Peter A. Coclanis, "Death in Early Charleston: An Estimate of the Crude Death Rate for the White Population of Charleston, 1722–1732," *South Carolina Historical Magazine* 85 (1984): 280–91; H. Roy Merrens and George D. Terry, "Dying in Paradise: Malaria, Mortality, and the Perceptual Environment in Colonial South Carolina," *Journal of Southern History* 50 (1984): 533–50.

colonies enjoyed phenomenal wealth that enabled them to live splendidly in the English manner and to build elaborate public buildings, private houses, and showy cultural institutions, while at least the wealthiest among them even managed altogether to escape the unhealthy disease environment that characterized both colonies.

If, however, the parallels were so striking, how do we explain why in the American Revolution Jamaica stayed within the British Empire, while South Carolina joined the other continental colonies in revolt? This question becomes more salient when we realize that the Jamaican assembly in 1774 petitioned the crown endorsing the American arguments against the Coercive Acts and other measures that led directly to the Revolution but indicating that its enormous population of slaves made it too weak to offer any physical resistance.[20]

We may search for the answers to this puzzle in South Carolina's continental situation or in the many ways it had fallen short of Jamaica in realizing the full potentiality of the Barbados model in a larger physical setting. South Carolina did not have such a large or disproportionately black and slave population as did Jamaica, it had not had nearly so much overt slave unrest, and it had far less absenteeism and, perhaps, a white settler elite that was considerably more committed to maintaining its ties with the colony. Notwithstanding these important differences, however, South Carolina did have a lot of slaves, and in 1775–76 it was, in fact, nearly paralyzed by the fear that if it carried resistance against Britain too far, political chaos and slave revolt might follow.[21]

John Drayton, one of South Carolina's earliest social analysts, had, perhaps, a better answer to this question. During the twenty years before the Revolution, Drayton observed in his *View of South Carolina*, published in 1802, the wholesale influx of white settlers into the backcountry of South Carolina "added thousands to her domestic strength." That influx, which raised the colony's white population from 25,000 in 1750 to 87,000 in 1780, was by the mid–1770s slowly altering South Carolina's racial composition. Instead of 2 to 1, the proportion of black slaves to white free people was falling to 1.1 to 1, almost to parity. Only with the augmentation of its "domestic strength" in the form of growing numbers of whites, Drayton

---

[20] Jamaica assembly's Petition to the King, Dec. 28, 1774, in Peter Force, ed., *American Archives* (Washington, D.C., 1837–53), 4th ser., 1:1072–74; George Metcalf, *Royal Government and Political Conflict in Jamaica, 1729–1783* (London, 1965), 167–91; Richard B. Sheridan, "The Jamaican Slave Insurrection Scare of 1776 and the American Revolution," *Journal of Negro History* 61 (1976): 199–301.

[21] See Robert Olwell, "'Domestick Enemies': Slavery and Political Independence in South Carolina" (seminar paper, Johns Hopkins University, 1985).

implied, did South Carolina have the wherewithal even to begin "collecting and preparing against a revolution." Without that vast immigration, Drayton thus suggested, South Carolina would have found it impossible to revolt—for the very same reason that deterred Jamaica. According to Drayton, this was the critical social fact that gave lowcountry South Carolina leaders the nerve to revolt.[22]

Of course, it was a social fact that obtained only temporarily. As soon as backcountry planters could secure the capital to buy slaves, they did so, and the successful introduction of cotton culture into the area in the 1780s and 1790s greatly accelerated the process. In a very real sense, the spread of cotton and slavery across the Lower South over the next half century testified to the continuing viability and adaptability of the Barbadian social model.

That model had not, in any case, ever been confined by national boundaries. Already by the late seventeenth century, it was being successfully adapted by the French in the small islands of Guadaloupe and Martinique. During the following century it would be established, again by the French, in the large island colony of St. Domingue. In the nineteenth century it was extended to the Spanish islands of Cuba and Puerto Rico. In the 1790s the continuing affinity of lowcountry South Carolina with the West Indies was pointedly underlined by the ease with which the many refugees from the St. Domingue revolt, the only genuine social revolution to take place during the so-called era of democratic revolutions, were first welcomed by and then settled happily into lowcountry society.

This essay was written for delivery as a lecture on Sept. 17, 1985, at the Caribbean Cultural Festival at the University of South Carolina, Columbia. It is reprinted with permission and minor corrections from *South Carolina Historical Magazine* 88 (1987): 192–210.

---

[22] John Drayton, *View of South Carolina* (Charleston, S.C., 1802), 102–3.

—FOUR—

Early South Carolina and the Psychology of British Colonization

O N May 8, 1753, during a debate in the House of Commons at Westminster over a proposed bill to require an annual census of people in Great Britain, the thoughts of several speakers turned to the perennial and, for some people, worrisome questions of how many people were leaving the country every year to settle in the American colonies, why they were going, and whether it was desirable for them to do so. William Thornton, M.P. for York, observed that most emigrants were those who could not "easily find the means of subsistence at home" and asserted that it was far "better [that] they should go and live by their industry there, than that they should live by pilfering, or be supported by their parish at home." Wills Hill, Viscount Hillsborough, M.P. for Warwick, who fifteen years later would become Britain's first secretary of state for the colonies, agreed "that some people go to settle in our colonies because they cannot . . . live at home." But he thought that there was another, equally significant, reason for emigration. "Multitudes of people," he remarked, "go thither yearly, who might live very well at home, and for no other reason but because they hope to live better, or to earn more money in those countries than they can do at home." They were encouraged in this hope, he complained, "by hearing every day of poor people having in a few years got great estates there." [1]

The problem Thornton and Hillsborough addressed in this debate was what might be called the psychology of colonization, a subject that has con-

---

[1] Speeches of Thornton and Hillsborough, May 8, 1753, in Leo F. Stock, ed., *Proceedings and Debates of the British Parliament respecting North America*, 5 vols. (Washington, D.C., 1924–41), 5:567–68.

tinued to fascinate students of European expansion down to the present. Except for a few specific sets of data, including the interview statements of emigrants from Britain in the early 1770s recently analyzed in detail by Bernard Bailyn[2] and the testimonies of late seventeenth-century Huguenots captured in flight now being studied systematically for the first time by Neil Kamil,[3] firsthand testimony on the rationale behind the vast transatlantic migration that issued out of Britain and Europe beginning with the early seventeenth century is largely limited to scattered letters and other personal accounts from individual emigrants.

If direct evidence on emigrant motivation is thus fragmentary and random, indirect evidence in the form of contemporary literature about the various colonial enterprises is both extensive and rich, and historians have relied heavily upon it in their efforts to reconstruct the several components of emigrant consciousness. Designed to define for settlers and prospective settlers the true character of these new countries and to explain why people might want to settle there and how the potentialities of these places could best be exploited, this literature included, especially in the case of the earliest colonies, chronicles or histories such as those published by Captain John Smith for Virginia and Richard Ligon for Barbados.[4] More commonly with the many colonies established during the late seventeenth and early eighteenth centuries, however, it consisted almost entirely of descriptive tracts that with few exceptions were unabashedly promotional in their intent.

On the plausible assumption that promotional writers had some clear sense of what their intended audiences might find appealing, scholars of the early modern English colonizing movement have long used the many tracts, pamphlets, and broadsides designed to lure emigrants from the Old World to the New as a vehicle for illuminating the psychology of colonization.[5] An especially large promotional literature, heavily concentrated during the first and second generations of settlement, appeared in association with the early

---

[2] Bernard Bailyn, *Voyagers to the West: A Passage in the Peopling of America on the Eve of the Revolution* (New York, 1986).

[3] Neil Kamil, "Reformation, Natural Science, and the Foundations of Artisanal Thought in Colonial America: La Rochelle, New York City, and the Huguenot Paradigm, 1517–1740" (Ph.D. diss., Johns Hopkins University, 1988).

[4] See John Smith, *The Generall History of Virginia, the Somers Iles, and New England* (London, 1623), and Richard Ligon, *A True and Exact History of the Island of Barbadoes* (London, 1657).

[5] Among the best examples are Howard Mumford Jones, "The Colonial Impulse: An Analysis of the Promotion Literature of Colonization," American Philosophical Society, *Proceedings* 90 (1946): 131–61, and Hugh T. Lefler, "Promotional Literature of the Southern Colonies," *Journal of Southern History* 33 (1967): 3–25.

years of Virginia during the first half of the seventeenth century, Carolina
and Pennsylvania during the late seventeenth and early eighteenth century,
and Georgia during the second quarter of the eighteenth century.[6]

For South Carolina, the two fullest, best informed, and most systematic
of all the many promotional tracts published about the colony before 1730
appeared early in the second generation of settlement, a full forty years after
the foundation of the colony in 1670. First published in London in 1710, *A
Letter from South Carolina* was published, also in London, in a second edition in 1718 and a third edition in 1732. All three editions were published
anonymously, but the British Library copy of the first edition identifies the
author as "Capt. Tho: Nairne a North Brittain," an attribution that has been
widely accepted by historians. Whether Nairne was indeed a native Scot or
the colonial-born son of a Scot is unclear, but he was resident in South
Carolina as early as 1698 and subsequently became a large planter near the
southernmost area of settlement in Colleton County, which he represented in
the elected Commons House of Assembly. In this role Nairne became a
prominent public figure and, as was compatible with his manifestly republican leanings, a powerful advocate of legislative supremacy, regularization
of the Indian trade, and toleration of dissenting religion. Sometime agent
for the colony in charge of relations with its large and powerful Indian
neighbors, Nairne was one of the first victims of the Yamasee War in April
1715. At the time his pamphlet was first published in 1710, he was in
London defending himself against charges brought by his political enemy,
Governor Sir Nathaniel Johnson.[7] Of uncertain provenance, a manuscript
copy of this pamphlet with several notable omissions is in the collections of
the John Carter Brown Library in Providence.[8]

The second, considerably longer, and much rarer pamphlet, *Profitable
Advice for Rich and Poor*, appeared in London in 1712 and was never reprinted. Although the title page lists no author, an introductory appeal is
signed by John Norris, a figure who was far less conspicuous than Nairne in

---

[6] For the Carolinas, the earliest examples of this literature are listed in William S. Powell,
"Carolina in the Seventeenth Century: An Annotated Bibliography of Contemporary Publi-
cations," *North Carolina Historical Review* 41 (1964): 74–104, and analyzed more fully in
Hope Francis Kane, "Colonial Promotion and Promotion Literature of the Carolinas, 1660–
1700" (Ph.D. diss., Brown University, 1930). See also Verner W. Crane, "The Promotion
Literature of Colonial Georgia," in *Bibliographical Essays: A Tribute to Wilberforce Eames*
(Cambridge, Mass., 1928).

[7] The fullest biographical sketch of Nairne may be found in *Nairne's Muskhogean Journals:
The 1708 Expedition to the Mississippi River*, ed. Alexander Moore, (Jackson, Miss., 1988),
3–31.

[8] The call number of the manuscript is Codex Eng 10.

the annals of colonial South Carolina. Indeed, very little is known about him. He was almost certainly from the west of England, probably from the county of Somerset, from where he wrote the Society for the Propagation of the Gospel in March 1710, and perhaps from Bridgewater, where *Profitable Advice* could be bought from a local bookseller, Robert Davis. In a letter of January 1711 soliciting a position for his son as missionary to the Yamasee Indians, he described himself as "a Planter of South Carolina" who had "settled" in St. Bartholomew's Parish about twenty miles from the Yamasees. His pamphlet also suggests that he had at least dabbled in various kinds of mercantile activity and probably had been involved with the colony for some time. Also in 1711 Norris published in London an almanac, *The Carolina Calendar for 4 Years, Beginning 1712 and Ending 1716*, which he described to the society as the first such publication especially "Calculated for that Province."[9]

Each author identified the ostensible purposes of his tract in a long subtitle. Nairne described his pamphlet as "An Account of the *Soil, Air, Product, Trade, Government, Laws, Religion, People, Military Strength, &c.* of that Province; Together with the Manner and necessary Charges of SETTLING a PLANTATION there, and the *Annual Profit* it will produce." Norris heralded his book as "A Description, or true Relation OF SOUTH CAROLINA, An *English* Plantation, or Colony, in *America*: WITH Propositions for the Advantageous Settlement of People, in General, but especially the Laborious Poor, in that Fruitful, Pleasant, and Profitable Country, for its Inhabitants."[10]

To deliver on the promises explicit in his subtitle, each author employed a familiar literary device. Insisting that he had not written "a regular Treatise," Nairne, assuming the persona of "*a* SWISS *Gentleman*," put his pamphlet in the form of a letter addressed "*to his Friend at* Bern," a place that was then supplying the people for the new settlement of New Bern in North Carolina, and explicitly directed his remarks at disbanded soldiers and mercenaries and possible sponsors of schemes to send such people to the British colonies. Whether Nairne's pamphlet ever reached its intended audience is unclear: it seems to have been translated into neither French nor German. But its initial publication in London renders it probable that Nairne wrote as much for English as for Swiss readers. The fact that the tract subsequently went through two further London editions also suggests that it found a ready

---

[9] Transcripts of the Journals of the Society for the Propagation of the Gospel, Jan. 26, May 18, Aug. 17, 1711, Manuscripts Division, Library of Congress, Washington, D.C.

[10] Thomas Nairne, *A Letter from South Carolina* (London, 1710), 1; [John Norris], *Profitable Advice for Rich and Poor* (London, 1712), 1.

audience in England among people who, as Nairne phrased it, "design[ed] to make their Fortunes in new Countries" or were thinking about "transport[ing] themselves [to America] for greater Advantage."[11]

For his part, Norris used the convention of an extended and folksy conversation arising out of a chance meeting between two old friends. Taking on the guise of "*James Freeman, a Carolina* Planter," Norris supplied answers to questions fed to him by "*Simon Question, a West-Country* Farmer." Hoping to hawk his work through such agencies of early modern English social communication as "Town and Country Shopkeepers, Parish-Clerks, Innkeepers, or Masters of Public-Houses," Norris identified the segments of the population that he was trying to reach. First, there were "the honest and labourious poor," including "*Labourers, Men or Women Servants, Boys, Girls, and Children*," as well as the "*Church-Wardens, Over-seers of the Poor, and Paymasters to their Relief*" who, in each parish, were responsible for raising and administering the enormous sums required for poor relief. Second, there were the "*Men of small Estates, or Jusment-Renters*" and "*provident Tradesmen*," "*whose Substance*" was "*small*" and who could not live in England "*without hard Labour and Toyl*." Third, there were the "*Rich . . . Merchants, Tradesmen, Gentlemen, Husbandmen, [and] Farmers*," who had "sufficient" estates to fulfill most of their desires but endeavored "for more." Although Norris's description applied to the colony as a whole, he specifically directed potential emigrants to the "Southern Part of *South Carolina*," where he himself had settled in the vicinity of Port Royal and may have had land for sale.[12]

Together, these pamphlets provide a wealth of information about two subjects: first, the psychology and expectations of immigrants who came to the colony, and, second, the nature of what they could expect to find there, including the costs, possible returns, and process of creating a plantation in the lowcountry wilderness during the first decades of the eighteenth century. Those interested in the psychology of colonization during these years will find the nature of the specific appeals made by Nairne and Norris of particular interest. They wrote in an already well-developed tradition associated with the colony. Not since the establishment of Virginia more than a half century earlier had the founding of any English colony on the North American mainland been so enthusiastically heralded as was that of the new province of Carolina following its creation in the mid–1660s. First settled in 1670, South Carolina, as it would subsequently be called, seemed to be particularly promising. This region, announced the English publicist Richard Blome in 1672, was "generally esteemed one of the best . . . that ever

[11] Nairne, *Letter*, 1, 3, 8, 51, 63.

[12] Norris, *Profitable Advice*, 3, 5, 7, 69–71, 77, 100–102, 111–12.

the English were Masters of." Without many of the liabilities English people found so unfamiliar and disorienting in tropical Barbados and Jamaica and with warmer winters than Virginia, South Carolina certainly appeared, as the former proprietor and governor John Archdale remarked in 1707, to have been blessed "in a most peculiar manner" with all "those Temporal Enjoyments that" most "other Nations and Provinces want[ed] the Benefit of." So congenial to vegetation and to animal life were its soil, water, and climate, early promotional writers asserted, that it yielded a rich abundance of all things essential for life. No person could possibly go wanting, and those willing to expend even modest labor could expect to reap substantial fortunes.[13]

"Health, Pleasure, and Profit," declared Blome in first articulating the central theme that would run through virtually all early writings on the colony, could not "be met with in so large measure, in any *Countrey* of the *Indies.*" Having surveyed those writings before composing his own proposal for establishing a new colony on the southern border of South Carolina in 1717, Sir Robert Montgomery was impressed by the universal agreement among the authors that South Carolina was "the most amiable Country of the Universe: that Nature has not bless'd the World with any Tract, which can be preferable to it, that *Paradise*, with all her Virgin Beauties, may be modestly suppos'd at most but equal to its Native Excellencies."[14]

Throughout its early history observers continued to extol South Carolina as a "Land that flows with Milk and Honey," "the American Canaan" that would certainly in just "a very few years" be "the most useful . . . of all the Plantations upon the continent of America" and, at least in terms of "Agriculture & Tillidge, vye with the Glory of the whole World." Few of South Carolina's early commentators dissented from the judgment that the country, as the Anglican missionary Francis Le Jau succinctly phrased it in early 1707, was "mighty agreable." It was a place, they mostly agreed, that left newcomers "ravisht with Admiration" and so beguiled its new European

---

[13] Richard Blome, "A Description of Carolina," in *A Description of the Island of Jamaica* (London, 1672), 127; John Archdale, *A New Description of That Fertile and Pleasant Province of Carolina* (London, 1707), in Alexander S. Salley, Jr., ed., *Narratives of Early Carolina, 1650–1708* (New York, 1911), 308.

[14] Blome, *Description*; Sir Robert Montgomery, *A Discourse Concerning the Design'd Establishment of a New Colony to the South of Carolina* (London, 1717), reprinted as *Azila: A Discourse by Sir Robert Montgomery, 1717, Projecting a Settlement in the Colony Later Known as Georgia*, ed. J. Max Patrick (Atlanta, 1948), 18. The appraisal of South Carolina's physical environment by contemporary writers is discussed cogently by H. Roy Merrens, "The Physical Environment of Early America: Images and Image Makers in Colonial South Carolina," *Geographical Review* 59 (1969): 530–56.

inhabitants as to establish a permanent claim upon their affections. For nearly a hundred miles back from the seacoast the land was flat and sandy. On first encounter, it conveyed an impression of monotony and barrenness. But closer inspection quickly revealed that, notwithstanding these conditions, it was a natural garden of exceptional beauty and abundance. Wherever settlers looked, reported Robert Ferguson, an associate of one of the Carolina proprietors who himself had never been in the colony, they found "imbellished Meadows, fertil[e], and flourishing Savan[n]a's . . . guarded with pleasant and solitary Woods." Broad grassy plains with few trees, the savannas invited people "to compare *Carolina* to those pleasant Parks [they had left behind] in *England*," while the woods, throughout "beautified with odoriferous and fragrant" plants, were "pleasantly green all the year" and so full of animals and so open that one could there "hunt the Hare, Fox, and Deer all day long in the shade, and freely spur . . . [his] Horse through the *Woods* to follow the chase."[15]

"Rather . . . a garden than an untilled place," much of South Carolina throughout much of the year appeared "like a bowling alley, full of dainty brooks and rivers of running waters." Even in its natural, unimproved state, Archdale was persuaded, "no Prince in Europe, by all their Art," could "make so pleasant a Sight for the whole Year." "Can Windsor or St[.] James Gardens," the Scottish immigrant William Dunlop asked rhetorically in April 1690, "show so much variety, delight, and native fertility even when advanc'd by all that art and wealth can doe, as rude nature spontaneously put[s] forth with us?"[16]

What seemed to make South Carolina "the most Hopeful Settlement the King of *England* has in *America*" and served as its primary appeal to immigrants, however, was less its beauty than its luxuriance. Like Barbados, Jamaica, and other of Britain's tropical colonies in the West Indies, it had

---

[15] Archdale, *New Description*, 290, 308; Robert Ferguson, *The Present State of Carolina with Advice to the Settlers* (London, 1682), 16, 18–19; Edward Randolph to the Board of Trade, Mar. 16, 1699, in Salley, *Narratives of Early Carolina*, 209; Francis Le Jau to Philip Stubs, Apr. 15, 1707, *The Carolina Chronicle of Dr. Francis Le Jau, 1706–1717*, ed. Frank J. Klingberg (Berkeley and Los Angeles, 1956), 23–24; Thomas Ash, *Carolina; or A Description of the Present State of That Country* (London, 1682), in Salley, *Narratives of Early Carolina*, 138; Norris, *Profitable Advice*, 22; Nairne, *Letter*, 6; *Carolina Described More Fully Than Heretofore* (Dublin, 1684), 1–2; R[ichard] B[urton], *The English Empire in America* (London, 1685), 143.

[16] Archdale, *New Description*, 290; "An Old Letter," [Mar. 1671], in W. Noel Sainsbury et al., eds., *Calendar of State Papers, Colonial Series*, 44 vols. to date (London, 1860—), *1669–71*, 186; Burton, *English Empire*, 143; John Stewart to William Dunlop, Apr. 27, 1690, in J. G. Dunlop and Mabel L. Webber, eds., "Letters from John Stewart to William Dunlop," *South Carolina Historical Magazine* 32 (1931): 6.

"alwayes one thing or other Springing and green all the year long." No other English continental colony in America, not even Virginia, seemed to be so obviously conducive to plant and animal life. South Carolina's rich and well-watered soils and moderate climate, especially its short and mild winters, meant, its proponents said with enthusiasm, that it had "great plenty of all things" necessary for plentiful and easy living. It contained a profusion of timber to use for building houses and shelters and a surplus of game and fish to serve as an instant food supply; and it was suitable for the rapid multiplication of all traditional European domestic animals and the generous growth of both native American and European grains, vegetables, and fruit. "Lying in the very bosom of fruitful Florida," the colony was "strech't out on a Bed of Roses so famous and so much celebrated by all the Spanish pens that," one immigrant declared, it was "the admiration to every bookishman at Madrid as well as at Charalestoun." South Carolina, in short, appeared to an extravagant degree, as writer after writer declared, to be governed by the "Law of Plenty, extended to the utmost limits of Sanity." [17]

The tracts of both Nairne and Norris represent a perpetuation of this tradition. Yet the fact that writers were still producing promotional tracts forty years after the colony's founding was a testimony less to its success than to its failure. Like those earthly Edens earlier forecast for Virginia, Barbados, Jamaica, and other colonies, this newest American paradise did not immediately fulfill the promise suggested by its rich natural endowments. Notwithstanding the rapid emergence of livestock as an easy road to economic competence in the 1670s and 1680s and the development of rice as a profitable agricultural staple in the 1690s, hostile neighbors, ineffective governing institutions, disease, hot summers, serious shortages of labor and capital, internal religious and political divisions among Anglicans and dissenters and between rival ethnic and economic groups, and perhaps the colony's predominantly slave labor system all combined to give South Carolina a highly negative image as a hot, unhealthy, dangerous, disorderly, and crude society and thereby to discourage immigration and retard the colony's growth. Lagging far behind that of Pennsylvania which had been founded a decade later, its population in 1710 included at most no more than 5,000 to

---

[17] *A True Description of Carolina* (London, [1682]), 1–2; Ferguson, *Present State*, 6–7, 9, 15, 27–28; Thomas to William Newe, May 17, 1682, "Letters of Thomas Newe, 1682," in Salley, *Narratives of Early Carolina*, 181; Maurice Mathews, "A Contemporary View of Carolina in 1680," *South Carolina Historical Magazine* 55 (1954): 156–57; Norris, *Profitable Advice*, 21–23; Blome, *Description*, 126–27, 129; Archdale, *New Description*, 288; Nairne, *Letter*, 7–8; Stewart to Dunlop, Apr. 27, 1690, in Dunlop and Webber, "Letters from Stewart," 4–5; Burton, *English Empire*, 137–42, 147; Peter Heylyn, *Cosmography in Foure Books* (London, 1713), 961.

6,000 settlers of European descent and perhaps a similar number of African slaves, and they were very thinly scattered over a small area within twenty to forty miles of the seacoast.[18]

Neither Nairne nor Norris denied that South Carolina was in many respects a "Strange Country" with many continuing problems. Like their predecessors, however, they concentrated upon its extraordinary material promise. Endeavoring to counter its negative reputation in Britain, they depicted it—in terms that seemed to them best calculated to entice immigrants to come to South Carolina—as a safe and inviting place where there was virtually no poverty, people could live in plenty with little labor, and riches were easily accessible to the industrious.[19]

What they primarily stressed was the astonishing ease with which people in South Carolina could live and accumulate wealth. There was "no Place in the Continent of *America*," Nairne wrote, "where People can transport themselves to greater Advantage." "With moderate Industry," he observed, a person could "be supplied with all the Necessaries of Life." South Carolina, Norris agreed, was a place where people could not only "live with greater Plenty and Content" than ever they could in England but also "advance themselves in Riches, Honour, and good Repute" and in just a "few Years become of good Substance and Worth." Whereas a large proportion of the English population had to live in "Scarcity, Poverty, and Want," no one in South Carolina, Nairne insisted, was "obliged to beg for want of food" except "Widows or Children of such Strangers, who die[d] before they" were "comfortably settled." Norris echoed this judgment. South Carolina had no poor rates, Norris assured his readers, because free people could "forthwith imploy themselves so Advantageously to their own Benefit, for themselves, or under some other Planter, that they need not any such supply." Nor, Norris insisted, was opportunity for betterment limited to the poor. In England, he contended, even men with some resources were "never like to be in a Capacity of otherwise Advancing their Fortune from their present State and Condition they are now in, to any higher Degree of Riches, Content, or Repute." By contrast, South Carolina presented them with "the Opportunity . . . of Benefiting themselves, during the Remainder of their Life."[20]

What made South Carolina such a land of opportunity for all classes of

---

[18] On South Carolina's early development, see Peter H. Wood, *Black Majority: Negroes in Colonial South Carolina from 1676 through the Stono Rebellion* (New York, 1975), and Converse D. Clowse, *Economic Beginnings in Colonial South Carolina, 1670–1730* (Columbia, S.C., 1971).

[19] Norris, *Profitable Advice*, 10.

[20] Ibid., 6–7, 61–62, 74, 107; Nairne, *Letter*, 3, 8, 42.

prospective immigrants was cheap land, fertile soil, and natural abundance. "Nothing can be more reasonable," Nairne wrote, "than the Price of Lands" which, he emphasized, were held in "Free and common Soccage" with only "a small Quit-Rent being paid annually to the Proprietors." As "an Encouragement to People to resort thither," Norris pointed out, the proprietors had deliberately made lands available "*on very easy and cheap Terms.*" One hundred acres, he reported, could be bought for less than ten acres in England. Moreover, even an impecunious servant who had finished his term could "have Land assign'd him from the Lords Proprietors."[21]

Land was not only cheap and accessible but also extraordinarily fecund. Producing "the best *Rice* that is brought to *England* from any Part of the World," the soil of the colony was so prolific that agricultural yields were much "greater than . . . in *England.*" "Ten Acres there, well Husbanded in [rice, the] proper Grain of that Country," according to Norris, generated "more Profit than Twenty Acres" in England cultivated according to "the general Way of Husbandry." A half bushel of corn and peas to an acre routinely yielded twelve to fifteen bushels of peas and twenty or twenty-five bushels of corn, and some people got as much as twenty bushels of peas and forty bushels of corn. One good laboring man, Norris asserted, could in a year clear, fence, plant, hoe, harvest, and thresh at least four acres of corn and peas besides land planted with food for the family's use and three acres of rice, an acre of which was "as Valuable as two or three Acres of *English* Grain." With such "Fertile Soil," any "Laborious and Industrious Man, being settled for himself," could, merely "with his own Labour and Industry, [easily] maintain a Wife and Ten Children, sufficient with *Corn, Pease, Rice, Flesh, Fish, and Fowl.*" Having many other marketable products and foodstuffs generated by the colony's natural abundance, including naval stores and cattle, with which South Carolina abounded "to a Degree much beyond any other *English* Colony," and stocked with large quantities of wood, fish, and game that, in contrast to England, was not reserved to the wealthy by game laws, South Carolina was obviously "*a very plentiful Country for Food*" and other essentials, a place where people could escape poverty and want and "*live well*" and "in great Affluence of most things necessary for Life."[22]

The argument that immigrants in such a yielding and beneficent environment could scarcely avoid improving their material circumstances while those who desired riches were virtually assured of success was the main

---

[21] Nairne, *Letter*, 46–47; Norris, *Profitable Advice*, 13, 56.

[22] Norris, *Profitable Advice*, 12–13, 23–24, 26–28, 39–40, 53, 61–62, 66, 86; Nairne, *Letter*, 7–13, 41, 50.

theme of both Nairne and Norris and a reiteration of what had been an important component in the colony's appeal from its first foundation. For those who, already having some resources, were interested in the "Advancement of their Fortunes," Norris wrote, no country offered better prospects. Except for "Gentlemen of Great Estates, or great Userers," he believed, every category of independent people could by settling in South Carolina "advance and prefer themselves to a [vastly] more plentiful and profitable Way to Live" than they could ever do in England.[23]

Both Nairne and Norris refined and considerably expanded upon John Archdale's calculation in an earlier promotional pamphlet, published in 1707, that, with prudent management, a man with £500 to invest could, "in a few Years, live in as much Plenty, yea more, than a Man of 300£ a Year in England; and if he continue[s] Careful . . . shall increase to great Wealth[,] as many there are already Witnesses." Whereas a person in England with £1,000 sterling to invest could expect a return of only about £50 a year, Nairne estimated that in South Carolina a similar sum would enable a person to establish a well-equipped 1,000-acre estate with thirty slaves that would yield annual profits of nearly £340. Similarly, Norris calculated that the same sum would permit the foundation of a working plantation of between 1,000 and 1,500 acres with thirty-six slaves producing yearly returns of at least £400. With such high profits, almost six to eight times what could be expected in England, a planter, in Norris's words, could acquire "great quantities of Land as well as Stock" and many slaves who could in turn be employed in planting corn and rice and making naval stores to the "great Profit and Advantage" of their masters, who, "in Time, [would] thereby become able to build fine Brick Houses" and otherwise maintain their families "*with Credit and Honour*."[24]

But one did not have to have such a large sum to do well in South Carolina. With only £100 sterling to invest, enough, by Nairne's figures, to buy two slaves and 200 acres and, by Norris's calculations, to purchase three slaves and 150 acres, a man could settle "with Comfort and Decency" and eventually "get a competent Estate, and live very handsom[e]ly." Those with still less who could pay their own passage or even had to go as servants had several avenues by which they could rise in the world. Either they could work for wages and thereby get £25 or £30 per year, a rate much higher than they could obtain in England, or they could work as shareholders on terms favorable enough to give them housing, food, and up to half of all the

[23] Norris, *Profitable Advice*, 96, 108.

[24] Archdale, *New Description*, 290; Norris, *Profitable Advice*, 49, 92–96; Nairne, *Letter*, 52–54.

produce they made in return for nothing more than their labor. Alternatively, with credit for all the "necessary Implements" easily obtainable from local merchants, Nairne explained, individuals could simply occupy "a Piece of Ground, improve it, build, raise, stock, plant Orchards, and make such Commodities, which being sold, procur'd . . . Slaves, Horses, Hous[e]hold-Goods, and the like Conveniencies; and after this was done, in seven or eight Years . . . to think it Time to pay the Lords something for their Land."[25]

Whatever route they chose, whether by squatting and improving a piece of land to which they did not have title or by working for another man for wages or shares, both Nairne and Norris emphasized, a poor, diligent, and "careful Man and his Wife" could in "a few Years" become "Masters and Owners of Plantations, Stocks, & Slaves, on which they [could] Live very plentifully." "I knew a Man, that at his first coming into the Country, was a Servant for Four Years," Norris explained, "yet before his Death, it was computed [that] he had at least Three Thousand Head of Cattle, Young and Old; and a Hundred Horses; and Three Hundred Calves Yearly." Indeed, he reported, "many Men" who could scarcely purchase a cow or two "at their first beginning" had merely "by their Stocks of Cattle and Hogs, in a few Years, become Rich" and were then "settle[d] well on a Plantation of their own." Only lazy people, intemperate drinkers, or "extravagant, careless, and bad Husbands" could fail to succeed in the rich and bountiful environment of South Carolina.[26]

Although South Carolina was especially advantageous for husbandmen and planters, it also held out bright prospects to those in nonagricultural employment. By English standards artisans could command extravagant wages, which Nairne listed for several of the most prominent categories of tradesmen, while merchants who settled in Charleston "with a quantity of Goods," including both importers and shopkeepers, could expect, "as many there have done," to "grow very Rich, in a few Years . . . from a small Beginning." Those traders who were willing to settle "with good Stocks of Goods . . . to furnish the Inhabitants, and *Indian* Traders" in the new town of Port Royal, which Norris predicted would soon "become a Place of great Trade," could expect to do even better, "soon grow[ing] extreamly Rich, as many Merchants, Shopkeepers, and others did, at the first settling their Trade in that Town, and doth still so continue getting Riches, to Admiration, many of them now being worth many *Thousand Pounds*, from a very small Beginning." A mercantile partnership that could put together ten to twelve

[25] Nairne, *Letter*, 47, 51–56; Norris, *Profitable Advice*, 59–60, 92–96.

[26] Norris, *Profitable Advice*, 46–48, 61, 76, 84.

thousand pounds of goods, Norris predicted, "might clearly get . . . (with good Success at Sea) at least 5 or 6000*l.* on their Returns" every year.[27]

What greatly enhanced the prospects of escaping want and acquiring wealth in South Carolina, both Nairne and Norris emphasized, was the simplicity and cheapness of government. Compared with England, the public realm was minute. The civil establishment was small. The members of the governor's executive council and the legislature received no "allowance for attending publick Service" but served "at their own Expence," and the only public officials who received a salary were the governor and ten ministers of the Church of England. With little poverty, the colony had no expenses for maintaining the poor. With "no regular troops in *Carolina*, except a very few in the Fort, and Sentinals in several Places along the Coast," defense costs, even including fortifications built to protect the colony against invasion by the Spaniards, were low. Altogether, Nairne reported, the public expenses were less than £3,500 a year. Moreover, the representatives of the freeholders in the legislature, Nairne pointed out, scrupulously kept the appointment of all revenue collectors in legislative hands, gave no discretionary spending power to proprietary governors, and required a strict accounting of any disbursements of public funds. "Frugality being a Vertue very useful in large Governments," Nairne remarked, was "absolutely necessary in small and poor ones."[28]

All of these conditions meant both that there were "very few Countries where public Credit" was "better preserved than" in South Carolina and that taxes were exceedingly low. Indeed, as Nairne pointed out, there were not yet any "Taxes in *South Carolina*, either upon real or personal Estates" and the public revenues were supplied wholly by duties on imports and exports, which he claimed produced nearly 25 percent more in funds than were needed to meet public costs. With such low "common Publick Taxes on the Province," the proportion of private income that went for public expenditures, Norris declared in underlining a point he made over and over, was "very small" in comparison "with what they are in *England*." In England, he wrote, the "many Taxes, Rates, Assessments, and other Disbursements" to which "all Estates" were liable were so high that they took "away *one* Half, if not two Thirds, of the Value" of annual returns and thereby rendered it impossible even for "an *Industrious* Man" to accumulate much profit from "his own laborious Care and Industry." By contrast, low public expenditures in South Carolina meant that people there did not have "to straighten themselves . . . Quarterly, or oftener, to pay great Taxes, Rates[,] Rents, and

---

[27] Nairne, *Letter*, 54–55; Norris, *Profitable Advice*, 70, 96–99.

[28] Nairne, *Letter*, 22–23, 30, 32–33, 38–39; Norris, *Profitable Advice*, 61.

Assessments" and that there were *"few Occasions for the Planter to expend his Profits that arises from his Labour."* As a consequence, Norris asserted, a family in South Carolina had a better chance both to obtain all *"reasonable Necessaries from their own Industry"* and to *"live very plentiful*[,] . . . *thrive in the World, and become Rich."*[29]

Nairne and Norris thus summoned people to South Carolina by what David Bertelson has called the doctrine of allurement, the prospects that its extraordinary material promise would enable them to live there without want in ease and abundance and perhaps even become rich. Every species of person, Norris proclaimed, could in South Carolina expect to improve their material circumstances and to rise in the world. To *"live . . . Plentiful, and get Riches withal to Admiration,"* these were the primary appeals employed by Nairne and Norris to persuade people to immigrate to the colony and probably also the major considerations in the decisions of immigrants to come.[30]

But these were by no means the only attractions held out by Nairne and Norris. Also important was the possibility that wealth in South Carolina could be acquired with relatively little labor. They did not claim that riches could "be got without Industry." But they did argue, in Nairne's words, that in South Carolina "as little will serve to put a Person into a Way of living comfortably, as in any Place whatever, and perhaps less." What made this fetching situation possible was not just the colony's natural abundance which made the work even of servants and slaves much less onerous than "that [of] many Thousand[s of] Servants and poor Laboure[r]s . . . in *England, Wales, Scotland,* and *Ireland"* but the institution of slavery itself. Far from condemning slavery, Nairne and Norris, like most of their British contemporaries, presented it as a boon to independent families. Employable "in any sort of Labour, either in Town or Country, in whatever their Masters, or Owners, have occasion to be done," slaves offered several advantages over servants or hired labor. "With good Management and Success," Norris pointed out, "a Man's Slave will by his Labour, pay for his first Cost in about Four Years at most, besides his Maintenance," which did not cost much, slaves largely feeding themselves and requiring but little clothing. Moreover, because masters had "as good a Right and Title to them, during their Lives, as a Man has here to a Horse or Ox, after he has bought them," every slave's labor, once his initial cost had been recovered, was "free Gain" for "the Remainder of his Life." As much as anything else, Norris thus suggested, slavery enabled people in South Carolina to live easily "without

---

[29] Nairne, *Letter,* 38–39; Norris, *Profitable Advice,* 33–34, 61, 69, 90.

[30] David Bertleson, *The Lazy South* (New York, 1967), 9–14; Norris, *Profitable Advice,* 100.

being oblig'd to Labour themselves, as most Jusment-renters are here, or Men of small Estates."[31]

As important as the prospect of escaping poverty, rising above meanness, and obtaining wealth and substance with little labor was in the appeals of both Nairne and Norris, neither seems to have presented it as an end in itself. Rather, material betterment was for each the vehicle by which dependent men in Britain and Europe could become independent, masterless men with dependents of their own in South Carolina. Free people were uninterested in working for wages for others, Norris reported, because, "by Planting . . . Corn and Rice" on "their own Land," they could "employ themselves very advantageously in their own Business." "How much better for Men to improve their own Lands, for the Use of themselves, and Posterity; to sit under their own Vine, and eat the Fruits of their Labour," than to work for others, declared Nairne, invoking a popular biblical metaphor. In a place where the road to independence and a comfortable subsistence was so open, Norris observed, people soon came to rely entirely upon themselves and to scorn charity. In South Carolina, he wrote, "I never yet saw . . . any Family so Poor and in Want, but that, if a small Gift of any kind of Provisions was offer'd them, because 'twas suppos'd they could not subsist without such Helps, they would refuse it, and scorn the Acceptance thereof." If few people in the colony had yet acquired large fortunes, Nairne wrote, most people quickly and easily had been able to achieve "that State of Life which many People reckon the happiest, a moderate Subsistance, without the Vexation of Dependance."[32]

But the prospect of obtaining wealth with ease and escaping the dependence that was the lot of the vast majority of the population of England would have meant little in a menacing environment, and both Nairne and Norris took pains to minimize the unpleasant and dangerous features that already had combined to give South Carolina an ambiguous reputation. They had to admit that throughout the summer temperatures were "indeed troublesome to Strangers." But they contended that settlers had quickly found satisfactory remedies in the form of "open airy Rooms, Arbours and Summer-houses" constructed in shady groves and frequent cool baths and insisted that the discomfitures of the summers were more than offset by the agreeableness of the rest of the seasons. Similarly, they denied that there was much danger from any of the terrifying creatures who made the colony their habitat. Despite having names that were "frightful to those who never saw them," alligators, wolves, panthers, bears, and other wild animals usually

---

[31] Nairne, *Letter*, 51; Norris, *Profitable Advice*, 17, 20, 31, 58, 61.

[32] Norris, *Profitable Advice*, 55, 61–62; Nairne, *Letter*, 3, 56.

tried to avoid people unless attacked, while the woods contained an effective antidote to the poisonous venom of the rattlesnake, the "most dangerous Creature" in the colony. Finally, Nairne and Norris tried to counter reports, which were all too accurate, about the colony's seemingly increasingly malignant disease environment, suggesting that ill health was largely limited to newcomers before they were seasoned to the climate, to people who insisted upon living in low marshy ground, and to those who were excessive and careless in their eating, drinking, and personal habits. "If temperate," they asserted, those who lived on "dry healthy Land" were "generally, very healthful."[33]

The discomfort of summers and the dangers presented by strange and ferocious animals and serpents and ill health were matched by the risks of war and destruction arising out of South Carolina's proximity to colonies of England's European rivals, Spanish Florida and French Louisiana, and its growing commercial involvement with the many powerful Indian nations in southeastern North America. Except for a brief Spanish foray into the southern portion of the colony in 1686 and some occasional skirmishes on the frontier between Carolina Indian traders and their French and Spanish rivals, South Carolina had been free from invasion throughout its early history. Indeed, during the early years of Queen Anne's War, South Carolinians had actually carried the attack to their foreign neighbors with an only partially successful expedition against the Spanish capital of Florida at St. Augustine in 1702 and a victorious thrust against them at Apalache in 1704. In 1706, moreover, they had managed to drive off a joint Franco-Spanish invasion force.[34]

Although they remained anxious about the possibility of Franco-Spanish retaliation until the conclusion of war in 1713, these early military successes seem to have contributed to a growing self-confidence and to have demonstrated the efficacy of the militia system. Denouncing professional armies as "Instruments in the Hands of Tyrants, to ravage and depopulate the Earth," Nairne did not deny that South Carolinians had to be concerned with defense. Rather, he argued that every "Planter who keeps his Body fit for Service, by Action and a regular Life" was the military superior of every

---

[33] Nairne, *Letter*, 14–15; Norris, *Profitable Advice*, 21–22, 28, 63–65. On the high mortality in South Carolina, see H. Roy Merrens and George D. Terry, "Dying in Paradise: Malaria, Mortality, and the Perceptual Environment in Colonial South Carolina," *Journal of Southern History* 50 (1984): 533–50.

[34] M. Eugene Sirmans, *Colonial South Carolina: A Political History* (Chapel Hill, N.C., 1966), 44, 83–86; Verner W. Crane, *The Southern Frontier, 1670–1732* (Durham, N.C., 1928).

regular soldier "whose Spirits and Vigour are soon pall'd by an idle effeminate Life, in a warm Climate." Praising the expertise of native white Carolinians in the use of firearms, a skill "very well . . . acquir'd by the frequent Pursuit of Game in the Forests," Nairne, writing in the English republican tradition associated with the political philosopher James Harrington, extolled the virtues of a citizen army. Carolinians, he observed, had "the same Opinion of Arms as the *Romans*, and other free People, generally had," believing that no one was "so fit to defend their Properties as themselves." To enjoy "the many Pleasures and Delights of a quiet peaceable Life," a "free People, surrounded with potent Neighbours," he insisted, had to take responsibility "for their own Defence" and therefore needed "to be brave, and military, [and] perfectly vers'd in Arms."[35]

As proof of the efficacy of the militia system and the colony's safety, Nairne pointed to the fact that Carolinians solely by their own exertions had "intirely broke and ruin'd the Strength of the *Spaniards* in *Florida*, destroy'd the whole Country, burnt the Towns, brought all the *Indians*, who were not kill'd or made Slaves, into our Territories, so that there is not now, so much as one Village with ten Houses in it, in all *Florida*, that is subject to the *Spaniards*." By thus "reducing *Spanish* Power in *Florida* so low, that they are altogether incapable of ever harming us" and "by training our *Indian* Subjects in the Use of Arms, and Knowledge of War, which would be of Service to us, in case of any Invasion," these expeditions, Nairne explained, along with "strong and regular Works" built to fortify Charleston had "added very much to our Strength and Safety."[36]

Nairne and Norris thus appealed to prospective settlers on the grounds that they could live in South Carolina in abundance, ease, independence, and safety; equally important, they also argued that the colony was a society that was rapidly becoming more cultivated and improved, another new Albion on the western shores of the Atlantic. The people who created and perpetuated the new societies of colonial British America sought not merely wealth and personal independence as individuals and the welfare of their families but also the social goal of improved societies that would both guarantee the independence they hoped to achieve and enable them to enjoy its fruits. Indeed, demands and aspirations for improvement were nearly as prominent in the promotional literature as were those for affluence and independence. Ubiquitous in the economic writings of early modern Britain, the language of improvement as it took shape in Britain primarily referred to schemes,

[35] Nairne, *Letter*, 3–4, 31–34.

[36] Ibid., 31–35.

devices, or projects through which the economic position of the nation might be advanced, the estates or fortunes of individuals bettered, or existing resources made more productive.[37]

In the new and relatively undeveloped societies of colonial British America, the term *improvement* carried similar connotations, but it also acquired a much wider meaning. It was used to describe a state of society that was far removed from the savagery associated with that "Primitive Race of Mankind," the native Indians. An improved society was one defined by a series of negative and positive juxtapositions. Not wild, barbaric, irregular, rustic, or crude, it was settled, cultivated, civilized, orderly, developed, and polite, and the primary model for an improved society was the emerging and more settled, orderly, coherent, and developed society of contemporary Britain.[38]

Neither Nairne nor Norris argued that South Carolina was yet a fully improved and anglicized society. Indeed, they both took pains to point out the many differences between the colony and its metropolitan model. The most striking difference was in the composition of the labor force. Because servants were so difficult to procure and slavery was a more profitable form of labor, most of "the Business of the Country," including all of "the greatest Drudgeries," was performed by black and Indian slaves, and servants were "seldom put to other Employments than to exercise some Trade, oversee a Plantation, or to carry Goods to Market." As a result, only about 12 percent of the total population was of European descent, 22 percent was black, and a whopping 66 percent were still "*Indian* subjects." Agricultural units were not called farms but plantations, and estate owners not farmers but planters, and the short and mild winters meant that the agricultural cycle was different "in all Respects from Seed-Time 'till Harvest." The great many stumps remaining in the fields after they had been cleared prevented the use of ploughs; neither orchards nor vineyards were "yet common"; few planters produced much butter or cheese; and English grain was neglected in favor of rice because it was much less profitable, an acre of rice being "as Valuable as two or three Acres of *English* Grain." The intensity of the summer heat forced people to "leave their Labour" and confine themselves to the shade for "Three or Four Hours in the Middle of the Day . . . and Refresh and Divert themselves in Bathing in Cool-Water; and retiring to the Shady

[37] See Joan Thirsk, *Economic Policy and Projects: The Development of a Consumer Society in Early Modern England* (Oxford, 1978), and Joyce Appleby, *Economic Thought and Ideology in Seventeenth-Century England* (Princeton, N.J., 1978).

[38] Nairne, *Letter*, 8; Jack P. Greene, "Search for Identity: An Interpretation of Selected Patterns of Social Response in Eighteenth-Century America," *Journal of Social History* 3 (1970): 189–224 [chap. 6 below].

Groves, Arbours, or Houses." For the same reason, for the "greatest Part of the Year" most people went "very thin clad, and airy," making their clothing half cotton instead of all wool as was the custom in England. The absence of building stone forced people to build their houses and other buildings with either brick or timber.[39]

If these many differences were ones to which most immigrants could easily adapt, there were still others that, in the eyes of Nairne and Norris, made South Carolina clearly superior to Britain. The greater productivity of the soil meant that agricultural yields were considerably higher and that there was no need to manure it. Domestic animals of all sorts—cattle, hogs, and fowl—were much more prolific, and there were no game laws. Still other areas of obvious superiority included those that had been deliberately built into the institutions of the colony by its early leaders. As Daniel Defoe remarked in a pamphlet published in 1705, the proprietors of Carolina had consciously set out to build a colony "upon some better Foundations . . . than the rest of the English Colonies." What Defoe specifically had in mind and what Nairne and Norris also emphasized were the provisions that people of all Protestant religious persuasions were to "have free *Toleration* to exercise and enjoy the same without Interruption" and that "All foreign Protestants, of what Denomination soever," were to be "made Denizens within three Months after their Arrival." Following the revocation of the Edict of Nantes, these provisions, Nairne noted, attracted large numbers of French Huguenots who "live[d] in good Friendship with . . . the *English*" and "contributed not a little to improve the Country." With 40 percent Anglicans, 20 percent Presbyterians, 20 percent French Calvinists, 10 percent Anabaptists, and 10 percent Quakers and others, the religious diversity of the settler population, Norris suggested, testified to the success of this policy. Nor was the religious area the only one in which South Carolina had shown some improvement over the society of metropolitan Britain. "In several things," Nairne observed, citing as evidence the choosing of juries by ballot from among a select list "of all the best qualified Persons in the Country," "we have . . . refin'd upon the *English* Laws."[40]

Notwithstanding these many differences between South Carolina and Britain, the message projected by both Nairne and Norris was that during its brief existence South Carolina had become increasingly English. If its new

[39] Norris, *Profitable Advice*, 16–18, 26, 30, 36–42, 44, 48, 50–51, 53–54, 68–69; Nairne, *Letter*, 43–44.

[40] Norris, *Profitable Advice*, 13, 15, 39–42, 46, 62; Nairne, *Letter*, 25, 41, 44; Daniel Defoe, *Party-Tyranny . . . in Carolina* (London, 1705), in Salley, *Narratives of Early Carolina*, 227.

European inhabitants had taken an area that had lain "for several Ages of Time unimprov'd and neglected," they had quickly transformed it into a country that, "in proportion to the Length of Time, and Stock of *English* Mon[e]y originally expended in Settling it," was, as Nairne contended, "much better improv'd than any other *English* colony on the Continent of *America*." The landscape was being increasingly anglicized, trade was expanding rapidly, and they had already created a settled and hierarchical social structure dominated by the planters, who, composing 85 percent of the independent white population, like the English gentry lived "by their own and their Servants['] Industry, improve[d] their Estates, follow[ed] Tillage or Grasing, and" produced "those Commodities which are transported from hence to *Great Britain*, and other Places," to the great profit of themselves and the colony. Moreover, since the legislature had "divided the Inhabited Part of the Country into Parishes, and caus'd Churches . . . and Parsonage-Houses" to be built with 200 to 300 acres of glebe land attached to them, the colony had attracted many ministers of the established church and had fifteen ministers of all denominations.[41]

With stronger and more plentiful religious institutions, Nairne wrote proudly, "Religion and Piety have increas'd and flourished among us, in good Measure," a development that, he thought, had in turn "greatly contributed to the Good of Society, by refining those Dispositions which were otherwise rude and untractable." Indeed, he insisted, the "*European* Inhabitants of the Province" were, "for the most part, People of Sobriety and Industry" who were both "very temperate, and have generally an Aversion to excessive Drinking." Without "that Moroseness and Sullenness of Temper, so common in other Places," South Carolinians, according to Nairne, retained all the best characteristics of English people. "Very . . . liberal in assisting" newcomers, orphans, and unfortunates, "no People," he averred, were "more hospitable, generous, and willing to do good Offices to Strangers; every one is ready to entertain them freely, with the best they have." Nor were they in any way a dull people. Rather, they were mostly "ingenious, of good Capacities, and quick Apprehensions, and have Heads excellently well turn'd for mechanical Works and Inventions." "With little or no teaching," he observed, "they'll make Houses, Mills, Sloops, Boats, and the like."[42]

Not surprisingly, South Carolina by the early eighteenth century also had

---

[41] Defoe, *Party-Tyranny*, 227; Nairne, *Letter*, 8–9, 15–16, 41–46; Norris, *Profitable Advice*, 14, 34–35.

[42] Nairne, *Letter*, 41–43, 45.

"many wise & honest men" to attend to the public service. For "the better and more effectual Preservation of the Lives and Estates of the Inhabitants," Nairne reported, the colony's early leaders had taken full advantage of the "generous Principles of civil and religious Liberty" offered by the proprietors to institute a government that in form was "as nigh as convenient can be to that of *England*," with representative institutions and guarantees of English liberties and English laws. From these "noble Foundation[s]," they and their successors had gradually fashioned an admirable constitution by which "known Laws" were the sole "Measure and Bounds of Power" and liberty was "so well and legally established" that no laws or regulations could be enforced without the explicit sanction of the representatives of the citizens meeting in an elected assembly modeled "as nigh as possible" after the British House of Commons. This assembly, moreover, not only "claim[ed] all the Power, Priviledges, and Immunities, which the House of Commons, have in Great Britain" but also took pains to "retain that Power they have by Law, and preserve the just Ballance of the Government." As if to symbolize their deep commitment to the establishment of a government of laws, a courthouse had been the first public building erected by South Carolina's earliest leaders; and they ever after, Nairne approvingly told his readers, took pains to provide proper officers and courts that would ensure impartial administration of justice. In just a few decades, Nairne and Norris thus argued, British settlers in South Carolina had managed to create a civilized British society with a system of governance every bit as conducive to order, liberty, and security of property as that of the metropolis itself and a liberal religious climate in which people of all Protestant faiths could feel comfortable.[43]

Notwithstanding these several evidences of the anglicization of the South Carolina social landscape, neither Nairne nor Norris suggested that South Carolina was yet the fully improved English society its settlers had hoped to build. Like the earlier promotional writer Robert Ferguson, they could point with pride "to the Growth, Conveniency, and Manufacture of the Country; the Regularity of Living, and Reformation of Life: the Medium of Manners, and the good and happy issues of Prosperity to the Settlement." They could also look forward to the time when, in Ferguson's words, the colony would "grow up to such compleat maturity" that it would finally "bring forth more *Cicero's*, than boasting Thraso's." But they could not argue that South Carolina as yet "abound[ed] with those gay and noisie amuse-

---

[43] Norris, *Profitable Advice*, 32–33; Nairne, *Letter*, 17–27; Mathews, "A Contemporary View of Carolina," 154; Francis Le Jau to Secretary, Mar. 19, 1716, *Le Jau Chronicle*, 175.

ments" or that richly textured social, cultural, and political life characteristic of the urban centers and densely populated rural areas of contemporary Britain.[44]

Seeking to make a virtue of the colony's still primitive social character, Nairne and Norris depicted it as a new Arcadia that offered "a safe and pleasant Retreat" from the bustle of so much of metropolitan Britain, the perfect place for those who took pleasure in the "innocent Delights of plain simple Nature" and could be content with "a Blissful, Retir'd Country Life" of "Solitude, Contemplation, Planting, Gardening, Orchards, Groves, Woods, Fishing, Fowling, [and] Hunting Wild Beasts." If South Carolina did not yet have the dense society and cultural amenities suitable for satisfying the tastes of the "great and [the] rich" of Britain, they observed, there was no better place in all of the British dominions for those who had "experienc'd the Frowns of Fortune . . . to make a handsome Retreat from the World." With only a small public stage, this "remote Country," both writers emphasized, was perfect for people who preferred to seek their happiness in the private realm. In contrast to Britain, there was not that "Multiplicity of Publick Affairs to molest or disturb" a man's "quiet innocent Pleasure." Even the method of jury selection prevented any "one set of Persons" from being "too much burthen'd" by that essential public obligation but ensured that "all should have an equal Share of the Trouble." With so few public duties, every man could concentrate upon his own private affairs, thus ensuring that he would "with moderate Industry be supplied with all the Necessaries of Life" and "plentifully enjoy the Fruits of his Diligence, and Delight, in Improvements, on a large and pleasant Plantation, adorn'd . . . with Buildings, Fish-Ponds, Park, Warren, Gardens, Orchards, or whatever else best delights him" in the full enjoyment of his "Family, Neighbours, and Friends, with all the innocent, delightful Satisfaction imaginable." A man who could be happy with a quiet peaceable life and wanted nothing more than simply to improve his estate for the benefit of himself and his posterity, they suggested, could live "with greater Content" in South Carolina than anywhere in the contemporary British world.[45]

The promise for individuals of a quiet, regular, abundant, and comfortable life in surroundings that were becoming increasingly British was the primary but by no means the only motive cited by Norris and Nairne for emigrating to South Carolina. By pursuing *their own Private Interest*," they suggested, immigrants would unavoidably also contribute to the "*Publick*

---

[44] Ferguson, *Present State*, 31, 34; Norris, *Profitable Advice*, 104.

[45] Nairne, *Letter*, 3, 5, 26, 41, 56; Norris, *Profitable Advice*, 6–7, 11, 65, 85, 104.

Good" of the entire British nation. Both writers stressed the potential national and public benefits of emigration. Norris explicitly heralded emigration as a device for taking poor families off the poverty rolls and thereby reducing local expenditures for poor relief and providing members of an unproductive segment of the population with the opportunity to contribute both to their own support and to the wealth of the nation. In an attempt to interest the Carolina proprietors and the British Board of Trade in a scheme to provide public money to assist emigrants, Nairne even supplied precise calculations of the specific returns that might be expected from an investment of £6,000 to transport and settle ninety laboring men in South Carolina. Estimating that each of these people would "add 5*l.* yearly to the Wealth of *Great Britain*" and would soon be employing at least four slaves, each of whom would add an equal amount, Nairne calculated the annual return from them for the nation at £2,250 at the end of seven years and £3,375 at the end of twenty years. On the basis of these rough figures, Nairne projected a total return to Britain during the first twenty years of over £36,000. Adding this figure to the value of estates in land and slaves created by these settlers, which he estimated at £67,500, Nairne put the total yield for the first twenty years at slightly more than £104,000, almost seventeen times the amount of the original investment. At the same time, according to Nairne, that investment would have added 225 families to the colony's settler population, brought 44,800 acres of land under occupation, and produced yearly quit-rents to the proprietors in excess of £300.[46]

Whatever returns additional settlers in South Carolina might bring to the British nation, the colony's main attraction as depicted by Nairne and Norris was the promise it held for individual immigrants and settlers to advance themselves and their families economically and socially, and they filled their tracts with a variety of data and advice on what economic resources, tools, labor, and provisions were necessary to establish a plantation, what procedures ought to be followed to make a plantation profitable, and what returns settlers might expect from their investments of money and labor. Both writers offered data on the establishment costs, necessary items, and rates of return for a plantation with an initial investment of £100 or £1,000 sterling. Both authors proffered advice on the best time and methods of settling and information on the proper seasons for sowing and harvest, the usual yields of corn, peas, and rice, and techniques for producing rice, silk, rosin, tar, and pitch, none of which was familiar to most English farmers. Nairne

---

[46] Norris, *Profitable Advice,* 5–8, 73, 83, 104–5; Nairne, *Letter,* 56–63. Norris calculated the annual return for each laboring settler at £4, 20 percent less than Nairne.

offered data on wages for several kinds of employment, and Norris described in detail the terms on which impecunious emigrants might get passage to the colony and provided information on the cost of transport: £7 from London and £5 to £6 from the outports of Bristol, Bideford, Exeter, Topsham, and Liverpool. This information constitutes some of the most detailed and authoritative evidence available on these subjects for late proprietary South Carolina.[47]

With £100 for an initial investment, both authors calculated that a family could live, in Nairne's words, "with Comfort and Decency." According to Nairne, that sum would purchase 200 acres of land, two black slaves, four cows and calves, four sows, a canoe, a steel mill for grinding corn, and all the food and tools, including axes, hoes, wedges, handsaws, and hammers, necessary to build a small temporary house and to clear enough land to become self-sufficient in foodstuffs by the end of the year with nearly £10 left for contingent expenses. For the same amount, Norris calculated that a couple could buy the same items promised by Nairne plus six ewes and a ram, sixteen "good Cows and Calves, and a Bull," an unspecified number of breeding poultry, and all the equipment necessary to enable the wife to produce butter and cheese with nearly £7 left for unforeseen expenses.[48]

For £1,000 a family could establish a magnificent estate. By Nairne's estimate, that sum would buy 1,000 acres of land; a labor force consisting of thirty black slaves equally divided between men and women; a vast stock, including twenty cows and calves, three horses, six sows and a boar, and ten ewes and a ram; a large pirogue and a small canoe for water transportation; a steel mill and all the tools, ploughs, and carts necessary to clear and plant 90 acres of land, half of it in rice, and to build a small house; and enough provisions to feed the family and slaves for the first year with nearly £25 left over for contingencies. Such a plantation, according to Nairne, would return over £300 annually. By Norris's calculations, the same sum would buy between 1,000 and 1,500 acres with a labor force of thirty-six slaves, including fifteen black men, three black women, and eighteen Indian women; livestock consisting of thirty cows and calves and two bulls, three horses, six sows and a boar, twenty ewes and a ram, four oxen, and "Fowls of several Sorts for to kill, and also to breed from"; a large pirogue, a small canoe, and carts for transportation of goods and produce; the tools needed to clear and plant 90 acres, sixty in rice and thirty in corn and peas; a year's provisions; dairy equipment; and the labor of carpenters to produce a small house,

---

[47] Norris, *Profitable Advice*, 35–41, 72–96; Nairne, *Letter*, 10-11.

[48] Nairne, *Letter*, 51–52; Norris, *Profitable Advice*, 85–90.

with over £60 left for contingencies. Such an estate, Norris predicted, would yield £400 per year, a quarter more than promised by Nairne.[49]

Both Nairne and Norris advocated beginning this process in the early fall. By immigrating in September, they agreed, an immigrant gave himself, as Nairne put it, "eight Months moderate Weather" in which to acclimate himself to the climate "before the Heat comes." But September was also the best time to start a plantation because it gave the planter up to six months to clear land at the rate of about three acres per laboring hand, build shelters for his slaves and family, and fence his corn ground before it was time to plant about March 1. If the first year was thus spent clearing land, constructing shelter, and planting essential crops to feed and return a small profit for the plantation, the second was the time both to clear more land and to make gardens, plant orchards, and build barns and other necessary buildings, while the third and fourth winters could be employed in clearing still more land and building a more substantial house for the planter, the original house thenceforth serving as a kitchen and the more successful planters building their new dwellings of brick. In just three or four years, according to both authors, new settlers could be living in a plentiful and comfortable way, free of the "Scarcity, Poverty, and Want" the poorest of them had known in the old country and with every prospect of obtaining wealth, substance, and honor in their new country.[50]

Nairne and Norris thus beckoned people to South Carolina to pursue their own individual happinesses. They either minimized or sought to translate into advantages the several conditions that had operated to prevent the colony from developing more rapidly during its first four decades—its malignant disease environment, hot summers, divisive public life, cultural crudeness, and situation close to powerful Indian nations and the colonies of hostile European powers. Above all, they sought to depict South Carolina as a place where immigrants could find "a more plentiful and profitable Way to Live." In articulating this vision, in inviting prospective immigrants "to go thither to advance themselves," Nairne and Norris appealed to what appears to have been the most powerful animating impulse in the thousands of individual decisions by early modern Britons and Europeans to pull up stakes in the Old World and move to the New: the desire to begin anew in a place with manifold opportunities for individual economic and social advancement in which—in the new field of action that was America—men might be active agents in their quest for competence, substance, independence, and the ca-

[49] Nairne, *Letter*, 52–54; Norris, *Profitable Advice*, 92–96.
[50] Nairne, *Letter*, 49–50, 55; Norris, *Profitable Advice*, 72–96.

pacity to shape their own lives however they wanted. That, at least insofar as Nairne and Norris perceived the situation, those goals had to be achieved through the systematic subjugation of dependent African and Indian slaves was far less of a disincentive to immigration than readers with modern sensibilities might suppose.[51]

This essay was written for and with permission and minor corrections is reprinted from "Introduction: Early South Carolina and the Psychology of British Colonization," in Jack P. Greene, ed., *Selling a New World: Two Colonial South Carolina Promotional Pamphlets by Thomas Nairne and John Norris* (Columbia: University of South Carolina Press, 1989), 1–30.

---

[51] Norris, *Profitable Advice*, 77, 96.

—FIVE—

Travails of an Infant Colony:
The Search for Viability,
Coherence,
and Identity in Colonial Georgia

W HO WE ARE, what kind of a society we live in, and what sort of a
place we inhabit are important, if usually only implicit, questions
for the members of all human societies. For new societies without clear shape
or a well-defined sense of social purpose, they take on a heightened importance. The inhabitants of most of the early modern British-American colonies only gradually found satisfactory answers to these questions as their
society slowly developed a definition of itself both as a corporate unit—as a
place and as a society—and as a collection of inhabitants who had a common
membership in a social order and held a common set of values and orientations, one that provided them with a basis for approved social behavior and
the interpretation of contemporary events and developments. Only as these
necessarily stereotypical definitions of the collective self were gradually articulated and refined by inhabitants and outside observers alike and then
internalized by the inhabitants did the settlers begin to understand what they
and their societies were about. Eventually, through that understanding, they
constructed a coherent sense of themselves and their enterprises—that is, a
collective identity.

As the clearest expression of what a people was "*wanting or trying to be, or
wanting to do with what it*" was,[1] a colony's corporate sense of self thus provides a key to the contemporary meaning of its inhabitants' collective experiences in founding and developing their new societies. At the same time,

---

[1] Américo Castro, *The Spaniards: An Introduction to Their History* (Berkeley, Calif., 1971),
127.

[113]

the analysis of the changing content of those collective identities reveals, perhaps as well as can the study of any other single phenomenon, the character of their responses to the successive social and political transformations they experienced. This essay, based on my reflections upon some of the voluminous published contemporary descriptions, analyses, and histories, seeks to describe and explain the changing reputation and identity of colonial Georgia and Georgians from the early 1730s to the mid–1770s.

Two general methodological or procedural points must be stated at the outset. First, as I have discovered in trying to construct a much more ambitious analysis of the process of identity formation in four other early modern plantation societies—Virginia, Barbados, Jamaica, and South Carolina—the collective identities of the new societies of colonial British America can be plotted around the answers to four general questions.[2] The initial question was posed before the settlers left England: What did they hope to do in this new place or why should they go there? The second question confronted the settlers upon arrival: What was the place like and what could be done there? The third question arose during the first generations of settlement out of the dialectic between the first two questions: What, given their original intentions and the possibilities offered by the environment, should they do there? The final question impressed itself ever more powerfully upon each succeeding generation of inhabitants: Who were they, that is, on the basis of their shared experiences in this new place what had they become? From the answers to these four questions—questions about objectives, circumstances, standards, and history—a sense of corporate self in each colony gradually took shape.

My second procedural point is that this process of collective identity formation in new societies seems to go through three sequential but not sharply distinguishable stages. In the first stage, characteristics of place usually assumed primacy. That is, the inhabitants identified themselves and their societies largely on the basis of the nature and potentiality of the places in which they had settled. During a second stage, they tended to define themselves more according to the way they were organizing their social landscapes and the extent to which those landscapes did—or did not—conform to inherited notions and standards. Finally, during a third stage, the inhabitants defined themselves on the basis of their predominant characteristics as a people.

---

[2] This larger study, still in process, is tentatively entitled *Paradise Defined: Studies in the Formation and Changing Character of Corporate Identities in Early Modern Plantation America, 1585 to 1820.*

In contrast to many other early modern British-American colonies, the set-tlers of Georgia from its very beginning had an unusually clear sense of what they hoped to do. Indeed, it is probable that no other early modern British colony began with a more fully articulated set of goals. These goals were revealed in an extensive promotional literature that in volume probably exceeded that for any of the earlier colonies, except possibly Virginia and Pennsylvania. Georgia was the first entirely new British colony founded in America since Pennsylvania almost fifty years before and the last until the establishment of East and West Florida and several new island colonies in the West Indies at the close of the Seven Years' War. Not since the founding of England's first colony in Virginia at the beginning of the seventeenth century had the establishment of any colony attracted so much public atten-tion in Britain or such wide public support, the extent of which was indicated not only by large private contributions but by an unprecedented outlay of government funds.

In some ways, the initial projections for Georgia do not appear very dif-ferent from those for most other colonies. Like most of its predecessors, Georgia was intended to enhance the power and wealth of the British nation and to provide an outlet and a field of opportunity for the unfortunate, the persecuted, and the adventurous of the Old World. Its specific strategic role as a barrier to render the increasingly valuable but black colony of South Carolina "safe from Indians and other enemies," particularly the Spanish in Florida, was not unlike that foreseen for Jamaica in the 1650s and New York and the Carolinas in the 1660s. Ever since the establishment of Virginia, moreover, colonies had been seen as "Asylum[s] to receive the Distressed," and, especially since the founding of the Carolinas, New Jersey, and Penn-sylvania during the last half of the seventeenth century, they had been pro-moted as places of religious refuge, where besieged and "distressed Protes-tants" from the continent of Europe could find "Liberty of Conscience and a free Exercise of Religion."[3]

Similarly, Georgia's depiction in the promotional literature as a land of

---

[3] "Some Account of the Designs of the Trustees for Establishing the Colony of Georgia in America," Georgia Historical Society, *Collections* 20(1980): 4–6; "Reasons for Establishing the Colony of Georgia," ibid., 1(1840): 216–17, 224, 226; Francis Moore, *A Voyage to Georgia Begun in the Year 1735* (London, 1774), in Trevor R. Reese, ed., *Our First Visit in America: Early Reports from the Colony of Georgia, 1732–1740* (Savannah, 1974), 99; Henry Newman to Reverend Mr. Samuel Urlsperger, May 18, 1733, *Henry Newman's Salzburger Letterbooks*, ed. George Fenwick Jones (Athens, Ga., 1966), 44–45.

promise, a new Eden, was not significantly different from the early portraits of other colonies in regions south of New England. With a warm, temperate climate and rich soil, which required "slight" husbandry and little work to yield a rich abundance, Georgia was presented as a place where the settlers could easily achieve both prosperity and contentment. Not only would its "fertile lands" and generous climate yield up all of the crops and other commodities produced in South Carolina, including corn, grains, rice, livestock, naval stores, and deerskins, it also promised to be suitable for the production of flax, hemp, and potash, which Britain then imported in substantial quantities from Russia. Most important, because it occupied "about the same latitude with part of China, Persia, Palestine, and the Made[i]ras," it was "highly probable," Georgia's promoters predicted, that as soon as the new colony was "well peopled and rightly cultivated," it would supply Britain with many of the exotic products—"raw silk, wine, [olive] oil, dies, drugs, and many other materials"—which it then had to purchase at vast expense from other "Southern Countries." Because it already had "white mulberry-trees [growing] wild, and in great abundance," silk, the production of which was "so Easy a work that Every Person from Childhood to old Age can be Serviceable therein," would, it was thought, be to Georgia what sugar was to Barbados and Jamaica, tobacco to Virginia and Maryland, and rice to South Carolina. Georgians at the same time would grow prosperous through such easy and potentially profitable productions and contribute to the prosperity and power of the entire Anglophone world.[4]

Nor until they had succeeded in such enterprises would Georgians have to worry much about either sustenance or defense, "difficulties" that had frequently "attended the planting" of earlier colonies. Just across the Savannah River, South Carolina abounded with cattle, grain, and other provisions that would be easily and cheaply available to feed the settlers of the new colony until they could support themselves. And although they would have to be on guard against the treacherous Spaniards, they had little to fear from Indians. Unlike both Virginians and Carolinians in their early days, Georgians would be "in no danger" from the Indians, whose numbers had so "greatly decreased" over recent decades that they "live[d] in perfect amity with the English." Such a safe and "fine Land . . . in a Temperate Climate"

---

[4] [Jean Pierre Purry], *A New and Accurate Account of the Provinces of South-Carolina and Georgia* (London, 1732), in Trevor R. Reese, ed., *The Most Delightful Country of the Universe: Promotional Literature of the Colony of Georgia, 1717–1734* (Savannah, 1972), 124, 127, 143–44, 147; "Reasons for Establishing," Georgia Historical Society, *Collections*, 1(1840): 205–6, 208–12, 216, 223; Newman to Urlsperger, May 18, 1733, *Newman's Letterbooks*, 44–45; "Some Account of the Designs," Georgia Historical Society, *Collections* 20(1980): 4, 6.

that would yield "a vast variety of Productions fit for the Benefit of Trade and Comfort of Life" was obviously "capable of great improvements." The colony's promoters assured potential supporters and settlers that the newcomers "must in a few Years be a flourishing and happy People." Like Pennsylvania, which a mere fifty years earlier had been "as much a forest as Georgia is now, and in those few years, by . . . wise economy . . . now gives food to 80,000 Inhabitants, and can boast of as fine a City as most in Europe," Georgia could not fail to grow into "a mighty Province."[5]

But the trustees had no intention of permitting this extraordinary promise to be frittered away in the egocentric pursuit of wealth. They knew that many earlier colonies had been undertaken with the best of intentions and the most elaborate plans and that in every one, with the possible exceptions of the orthodox Puritan colonies of New England, the plans of the organizers had quickly given way before the uncontrollable pursuit of self-interest. Placing their own welfare over all social concerns, the colonists had settled in a pell-mell and dispersed fashion, monopolized as much land as they could, and done everything possible to enhance their own private wealth. With their small white populations, legions of dangerous and discontented slaves, and large concentrations of land in the hands of a few proprietors, South Carolina and Jamaica were exactly what Georgia's organizers were determined that it would never become. Having learned from the mistakes of earlier promoters, the trustees were determined that Georgia would be "founded upon Maxims different from those on which other Colonies have been begun."[6]

The Georgia plan as devised by the trustees was less a throwback to seventeenth-century ventures than a preview of the later doctrines of "systematic colonization" advocated by Edward Gibbon Wakefield and others for the settlement of Australia and New Zealand in the 1830s and 1840s. In contrast to such places as Jamaica and South Carolina, Georgia was to be "a regular Colony," by which its promoters meant "methodical; orderly," "agreeable to rule," "instituted . . . according to established forms of discipline," "constituent with the mode prescribed," and "governed by strict regulations."[7]

---

[5] "Some Account of the Designs," Georgia Historical Society, *Collections*, 20(1980): 6–7; "Reasons for Establishing," ibid., 1(1840): 223–24; [Purry], *New and Accurate Account*, 127; Newman to Urlsperger, Nov. 21, 1732, May 18, 1733, *Newman's Letterbooks*, 31, 43.

[6] Moore, *Voyage to Georgia*, 99.

[7] "Some Account of the Designs," Georgia Historical Society, *Collections* 20(1980): 6. The definitions in this paragraph are taken from Samuel Johnson, *A Dictionary of the English Language*, 8th ed., 2 vols. (London, 1799).

Georgians would have "Civil liberty . . . in its full extent" in the manner of the free people in all British colonies. But this civil liberty would not include the freedom to pursue individual interests at the expense of the trustees' overall design. Thus the colonists were to be settled "in an orderly manner so as to form . . . well regulated town[s]" and close settlements and not in the dispersed manner that was common in other colonies and for which Virginia was particularly infamous. Experience had "shown the inconvenience of private persons possessing too large quantities of land in our colonies, by which means, the greatest part of it must lie uncultivated" to the prejudice of the "well-settling" of those colonies. The trustees therefore were determined that Georgia should have "a more equal distribution of lands." To that end they stipulated that land "be divided in small Portions" of fifty acres, none of which could subsequently be united through "Marriage or Purchase." By this "strict *Agrarian* Law," the trustees hoped to prevent "the Rich [from] . . . monopolizing the Country." Because they had only small tracts, the settlers would not need the slaves that had helped undermine both the social happiness and the individual moral fiber of South Carolina and colonies in the West Indies. Rather, they would be able and would be expected "to labor themselves for their support." They would not, "like the old Romans," be sucked by slavery into indolence and passivity but would be rendered "more active and useful for the defence of their government." Finally, the trustees vowed to give "all Encouragement . . . to Virtue and Religion & all Discouragement to Immorality and Profaneness" and to maintain "good discipline" through the introduction of "such regulations . . . as . . . would best conduce to the . . . encouragement of industry and virtue among" the settlers.[8]

As one looks more deeply into the Georgia plan, it becomes obvious that it was designed to avoid not only the mistakes of earlier colonies but the contemporary social evils of Britain as well. As is well known, Georgia was conceived as a charitable trust that would employ a combination of lightly occupied land between the Savannah and the Altamaha rivers, the private contributions of the benevolent in Britain, and public funds to relieve the nation's growing population of the impoverished and the imprisoned. Hence the founding of the colony was widely heralded in Britain as an act of beneficence by which "many families who would otherwise starve" would "be provided for & made masters of houses and lands," and many other unfortunates then languishing in prison would be once again rendered useful to

---

[8] "Some Account of the Designs," Georgia Historical Society, *Collections* 20(1980): 5–6; "Reasons for Establishing," ibid., 1(1840): 214, 221, 225–26; Newman to Urlsperger, May 18, 1732, *Newman's Letterbooks*, 44–45; Moore, *Voyage to Georgia*, 99–100.

the nation. That this charitable assistance would also free the British public from some of the economic burdens of poor relief was also a consideration. Contemporary cynics could dismiss this aspect of the Georgia enterprise as a clever device to get the poor and the imprisoned out of the country and off the public charge: to rephrase the old aphorism, out of sight, out of mind—and not out of pocket.[9]

But the impulse behind the founding of Georgia obviously went far deeper than such expedient calculations. Established during what one con-temporary social critic called "the very age of retention, [an age] in which every man's benevolence is centered in himself, and publick spirit is ab-sorbed by private interest," Georgia was to be not just a model colony but a model society for Britain, a mirror or counterimage that would stand as both a reaffirmation of old values and a repudiation of the baser tendencies then rampant in British life. For throughout the first half of the eighteenth cen-tury, one social commentator after another sounded the theme that Britain's rising wealth and growing involvement in an expanding and volatile money economy were the primary sources of the blatant social miseries that Georgia was in part designed to relieve. These developments, critics asserted, had produced not only a decline in virtue and other traditional English values but social evils unknown to earlier generations. As the rich grew ever richer and wallowed in more and more luxury, it seemed, the gap between rich and poor grew ever wider, poverty increased, the number of poor in work-houses, poorhouses, and prisons rose dramatically, and private virtue and public spirit fell victim to a deluge of possessive individualism and a riot of self-indulgence.[10]

The ubiquity of such concerns in Britain strongly suggests the possibility that the Georgia project elicited such deep public resonances and exerted such a powerful and widespread appeal among the comfortable and the wealthy because it proposed to relieve not just some of the nation's growing social problems but also the social guilt created by those problems. By giving money to the Georgia trustees instead of spending it on "luxury and super-fluous expenses," the people considered responsible for the country's social ills could at the same time allay their guilt over their own good fortune in the lottery of life, absolve themselves of any personal responsibility for ex-isting social ills, prove—to themselves and to others—their generosity, and

---

[9] "Some Account of the Designs," Georgia Historical Society, *Collections* 20(1980): 4–7; "Reasons for Establishing," ibid., 1(1840): 216, 218, 221–22.

[10] See esp. Isaac Kramnick, *Bolingbroke and His Circle: The Politics of Nostalgia in the Age of Walpole* (Cambridge, Mass., 1968). The quotation is from *State of the British and French Colonies in North America* (London, 1755), 67.

show that, doomsayers to the contrary notwithstanding, all "public spirit" was not "lost" in Britain.[11]

Georgia may thus have become a great national undertaking not only because of the growing appreciation of the worth of colonies and a desire to enhance the wealth and power of the nation but also because it spoke directly—and positively—to some of the British elite's deepest social anxieties. If Georgia could prove that the habits and character of such "miserable objects" as the poor and the indebted could, under proper regulations, be reformed and such people given a new sense of purpose and self-worth, there was still hope for Britain itself. The "example of a whole Colony" behaving "in a just, moral and religious manner" would, it was hoped, strike a blow against profligacy throughout the entire Anglophone world. Georgia could become a model, indeed, the inspiration, for Britain's own social salvation. As the patrons and promoters of such a glorious enterprise, the trustees became national social heroes, and James Oglethorpe was lionized for his selfless patriotism and public spirt. "That a Gentleman of his Fortune possessed of a Large and Valuable Acquaintance[,] a Seat in Parliament, with the Genius to make a Figure in any Senate in the World, Should renounce all these Pleasures to cross a perilous Ocean for the Sake of establishing a few distressed families undone by Idleness, Intemperance, Sickness, with other ill habits and all Oppressed with Poverty, to Found a Colony in a Wilderness wholly uncultivated," was, declared one observer, "one of the greatest pieces of Self Denial this Age has afforded."[12]

For more than a decade, people hoped that this ambitious enterprise would succeed in its original design. Indeed, for the first few years, reports from the colony were largely encouraging. "A very pleasant country" with a "good . . . climate" that, one visitor noted, would produce, "with God's blessing, everything which grows in the West Indies" and afforded "the opportunity of cultivating olives, grapes, and silk," Georgia seemed to be a "great success." Despite some sickness and predictable intemperance and disobedience on the part of a few of the settlers, Oglethorpe reported to the trustees eleven

---

[11] "Some Account of the Designs," Georgia Historical Society, *Collections* 20(1980): 5–6; "Reasons for Establishing," Georgia Historical Society, ibid., 1(1840): 231–32.

[12] "Some Account of the Designs," Georgia Historical Society, *Collections* 20(1980): 6; Robert G. McPherson, ed., "The Voyage of the *Anne*—A Daily Record," *Georgia Historical Quarterly* 44 (1960): 222; Newman to John Vat, Oct. 10, 1735, *Newman's Letterbooks*, 175.

months after the arrival of the first settlers that the colony had "increased and flourished." Savannah had been laid out and contained fifty houses; several necessary public works had been begun; the population was approaching five hundred. During the next year, the number of houses in Savannah almost doubled, and many additional settlers swelled population figures. By June 1735 one new arrival claimed that people were flooding in so rapidly "from all parts of America as well as from England" and the Continent that "the builders and brick-makers cannot make and build [houses] fast enough for [all] the [new] inhabitants." "Trade and planting" were developing "very fast"; cattle exceeded two thousand head; naval stores, corn, and peas were being produced in abundance; oranges were coming "on finely"; and silk culture appeared so promising that, it was said, "the name of it fills the colony so full [of hope] that if it goes on so for seven years," Savannah would "be the largest city or town in all the Continent of America."[13]

Although a few lazy and improvident people among the new settlers neglected "to improve their Lands," got into debt, and were "generally discontented with the Country," the "Industrious ones," another visitor told his London readers, "have throve beyond Expectation" and "made a very great Profit" out of provisions and cattle. Obviously, remarked the young Baron Philipp Georg Friedrich von Reck, who conducted the first transport of Salzburger immigrants to Georgia, God had "so far . . . blessed" the enterprise as to permit industry, justice, and good order to triumph over "[self-]indulgence and idleness," "Discord and disorder." The pious Salzburgers at Ebenezer seemed to do particularly well. When one of them had to travel into South Carolina, he recoiled in horror at the sinful lives of both masters and servants on the rice plantations and vowed to "remain in Ebenezer with water and bread rather than to live in a place [like South Carolina] where people walk[ed] the straight path to hell." By contrast, von Reck concluded, the "arrangements made for Georgia by the Trustees" indeed seemed to be "very praiseworthy and Christian."[14]

---

[13] James Oglethorpe to Trustees, December 1733, Francis Piercy to Rev. Forster, June 1, 1735, and Phillip Thicknesse to His Mother, Nov. 13, 1736, in Mills Lane, ed., *General Oglethorpe's Georgia*, 2 vols. (Savannah, 1975), 1:27–30, 180–81, 282; George Fenwick Jones, trans., "Commissary Von Reck's Report on Georgia," *Georgia Historical Quarterly* 47 (1963): 100.

[14] Jones, "Commissary Von Reck's Report," 101; *The Journal of the Earl of Egmont*, ed. Robert G. McPherson (Athens, Ga., 1962), 71, 307; Moore, *Voyage to Georgia*, 98; "Travel Diary of Commissioner Von Reck," in Samuel Urlsperger, comp., George Fenwick Jones et al., eds., *Detailed Reports on the Salzburger Emigrants Who Settled in America . . .* , 7 vols. to date (Athens, Ga., 1968—), 1:142; "Daily Register," ibid., 2:193.

Although Georgia continued into the late 1730s to receive glowing reports in the British press,[15] the initial euphoria gave way to doubt as the settlers slowly began to come to terms with the questions of what kind of a place Georgia was and what could or ought to be done there. Reports began to filter back across the Atlantic that all was not well in the new Eden. Within two years, there were complaints about a variety of problems, including incompetent magistrates, ethnic antagonisms, political contention, social dissipation, and the engrossment of trade by a handful of Scottish merchants. Most important were the complaints that, despite all the money being poured into the colony, it was making but "small progress." Contrary to the "extravagant representations . . . in favour of this settlement" circulated in the London press, John Brownfield wrote the trustees from Georgia in May 1737, a little over four years after the initial settlement, Georgians could not yet feed themselves, few settlers could "subsist independent of" public support, and there was no credit and almost no foreign trade. Instead of becoming the prosperous, well-regulated, regenerated, and contented people initially projected by the trustees, some significant part of them were slowly falling into an "indolent and dejected" state, and many of the "best workmen" were "beginning to leave the place in order to get employment in Carolina and by that means prevent their families from starving." Far from being "so flourishing as our public papers would persuade us," Georgia was, Brownfield noted, "never yet so low as at this time," and all the inflated reports of its "great improvements" were nothing more than "great chimerical idea[s]" designed to deceive the trustees and the British public.[16]

Nor, according to a significant and articulate section of the population, did this downward trajectory change over the next few years. The trustees continued to sponsor publication of favorable reports, which as late as the early 1740s insisted that most settlers had found "Means to live comfortably" and that those of industry and frugality, such as the Salzburgers at Ebenezer and the Highland Scots at Darien, were thriving. Moreover, these reports asserted, continued progress in the culture of silk and wine, the intended "Staple[s] of the Country of *Georgia*," enhanced the hope that with perseverance these two products could yet be brought "to Perfection."[17]

---

[15] See John Brownfield to Trustees, May 2, 1737, in Lane, *General Oglethorpe's Georgia* 1:305–9.

[16] *The Journal of Peter Gordon, 1732–1735*, ed. E. Merton Coulter (Athens, Ga., 1963), 49–51, 59; Brownfield to Trustees, Mar. 6, 1736, May 2, 1737, in Lane, *General Oglethorpe's Georgia* 1:248–50, 306–9.

[17] William Stephens, *A State of the Province of Georgia* (London, 1742), in Trevor R. Reese, ed., *The Clamorous Malcontents: Criticisms and Defenses of the Colony of Georgia, 1741–1743*

In opposition to such rosy projections, a rising chorus from people the trustees tried to dismiss as "clamorous malcontents" argued that the colony was an abysmal failure. The first history of Georgia—entitled *A True and Historical Narrative of the Colony of Georgia*, published in Charleston and London in 1741 and composed by three of the trustees' most vehement critics, Patrick Tailfer, Hugh Anderson, and David Douglas—provided a detailed account of that failure. The promotional literature, these critics complained, had depicted Georgia "as an *Earthly Paradise*, the soil far surpassing that of England; the air healthy, always serene, pleasant and temperate, never subject to excessive heat or cold, nor to sudden changes." Such reports had led the early immigrants to expect a "Land of Promise, overflowing with the abundance of all good things necessary and desirable for the comfortable support of life, and those to be obtained with half the labour, industry and application" required in the Old World "for the lowest subsistance." Instead, the settlers found an excessively hot and, by European standards, inhospitable climate in which sickness and disease were rife and people could feed themselves only with the most debilitating labor without hope of ever achieving more than simple subsistence. Despite the large sums poured into the colony, its critics contended, Georgia during its first decade remained a poor, "miserable colony," a place, indeed, that did not even deserve "the *Name* of a Colony."[18]

The reasons for this failure, according to the malcontents, did not lie in the place. Just across the Savannah River, in South Carolina, people were prospering in the same climate and with the same soil. Nor was the problem in the settlers themselves, most of whom had worked hard, and many of whom, having given up on Georgia, had succeeded elsewhere. Rather, Georgia's desolate state was entirely traceable to its initial design and to the implementation of that design by the trustees and their subordinates in Georgia. Specifically, the restrictions on land acquisition and inheritance had "ex-

(Savannah, 1973), 3–5, 8, 10–11, 14; [Benjamin Martyn], *An Account Showing the Progress of the Colony of Georgia . . .* , (London, 1741), in ibid., 224–25; [Thomas Christie], *A Description of Georgia* (London, 1741), in Peter Force, comp., *Tracts and Other Papers Relating Principally to the Origin, Settlement, and Progress of the Colonies in North America*, 4 vols. (Washington, D.C., 1836–46), 2:3–4.

[18] Patrick Tailfer, Hugh Anderson, and David Douglas, in Clarence L. Ver Steeg, ed., *A True and Historical Narrative of the Colony of Georgia* (Athens, Ga., 1960), 4–5, 40–41; *Journal of Peter Gordon*, 25; Inhabitants of Savannah to Trustees, Nov. 22, 1740, Hugh Anderson and Others to Trustees, Dec. 2, 1740, Petition to George II or Parliament, Dec. 29, 1740, Joseph Avery to Harman Verelst, Jan. 31, 1743, in Lane, *General Oglethorpe's Georgia* 2:486–89, 492, 513, 519, 522–23, 654; [Thomas Stephens], *A Brief Account of the Causes That Have Retarded the Progress of the Colony of Georgia, in America* (London, 1743), in Reese, *Clamorous Malcontents*, 287.

tinguish[ed] every Incitement to Industry and Improvement" and had been "a *great Means of de-peopling the Colony, as fast as you can people it*." In their passion for system and regularity, the trustees had assigned lands without regard to fertility or worth and had thus left many people both with inferior plots and at a serious disadvantage. Most important, by excluding black slavery, the trustees had deprived the colonists of the means by which to develop lands in a hot climate. "It has hitherto been a received maxim in all owr southerne setlements, not only in the West Indies, but also in Carolina," one discontented Georgian noted, "that negroes are much more profitable to the planter (as being naturalisled to the extreame heats) than any European servants," who were both less reliable and more expensive. Indeed, "without the help and assistance of negroes," the malcontents concluded, it would be "morrally impossible that the people of Georgia can ever gett forward in their setlements or even be a degree above common slaves" because "the people of Carolina, who are remarkable for their industry and who inhabit a country equally as fine and productive as Georgia, will at all times, by the help of their negroes be able to undersell the people of Georgia in any commodities they can possibly raise, at any market."[19]

Finally, as if these difficulties were not enough, the malcontents charged that the interior government of the colony had been conducted in an arbitrary manner that was wholly inconsistent with the customary rights of Britons and was utterly "unexampled under any *British* Government." "While the nation at home was amused with the fame of the happiness and flourishing of the colony, and of its being *free from lawyers of any kind*," the malcontents reported, "the poor miserable settlers and inhabitants were exposed to as *arbitrary* a government as Turkey or Muscovy ever felt. Very looks were criminal, and the grand sin of *withstanding*, or any way *opposing* authority, (as it was called, when any person insisted upon his just rights and privileges) was punished without mercy." The result was that "for some time there were more imprisonments, whippings, &c. of white people, in that *colony of liberty*, than in all British America besides." Instead of the silkworm, the "Georgia stocks, whipping-post, and logg-house" came to symbolize the colony "in Carolina and every where else in America, where the name of the Province was heard of, and the very thoughts of coming to the colony became a terror to the people's minds." "By all appearance[s]," Georgia thus

---

[19] *Journal of Peter Gordon*, 53–54, 56–59; Tailfer and Others to Trustees, Aug. 27, 1735, Petition to Trustees, Dec. 9, 1738, Hugh Anderson to Oglethorpe, Jan. 9, 1739, Inhabitants of Savannah to Trustees, Nov. 22, 1740, Hugh Anderson and Others to Trustees, Dec. 2, 1740, Petition to George II or Parliament, Dec. 29, 1740, Avery to Verelst, Jan. 31, 1743, in Lane, *General Oglethorpe's Georgia* 1:225–27, 2:372, 374, 382–83, 489–90, 494, 513, 515, 519–21, 656; [Stephens], *Brief Account of the Causes*, 279–80, 284.

seemed "to have been calculated and prepared" not as a settlement of British subjects but as "a colony of vassals, whose *properties* and *liberties* were, *at all times*, to have been disposed of at the discretion or option of their superiors." "Not even the flourishing of wine and silk," the malcontents declared, could "make a colony of British subjects happy if they" were "deprived of the liberties and properties of their birthright."[20]

Although first set forth in a conciliatory, even deferential, tone, the criticisms of the malcontents represented a demand for precisely what the trustees were determined to avoid: placing Georgia on the same "foot of the other American Colonies." In demanding liberty for individuals to acquire as much land as they wished, to dispose of their possessions without restraint, to settle where they liked, to have as many slaves as they saw fit, and, ultimately, to enjoy a government that provided the benefits of British law and assured that they would neither be deprived of liberty and property without due process of law nor governed by laws passed without their consent, they were asking that Georgia be permitted to follow the time-tested pattern of British colonization—the "ancient Custom of sending forth Colonies, for the Improvement of any distant Territory, or new Acquisition," as it had been "continued down to ourselves." "By enjoying the freedom we crave," they declared, "New York and the rest of His Majesty's colonies," including the "famous province of Pennsylvania," were "all doing well," permitting their inhabitants to accumulate "large and plentiful fortunes . . . while this poor province and the people in it, for want of such liberty, are a load and burden to the mother country." South Carolina, which they praised without irony as "a land of liberty, property and plenty," was a dramatically successful model of the traditional mode of British colonization using slaves to work in the "scorching rays" of the summer sun.[21]

Indeed, the success of all the other British colonies seemed to the malcontents to underline the absurdity and visionary character of the Georgia scheme. Whereas the founders of those colonies "fondly imagin'd it neces-

---

[20] *Journal of Peter Gordon*, 51–53; Inhabitants of Savannah to Trustees, Nov. 22, 1740, Petition to George II or Parliament, Dec. 29, 1740, in Lane, *General Oglethorpe's Georgia* 2:490, 517–18; [Stephens], *Brief Account of the Causes*, 275–76, 281; Robert Pringle to James Henderson, June 22, 1739, *The Letterbook of Robert Pringle*, ed. Walter B. Edgar, 2 vols. (Columbia, S.C., 1972), 1:101; Tailfer, Anderson, and Douglas, *True and Historical Narrative*, 8, 17, 52–54, 58–59, 129–30, 141; [Thomas Stephens], *The Hard Case of the Distressed People of Georgia* [London, 1742], in Reese, *Clamorous Malcontents*, 266.

[21] Tailfer, Anderson, and Douglas, *True and Historical Narrative*, 3, 17, 20; *Journal of Peter Gordon*, 52; Tailfer and Others to Trustees, Aug. 27, 1735, Inhabitants of Savannah to Trustees, Nov. 22, 1740, Hugh Anderson and Others to Trustees, Dec. 2, 1740, in Lane, *General Oglethorpe's Georgia* 1:225, 2:489–91, 496.

sary to communicate to such young Settlements the fullest Rights and Properties, all the Immunities of their Mother Countries, and Privileges rather
more extensive" so that their colonies would flourish "with early Trade and
Affluence," the trustees, considering "Riches . . . as the *Irritamenta Malo-
rum* . . . that . . . inflate[d] weak Minds with Pride[,] . . . pamper[ed]
the Body with Luxury, and introduce[d] a long variety of Evils," had, the
malcontents acidly wrote, thus

> *Protected us from ourselves* . . . by keeping all Earthly Comforts from
> us: You have afforded us the Opportunity of arriving at the Integrity
> of the *Primitive Times*, by intailing a more than *Primitive Poverty* on
> us: The Toil, that is necessary to our bare Subsistence, must effectually
> defend us from the Anxieties of any further Ambition: As we have no
> Properties, to feed Vain-Glory and beget Contention; so we are not
> puzzled with any System of Laws, to ascertain and establish them: The
> valuable Virtue of Humility is secured to us, by your Care to prevent
> our procuring, or such much as seeing any *Negroes* (the only human
> Creatures proper to improve our Soil) lest our Simplicity might mis-
> take the poor *Africans* for greater Slaves than ourselves: And that we
> might fully receive the Spiritual Benefit of those wholesome Austeri-
> ties; you have wisely denied us the Use of such Spiritous Liquors, as
> might in the least divert our Minds from the Contemplation of our
> Happy Circumstances.[22]

After "seven years . . . of fruitless and misspent time and labour," the
malcontents concluded in 1740, "the present establishment" could "never
answer." Not only the example of other colonies but "trial, practice and experience" in Georgia itself had shown beyond doubt that the original plan
should be dismissed as merely some "noted refiner['s]" "theoretical" and
"*utterly impracticable*" scheme. The failure of the trustees' grand plan had
proven conclusively that "all Projects to devise a better Constitution of Government than the *British*, for *British* Subjects," were "sad Quack Politicks,"
remarkable for at once "destroying or torturing the Patients, and disgracing
the Prescriber." Now that a "sufficient Term" had "been allowed for the
Experiment," it was time to turn to modes of settlement that had worked
elsewhere. Why, they asked, should Georgia, alone among all the British
colonies, be "singled out for a state of misery and servitude"? The trustees'

---

[22] Tailfer, Anderson, and Douglas, *True and Historical Narratives*, 3–4.

clerical minion John Wesley might desire *"never . . . to see* Georgia *a rich, but a Godly Colony."* The malcontents wanted precisely the opposite.[23]

This frontal assault upon virtually every element that had given the Georgia plan its distinctive character stimulated an increasingly strident and uncompromising verbal battle that lasted for the five years from 1738 to 1743 and produced a continuous round of petitions, counterpetitions, and pamphlets. At first, the trustees and their supporters held fast to all aspects of their initial plan, and, although they eventually agreed to modify the restrictions on inheritance and land distribution, they refused to abandon the prohibition on slavery on the grounds that it was thoroughly "inconsistent" with "the first Design of the Establishment." Not only, they argued, were slaves unnecessary for the production of "Silk, Cotton, Cochineal, [wine,] and the other designed Products of the Colony," all of which were "Works rather of Nicety than Labour," but they were "absolutely dangerous." Recent "Insurrections of Negroes in *Jamaica* and *Antigua*" had revealed that slaves were "all secret Enemies" who were "apt . . . to rise against their Masters, upon every Opportunity." For that reason, they were wholly inappropriate for a frontier colony such as Georgia. Much more important, however, slavery was a primary source of most of the evils that were present in the other colonies and that the trustees were determined to avoid in Georgia. Slaves, they argued, citing South Carolina and the West Indies as examples, discouraged white immigration, led to the concentration of wealth and the engrossment of lands in the hands of those who could afford them, destroyed the industry of poor whites, who invariably "disdain[ed] to work like Negroes," and ultimately drove even the slaveholders "to absent themselves, and live in other Places, leaving the Care of their Plantations and their Negroes to Overseers."[24]

Pointing out that "none of our most beneficial Colonies have yielded an early Profit," the trustees admitted in their counterattacks that Georgia's progress had been slow. But they attributed that slowness not to the prohi-

---

[23] *Journal of Peter Gordon*, 54; Petition to Trustees, Dec. 9, 1738, Hugh Anderson to Oglethorpe, Jan. 6, 1739, Inhabitants of Savannah to Trustees, Nov. 22, 1740, Petition to George II or Parliament, Dec. 29, 1740, Avery to Verelst, Jan. 31, 1743, in Lane, *General Oglethorpe's Georgia* 2:372, 382, 384, 487–88, 518, 656; Tailfer, Anderson, and Douglas, *True and Historical Narrative*, 4–5, 40, 67–68; [Stephens], *Hard Case of the Distressed People*, 260–62, and *Brief Account of the Causes*, 279–81, 283, 288.

[24] [Benjamin Martyn], *An Impartial Enquiry into the State and Utility of the Province of Georgia* (London, 1741), in Reese, *Clamorous Malcontents*, 126–47; [Martyn], *Account Showing the Progress*, 191–92; Urlsperger, *Detailed Reports of the Salzburger Emigrants* 3:311; Tailfer, Anderson, and Douglas, *True and Historical Narrative*, 103.

bition of slaves or to any of the other regulations called into question by the malcontents but to the quality of the early immigrants, many of whom were "low and necessitous People" who had been difficult "to form . . . into Society, and reduce . . . to a proper Obedience to the Laws." The colony's recent problems, the trustees professed, resulted from the activities and example of the malcontents, those profligate lovers of Negroes, who had fomented a spirit of idleness, dissipation, and contention that discouraged the entire colony. Citing the success of the industrious Salzburgers in Ebenezer and Highland Scots in Darien, the trustees' protagonists argued that the initial design was viable for any people who were willing to expend the necessary labor and be content with moderate and moral lives. They insisted that Georgia could still be made to work according to its original plan and predicted that silk and possibly even wine would eventually make both the colony and its inhabitants prosperous—without the use of black slaves.[25]

Participants on both sides of this long and bitter public debate agreed on two points: first, that Georgia had not made as much progress in its first decade as had been originally hoped, and second, that it was still a place of extraordinary promise. Their disagreement was over the means by which that promise could best be achieved. When the trustees continued "their inflexible Adherence to" their "pernicious and impracticable Schemes and Maxims of Government," the malcontents appealed twice to Parliament for redress, in 1742 and 1743. During the second appeal, one member of Parliament indicated in debate that he had "always thought the affair of Georgia a jobb" and averred that the trustees, though honest men, must have been "misled and misinformed of the [true] state of the colony, or they would [have] change[d] their measures of proceeding." On both occasions, however, Parliament sided with the trustees on the major issues. Thereafter, the controversy gradually became less intense. Some Georgians continued to press for slavery, but the trustees resisted their demands until later in the decade.[26]

In the meantime, Georgia continued to grow slowly. By the mid–1740s Savannah may have had three hundred houses, its famous public garden was still "in a very thriving Way," and in its immediate vicinity were "several very pretty Plantations," including Wormsloe, the seat of the trustees' trea-

---

[25] [Martyn], *Impartial Enquiry*, 127–29, [Martyn], *Account Showing the Progress*, 187, 217; Stephens, *State of the Province of Georgia*, 11; [Christie], *Description of Georgia*, 6; *Egmont's Journal*, 71; Tailfer, Anderson, and Douglas, *True and Historical Narrative*, 17, 21, 39–40, 59, 158.

[26] [Stephens], *Hard Case of the Distressed People*, 267; Leo F. Stock, ed., *Proceedings and Debates of the British Parliament respecting North America*, 5 vols. (Washington, D.C., 1924–41), 5:140–41, 151–52, 164, 167.

surer Noble Jones and a place with many "extraordinary" improvements. Nearby was the Reverend George Whitefield's famous orphan house, a large "Superstructure . . . laid out in a neat and elegant Manner" with rooms that were "very commodious, and prettily furnished." Except for Savannah, Ebenezer, and a few other small, scattered settlements, however, the Salzburger spiritual leader Johann Martin Boltzius reported in the early 1750s, Georgia was mostly "still forests" with "small plantations . . . established only here and there." Between 1740 and 1750 population had increased at a rate of less than two hundred per year, and many settlers, who preferred to "run around rather than work," were primarily hunters with no permanent abode. If, as Boltzius contended, Georgia had "nearly all things" that were "necessary for the wants and refreshments of human life," it was still crude and relatively undeveloped. Almost all of its houses were built of wood; many of its public works, buildings, and fortifications were in disrepair; there was a shortage of craftsmen; and there were few mills or roads. So far, the colony had only two "rich merchants," no ships came directly to Georgia for freight, and there was "very little Business stirring." Although silk production had "for several years . . . rather gathered momentum" and there was "no lack of people who" knew "well how to handle it," the annual volume produced was modest, and Georgia contained no vineyards.[27]

Notwithstanding the colony's slow development, Georgia and the trustees did not suffer from a wholly unfavorable reputation as a result of the campaign of the malcontents. In the section on Georgia in the second edition of *The British Empire in America*, published in 1741, John Oldmixon praised the trustees' original design and the colony's subsequent progress. Edward Kimber, whose journal of his visit to Georgia was published in the *London Magazine* in 1745, attributed the fact that Georgia was "so much less flourishing than it was at the Beginning of the Settlement" not to flaws in the trustees' design but to the "cursed Spirit of Dissension" fomented by the malcontents. The antiquarian John Harris, a friend of Oglethorpe, who included a long section on Georgia in his two-volume collection of voyages and travels, published in 1748, was even more lavish in his praise of the trustees and their "worthy, disinterested, and public-spirited . . . Design." Formed "upon the truest Principles of Virtue, Industry, and Freedom," Harris declared, this design was "the best" of "all the Methods that have

[27] [Edward Kimber], "Itinerant Observations in America," Georgia Historical Society, *Collections* 4(1878): 15–19; Klaus G. Loewald, Beverly Starika, and Paul S. Taylor, eds., "Johann Martin Bolzius Answers a Questionnaire on Carolina and Georgia," [March 19, 1751], *William and Mary Quarterly*, 3d ser., 14 (1957): 242, 246–50, 252, 254, 15 (1958): 232, 243, 250.

been hitherto tried, in fixing Colonies in distant Parts of the World." All it needed "to render it, in every respect, a fertile and a pleasant Settlement" was "a sufficient Number of Inhabitants," and, Harris predicted, it could not "fail of striking firm and deep Root" and "would very soon be full of People, and useful People," not masters and slaves.[28]

But the truth was that the old design no longer had any vigor. Through their intensive public campaign, the malcontents had undermined its appeal, if not its credibility, and that battle had taken much of the enthusiasm for the project out of the trustees. As a result, Georgia during the 1740s was left without any clear sense of direction. Between an old design that was no longer fully in operation and the alternative model of the ordinary British colony that had not yet been tried, Georgia had no agreed-upon set of goals and priorities, no coherent sense of place, no acceptable collective sense of self. Oldmixon, Kimber, and Harris to the contrary notwithstanding, by the mid–1740s it was clear that Georgia would never become the well-regulated, egalitarian yeoman utopia initially envisioned by the trustees. Whether it could by another route achieve an equality with other British colonies remained to be seen.

At their first general meeting in July 1732 the Georgia trustees had ordered a common seal for their new colony. Like all the colonial seals, that of Georgia was a representation of aspirations, an emblem of what its founders hoped Georgia would become. On one side "was a representation of silk worms, some beginning and others having finished their web," with a motto signifying "that neither the first trustees nor their successors could have any view of [private] interest" and that the colony was "entirely designed for the benefit and happiness of" the settlers. The reverse side expressed more directly, one suspects, the expectations of the settlers themselves. It had "two figures resting upon urns, representing the rivers Altamaha and Savanna, the boundaries of the province." Between them was seated another figure representing "the genius of the colony . . . with a cap of liberty on his head, a spear in one hand and a cornucopia in the other." Liberty, strength, and abundance—these were the qualities, the seal projected, that would form the "genius" of Georgia.[29]

---

[28] John Oldmixon, *The British Empire in America*, 2d ed., 2 vols. (London, 1741), 2:525–41; [Kimber], "Itinerant Observations," 19; John Harris, *Navigantium atque Itinerantium Bibliotheca*, 2 vols. (London, 1748), 2:323–47.

[29] Alexander Hewatt, *An Historical Account of the Rise and Progress of the Colonies of South Carolina and Georgia*, 2 vols. (London, 1779), 2:18.

All of these qualities had effectively escaped the colony during its first twenty years. "Great had been the expence which the mother country had already incurred, besides private benefactions, for supporting this colony," one contemporary commentator noted, "and small had been the returns yet made by it. The vestiges of cultivation were scarcely perceptible in the forest, and in England all commerce with it was neglected and despised." When the German engineer William Gerard De Brahm planted a settlement of 160 Germans at Bethany in 1751, he found the colony "so lowly reduced that, had it not been for the few English in the Government[']s Employ, and the Salzburgers," the province would have been "intirely deserted of Inhabitants." De Brahm later recalled that a "few days before he arrived, a Lot with a tolerable House on it in the City of Savannah had been sold for [a] few shillings." He said that he "might have bought at that time with twenty Pounds Sterling nearly half the City." If Georgia had become neither rich nor strong, its inhabitants had also failed to acquire the cap of liberty. Without a representative assembly such as was enjoyed by the other colonies, Georgia, as the New England historian William Douglass remarked disparagingly in the late 1740s, could only be considered as "not [yet] colonized."[30]

Once the trustees had surrendered their charter, and Georgia, now "new modelled," was finally put upon "the same footing with Carolina," the colony was at last to have a new—the malcontents would have said, a proper— beginning. Following the removal of the restrictions on slavery, De Brahm remembered, "many rich Carolina Planters . . . came with all their Families and Negroes to settle in Georgia in 1752," and "the Spirit of Emigration out of South Carolina into Georgia became so universal that year, that this and the following year near one thousand Negroes were brought in Georgia, where in 1751 were scarce above three dozen." Formal establishment of royal government under the first crown governor, John Reynolds, in late 1754 seemed at last, as one older resident declared, to bring the colony "the greatest prospect to being . . . happy." "People were then crowding in every day, fill'd with expectations of being Settled in a Country which" had "all the Advantages of Air & Soil and was [finally] founded upon liberty"—a country that at last, in Douglass's terms, had been "colonized." But Reynolds turned out to be a disaster, "a lawless tyrant" whose "iron rod" created so much "Discord" and faction that migration once again flowed out rather than

---

[30] Ibid., 2:165; *De Brahm's Report of the General Survey in the Southern District of North America*, ed. Louis De Vorsey, Jr. (Columbia, S.C., 1971), 141; William Douglass, *Summary, Historical and Political, of the First Planting, Progressive Improvements, and Present State of the British Settlements in North-America*, 2 vols. (Boston, 1749–51), 1:207.

in and Georgia, one disappointed inhabitant lamented, seemed likely to "be reduced to as low an ebb as it was under the Late unhappy Constitution under the Trustees." Several more years would have to elapse before the colony would achieve an identity as a free and flourishing place.[31]

If Georgia "drooped and languished" under Reynolds, his term was mercifully short. Under his politically more adroit successor, Henry Ellis, the colony began "to emerge, though slowly, out of the difficulties that [had] attended [it from] its first establishment," and Georgians at last seemed to be acquiring an unambiguous answer to the question of what they ought to be doing. The colony suffered from a very low base of both people and wealth. The population, Ellis reported shortly after his arrival, was small and mostly "so very poor that they but barely subsist themselves." But the Seven Years' War turned out to be a boon for Georgia, which became a refuge for many people fleeing from the warfare along the Virginia and Pennsylvania frontiers. In the two previous years, Ellis reported in January 1759, white population had jumped almost 40 percent to around seven thousand people, and "other things" were "increasing in proportion," the "produce of the Country" having "more than doubled." With growing numbers and production and a new sense of "happiness & tranquillity" in public life, Georgia was finally beginning to manifest "a visible spirit of industry & improvement."[32]

For the last fifteen years of the colonial period Georgia rapidly acquired a reputation for having an abundance of rich land and a growing population, animated by a building "spirit of industry" that was putting the colony into a "happy" and "most flourishing Condition." Because the "Climate & Soil is at least equal, the Spirit of Industry very Great, and the People beginning to have Property & Foundation Sufficient to Enable them to make Considerable Progress," Governor James Wright, who, as Ellis's successor, presided over Georgia during these boom years, observed in early 1763 that

---

[31] [Edmund Burke], *An Account of the European Settlements in America*, 2 vols. (London, 1808), 2:311; Hewatt, *Historical Account* 2:165; *De Brahm's Report*, 142; Jonathan Bryan to Earl of Halifax, Apr. 6, 1756, Allen D. Candler et al., eds., *The Colonial Records of the State of Georgia*, 31 vols. to date (Atlanta, 1904—) 27:114–15; Douglass, *Summary* 1:207; "On Governor Ellis's Arrival in Georgia," [1757], Georgia Historical Society, *Collections* 20 (1980): 942; Anthony Stokes, *A View of the Constitution of the British Colonies in North America and the West Indies, at the Time the Civil War Broke Out on the Continent of America* (London, 1783), 115.

[32] John Huddlestone Wynne, *A General History of the British Empire in America*, 2 vols. (London, 1770), 1:315, 318; Henry Ellis to Board of Trade, Aug. 1, 1757, Jan. 1, 1758, Jan. 29, 1759, and to William Pitt, Aug. 1, 1757, *Colonial Records of Georgia* 28, pt. 1:41–42, 44, 104, 178.

"the only thing now wanting to make this in a few years a Province of as much Consequence to Great Britain as some others in our Neighbourhood" was "a great Number of Inhabitants."[33]

The close of the Seven Years' War brought peace to the colony and, by placing Florida under British control, removed all apprehension of danger from the Spaniards. Wright negotiated a series of treaties with Indians that brought at least seven million more acres under British jurisdiction. Spurred by these inducements, inhabitants poured into Georgia. The number of whites tripled between 1761 and 1773, rising from just over six thousand in 1761 to ten thousand in 1766 and eighteen thousand in 1773. At the same time, the number of blacks, virtually all of whom were slaves, more than quadrupled, increasing from thirty-six hundred in 1761 to seventy-eight hundred in 1766 and fifteen thousand in 1773.[34] With these growing numbers, the face of the landscape changed. The Savannah River and other areas near the coast now were described as having an "abundance of very fine Settlements and Plantations." But the most dramatic change occurred in the backcountry, where by 1772 the number of whites substantially exceeded that of the lowcountry. By 1773 the colony was "well laid out with Roads," and "the many Plantations and Settlements" along them made "travelling very convenient and easy." "Increasing . . . extreamly fast" since 1760, Savannah had many new houses which were spreading west to the new suburbs of "Yamacraw" and the "Trustees Garden," while Savannah Bay was already "nearly fronted with contiguous Wharfs," all built to handle Georgia's expanding volume of trade.[35]

Indeed, Georgia increased not only in population and settledness during these years but also in production, credit, shipping, and wealth. Its rising production can best be measured by the growing value of its exports, which jumped from around £40,000 in 1761 to almost £85,000 in 1766 to over £100,000 in 1773. The expansion of credit was revealed by the adverse

---

[33] Hewatt, *Historical Account* 2:165; James Wright to Board of Trade, Feb. 22, 1763, Dec. 23, 1763, *Colonial Records of Georgia* 28, pt. 1:406, 455.

[34] "Report of Sir James Wright on the Condition of the Province of Georgia," Sept. 20, 1773, Georgia Historical Society, *Collections* 3(1873): 160, 167; Wright to Board of Trade, Apr. 15, 1761, *Colonial Records of Georgia* 28, pt. 1:309; Wright's Answers to Board of Trade's Queries, Feb. 15, 1762, and 1766, ibid., pt. 2:186; *De Brahm's Report*, 162.

[35] "Journal of Lord Adam Gordon," 1765, in Newton D. Mereness, ed., *Travels in the American Colonies* (New York, 1916), 394–95; Wright to Board of Trade, June 24, 1765, Wright's Answers to Board of Trade's Queries, Feb. 15, 1762, and 1766, *Colonial Records of Georgia* 28, pt. 2:94, 180; James Habersham to Earl of Hillsborough, Apr. 24, 1772, Georgia Historical Society, *Collections* 6(1904): 173; "Report of Sir James Wright," Sept. 20, 1773, ibid., 3(1873): 160; *De Brahm's Report*, 153, 158, 161.

balance of trade. The annual value of imports often exceeded that of exports by nearly £50,000, and much of that difference went for the purchase of slaves, who, in a remark that showed how far Georgia had departed from the trustees' initial plan, Governor Wright described as the "wealth & strength of the Southern American Colonies" and the "chief means of their becoming Opulent & considerable." Over the period from 1761 to 1773 the number of vessels annually loading out of Georgia rose from 42 to 185. With "Produce & Trade" increasing so "amazingly," personal wealth also grew. Most Georgia planters, the anonymous author of *American Husbandry* reported in 1775, were "very much on the thriving hand." Most were not "yet . . . rich," but a few were doing extremely well. The Savannah merchant James Habersham had an income of £2,000 per year, and Wright himself had "in a few years" acquired "a plentiful fortune." His "example and success," one commentator noted, "gave vigour to industry, and promoted a spirit of emulation among the planters for improvement."[36]

Silk was of little importance in this expansion. Georgians continued to produce silk until the early 1770s, and, for a time in the early 1760s, it appeared to be "in a Flourishing State." Within the decade, however, Wright had concluded that it was a "Precarious & uncertain" crop and "that nothing but the Bounty of Parliament" kept "Silk Culture alive" in the province. After the bounty was lowered in the late 1760s, production declined precipitously, and Habersham noted that silk would never become "a considerable Branch of Commerce" in Georgia until, like the Italian silk-producing region of Piedmont, it had "a number of white people in middling circumstances" who would invest the care necessary for its success. Olive trees and vineyards, two of the other exotic staples Georgia had originally been intended to produce, had "not . . . yet [even] become an Object of . . . Attention."[37]

Georgia's new prosperity was based almost entirely upon the same commodities that had been so successful in South Carolina: rice, indigo, naval

---

[36] Wright's Answers to Board of Trade's Queries, Feb. 15, 1762, and 1766, and Wright to Board of Trade, June 8, 1768, *Colonial Records of Georgia* 28, pt. 2:183–86, 251, 258; "Report of Sir James Wright," Sept. 20, 1773, Georgia Historical Society, *Collections* 3(1873): 167; Habersham to Ellis, Jan. 27, 1772, and to John Nutt, July 31, 1772, ibid., 6(1904): 12, 196; *De Brahm's Report*, 163–64; Harry L. Carman, ed., *American Husbandry* (New York, 1939), 351; Hewatt, *Historical Account* 2:266–67.

[37] Wright to Board of Trade, Apr. 23, 1765, Oct. 21, 1766, *Colonial Records of Georgia* 28, pt. 2:92, 172; Habersham to Hillsborough, Apr. 24, 1772, Georgia Historical Society, *Collections* 6(1904): 173–74; *De Brahm's Report*, 142; Guillaume Thomas François Raynal, *A Philosophical and Political History of the Settlements and Trade of the Europeans in the East and West Indies*, trans. J. O. Justamond, 2d ed., 6 vols. (New York, 1969), 6:69–70.

stores, provisions, lumber, and wood products. "Without Exception," one author proclaimed, all of these commodities could be produced "to the same Perfection, and in every respect equal to South Carolina," and they "arrived at the markets in Europe [and the West Indies] in equal excellence and perfection, and, in proportion to its strength, in equal quantities with those of its more powerful and opulent neighbours in Carolina." Alexander Hewatt claimed that because it contained "more good River Swamp," Georgia was actually "a better rice Colony than South Carolina." As proof, several "planters of Carolina, who had been accustomed to treat their poor neighbours with the utmost contempt," had "sold their estates in that colony, and moved with their families and effects to Georgia." Cotton, which was reported to agree "well with the soil and climate of Georgia" and in a few decades would be Georgia's premier staple, was only beginning to be produced in small quantities.[38]

The Georgia seal of 1732 had represented the genius of Georgia as embodying three qualities—abundance, strength, and liberty. The colony's steady growth had finally brought abundance and a considerable degree of strength; liberty, that is, the sense among its free inhabitants of being as much in control of their own destinies and as free as the people of other colonies, was more elusive. With the implementation of royal government in 1754 and the immediate establishment of a representative assembly and a regular judicial system, Georgians appeared finally to have obtained those "English freedom[s]" enjoyed by "all English Colonies"—except Georgia under the trustees. Once Reynolds was removed as governor, it would be accurate to say, as did a contemporary, that Georgia contained "no trace of a despotic government." But the conversion to a royal colony occurred just when colonial authorities in Britain were strongly advocating limiting the autonomy of all of the older colonies and bringing them under much tighter metropolitan control. The officials who designed and oversaw the establishment of royal authority in Georgia had no intention of permitting Georgians to exercise the same autonomy then enjoyed by the other colonies. Once again, Georgia, along with contemporary Nova Scotia, was to be a model colony, this time a model royal colony, a place where "Royal Government" would be "settled in it's greatest purity" and the errors of other governments would be corrected. Georgians were indeed to be "intitled to British Liberty," but their "Mode of Government," as Henry Ellis later declared, was

[38] Ellis to Board of Trade, Apr. 24, 1759, and Wright's Answers to Board of Trade's Queries, Feb. 15, 1762, and 1766, *Colonial Records of Georgia* 28, pt. 1:207, pt. 2:185; *De Brahm's Report*, 140, 150; Carman, *American Husbandry*, 345, 357; Hewatt, *Historical Account* 2:267; Stokes, *View of the Constitution*, 116.

to be "the freest from a Republican Mixture, and the most conformable to the British Constitution of any that obtains amongst our Colonies in North America." In practical terms, this meant that metropolitan officials in the colony—the royal governor and the council—were to have more authority and the representative assembly less than was the case in the other colonies. Even as a royal colony, Georgia would be swimming against the mainstream of British colonial development.[39]

Again, as with the trustees' plans, however, South Carolina acted as the serpent in Eden. "Influenced by the example of South Carolina," the Georgia assembly, Henry Ellis complained soon after his arrival in the colony, "was industriously attempting to usurp the same power" enjoyed by the South Carolina assembly "& had indeed made a considerable progress therein during the Administration of my Predecessor." Indeed, what Ellis called "Carolina notions" seemed in "many instances" to "have prevailed with our people over every other consideration," as Georgians continued "incessantly urging & aiming at the privileges enjoyed there." "It would be happy for us if South Carolina was at a greater distance," Ellis lamented. "So long as our present intercourse with & dependence upon that Province subsists," he despaired that Georgians would ever "alter their ideas" or that he would be able to make the Georgia government conform to the model designed by his superiors in London.[40]

With judicious administration and much help from London, however, Ellis and Wright managed to a remarkable extent to do just that during the late 1750s and early 1760s, albeit the assembly continued sometimes to grasp "at powers that did not belong to them." When the Treaty of Paris brought many new territories under British control in 1763, the governments of Georgia and Nova Scotia were indeed held up as models for those to be established in the new territories, and a visitor to Georgia just before the Stamp Act crisis found the colony's public life full of "love and unanimity." Its behavior during that crisis seemed to indicate that in Georgia, the only older British continental colony except for Nova Scotia in which the designs of the act were not totally frustrated, the crown's new experiment was working. Georgians did not like the Stamp Act, but, as Habersham said, they did not let their "dislike to this Law" lead them into the "unjustifiable ex-

---

[39] Loewald, Starika, and Taylor, "Bolzius Answers a Questionnaire," *William and Mary Quarterly*, 3d ser., 14(1957): 254; Verner W. Crane, ed., "Hints Relative to the Division and Government of the Conquered and Newly Acquired Countries in America," May 5, 1763, *Mississippi Valley Historical Review* 8 (1922): 371–72.

[40] Ellis to Board of Trade, Jan. 1, 1758, Mar. 15, 1759, *Colonial Records of Georgia* 28, pt. 1:101, 193.

cess[es]" of "the Northern people"—even though "No pains" had "been Spared in the Northern Colonies to Spirit up and inflame the People here." Wright confidently predicted that "A Small Check from Home or disapprobation of their Proceedings" and his own diligent attention would "Set all Right here."[41]

Wright was wrong. Despite several small checks from home, Georgia proved to be "a very fertile Soil" for northern ideas. As the quarrel with Britain intensified during the late 1760s and early 1770s, Georgia came increasingly into the orbit of the discontented colonies to the north until, Wright lamented, "the Spirit of Assuming Power, and Raising the Importance of the Assembly" rapidly became "the Ruling Passion." Inspired by the "Example of . . . Carolina," Georgians seemed to be growing just as licentious as other colonists. In the final crisis in 1774–76, when, partly because of Wright's efforts and influence, Georgians hesitated to throw their unreserved support into the opposition to the Coercive Acts, they were in effect shamed or goaded into doing so by the revolutionary leaders in South Carolina. To prove that they were just as free and just as committed to liberty as people in other colonies, to make it clear to themselves as well as to others that they deserved to wear the cap of liberty displayed by the genius of the colony in their great seal, they had no choice. Georgians could at last become equal to the other colonists in this respect only by being equally firm in the cause of liberty.[42]

As Georgians, through their economic, social, and political behavior, were establishing during the 1760s and early 1770s the credibility of their claims to the positive attributes of abundance, strength, and liberty forecast by their seal, they also came to a new understanding of their history, of their collective experiences as a people. "Few countries," one commentator remarked during the American Revolution, had "undergone so many changes as Geor-

---

[41] Stokes, *View of the Constitution*, 137; Crane, "Hints Relative to the Division and Government," 367–73; "Journal of Lord Adam Gordon," 396; Habersham to William Knox, Oct. 28, 1765, Georgia Historical Society, *Collections* 6(1904): 46; Wright to Board of Trade, Jan. 15, 22, Feb. 1, 1766, May 15, 1767, *Colonial Records of Georgia* 28, pt. 2:133–36, 217.

[42] Wright to Board of Trade, June 8, 1768, *Colonial Records of Georgia* 28, pt. 2:253; Habersham to Nutt, July 31, 1772, Georgia Historical Society, *Collections* 6(1904): 197; "Report of Sir James Wright," Sept. 20, 1773, and Wright to Lord Dartmouth, Aug. 24, 1774, ibid., 3:164, 180; *South Carolina Gazette* (Charleston), Sept. 12, 1774, Feb. 27, Mar. 5, 1775.

gia has, in the course of fifty years." But the most dramatic of these changes was the colony's sudden rise to prosperity: "Under the long administration of Sir James Wright . . . it made such a rapid progress in population, agriculture, and commerce, as no other country ever equalled in so short a time." From the perspectives supplied by that change, on the basis of the observable fact that Georgia did not begin "to flourish" until after "the original Constitution framed by the trustees" had been altered, Georgians and other observers could only conclude that the colony's difficulties under the trustees were not attributable to the character of the settlers, who with some exceptions had worked hard enough to ensure that Georgia, as De Brahm declared, had been "a Place of Industry ever since its very Beginning." Rather, Georgia's "Backwardness seemed only to be owing, first to the Prohibition of introducing African Servants, [and] . . . secondly for not being governed in a manner as other Provinces [with] . . . Representatives, with the Liberty to make their own Laws." As soon as the colony had been "freed from those Prohibitions, and invested with Privileges and Liberties, as other Provinces," as soon as its "planters," as another writer put it, "got the strength of Africa to assist them" (and it might be said that the planters enjoyed the abundance and liberty forecast by the seal while the Africans supplied the strength), they immediately began to labor "with success, and the[ir] lands every year yielded greater and greater increase." In the face of this success, no conclusions could be drawn other than those put forth by Wright in 1767 to explain the colony's sudden success: the trustees' plan was obviously "not properly adapted for settling an American Colony," and Georgia's dramatically improved condition was "owing to the great alteration" in that plan.[43]

The writers who supplied the earliest histories of the colony written after the trustee period—Edmund Burke, John Huddleston Wynne, the Abbé Raynal, Alexander Hewatt—all agreed with Wright. They treated the trustees and Oglethorpe as "humane and disinterested" men whose designs for their new colony could scarcely have been more "Laudable . . . in every respect." "The benevolent founders of the colony of Georgia," wrote Hewatt, "perhaps may challenge the annals of any nation to produce a design more generous and praiseworthy than that they had undertaken." Generous and

---

[43] Stokes, *View of the Constitution*, 113, 115; Ellis to Board of Trade, Aug. 1, 1757, William Knox's Memorial to Board of Trade, Dec. 7, 1762, Wright's Answers to Board of Trade's Queries, Feb. 15, 1762, and 1766, *Colonial Records of Georgia* 28, pt. 1:41, 385, pt. 2:187; *De Brahm's Report*, 163; Hewatt, *Historical Account* 2:267; "Report of Sir James Wright," Sept. 20, 1773, Georgia Historical Society, *Collections* 3(1873): 167.

laudable—but not, in Burke's understated phrase, "altogether answerable." Answerable plans for settlement, Georgia's experience under the trustees powerfully seemed to indicate, should have arisen "from the nature of the climate, country, and soil, and the circumstances of the settlers, and [to have] been the result of experience and not of speculation." Certainly, as Wynne remarked, "a levelling scheme, in a new colony," seemed to be "extremely unadviseable," especially, added Burke, when its inhabitants could "see their neighbours . . . in a much more easy condition." The new hero of Georgia, its founding father, became not Oglethorpe but James Wright.[44]

But if the malcontents gained a victory in these early histories, all of which accepted the contention that work in such a hot climate "was too heavy for . . . white men," most of the historians and indeed governors Ellis and Wright recognized that the trustees had not been wholly wrong in their intentions. The trustees' plan had been designed to prevent the irregular settlement, the dispersion, the unequal concentration of property, and the absenteeism and fear associated with a large population of slaves. By 1775 Georgia was displaying strong tendencies in all of these directions; during the period leading up to the Revolution, Georgia's large black population was seen as both a strength and a weakness of the colony.[45]

Notwithstanding the anxieties that slavery brought to the colony, Georgia during the royal period finally achieved a positive sense of itself as a place and as a people. Some areas were unhealthy; indeed, disease seemed to increase with prosperity, population, and trade.[46] As a "young new settled Country," Georgia society was still crude and culturally undeveloped. "We have no Plays, Operas, or public Exhibitions, either in point of Literature or Amusements, to animadvert upon," wrote Habersham in 1772. Or, to

---

[44] Robert Rogers, *A Concise Account of North America* (London, 1755), 142; Hewatt, *Historical Account* 2:16–17, 151; [Burke], *Account of the European Settlements* 2:304–5, 307–8; Raynal, *Philosophical and Political History* 6:65–67; Wynne, *British Empire in America* 1:311.

[45] Carman, *American Husbandry*, 343; [Burke], *Account of the European Settlements* 2:307–12; "Report to Sir James Wright," Sept. 20, 1773, Georgia Historical Society, *Collections* 3(1873): 158; Ellis to Board of Trade, Apr. 24, 1759, Wright to Board of Trade, June 10, 1762, Dec. 23, 1763, June 15, 1767, Knox's Memorial to Board of Trade, Dec. 7, 1762, Wright's Answers to Board of Trade's Queries, Feb. 15, 1762, and 1766, *Colonial Records of Georgia* 28, pt. 1:207–8, 377, 384, 455, pt. 2:179, 232.

[46] *De Brahm's Report*, 160; Wright's Answers to Board of Trade's Queries, Feb. 15, 1762, and 1766, *Colonial Records of Georgia* 28, pt. 2:179; Rogers, *Concise Account*, 145; John Mitchell, *The Present State of Great Britain and North America* (New York, 1767), 178, 184–85, 188–91; Hewatt, *Historical Account* 2:259.

put the matter more positively, although Georgia had "some brilliant . . . [public] Assemblys" and at least five "fine [private] Libraries" and there was talk of turning George Whitefield's orphanage into the first college south of Williamsburg, Georgia, in De Brahm's words, had "not as yet [been] debauched by European Luxuries, such as Balls, Masquerades, Operas, Plays, etc.," and Georgians who sought cultural enrichment had little choice but to apply "themselves to reading good Authors."[47]

In spite of these deficiencies in health and culture, Georgia obviously was becoming a place of which its free white inhabitants could be proud. With large amounts of unoccupied land that, especially in the interior, was said to be "the finest in all America," Georgia was rapidly becoming known and was usually depicted as a "rich and plentiful country" with great opportunity not just for rich slave owners but even for "people of small fortunes" who did "not dislike retirement" in a place of rural delights. As it became increasingly clear that Georgia was "Making a very Rapid Progress towards being an Opulent & Considerable Province" and that that progress finally afforded Georgians "a Prospect of . . . soon becoming a rich, commercial People," and even outsiders began to suspect that Georgia would "become one of the richest, and most considerable provinces in British America, and that[,] in a very few years," Georgians gradually acquired a positive sense of themselves as a demonstrably prosperous and liberty-loving people.[48]

At the same time, their home and their society—their country—was gaining an increasingly flattering reputation as a place of opportunity, freedom, and ease. Like all of the other new plantation societies at a comparable point in their development, Georgians had not been together long enough to articulate any very well developed sense of whether as individuals they were acquiring in common any distinctive characteristics, that is, a collective identity. Georgians were just beginning to attribute special defining qualities to themselves—"a Volatile, but kind people," in the estimation of Habersham; a people who were, "in general of very elevated Spirits," according to De Brahm; a people who, not caring "for a small profit" or a modest way of living, were prone, in the words of Boltzius, to "abuse . . . [their] free-

---

[47] Wright's Answers to Board of Trade's Queries, Feb. 15, 1762, and 1766, *Colonial Records of Georgia* 28, pt. 2:185; Habersham to Wright, Feb. 17, 1772, Georgia Historical Society, *Collections* 6(1904): 166–67; *De Brahm's Report*, 143–44; "Journal of Lord Adam Gordon," 395; Carman, *American Husbandry*, 345.

[48] Carman, *American Husbandry*, 335–37, 344–45, 351; "Journal of Lord Adam Gordon," 396; Wright to Board of Trade, June 8, Nov. 24, 1768, *Colonial Records of Georgia* 28, pt. 2:258, 309; Habersham to Ellis, Jan. 27, 1772, to Wright, Feb. 17, 1772, Georgia Historical Society, *Collections* 6(1904): 162, 167; *De Brahm's Report*, 150; Stokes, *View of the Constitution*, 115.

dom." But their sense of self was primarily expressed through their understanding of their physical and social landscapes.[49]

Especially in view of the destructive effects of the War for Independence
in Georgia, the colony's many loyalists and two of its earlier historians,
Anthony Stokes and Alexander Hewatt, wondered why Georgians put their
new prosperity and positive identity at risk by joining the rebellion against
Britain in 1776. "No country ever enjoyed a greater share of liberty than
Georgia did from the time it became a King's Government, down to the
breaking out of the Civil War," Stokes wrote in 1782. "Justice was regularly
and impartially administered—oppression was unknown . . . taxes . . .
were trifling—and every man that had industry, became opulent." "The
people there were more particularly indebted to the Crown, than those in
any other Colony," he noted; "immense sums were expended by Government
in settling and protecting—that country—troops of rangers were kept up
by the Crown for several years—the Civil Government was annually provided for by vote of the House of Commons of Great Britain, and most of
the inhabitants owed every acre of land they had to the King's *free* gift: in
short, there was scarce a man in the Province that did not lie under particular
obligations to the Crown."[50] Stokes did not understand that Georgians could
never feel that they were equal to the other colonies until they had done
exactly what he found so incomprehensible: shown that, like the others, they
were willing to put all the prosperity they had gained at risk in behalf of the
liberty they claimed as Britons, including their liberty to have slaves.

That Georgia's success in achieving a positive sense of self in the 1760s
and 1770s was so heavily dependent upon the massive adoption of black
slavery was thoroughly consistent with its entire colonial history. For one of
the most interesting facets of the history of colonial Georgia, one that provides some consistency over the entire period, was that it seemed forever to
be destined to go against history. Started as a place that would be free of the
social evils of other British-American colonies, it had been reconstituted as
an entity that would be as free as possible from the centrifugal impulses
toward autonomy that, at least to metropolitan authorities, had seemed to
make the colonies politically fragile and increasingly difficult to control. By
managing to subvert both of these designs, Georgians had succeeded in placing themselves on an equal footing with the other colonies. But in thus
thrusting themselves into and thereby showing that they belonged in the

---

[49] Habersham to William Symonds, Dec. 4, 1765, Georgia Historical Society, *Collections*
6(1904): 51; *De Brahm's Report*, 143; Loewald, Starika, and Taylor, "Bolzius Answers a
Questionnaire," *William and Mary Quarterly*, 3d ser., 15(1958): 243.

[50] Stokes, *View of the Constitution*, 137, 139; Hewatt, *Historical Account* 2:267.

mainstream of British-American colonial history, they were at the same time once again going against much larger currents in Western history. For at the very time Georgia was moving so heavily into slavery, that institution was beginning—for the first time—to be widely condemned in western Europe as a moral evil that was inappropriate for civilized societies. Although this movement seems to have created no problems for Georgians during the colonial period, the rapid triumph of the point of view it represented, which was nearly as sudden as, and far more revolutionary than, Georgia's rise to prosperity, would soon put Georgians at the same point where they had repeatedly found themselves: on the defensive. No doubt the earl of Egmont and the other authors of the trustees' Georgia plan would have found this development disquieting, as they would have found almost everything else that happened to their colony. But they might also have gained a certain amount of satisfaction in the knowledge that their early forebodings about slavery had not been without foundation.

This essay was written to be given on Feb. 10, 1983, as the closing address at "Forty Years of Diversity: A Symposium on Colonial Georgia," held in Savannah, and is reprinted with permission and minor corrections from Harvey H. Jackson and Phinizy Spaulding, eds., *Forty Years of Diversity: A Symposium on Colonial Georgia* (Athens: University of Georgia Press, 1984), 278–309.

Six

Search for Identity:

An Interpretation of the Meaning of Selected Patterns of Social Response in Eighteenth-Century America

RAPID GROWTH, successful social adjustment, phenomenal material ac-complishments, increasing maturity, exuberant self-confidence, buoy-ant celebration—these are the terms in which the story of eighteenth-century American social development has been told.[1] The conventional—and, I sus-pect, still dominant—interpretation is that the original goals and values of the founders of the colonies were, as Daniel J. Boorstin has phrased it, quickly "dissipated or transformed by the American reality."[2] This process had exacted a heavy psychic toll, of course, especially in New England where Puritan leaders of the second and even third generations clung desperately to their original vision of building a "city on a hill," but it presumably had resulted, at least by the middle decades of the eighteenth century, in the successful adjustment of the vast majority of the English settlers to the con-ditions of life they found in America. With this adjustment came new and more appropriately American values and, despite marked regional—even community—differences, a strong sense of group identity deriving from a set of similar experiences in the New World and manifest in a series of flattering self-images that emerged out of their satisfaction with present achievements and boundless optimism about future prospects. This process

---

[1] I wish to thank Kai T. Erikson, Norman S. Grabo, P. M. G. Harris, David F. Musto, and James T. Lemon, the other participants in the OAH session, as well as John E. Crowley for their many helpful suggestions.

[2] Daniel J. Boorstin, *The Americans: The Colonial Experience* (New York, 1958), 1. This book is the most sophisticated and comprehensive statement of the view summarized in this paragraph, though that view serves as an implicit framework for the vast majority of works published on early American history over the past century.

was irreversible, and few wanted to reverse it. So naturally had Americans slipped into the easy pragmatism and undeviating and compulsive pursuit of wealth and so eagerly had they taken to the new ethic of "autonomy and initiative," of virile individualism, social fluidity, atomistic social freedom, and exaltation of the present that the ethic encountered no more than feeble resistance from a few maladjusted groups or individuals.[3] The American Revolution simply accelerated the process by freeing the colonists from a wide assortment of externally imposed institutions and traditions that had constituted the only remaining barriers to their total self-realization, to their coming to be completely themselves.

The extraordinary staying power of this conception is a testimony to its continuing utility in interpretation. Obviously, the remarkable amount of economic and social energy that lay behind the initial settlement of the colonies was not only sustained but vastly increased by the extensive opportunities Englishmen found—and created—in the New World, with the result that colonial societies put a very high premium upon economic and social success and exerted strong pressures, especially upon young men in the middle strata of society, as young Henry Laurens put it, to get ahead "in their Career[s]."[4] Whatever their power, however, and it should not be minimized, these pressures were not—except in the West Indies and possibly South Carolina after 1745 and Georgia after 1760—so great as to exempt men from other kinds of psychological imperatives. They did not necessarily exercise the determinative influence upon the ways men conceived of themselves and their societies, and at no point during the colonial period do they seem to have achieved the kind of full intellectual legitimation that they would attain in the nineteenth century.

What I would like to suggest, in fact, is that for much of the eighteenth century these pressures along with the mood of optimism and rhetoric of success with which they are traditionally associated were counterbalanced by, and existed in an uneasy state of tension with, a deep, pervasive, and probably growing sense of failure and that, far from having developed any explicit or new sense of "American" identity, the colonists continued even as late as the 1760s and 1770s to be remarkably dependent for their normative values—their conceptions of what they would like for themselves and their

---

[3] For a suggestive analysis of the central components of the American identity as it had developed by the middle of the twentieth century, see Erik H. Erikson, "Reflections on the American Identity," in his *Childhood and Society*, 2d ed. (New York, 1963), 285–325.

[4] Henry Laurens to Thomas Mears and Co., Sept. 26, 1755, *The Papers of Henry Laurens*, ed. Philip H. Hamer et al., 12 vols. to date (Columbia, S.C., 1968—), 1:347.

societies to be[5]—upon two externally derived, overlapping, and occasionally conflicting social models, models that both supplied them with "common images of good and evil" and served as prototypes against which good and evil, success and failure, might be measured.[6] So compelling were these models that they inhibited the colonists from fully adjusting to conditions of life in America by developing either an appropriate sense of their own identity or a new set of values that would more accurately correspond with prevailing modes of behavior. For many contemporaries, the extent to which the colonists actually had succeeded in making this psychological adjustment seemed to be almost an exact measure of their moral and cultural failure.

The first of these models—an idealized conception of the character and achievements of the several colonial societies during their early years of settlement—was external in the sense that it derived from the colonial past rather than from the colonial present. The "powerful psychological reality"[7] of this conception in the New England mind during the half century from 1680 to 1730 has of course been described at length by Perry Miller.[8]

[5] See W. G. Runciman, *Relative Deprivation and Social Justice: A Study of Attitudes to Social Inequality in Twentieth-Century England* (London, 1966), 11–13, for the useful distinction there made between normative and comparative reference groups. The same terms may be applied to social models, comparative models being those which furnish a contrast to the existing situation and normative models being those which supply approved standards. Among the former, Indians, blacks, Frenchmen, Spaniards, Turks, and, for the continental colonists, even British West Indians, served as negative reference groups which, by providing Englishmen in America with models of what, to quote Roy Harvey Pearce, "they were not and must not be," helped them to discover who it was they were. Excellent studies of the functioning of two of these groups are Pearce's *The Savages of America: A Study of the Indian and the Idea of Civilization* (Baltimore, 1953) and Winthrop D. Jordan's *White over Black: American Attitudes toward the Negro, 1550–1812* (Chapel Hill, N.C., 1968). The above quotation is from Pearce, 5. An important underlying assumption of this essay, however, is that normative groups exercise a more powerful influence in the process of identity formation among groups, and it is with such groups that I am primarily concerned here.

[6] Erik H. Erikson, "Identity and the Life Cycle," *Psychological Issues* 1 (1959): 18. My assumption is that these models impinge most powerfully upon elite groups but also are widely diffused throughout all strata of society as a result of their intentional popularization by elites and the familiar tendency of middle- and lower-class groups to emulate their betters.

[7] Ibid., 21.

[8] Perry Miller, "Declension in a Bible Commonwealth," in *Nature's Nation* (Cambridge, Mass., 1967), 14–49, and *The New England Mind: From Colony to Province* (Cambridge, Mass., 1953).

Within a generation after the Great Migration to Massachusetts, the Puritan clergy had begun to indict the people for "'declension' from the virtues of their fathers"[9] and to call for a return to "the Primitive Zeal, Piety, and Holy Heat found in the Hearts of our Parents."[10] In one jeremiad after another, the clergy decried the "Visible Decay in Life and Power of Godliness" among later generations and denounced their growing accommodation to the world,[11] interpreting every calamity that befell New England as a chastisement from God and a warning of still greater disasters to come if the people did not desist from their sinful ways.

As the clergy continued to dilate upon the theme of New England's decline, the great "Leaders of the first Generation" assumed heroic, almost saintly, proportions. "They were," said Thomas Foxcroft in his centenary sermon in 1730, "Men of an extraordinary Character, remarkable for their strict piety, simple purity, and brilliant Accomplishments."[12] To "get the World," as Samuel Whitman declared in 1716, could not possibly have been any "part of their Errand: It was not," he said, "any Worldly Consideration, that brought them over hither; but Religion, that they might Build a Sanctuary to the Name of the Lord, where it had not been known before." For later generations of New Englanders wallowing in their own "Great Worldliness,"[13] this idealized vision of the towering figures of the founders, the unavoidable tendency "to magnify their exemplary achievements,"[14] gave them a vivid and exaggerated sense of their own inadequacies and led them irresistibly to the conclusion drawn by the clergy: that, as Foxcroft remarked, by any standard of comparison with their "Forefathers" they fell

---

[9] Quotation from Alan Heimert, *Religion and the American Mind from the Great Awakening to the Revolution* (Cambridge, Mass., 1966), 27.

[10] Joshua Scottow, *Old Men's Tears, for their own Declensions . . .* (1691; rept. Boston, 1715), 19.

[11] Samuel Whitman, *Practical Godliness the Way to Prosperity* (New London, 1714), 27. See also Increase Mather, *An Earnest Exhortation to the Children of New-England to Exalt the God of the Fathers* (Boston, 1711), 29–30.

[12] Thomas Foxcroft, *Observations Historical and Practical* (Boston, 1730), 30.

[13] Quotations from Whitman's *Practical Godliness*, 28–31. See also, among many other examples of similar complaints about growing worldliness, Ebenezer Thayer, *Jerusalem Instructed and Warned* (Boston, 1725), 31–32; John Barnard, *Two Discourses Addressed to Young Persons* (Boston, 1727), 92–94; Samuel Wigglesworth, *An Essay for Reviving Religion* (Boston, 1733), 15–16; and John Webb, *The Duty of a Degenerate People to Pray for the Reviving of God's Work* (Boston, 1734), 3, 25–26.

[14] Alan Heimert, "Puritanism, the Wilderness, and the Frontier," *New England Quarterly* 26 (1953): 371.

"vastly short . . . of their bright example."[15] In Joshua Scottow's words, the "Noble Vine" had obviously degenerated "into a Strange Plant."[16] And it was the strangeness and hence the unrecognizability of the plant that was so disturbing. So vast and apparently unclosable was the gap between present modes of actual behavior and the way of life represented by the founders and recommended by the clergy that, as Perry Miller has written, by the centennial of New England settlement in 1730 the people "were forced to look upon themselves with amazement, hardly capable of understanding how they had come to be what they were"[17] or, I would add, exactly what and who they had become.

Outside New England, where these atavistic impulses were neither so carefully cultivated by the clergy nor conventionally put in such public and highly ritualized forms, they were much less obvious and, at least for the early portion of the eighteenth century, probably much less vividly and finely developed. But in every economically advanced region and among all elite groups which were at least a generation away from the frontier, they lurked just below and occasionally rose above the surface of public life. Throughout the early decades of the century, Pennsylvania Quakers, as Frederick B. Tolles has shown, were bothered by a growing concern over their obvious fall from the "primitive Simplicity" of their forefathers and a deepening "sense of failure" over their inability to live up to the original goals of the "Holy Experiment" envisioned by William Penn and the first leaders of the colony.[18] Because colonies like Virginia, the Carolinas, and New York had not been founded by quite such transcendent figures with such lofty, coherent, and well-defined aims, the tendency there was to complain less about declension from a virtuous past and more about the failure to achieve the full potential of their society. But there was, nonetheless, a widespread conviction that the current generation was inferior in industry, enterprise, frugality, strength, and virtue to the groups who had performed the Herculean task of wresting plantations out of the wilderness.[19]

---

[15] Foxcroft, *Observations Historical and Practical*, 41.

[16] Scottow, *Old Men's Tears*, 19; see also Webb, *Duty of a Degenerate People*, 25–26.

[17] Miller, *From Colony to Province*, ix.

[18] Frederick B. Tolles, *Meeting House and Counting House: The Quaker Merchants of Colonial Philadelphia* (Chapel Hill, N.C., 1948), esp. viii, 123–24, 234–36. See also *Advice and Information to the Freeholders and Freemen of the Province of Pennsylvania* (Philadelphia, 1727), 1, 4.

[19] See, e.g., [Benjamin Whitaker], *The Chief Justice's Charge to the Grand Jury* (Charleston, S.C., 1741), 10–11, and Lewis Morris, Sr., "Views about the Seat of Government" (n.d.),

The specific forms of behavior identified as evidences of this decline varied somewhat—but only somewhat—from region to region. The concern of New England Puritans and Pennsylvania Quakers with what Kenneth A. Lockridge has referred to as "gradually waning spiritual energies"[20] was much less pronounced elsewhere, while, as David Bertelson has suggested, complaints about the rise of "slothful Indolence" were probably slightly more common among the southern colonies.[21] From all over the colonies, however, came complaints about a growing contentiousness in all areas of colonial life, insubordination and declining deference among social inferiors, rankly antisocial individualism, neglect of calling and of public duty, deceit, avarice, extravagance, and pursuit of pleasure.[22] What was most alarming was the "'Exorbitant Reach after Riches' that had come to be 'the reigning Temper of Persons of all Ranks.'"[23] "The generally prevailing cry is the World," lamented the Reverend William Williams in his Massachusetts election sermon in 1719. "How many seem to have taken up that Resolution that they will be Rich? How many are in haste to be Rich?"[24] And with the quest for riches came a manifest and frightening increase in "carnal Appetites."[25] In New England clergymen and laymen alike deplored the "great Extravagance that People, and especially the Ordinary sort, are fallen into, far beyond their Circumstances, in their Purchases, Buildings,

---

Morris Family Papers, Rutgers University Library, New Brunswick, N.J. Robert E. Kehoe called to my attention this and other documents from the Morris Family Papers cited in this essay.

[20] Kenneth A. Lockridge, *A New England Town, the First Hundred Years: Dedham, Massachusetts, 1636–1736* (New York, 1970), 89.

[21] David Bertelson, *The Lazy South* (New York, 1967), 61–97. The quotation is from Robert Beverley, *The History and Present State of Virginia*, ed. Louis B. Wright (Chapel Hill, N.C., 1947), 319. For an analysis of how William Byrd II of Westover internalized this fear of laziness, see Kenneth S. Lynn, *Mark Twain and Southwestern Humor* (Boston, 1959), 3–22.

[22] An excellent case study of these lamentations as well as of the conditions that gave rise to them and the psychological functions they fulfilled is Richard L. Bushman's *From Puritan to Yankee: Character and the Social Order in Connecticut, 1690–1765* (Cambridge, Mass., 1967).

[23] Heimert, *Religion and the American Mind*, 31, quoting Wigglesworth, *Essay for the Reviving of Religion*, 25.

[24] William Williams, *A Plea for God, and an Appeal to the Consciences of a People Declining in Religion* (Boston, 1719), 23–25.

[25] James Blair, *Our Saviour's Divine Sermon on the Mount*, 2d ed., 2 vols. (London, 1740), 1:58; the phrase "carnal Appetites" was later used with great frequency by the evangelical clergy during and after the Great Awakening.

Families, Expenses, Apparel, and generally in the whole way of Living,"[26] while in Virginia Commissary James Blair chided his Anglican parishioners in a thinly veiled allegory for their inability to resist the "temptations of pleasure" and their addiction to "all manner of Gratifications of their Luxury, stately Houses, Furniture, and Equipage, plentiful Tables, Mirth, Musick, and Drinking."[27] Such an "expensive" and "sumptuous" style of life, remarked another critic, had been completely "unknown to their Forefathers forty years ago."[28] In Pennsylvania Chief Justice James Logan questioned "whether the Attractions of Pleasure and Ease" had not come to be far "Stronger than those of Business,"[29] and Benjamin Whitaker, Logan's counterpart in South Carolina, called upon the people "to abstain from that Luxury and Excess, which within a few Years last past, has pour'd in upon us like a Torrent" and "so greatly contributed to enervate and soften our Minds, and to sink us, into Indolence and Inactivity."[30]

What this intercolonial chorus of jeremiads was objecting to, of course, was, in Perry Miller's words, "the outward and visible signs of prosperity and its abuses."[31] The rapid economic and demographic growth of the colonies after 1680 and more especially after 1713 opened up vast new economic opportunities in land, trade, and services and greatly accelerated the transformation of the colonies from the largely traditional and relatively static societies most of them had been throughout much of the seventeenth century into the market-oriented, rapidly changing societies most of them would become by the middle of the eighteenth century. There were, of course, eddies and backwaters among older settled areas and in remote regions with unfavorable locations or poor natural resources which were largely unaffected by these developments and did not share in the rising levels of prosperity that accompanied them. But for a great many people and for most regions the American continent seemed to be, in the later phrase of William Smith, Jr., of New York, an "inexhaustible Source of a profuse Abun-

---

[26] Paul Dudley, *Objections to the Bank of Credit Lately Projected . . .* (Boston, 1714), 24. See also *The Present Melancholy Circumstances of the Province Consider'd and Methods for Redress Humbly Proposed in a Letter from One of the Country to One in Boston* ([Boston], 1719), 3–5.

[27] Blair, *Our Saviour's Divine Sermon on the Mount* 1:127, 132.

[28] *A Reply to the Vindication of the Representation of the Case of the Planters of Tobacco in Virginia* (London, 1733), 4–5.

[29] James Logan, *The Charge Delivered from the Bench to the Grand Jury . . .* (Philadelphia, 1723), 9.

[30] [Whitaker], *The Chief Justice's Charge*, 10–11.

[31] Miller, *Colony to Province*, 307–8.

dance."[32] Relatively few in the colonies were "very rich," but, as several observers began to point out during the early decades of the eighteenth century, there were almost "none who" were "miserably poor (unless per accident),"[33] and "such a favoring material environment"[34] whetted the social and economic appetites and increased the material aspirations of men at all levels of society.

For men who had already realized their economic ambitions or were otherwise exempt from the imperatives of the success syndrome that operated so powerfully upon upwardly mobile groups—for members of established elites, older and successful men among first-generation elites,[35] residents of regions no longer occupied with the elemental frontier concerns for simple survival, clergy who took upon themselves the task of keeping watch on the moral health of society, and foreign observers—for all of these groups it was obvious, however, that such a bounteous environment was not an unmixed blessing.[36] An inbred Christian fear of the adverse moral effects of wealth predisposed them[37] to believe that "the sunshine of affluence," as a young Scottish tutor in Virginia later observed, would engender "many more reptile than ethereal friends,"[38] and the central paradox of colonial life

[32] William Livingston et al., *The Independent Reflector . . .* , ed. Milton M. Klein (Cambridge, Mass., 1963), 103.

[33] The quotation is from George Vaughan to Board of Trade, May 10, 1715, in W. Noel Sainsbury et al., eds., *Calendar of State Papers, Colonial Series*, 44 vols. to date (London, 1860—), *1714–15*, 171.

[34] Tolles, *Meeting House and Counting House*, 11.

[35] Some evidence for the peculiar concern of middle-aged and older men over the moral state of colonial society is presented by Cedric B. Cowing, "Sex and Preaching in the Great Awakening," *American Quarterly* 28 (1968): 635–36. Cowing notes the strong appeal of the Great Awakening to "'middle aged' men."

[36] There were some groups, of course, who seem neither to have been wholly caught up in the success syndrome nor to have shared the fears of prosperity described below. These were mostly groups who were either on the peripheries of colonial society or almost totally engaged in providing for themselves and their families at a subsistence or slightly higher level. For a suggestive discussion of some of these groups in New England, see *A Plea for the Poor and the Distressed . . .* (Boston, 1754), 3–10.

[37] Among many examples of this fear: *A Rich Treasure at an Easy Rate: or The Ready Way to True Content* (London, 1657), which was twice reprinted in Boston in 1683 and 1763 (Miller, *Colony to Province*, 42); Blair, *Our Saviour's Divine Sermon on the Mount* 1:121–24; Tolles, *Meeting House and Counting House*, 81–84.

[38] James Reid, "The Religion of the Bible and Religion of K[ing] W[illiam] County Compared" (1769), in Richard Beale Davis, ed., *The Colonial Virginia Satirist: Mid-Eighteenth Century Commentaries on Politics, Religion, and Society*, American Philosophical Society, *Transactions*, n.s., 57, pt. 1 (Philadelphia, 1967), 65.

seemed to be that material improvement led ineluctably to moral degeneration, that the conquest of the physical wilderness only made it easier for a
psychological and social wilderness of unknown dimensions and unknown
power to creep in upon them, choke off all morality, and eventually even to
reduce them to the barbarous—and, most frightening of all, undifferentiated—level of most of the rest of mankind.[39] God had given the colonists
"Plenty; but Plenty begat Ease, and Ease begat Luxury; and Luxury," it
seemed, had "introduced a fatal corruption of every good and virtuous principle."[40] Americans seemed merely to "have hardened under the Sun-Shine,"
to have repaid God's "bounteous Dispensations"[41] by turning them into
"Wantonness," abusing their "Peace to Security," their "Plenty, to Riot and
Luxury," and making "those good Things which should have endeared"
them to God "the occasion of estranging them from" Him.[42] Instead of
bringing out the better side of human nature, instead of enabling and encouraging men to use their material abundance as a foundation on which to
erect a society of virtue and benevolence, the affluent conditions of the New
World seemed largely to have resulted only in the almost total unfettering of
the darker side of human nature.

Increasing luxury and ingratitude to God were not the only ill effects of
the favorable conditions of economic life in the colonies. Equally, if not
more, alarming was the social chaos they seemed to generate: the uncertainty
and impermanence of social status, the blurring of traditional social grada-
tions and lines of social and political authority, defiance of established social
and political institutions, and the sacrifice of concern for the public good to
the unrestrained pursuit of individual wealth and ambition. Although it is
now clear that these social conditions and the modes of behavior they generated were normal in an early market society undergoing dramatic enlargement of economic opportunity and individual aspirations during a period of
rapid economic and demographic growth, colonials were operating out of a
set of social attitudes that had taken shape in an "economy of scarcity" in

---

[39] This theme is briefly developed by Heimert, "Puritanism, the Wilderness, and the Fron-
tier," 377–81. Note also Francis Rawle's comment that "Riches is the Mother of Luxury and
Idleness" and that "the Daughter [hath] devoured the Mother" in *Ways and Means for the
Inhabitants of Delaware to Become Rich* (Philadelphia, 1725), 12, as quoted by Tolles, *Meeting
House and Counting House*, 106.

[40] William Smith, *Discourses on Several Public Occasions during the War in America* (London,
1759), 77.

[41] *South-Carolina Gazette* (Charleston), Jan. 8, 1741. This quotation was called to my attention by Lewis Frisch.

[42] Richard Allestree, *The Whole Duty of Man* (London, 1658), 149; this widely influential—
among Anglicans—work was reprinted in Williamsburg in 1746.

which the middle and lower orders accepted their "subordination and the obligation to cultivate the qualities appropriate to" their "subordination, such as submissiveness, obedience, and deference."[43] From the perspective of those attitudes, such volatile and fragile social arrangements and such highly egoistical behavior as prevailed throughout the colonies could only be interpreted as evidence of a dramatic fall from the high standards set by the early founders and as the certain harbinger that society itself was on the verge of dissolution, about to "tail [off] into a State of Anarchy and Confusion."[44]

But these attitudes were clearly inappropriate to the conditions of colonial life,[45] and what Perry Miller has said about New England in 1730 applies equally to all the older colonies at that date: "the complex, jostling reality of this anxious society . . . demanded new descriptions. Ideas relative to these [new social] facts had to be propounded, and in words that could make the relation overwhelmingly felt." Colonial society "needed to establish its identity anew . . . and reconstruct its personality"[46] in such a way as to make it possible for individuals to adjust to conditions of abundance and to rationalize and thereby to make acceptable—and thus to render socially and morally valid—the new forms of behavior called forth by those conditions.

The tendency of most of those scholars who have been particularly concerned with this problem—Perry Miller, Frederick B. Tolles, Daniel J. Boorstin, Alan Heimert, David Bertelson, Richard L. Bushman—has been

---

[43] David M. Potter, *People of Plenty: Economic Abundance and the American Character* (Chicago, 1954), 205.

[44] Quotation from [Whitaker], *Chief Justice's Charge*, 10–11.

[45] This is not to say that these attitudes did not fulfill an important social function. Such attitudes had, of course, been a standard feature of the intellectual ambiance of England at least since the middle of the sixteenth century. In the colonies as well as in England, they obviously served a deep and persistent need to preserve the ideal of a more static and coherent social order amidst the constantly shifting and always potentially convulsive conditions of a market society. Whether they were actually "appropriate . . . to the more static society" of the seventeenth century, as Alan Heimert (*Religion and the American Mind*, 55–56) and many other students of colonial history have contended, is less important than that they were clearly incongruent with eighteenth-century colonial behavior. The meaning of the persistence of such attitudes from the sixteenth through the eighteenth centuries in England is explored briefly in my review of Isaac Kramnick's *Bolingbroke and His Circle: The Politics of Nostalgia in the Age of Walpole* (Cambridge, 1968) and David Bevington's *Tudor Drama and Politics: A Critical Approach to Topical Meaning* (Cambridge, 1968) in the *William and Mary Quarterly*, 3d ser., 26 (1969): 450–53. See also E. M. W. Tillyard, *The Elizabethan World Picture* (New York, 1958); Michael Walzer, "Puritanism as a Revolutionary Ideology," *History and Theory* 3 (1963): 59–90; and W. H. Greenleaf, *Order, Empiricism, and Politics: Two Traditions of English Political Thought, 1500–1700* (Oxford, 1964).

[46] Miller, *Colony to Province*, 482–85.

to emphasize how far the colonists had succeeded in making this adjustment by the middle decades of the eighteenth century, but there is a large volume of evidence to indicate that the revolution in day-to-day behavior denounced by the jeremiads was accompanied not by the development of a new and more appropriate set of values or of a new concept of identity but by a passionate adherence to the old. So heavily did the "weight of the past" hang upon the colonists that they were unable either to surrender the standards they had inherited from their ancestors or to face up to and accept the changes taking place in their societies.[47] The result was an ever greater divergence between behavior and values that left the colonists uncertain about their standards and capabilities, anxious about the present, and without full confidence in the future. Far from discovering "a deeper identity"[48] of their own, then, they never ceased to measure their own achievements against their idealized conception of their ancestors, and the blatant disparity between this mythic past and contemporary reality contributed to the formation and perpetuation of what Erik Erickson has referred to as a "guilt-culture" in which all tragedies—earthquakes, fires, epidemics, hurricanes, slave uprisings, and wars—were imputed to their own and their society's "inner" failings, and "a reactionary return to the content and to the form of historically earlier principles of behavior"[49]—the model of the early founders— was seen to be the only method to overcome those failings and to achieve the society's fullest potential.

In an important sense, the Great Awakening was just such a reactionary return. Alan Heimert has shown that the Awakening produced at least some rudimentary forms of millenarian thinking that looked forward to the eventual achievement of the kingdom of God in America.[50] But its primary appeal seems to have been for a renunciation of contemporary worldliness and a return to the simple uncorrupted, pious, and virtuous life of an earlier generation, and, as Richard L. Bushman has argued in the case of Connecticut, it seems to have fed upon the accumulation of anxiety and guilt that derived from the disparity between the idealized values associated with the founders and the customary patterns of contemporary behavior.[51] The Awakening seemed to result in a dramatic, if remarkably temporary, reversal of the tide of sin and extravagance that seemed to have swept the colonies. Dr. Alexander Hamilton noted how it had virtually ended "publick gay diver-

---

[47] Ibid., 375, 398–400.

[48] Ibid., 391–92.

[49] Erickson, "Identity and the Life Cycle," 28–29.

[50] Heimert, *Religion and the American Mind*, esp. 61–67.

[51] Bushman, *From Puritan to Yankee*, 147–266.

sions" in Philadelphia,[52] and a recent study has found that it had a similar effect upon Charleston.[53] But the frenzied enthusiasm and bitter religious and political animosities unleashed by the Awakening appeared, at least to its opponents, to portend social and political chaos of a magnitude never before imagined and to arouse still greater fears over the ultimate prospects for colonial society.[54]

Much of the spiritual energy and moral fervor spawned by the Awakening was in any case quickly dissipated by the rapid acceleration of the economy in the two decades after 1745.[55] So great was the economic boom in South Carolina, in fact, that it seems during the 1750s to have eroded most of the traditional fears of prosperity and to have produced a remarkably complete adjustment to the conditions of abundance, with the result that by the 1760s South Carolina may well have been far closer to the values and psychology of Jacksonian America than any other colony.[56] Nowhere else, however, was economic expansion sufficiently great to produce the same kind of unblinking acceptance of the modes of behavior that seemed to be the inevitable concomitants of prosperity. The extent of the colonists' uneasiness about their declining moral state was repeatedly revealed both in the jeremiads that followed every major disaster—the New England earthquake of November 1755, the humiliating defeats during the early years of the French and Indian War, the Boston fire of March 1760[57]—and in the grow-

---

[52] *Gentleman's Progress: The Itinerarium of Dr. Alexander Hamilton, 1744*, ed. Carl Bridenbaugh (Chapel Hill, N.C., 1948), 22–23 (June 9).

[53] Lewis Frisch, "Changing Social Attitudes in South Carolina" (undergraduate seminar paper, Johns Hopkins University, 1968), 6–12.

[54] See, e.g., *A Letter from a Gentleman in Boston, to Mr. George Wishart, One of the Ministers of Edinburgh, concerning the State of Religion in New-England* (Edinburgh, 1742), esp. 9, and the analyses in Bushman, *From Puritan to Yankee*, 190–95, 268–69, and Heimert, *Religion and the American Mind*, 159–293.

[55] There is no satisfactory study of this economic upsurge, but contemporaries frequently remarked upon it. See, e.g., William Smith, *History of New-York* (Albany, 1814), 323, and *The Power and Grandeur of Great-Britain, Founded on the Liberty of the Colonies* (Philadelphia, 1768), 7.

[56] Frisch, "Changing Social Attitudes in South Carolina." See also *The Private Character of Admiral Anson* (Dublin, 1747), 15–16, 21–23. The same process probably had already occurred in the West Indies, where the jeremiad seems to have persisted but only in a highly ritualized and, one suspects, psychologically less compelling form. See *Forms of Prayer to Be Used on the Island of Jamaica, on the Seventh Day of June, Being the Anniversary of the Dreadful Earthquake and on the Twenty Eighth Day of August, Being the Anniversary of the Dreadful and Surprising Hurricane* (London, 1748).

[57] See, among many examples, Gilbert Tennent, *The Late Association for Defence, Encourag'd, or The Lawfulness of a Defensive War* (Philadelphia, 1748), 39; *A Letter to a Gentleman on the*

ing volume of complaints—secular as well as religious—about the increasing sinfulness of colonial society. Pride, avarice, oppression, craft, prodigality, intemperance, wantonness, sensuality, adultery (even with blacks), idleness, ostentation, overreaching ambition, disobedience to superiors, ungovernableness in children, neglect of public duty, ingratitude to God, insubstantiality in religion—all of the old sins for which the clergy and other social critics had been rebuking the people for several generations were said to be not only still very much in evidence but rising at a dramatic rate.[58] Most alarming, however, was the great increase in extravagance, dissipation, and addiction to pleasure, a veritable "Deluge" which threatened to undermine and destroy the colonists' prosperity along with their virtue.[59] In the cities and in older settled rural areas, it was said, probably correctly, that the number of poor was already growing rapidly,[60] and, it was widely predicted, without a speedy reformation of character the whole society would be reduced to poverty as the wealth and possessions accumulated from the industry of earlier generations were squandered "to pay for . . . Pride, Pageantry and Lazyness."[61]

Newly emergent or declining elites seem to have been the greatest offenders and cities the worst centers of vice and corruption, but moral declension

---

Sin and Danger of Playing Cards (Boston, 1755); Timothy Harrington, *Prevailing Wickedness, and Distressing Judgments . . .* (Boston, 1756); Jonathan Mayhew, *Practical Discourses Delivered on Occasion of the Earthquakes in November, 1755* (Boston, 1760), and *God's Hand and Providence to Be Religiously Acknowledged in Public Calamities* (Boston, 1760); John Burt, *Earthquakes, Effects of God's Wrath* (Bristol, R.I., 1755); Samuel Davies, *Virginia's Danger and Remedy* (Williamsburg, Va., 1756), and *The Crisis . . .* (London, 1756); and Nathaniel Potter, *A Discourse on Jeremiah 8th, 20th* (Boston, 1758).

[58] See, in addition to the many other citations above and below to contemporary opinion in the 1740s, 1750s, and 1760s, James MacSparran, *A Sermon Preached at Naraganset . . .* (Newport, R.I., 1741), 15–16, 22–23; Andrew Eliot, *An Inordinate Love of the World Inconsistent with the Love of God* (Boston, 1744); Thomas Prince, *A Sermon Delivered at the South Church in Boston . . .* (Boston, 1746), 25, 35–37; Daniel Fowle, *A Total Eclipse of Liberty* (Boston, 1755), 31–32; *The Relapse* ([Boston], 1754), 2–3; James Sterling, *Zeal against the Enemies of Our Country Pathetically Recommended* (Annapolis, 1755), 7–8; Josiah Woodward, *A Disswasive from the Sin of Drunkenness* (Lancaster, Pa., 1755), 7–8.

[59] Quotation from Samuel Davies, *Religion and Patriotism* (Philadelphia, 1755), 10–12. For a sustained exploration of this theme, see the Antigallican essays in the *American Magazine* (Philadelphia), 1 (1757–58): 78–82, 116–19, 166–69, 231–34, 321–24.

[60] Among many such complaints, see *Industry and Frugality Proposed as the Surest Means to Make Us a Rich and Flourishing People* (Boston, 1753); *A Plea for the Poor and Distressed . . .* (Boston, 1754); and Thomas Bernard, *A Sermon Preached in Boston, New-England, before the Society for Encouraging Industry, and Employing the Poor* (Boston, 1758).

[61] Quotation from *Elixir Magnum: The Philosopher's Stone Found Out* (Philadelphia, 1757), 23.

appeared to have spread through all strata of society and to every corner of British America. Even tradesmen, formerly the most industrious and enterprising group in the colonies, had "grown as idle, and as extravagant . . . as so many Spaniards,"[62] and, if rural areas and smaller towns were somewhat less profligate than larger towns, it was only because they lacked the necessary means. The cities provided the "Pattern" for the countryside and were far "too closely imitated," one wag remarking that he "could tell his Distance from" Boston "by the Length of the Ruffles of a Belle of the Town he was in."[63] Everywhere the colonists seemed to have fallen into a "gay and expensive . . . Way of Living." The only exceptions, said the Reverend James MacSparran of Narragansett, were the "Irish, Dutch, Palatines, and other Germans," but, he added, "I think one may foretel . . . by the Symptoms beginning to shoot out on the Offspring of the Wealthy and Thriving among them, their Posterity will fall into the like destructive Indulgencies."[64] As Dr. William Douglass of Boston declared, it seemed to be a lamentable fact that "Idleness, intemperance, luxury in diet, extravagancies in apparel, and an abandoned way of Living" had come to be the distinguishing features of the "general character of many of the populace" in the colonies.[65]

Because such extraordinary "Vice and Wickedness" in "A Nation" were regarded as "the certain Forerunners and Cause of its Disgrace and Destruction,"[66] concerned colonials during the two decades after 1745 frantically sought some way to reverse the currents of corruption. They called upon the clergy "to preach up industry and frugality" and "to preach down idleness, a dissolute life, and fraud,"[67] exhorted the magistrates to enforce existing laws against vice and immorality, and urged the gentry to save their country by abandoning their lives of luxury and ease and fulfilling the social obliga-

---

[62] Benjamin Franklin to Richard Jackson, Mar. 8, 1763, *The Papers of Benjamin Franklin*, ed. Leonard W. Labaree et al. (New Haven, 1959—), 10:208–9.

[63] Livingston, *Independent Reflector*, 107; Hamilton, *Gentleman's Progress*, 192–93 (Sept. 19, 1744). See also John Hancock, *The Prophet Jeremiah's Resolution to Get Him unto Great Men* (Boston, 1734), 17; and "The Antigallican No. 1," *American Magazine* 1 (1757–58): 81–82.

[64] MacSparran, *America Dissected, Being a Full and True Account of All the American Colonies* (Dublin, 1753), 8–9.

[65] William Douglass, *A Summary, Historical and Political, of the First Planting, Progressive Improvements, and Present State of the British Settlement in North America*, 2 vols. (London, 1760), 1: 222–23.

[66] William Stith, *The Sinfulness and Pernicious Nature of Gaming* (Williamsburg, Va., 1752), 11–12.

[67] Douglass, *A Summary, Historical and Political* 1:250.

tion imposed upon them by their superior station in life to set proper examples for "the lower people" and thus "lead them on to every Thing, that is virtuous and honest."[68] Some people thought the situation demanded nothing less than more stringent laws prohibiting all forms of vice and a "sumptuary excise . . . upon extravagancies."[69] But none of these efforts seemed to meet with success. Adversity and misfortune occasionally appeared to bring about temporary and localized reformations but never any basic alteration in existing patterns of behavior.[70] Where or how it would all end were still in doubt, but one of the dominant assumptions of the age was that societies, like individuals, proceeded through cycles that led irresistibly to decay and extinction as "vigilance and economy" yielded "riches and honour" which produced "pride and luxury" which led to "impurity and idleness" which resulted in moral depravity, "indigence and obscurity."[71]

The prevalence of similar complaints about the "swift and Rapid Progress" of "Vice and Wickedness"[72] in Britain during the first half of the eighteenth century[73] suggests that much of this rhetoric of decline was simply another example of indiscriminate cultural borrowing by the colonials, having little social meaning in America, little effect upon the colonists' attitudes toward their societies, and little relationship to their actual perceptions of themselves. Indeed the "Topick of general Declamation against the Vice and Corruption of the Age" was, as William Stith, rector of Henrico Parish in Virginia, remarked in 1746, "trite and tedious."[74] As in the case of Stith, however, the rhetoric of decline, given existing social conditions in the colonies from the mid–1740s on, was also irresistible, not simply to the clergy and elite groups whose status was apparently being undermined by those conditions but probably also to those many segments among the general

---

[68] Stith, *Sinfulness . . . of Gaming*, 14–15; Livingston, *Independent Reflector*, 404–7; "My Country's Worth," in *The Poems of Charles Hansford*, ed. James A. Servies and Carl R. Dolmetsch (Chapel Hill, N.C., 1961), 62–67.

[69] Quotation from Douglass, *A Summary, Historical and Political* 1:259. See also Peter Clark, *The Rulers Highest Dignity, and the People's Truest Glory* (Boston, 1739), and *Some Observations Relating to the Present Circumstances of the Province of the Massachusetts-Bay* (Boston, 1750), 12–14.

[70] See, e.g., [George Churchman,] *A Little Looking-Glass for the Times* (Wilmington, Del., 1764).

[71] Quotations from James Reid, "The Religion of the Bible . . . ," in Davis, *Colonial Virginia Satirist*, 55.

[72] Andrew Eliot, *An Evil and Adulterous Generation* (Boston, 1753), 21.

[73] See Kramnick, *Bolingbroke and His Circle*.

[74] William Stith, *A Sermon Preached before the General Assembly at Williamsburg, 2 March 1745–46* (Williamsburg, Va., 1746), 31–34.

populace which yearned for a more stable and coherent social order. What made it so irresistible and what perhaps gave it a degree of explanatory power in the colonies far greater than it may have had in Britain itself were the force of the idealized model of the founders that colonials always had immediately before them and the chronic anxiety, passed along from one generation to another and never far below the surface of colonial life, over the failure of later generations of colonists to measure up to the standards imposed upon them by that model. For a century, each succeeding generation had watched, seemingly helplessly, as it failed to live up to the ethical norms of its immediate predecessor and, in the process, fell ever further away from the "exalted Goodness," the incorruptible virtue and simplicity, of the founders.

From the perspective supplied by this long record of failure, the new patterns of consumption and behavior, the further weakening of the moral fabric of society that accompanied the economic upsurge that began in the 1740s precipitated a psychological crisis of significant proportions, exacerbating the colonists' residual doubts about their own moral worth, further undermining their confidence in themselves and their societies, and increasing their uncertainties about who and what they were: "the genuine offspring of the first Settlers" or only a "spurious Race," a mere "possessing People" who had "risen up instead of them, but [were] very unlike them."[75] That the material "Felicity of . . . [the] Country" far transcended its virtue and that the colonists were undeserving of the "public Prosperity" with which God had provided them seemed painfully evident.[76] What their ultimate fate might be was less clear, but there was a widespread fear that without a major revolution in morals and behavior colonial society would either collapse from inner decay or be struck down by God's "Sin-revenging Justice upon a guilty land."[77]

The great British and colonial victories over the French, Spanish, and Indians during the last years of the Seven Years' War and the favorable conclusion of the war by the Treaty of Paris in 1763 opened up the prospects of even greater prosperity in the years ahead, but colonials faced the postwar world with great ambivalence. Afraid that the prosperity that they simultaneously desired and dreaded would bring such "an inundation of wealth and luxury" that it would result in moral collapse and social ruin, they nonetheless hoped that they would find some way to effect a return to the solid virtues

[75] Eliot, *An Evil and Adulterous Generation*, 8.

[76] East Apthorp, *The Felicity of the Times, a Sermon* (Boston, 1763), 21, 24.

[77] *A Letter to a Gentleman on the Sin and Danger of Playing Cards*, 8.

of their forefathers.[78] Their great material successes had opened up the possibilities of future greatness for the colonies, but they were under no illusions that the greatness could be realized until, as Governor Lewis Morris of New Jersey had remarked two decades earlier, they had first reformed "the genius of the people."[79]

A second and probably even more compelling model to which colonials looked for normative values was an idealized image of English society and culture.[80] The widespread colonial fascination with this model is simply another example of the familiar tendency of provincial societies to look to the metropolis for preferred values and approved modes of behavior. If, as Peter Laslett has remarked, English colonization contained within it a strong urge to create in America "new societies in its own image, or in the image of its ideal self,"[81] the impetus among the colonists to cast their societies in that same ideal image was (except possibly in places like Massachusetts Bay, where for a generation or more men actually hoped to improve upon and not merely to duplicate English patterns) infinitely more powerful. Conditions of life in new and relatively inchoate and unstable societies at the extreme peripheries of English civilization inevitably created deep social and psychological insecurities, a major crisis of identity that could be resolved, if at all, only through a constant reference back to the one certain measure of achievement: the standards of the metropolitan center. The result was a strong predisposition among the colonists to cultivate idealized English values and to seek to imitate idealized versions of English forms, institutions, and patterns of behavior. At work to some extent in all areas of colonial life from the very beginning of English colonization,[82] these mimetic impulses

---

[78] See James Horrocks, *Upon the Peace* (Williamsburg, Va., 1763), esp. 9–10, and Apthorp, *Felicity of the Times*, 9, 11, 21, 24–25.

[79] "Manuscript Verses about the Seat of Government," Morris Family Papers, Rutgers University Library.

[80] Portions of this and the two following paragraphs are adapted from my "Political Mimesis: A Consideration of the Historical and Cultural Roots of Legislative Behavior in the British Colonies in the Eighteenth Century," *American Historical Review* 75 (1969): 343–44.

[81] Peter Laslett, *The World We Have Lost* (New York, 1965), 183.

[82] In the absence of any substantial treatment of this theme for the early phase of European expansion, see Ronald Syme, *Colonial Elites: Rome, Spain, and the Americas* (London, 1958), and G. C. Bolton, "The Idea of a Colonial Gentry," *Historical Studies* 13 (1968): 307–28.

were given more power and made more explicit by three simultaneous developments during the late seventeenth and early eighteenth century.

The first of these developments was the emergence of recognizable and reasonably permanent colonial elites. As the society of each of the colonies became more complex and more differentiated during the second and third generations of settlement, the men who wound up at the top of the social scale, some of whom had actually come from gentry familes in England, sought to reproduce in the colonies a society that resembled that of England as closely as possible.[83] Whether they hoped to re-create "the country life of England" or the atmosphere of metropolitan London depended upon the nature and apparent potentiality of the particular society in which they lived, but everywhere they sought to assume to themselves "the outward and visible sign[s] of social and political consequence" by assimilating themselves to the model of the English gentry.[84]

The attempt to "perpetuate in the colonies the way of living, privileges, and standards of behaviour associated with the British upper classes"[85] was given additional impetus by the increasing involvement of the colonies with England and, more specifically, London. Much of this involvement was economic. As the business activities of the new elites in the colonies drew them directly into the mercantile life of London and, to a lesser extent, the outports, England became both "the Center, to which all Things [from the colonies] tend[ed]" and "the Great Fountain" from which they were supplied with all kinds of manufactured goods which they could not produce in the colonies.[86] But the involvement was also political. Following the Restoration, there was an extensive expansion of English governmental influence into the colonies as metropolitan officials sought with considerable success to substitute for a welter of existing political forms that had grown up in the colonies something resembling an English model of government and to bring the colonies more closely under the control of the administration in

---

[83] For case studies of this phenomenon, see Louis B. Wright, *The First Gentlemen of Virginia: Intellectual Qualities of the Early Colonial Ruling Class* (San Marino, Calif., 1940); Tolles, *Meeting House and Counting House*; and Bernard Bailyn, *The New England Merchants in the Seventeenth Century* (Cambridge, Mass., 1955), and "Politics and Social Structure in Virginia," in James Morton Smith, ed., *Seventeenth-Century America: Essays in Colonial History* (Chapel Hill, N.C., 1959), 90–115.

[84] Quotations from Wright, *First Gentlemen of Virginia*, 2, and Bolton, "Idea of a Colonial Gentry," 312; on this point, see also Miller, *Colony to Nation*, 170–72.

[85] Bolton, "Idea of a Colonial Gentry," 307.

[86] Henry St. John, Viscount Bolingbroke, *The Craftsman*, 4 vols. (London, 1731), 4:55; [John Wise], *A Word of Comfort to a Melancholy Country* (Boston, 1721), 38.

London.[87] This growing economic and political involvement with England both carried colonial elites directly into the ambit of English society and, in the personages of the new and increasing numbers of royal officials who swarmed to the colonies, "brought England . . . into the heart of colonial America."[88] The result was that elites in the colonies were subjected to an even greater degree than earlier colonials to the irresistible pull—what Bolingbroke called the "magnetick Force"—of English culture.[89]

Still a third development which helped to intensify the mimetic impulses among the colonists was the cultural degeneration that seemed to occur among the second and third generations. From the very beginnings of settlement there had been a persistent and gnawing fear of the corrosive effects of the wilderness environment upon the societies of the colonies. The alleged barbarism of the Indians and the disturbing tendency of the English on the frontiers—those "Pagan Skirts" of settlement—to "Indianize" themselves by relinquishing all concern with maintaining even the rudiments of English civilization[90] served as vivid evidence of the deleterious consequences of "the disintegrating forces which the liberty of a wild country unleashed." Even if they managed to avoid such a dismal fate, there was always the additional, and more probable, possibility that they would become either so absorbed in the business of making a living and getting on in the world or so overcome by "the deadening influences of isolation, loneliness, and lack of [intellectual] . . . stimulation" in corners so remote from the center of English culture that their societies would "insensibly decline" into "a State of Ignorance and Barbarism, not much superior to those of the native Indians."[91]

Faced with such ominous possibilities, emergent elites in the colonies, as Louis B. Wright has argued in the case of Virginia, worked as hard to retain and to pass on to their children their English cultural inheritance as they did to increase their fortunes. The disturbing fact was, however, that, despite

---

[87] See A. P. Thornton, *West-India Policy under the Restoration* (Oxford, 1955); Michael Garibaldi Hall, *Edward Randolph and the American Colonies, 1676–1703* (Chapel Hill, N.C., 1960); and Beverley, *History of Virginia*, 255.

[88] John Clive and Bernard Bailyn, "England's Cultural Provinces: Scotland and America," *William and Mary Quarterly*, 3d ser., 11 (1954): 207–8.

[89] Bolingbroke, *Craftsman* 4:55.

[90] Quotations from Jeremiah Wise's election sermon of 1729, in Miller, *Colony to Province*, 305; see also Leo Marx, *The Machine in the Garden: Technology and the Pastoral Ideal in America* (New York, 1964), 34–72.

[91] Louis B. Wright, *Culture on the Moving Frontier* (Bloomington, Ind., 1955), 12, 23–26, and *First Gentlemen of Virginia*, 77, 108; MacSparran, *America Dissected*, 10.

the most persistent efforts, later generations seemed to be far "less cultivated than their elders," and from the last decades of the seventeenth century through the first decades of the eighteenth the colonies seemed to be in a trough of cultural decline.[92] In the 1690s in Virginia, men complained that courts were much more deficient than "in former Times, while the first Stock of Virginia Gentlemen lasted, who having had their Education in England, were a great deal better accomplish'd in the Law, and Knowledge of the World, than their Children and Grandchildren, who have been born in Virginia, and have generally no Opportunity of Improvement by good Education."[93] Similarly, Samuel Johnson, later president of King's College in New York, recalled that in the New England of his youth during the early eighteenth century learning "(as well as everything else) was very low indeed[,] much lower than in earlier times while those yet lived who had had their education in England."[94]

Greatly intensified both by the growing volume of contacts with England which provided increased opportunities for colonials to measure colonial against British life and by the generally condescending and denigrative tone taken toward the colonies by metropolitans and by would-be sophisticates among the provincials themselves,[95] the fear of this "creolean degeneracy," as it was called by Cotton Mather,[96] both expressed and was expressive of a painful "sense of inferiority that pervaded the culture" of the colonies[97] and was manifest in several different forms of behavior. One form was a frank and usually apologetic admission of colonial cultural inferiority. Provincial authors addressing a metropolitan audience often excused the assumed deficiencies in their works on the grounds that they had spent most of their lives in the uncultivated "Woods of America, far from the Fountains of Science,

---

[92] Wright, *Culture on the Moving Frontier*, 20–21, 43–45.

[93] Henry Hartwell, James Blair, and Edward Chilton, *The Present State of Virginia and the College*, ed. Hunter Dickinson Farish (Williamsburg, Va., 1940), 45.

[94] Samuel Johnson, "Autobiography" in *Samuel Johnson: His Career and Writings*, ed. Herbert and Carol Schneider, 4 vols. (New York, 1929), 1:5. See also, among a large number of other similar impressions about New England, Samuel Dexter, *Our Father's God, the Hope of Posterity* (Boston, 1738), 33.

[95] On this point, see *The History and Life of Thomas Ellwood* (London, 1714), 416–17; *The Interest of Great Britain in Supplying Herself with Iron Impartially Considered* [London, 1756?], 20; John, Lord Bishop of Landaff, *A Sermon Preached before the Incorporated Society for the Propagation of the Gospel in Foreign Parts* (London, 1767), 6–7; and Lynn, *Mark Twain and Southwestern Humor*, 3–22.

[96] Bernard Bailyn, *Education in the Forming of American Society* (Chapel Hill, N.C., 1960), 79.

[97] Clive and Bailyn, "England's Cultural Provinces," 209–10.

and [with] . . . but very rare Opportunities of conversing with learned Men,"[98] and colonial writers and correspondents alike repeatedly found themselves apologizing for the peculiarities in their speech and manners, the crudity of their institutions, the meanness of their architecture, the pallor of their intellectual life, the unimportance of their affairs.[99]

Unable to make such self-deprecatory admissions, others turned instead to wishful and occasionally even extravagant boasting about the quality of colonial life. Their argument was usually not that the colonies were in any way superior to Britain but, as Samuel Keimer remarked about the West Indies, that the colonies were "Great Britain itself in Miniature,"[100] and they sought to establish the legitimacy of their claims to English identity by boldly asserting that colonial "habits, life, customs, . . . etc." were "much the same as about London," that "the Planters, and even the native Negroes generally talk[ed] good English without idiom or tone," and that the gentry lived "in the same neat manner, dress[ed] after the same modes, and behave[d] themselves exactly as the gentry in London."[101]

Still others retreated before the obvious fact of metropolitan superiority into the uneasy comfort of an arcadian image of the colonies.[102] This tendency was perhaps most clearly revealed in the extraordinary popularity among the colonists of Joseph Addison's play *Cato* (1713).[103] The ideal of the public man of honor who, like Addison's hero, flees from the corruption, luxury, pomp, and "empty show," the "doubled wealth and doubled care," of

---

[98] [Whitaker], *Chief Justice's Charge*, vi. Among many other examples, see Blair, *Our Saviour's Sermon on the Mount*, 1:xix-xx, xxviii, xxxii, and *A Letter from a Friend at J—, to a Friend in London* (London, 1746), 1.

[99] See Richard Lewis, "Dedication to Benedict Calvert," Maryland Historical Society, *Fund Publication*, no. 36 (1900): 60; Tolles, *Meeting House and Counting House*, 156–57; Heimert, *Religion and the American Mind*, 25; William L. Sachse, *The Colonial American in Britain* (Madison, Wisc., 1956), 202–3; Hugh Jones, *The Present State of Virginia*, ed. Richard L. Morton (Chapel Hill, N.C., 1956), 67; and Samuel Keimer, ed., *Caribbeana*, 2 vols. (London, 1741), 1:235.

[100] Keimer, *Caribbeana* 1:iv.

[101] Jones, *Present State of Virginia*, 70–71, 80. Other examples are in Keimer, *Caribbeana* 1:iii-vi; Beverley, *History of Virginia*, 288–91; *Some Modern Observations upon Jamaica* . . . (London, 1727), 16–20; Hamilton, *Gentleman's Progress*, 132 (Aug. 5, 1744); and Richard Fry, *A Scheme for a Paper Currency* . . . (Boston, 1739), 4–5. An excellent exploration of this theme is Lynn, *Mark Twain and Southwestern Humor*, 3–22.

[102] Two diverse examples are Thomas Nairne, *A Letter from South Carolina* (London, 1710), 56, and the extended development in William Livingston, *Philosophic Solitude: or, The Choice of a Rural Life* (New York, 1747).

[103] Bernard Bailyn, *The Origins of American Politics* (New York, 1968), 54.

the metropolis to a simple rural retreat where he can preserve his virtue and content himself with being "obscurely good" was so attractive to the colonists not only, as I have suggested elsewhere,[104] because it provided those members of the colonial elite who were unable to cope with the rough-and-tumble politics of the colonies with a rationale for withdrawing from public life but also because it served as a defense of their own provinciality, a way of disguising from others and hopefully even from themselves their own insecurities and guilt over their inability to measure up to the standards of the metropolis.

But there was little conviction, little genuine confidence, behind either their boasting or their arcadian conceits. As long as colonial societies continued to be so obviously provincial, London would continue to supply the "standards by which men and events were judged," the "definition of sophistication," and "the approved canons of taste and behavior," and the "passion with which Americans" would seek "to imitate English ways" would remain unabated.[105] For only by zealous imitation, only by raising the cultural level of the colonies by substituting English ideals for American practices, could colonials ever hope to throw off their provinciality and to achieve metropolitan recognition that they were indeed deserving of the English identity to which they so fervently aspired, that they were in fact still Englishmen. This fervor and all of the uncertainties that generated it lay behind the profound craving for metropolitan acceptance and approval that was manifest in such moving incidents as Philip Ludwell's ejaculations over the inclusion of Virginia as "the fourth kingdom" in the coronation oath given to James II in 1685[106] and Cotton Mather's prayer "that the Papers I am Sending to London, may be preserved thither, and accepted there" in 1712.[107] Only through metropolitan acceptance could the colonists ever be assured that they were actually what they hoped to be and thus come to accept themselves.

No example of empty cultural borrowing, colonial mimesis of English culture was thus expressive of the colonists' innermost psychological needs. The simple process of imitation was itself less important than its intensity, for it was the avidity with which colonials with literary interests and preten-

---

[104] See my *Landon Carter: An Inquiry into the Personal Values and Social Imperatives of the Eighteenth-Century Virginia Gentry* (Charlottesville, Va., 1965), 86–88.

[105] Clive and Bailyn, "England's Cultural Provinces," 209.

[106] As quoted by Sister Joan de Lourdes Leonard, "Operation Checkmate: The Birth and Death of a Virginia Blueprint for Progress, 1660–1676," *William and Mary Quarterly*, 3d ser., 24 (1967): 74.

[107] *The Diary of Cotton Mather for the Year 1712*, ed. William R. Manierre II (Charlottesville, Va., 1964), 96–97 (Dec. 6, 1712).

sions devoured and self-consciously sought to copy the latest English literary fashions and the assiduousness with which those who "aspired to gentility in a provincial setting"[108] emulated the life of the English gentry by acquiring estates, founding a family dynasty, building a country house in neoclassical style complete with the latest English furniture and a formal garden, forming clubs, dabbling in letters, and, in all too many cases in New England, abandoning the religion of their ancestors for the Church of England[109]—it was the enormous energy behind all of these familiar patterns of behavior that revealed their fullest social and psychological meaning, their intimate relationship to the colonists' desperate efforts to find their own identity in idealized images of England.

An examination of the system of values as well as the many outward signs of gentility cultivated by colonial elites reveals both just what it was about colonial life they found so disturbing and so much in need of improvement and the depth of their discontent with society as it had developed in the colonies. As is well known, that system of values was, preeminently, one of order. It was based upon assumptions that society was an organic unit which was distinct from and greater than the sum of the individuals who composed it and that individual considerations always had to give way before the interests of the society as a whole. It placed great stress upon reinforcing the authority of traditional social institutions such as the family, the church, and the community—all of which seemed to have lost much of their vigor as agencies of social control in the New World—and it looked forward to the achievement of a cohesive and coherent social order in which each man would move contentedly in his proper sphere, social distinctions would be visible and respected, the social functions assigned to each group diligently and faithfully performed, the individual values of thrift, diligence in callings, humility, moderation, and deference adhered to by all men, and a devotion to the public welfare substituted for the almost universal concern for self that seemed to be the single most manifest characteristic of the colonial personality.[110] Here, then, at the level of the specific values which colonists hoped would come to serve as the guiding principles for their so-

---

[108] Heimert, *Religion and the American Mind*, 170.

[109] On these points, see Tolles, *Meeting House and Counting House*, 114, 178, 196; Heimert, *Religion and the American Mind*, 28–29; Carl Bridenbaugh, *Rebels and Gentlemen: Philadelphia in the Age of Franklin* (New York, 1961) and *Cities in Revolt: Urban Life in America, 1743–1776* (New York, 1955), 141; and Miller, *Colony to Province*, 335–36, 395, 431.

[110] Two of the best statements of these ideas are James Logan's *The Charge Delivered from the Bench . . . April 13, 1736* (Philadelphia, 1736), and Samuel Johnson's "Raphael" (n.d.), in *Samuel Johnson* 2:519–600.

cieties, the two models that served as gauges for their own conduct and self-development came together, for the virtues of the founders and "the ancient British virtue"[111] in its purest form were isomorphic.

The attempt to impose these values upon colonial society has often, and correctly, been perceived as a species of elitism, an effort by colonial elites "to set themselves off" from those beneath them, to give lasting social sanction to their economic achievements, and to give the social system a static set with themselves firmly and, they hoped, perpetually entrenched at the top.[112] Far more fundamentally, however, it represented a compulsive yearning for stability and order. Just as the formal gardens they built on their estates were an implicit and somewhat touching effort to impose some symmetry and precision upon the rank and seemingly ungovernable natural environment in the colonies, so the cultivation of hallowed British values was an attempt to establish some sort of control over the chaotic and apparently untractable society that had grown up in that environment. To the very great extent that this attempt may be interpreted as a refusal to construct a new system of values that would correspond more closely to conditions of life in the colonies, it also constituted a clear rejection of many of the most manifest and basic tendencies in American society. Only when those tendencies had been reversed, the elite believed, could the ultimate promises of colonial life be fulfilled.

But the growing fear through the middle decades of the eighteenth century was that those promises might indeed never be fulfilled. As the economies of the home islands and the colonies became ever more tightly connected during those years, as increasing prosperity seemed to bring the material aspects of English culture ever closer to colonial grasp, as the last two intercolonial wars provided a new and compelling focus of common attention, and as the colonial elites developed an increasing amount of self-consciousness, the colonists became more and more unhappily aware of the tremendous social gulf between the colonies and Britain. Whatever comfort residents of older settled areas might take from the fact that their own regions were more stable and less crude than they once had been or than more recently occupied areas still were,[113] they were under no illusions that they had come anywhere close to matching the standards of the metropolis.

---

[111] Stith, *A Sermon Preached . . . 1745–46*, 31–34.

[112] Heimert, *Religion and the American Mind*, 12, 55–56; Miller, *Colony to Province*, 327; Bridenbaugh, *Rebels and Gentlemen*, 192–93.

[113] On this point, see John Callender, *An Historical Discourse on the Civil and Religious Affairs of the Colony of Rhode Island . . .* (Boston, 1739), 98–103; *A Word of Advice to Such as Are*

The knowledge that they were falling so far short of those standards, of their ideal image of what they might and hoped to be, only made that image infinitely more attractive and intensified the desire to anglicize colonial societies. In part at least a direct product of this desire, the spurt in college founding after 1745, and especially the establishment of the College of Philadelphia and King's College in New York, was interpreted as the first volley in an all-out "War upon Ignorance and Barbarity of Manners." The new colleges were to be seminaries for the instruction of virtue and public spirit which by "checking the Course of a growing Luxury" and "purging the Fountain, by making a lasting Provision for educating a Succession of true Patriots and Citizens" would "stem Corruption's all-devouring Tide," substitute "Light, Learning, Virtue and Politeness" for "Darkness, Immorality, and Barbarism," and make the colonies "polished, flourishing and happy." At last, the colleges would provide the colonies with suitable instruments for achieving their as yet unfulfilled promise by enabling them to reconstitute English civilization in its purest form in the New World.[114]

But neither the new colleges nor the many clubs, societies, schools, professional organizations, and other institutions founded for a similar purpose[115] could fill such a large prescription, and during the flush times beginning in the mid–1740s it became devastatingly obvious that what had begun as a movement to imitate the best features of English society had wound up by bringing on many of its worst. Everywhere, men seemed to have adopted the forms of English life without much of the substance, so that there were, as Dr. Alexander Hamilton remarked about New York, "severall men of sense, ingenuity, and learning" among the gentry "and a much greater number of fops." The American gentleman was turning out to be nothing more than a "ruffled Dunce!" What else could be expected, he added, from "aggrandized upstarts in these infant countrys of America who never had an opportunity to see, or if they had, the capacity to observe the different ranks of men in polite nations or to know what it is that really

Settling New Plantations (Boston, 1739); Hamilton, *Gentleman's Progress*, 68 (July 1, 1744); Lynn, *Mark Twain and Southwestern Humor*, 3–20.

[114] Livingston, *Independent Reflector*, 220; Hippocrates Mithridale, *Some Thoughts on the Design of Erecting a College in the Province of New-York* (New York, 1749), dedication, 2–5; William Smith, *A General Idea of the College of Mirania* (Philadelphia, 1753), 9–11, 76–77.

[115] On the goals of such institutions, see Alexander Hamilton's remarks in John Gordon, *Brotherly Love Explained and Enforced* (Annapolis, 1750), 21, and also Smith, *History of New-York*, 323–26, 382–83.

constitutes the difference of degrees?"[116] And, as young John Dickinson, who as a student at the Inns of Court had observed at first hand how deficient the colonial legal and educational systems were in comparison with those of London, wrote to his father from London in 1754, when such men came "to see the difference between themselves and the polite part of the world, they must be miserable."[117]

These unfavorable comparisons of American with English society must of course be considered against the significant amount of explicit criticism of—even outright revulsion against—many of the less attractive aspects of English life. From the beginning of settlement, colonial families had been cautioning their offspring who were returning to England for education or business to be wary of the lures of the metropolis,[118] and ministers and polemicists had raged against the corrupting influence of English imports. Starting with the 1740s, the evangelical clergy had spoken out against the dangers to be expected from the growing anglicization of the colonies,[119] and Americans who visited or studied in London had, like Dickinson and young Charles Carroll of Carrollton, expressed their shock and disappointment at the vice and extravagance of English society.[120] In connection with an apparently significant rise in the quantity of expressions of optimism about the future of America in every species of colonial literature,[121] these suspicions and criticisms of English society suggest the possibility of a continuous diminution of colonial mimetic impulses and a growing awareness of the inappropriateness of British models for American society, if not yet of the "need for another set of cultural standards and symbols" more suited to conditions in the colonies.[122]

But it would be a mistake, I submit, to read any of this evidence as

---

[116] Hamilton, *Gentleman's Progress*, 185–86 (Sept. 11, 1744); Mithridale, *Some Thoughts on the . . . College*, 2.

[117] John Dickinson to Samuel Dickinson, Aug. 15, 1754, in H. Trevor Colbourn, ed., "A Pennsylvania Farmer at the Court of King George: John Dickinson's London Letters, 1754–1756," *Pennsylvania Magazine of History and Biography* 86 (1962): 277–78.

[118] See Isaac Norris I to Joseph [?] Norris, April 1719, as quoted by Tolles, *Meeting House and Counting House*, 183–84.

[119] See Heimert, *Religion and the American Mind*, 34.

[120] See Bernard Bailyn, *Pamphlets of the American Revolution, 1750–1776* (Cambridge, Mass., 1965), 56–58.

[121] Max Savelle, *Seeds of Liberty: The Genesis of the American Mind* (Seattle, 1965), 564–82, discusses this subject.

[122] Quotation from Bridenbaugh, *Rebels and Gentlemen*, xi.

symptomatic of declining Anglophilia in the colonies. The literature of celebration in the 1740s and 1750s was no less defensive and no less expressive of a sense of American inferiority than similar literature had been earlier in the century, and, in any event, in the vision it presented, the America of the future usually bore a remarkable resemblance to contemporary Britain. For the bitter fact was, as John Singleton Copley remarked, "in comparison with the people [of England] . . . , we Americans are not half removed from a state of nature."[123] To paraphrase Constance Rourke, the colonies seemed to be perpetually condemned to follow English models "much as the lady-in-waiting follows the heroine in *The Critic*, at a distance, gawkily going through some of the same motions but by no means achieving the same grace."[124] Colonial cultural inadequacies might have been more bearable had the colonies been able to claim a measure of moral superiority over Britain.[125] It was by no means clear, however, that colonial corruption did not equal or even exceed that of Britain, and Benjamin Franklin was even afraid that instead of America's rising to the standards of Britain, Britain would fall to the level of the colonies as its wealth increased so rapidly and to such a point that it would come to equal the colonies in "Sloth, and . . . feverish Extravagance."[126] Britain did not, after all, have the stain of African slavery, which, more and more Americans were beginning to say, was both the prime symbol and an important cause of America's moral and cultural failure.[127]

---

[123] Quoted by Sachse, *Colonial Americans in Britain*, 202–3.

[124] Constance Rourke, *The Roots of American Culture* (New York, 1942), 47.

[125] This is not to say, of course, that some colonists did not decry the corruption of contemporary Britain. Among many expressions of such sentiments, see William Livingston, *A Funeral Eulogium on the Reverend Mr. Aaron Burr*, 2d ed. (Boston, 1758), 14–15. But it did not necessarily follow that the colonies were any less corrupt than the parent society.

[126] Lewis Morris, "The Dream and the Riddle: A Poem," 7–8, Morris Family Papers, Rutgers University Library; Franklin to Richard Jackson, Mar. 8, 1763, *Papers of Benjamin Franklin* 10:209–10.

[127] See [George Whitefield], *A Collection of Papers Lately Printed in the Daily Advertiser* (London, 1740), 5–11; John Bell, *An Epistle to Friends in Maryland, Virginia, Barbados, and the Other Colonies . . .* (London, 1741), 3; Charles Hansford, "My Country's Worth," *Poems*, 66–67; Anthony Benezet, *Observations on the Inslaving, Importing and Purchasing of Negroes* (Philadelphia, 1762), 31–34; and "Journal of Josiah Quincy, Jr., 1773," ed. Mark A. DeWolfe Howe, Massachusetts Historical Society, *Proceedings* 49 (1916): 454–57. It was even said that the white colonists had themselves grown so vicious that the danger was no longer that the white man would be corrupted by the black but that the black man, like the Indians, would be corrupted by the white. See Thomas Bacon, *Four Sermons upon the Great and Indispensible Duty of All Christian Masters and Mistresses to Bring Up Their Negro Slaves in the Knowledge and Fear of God* (London, 1750), 43–44, 48–49, 110. Among several

The probability is, in fact, that, far from having diminished, colonial mimetic impulses were never stronger than they were on the eve of the Stamp Act crisis. Importations of English goods and, probably, attention to English news by the colonial press were increasing perceptibly during the decade after 1755,[128] and as William L. Sachse has suggested, there seems to have been a marked rise in expressions of "full-blooded Anglophilism" during the last years of George II and the first of George III.[129]

These tendencies were stimulated not only by an overwhelming desire to close the cultural gap between the colonies and England but also by the obvious fact that the colonies, at least in the older settled areas, had come to look more and more like England in aspect and structure during the eighteenth century. The extent to which such areas had actually become more like England in substance as well as in appearance cannot be considered in detail here, though it is almost certainly true that elite cultivation of English models had, as those models had filtered down through society as a whole as a result of the widespread practice of social emulation, "acted as a powerful solvent of the customs, prejudices, and modes of action" in the colonies and had thereby helped to make the separate colonies far more alike than they had ever been at any earlier time.[130] But the important point is that however anglicized various segments of American society may have been by the 1760s, they were not sufficiently anglicized to fulfill the aspirations of a great many among the elite. It was not, as Kenneth Lockridge has recently contended, the "gradual 'Europeanization' of American society"[131] that was the source of their malaise but the possibility that American society would not become sufficiently Europeanized; it was this fear that moved a number of men on the eve of the pre-Revolutionary debate to propose the creation of

---

similar complaints about the colonists' impact on the Indian, see Samuel Hopkins, *An Address to the People of New-England . . .* (Philadelphia, 1757), 10, 12, 27, and *American Magazine* I (1757–58): 82–84, 274–77.

[128] See Richard L. Merritt, *Symbols of American Community, 1735–1775* (New Haven, 1966); Michael Kraus, *The Atlantic Civilization: Eighteenth-Century Origins* (Ithaca, N.Y., 1949).

[129] Sachse, *Colonial Americans in Britain*, 201–2.

[130] The process by which ideas and modes of behavior are diffused downward through society is discussed by Georges Duby, "The Diffusion of Cultural Patterns in Feudal Society," *Past and Present*, no. 39 (1968): 3–10. E. A. Wrigley, "A Simple Model of London's Importance in Changing English Society and Economy, 1650–1750," *Past and Present*, no. 37 (1967): 50–51, and H. J. Perkin, "The Social Causes of the Industrial Revolution," Royal Historical Society, *Transactions*, 5th ser., 18 (1968): 136–43, discuss this phenomenon with reference to provincial areas within Britain.

[131] Lockridge, *A New England Town*, 76–77.

an American aristocracy, a titled patriciate that would provide the colonies with a "complete" social structure on the British model and bolster colonial society against the forces of disorder and instability that had worked so effectively against the anglicization of the colonies from their initial settlement.[132]

Rather than shaking his mind loose "from the roots of habit and tradition," as John Clive and Bernard Bailyn have argued, the colonial provincial's peculiar position between his "familiar local environment" and the "higher sources of culture" in Britain thus seems to have fixed his attention so firmly upon those roots and to have made him so dependent psychologically upon them for a sense of his own identity and a model for his society that it was impossible for him to develop either his own cultural models or "distinctive status symbols."[133] Because he was as yet no more than vaguely aware that he needed such models and symbols, his inability to develop them was scarcely a source of major concern. What did concern him and what was an important cause of anxiety and a dark blot upon his own self-image was his and his society's failure to measure up to the cultural standards imposed upon them by the metropolis. That they could eventually overcome that failure was the desperate and single most important hope of the postwar world.

Obviously not everyone in the colonies faced the future with such doubts in the early 1760s. Many men were simply too involved in the race for material success to worry much about the larger moral and social issues posed by their societies, while others, as Alan Heimert has recently shown, were groping about trying to discern in America's present the seeds of a social and spiritual millennium that they confidently expected would characterize America's future.[134] For a large and powerful segment of colonial society, by contrast, the mood of the early 1760s seems to have been one of disappointment at not being able to live up to the imperatives of either of the two social models that shaped their expectations of themselves and their societies and concern over the great—and seemingly increasing—gulf between the ways they thought society should function and the realities of colonial life.

---

[132] Douglass, *A Summary, Historical and Political* 1:241–49; Edmund S. and Helen M. Morgan, *The Stamp Act Crisis: Prologue to Revolution* (Chapel Hill, N.C., 1953), 16–18.

[133] Bailyn and Clive, "England's Cultural Provinces," 212–13; Bolton, "Idea of a Colonial Gentry," 327.

[134] Heimert, *Religion and the American Mind*; Earnest Lee Tuveson, *Redeemer Nation: The Idea of America's Millennial Role* (Chicago, 1968), 28–30, 92–93, 96–97.

Even millennialist thinkers betrayed a deep-seated discontent with prevailing modes of behavior in the colonies when they chose to focus upon the future rather than upon the present.

This vivid sense of America's moral and cultural deficiencies helped to make colonial leaders hypersensitive to deviations from accepted norms in both the colonies and Britain, and this hypersensitivity helps to explain why the colonists responded so vigorously to what they took to be a series of instances of British corruption between 1763 and 1776. For in opposing British deviance from pure British values the colonists were at once demonstrating their own commitment to those values and, by rousing themselves out of their "inglorious ease," promoting a return to the primitive and manly virtues of their ancestors.[135] The Revolution thus provided the colonists with an opportunity to close in one heroic effort the long-existing chasm between their societies and the social models they so much admired. That they had failed to take full advantage of the opportunity was indicated by the apparently great increase in individualistic and antisocial behavior during the decade and a half following the Declaration of Independence; the Constitution of 1787 may be interpreted as an effort to counteract that behavior by imposing upon American society a series of political arrangements calculated to achieve the orderly world envisioned by the early founders and still thought to be characteristic of Britain and the Old World.[136]

But the impulses behind this effort could not in the long run sustain themselves against other and, for the moment at least, more appropriately American counterimpulses set free by the Revolution. For by impelling men to juxtapose the virtues of the New World against the vices of the Old and finally to rebel against the mother country—for so long the ultimate source of authority and the supreme arbiter of values—and by calling forth a new generation of heroes whose virtues and accomplishments matched—perhaps even exceeded—those of the early settlers, the Revolution became a cathartic event, serving as a psychological release, that at last enabled men to reject the oppressive social models on which they had so long depended and to begin to adjust emotionally and intellectually to the conditions of prosperity in America, to overcome the anxiety that derived from their inability to restrain their acquisitive instincts in a society of abundance, to accept the

---

[135] Bernard Bailyn, *The Ideological Origins of the American Revolution* (Cambridge, Mass., 1968), and Edmund S. Morgan, "The Puritan Ethic and the American Revolution," *William and Mary Quarterly*, 3d ser., 24 (1967): 3–41, esp. 12.

[136] See Gordon S. Wood, *The Creation of the American Republic, 1776–1787* (Chapel Hill, N.C., 1969), 391–532.

luxury of living in an environment in which, at least temporarily, unrestrained individualism was not necessarily or even usually antisocial, and to learn how to be free, not simply from the fetters of ancient social conventions and traditional models of behavior but from the want that had previously been the normal condition of mankind throughout most of recorded history.

Long after the Revolution some Americans would continue to be suspicious of prosperity and to yearn for what by European standards was a more complete and coherent society, and the new heroes created by the Revolution would exert a degree of authority over subsequent generations far greater than that imposed upon the men of the colonial period by the founders of the colonies.[137] But the Revolution finally made men aware, as Benjamin Franklin wrote in 1787, of the necessity of "breaking through the bounds, in which a dependent people" had "been accustomed to think, and act," so that they might "properly comprehend the character they had assumed."[138] To comprehend the character they had assumed, to come to terms with themselves and their environment, to appreciate themselves and their societies for what they were and had become—these were the necessary first steps in the development of a new conception of American identity that, by recognizing that Americans in the present were and ought to be different from either Americans in the past or Europeans, would during the following century bring values and behavior into at least a temporary degree of harmony for the first time since the founding of the colonies.

The initial draft of this essay was presented at the Sixty-second Annual Meeting of the Organization of American Historians in Philadelphia on Apr. 17, 1969, and is reprinted here with permission and minor corrections and revisions from *Journal of Social History* 3 (1970): 189–224. The essay was previously reprinted as no. H–396 in The Bobbs-Merrill Reprint Series in American History (Indianapolis: Bobbs-Merrill, 1972). Abbreviated versions were given as lectures at Wilson College in Chambersburg, Pa., on Sept. 23, 1969, the Trinity College Historical Society of Duke University in Durham, N.C., on Oct. 6, 1969, Princeton University in Princeton, N.J., on Dec. 9, 1969, and the Downstate Medical Center, State University of New York in Brooklyn on Dec. 15, 1969.

[137] On this theme, see Fred Somkin, *Unquiet Eagle: Memory and Desire in the Idea of American Freedom, 1815–1860* (Ithaca, N.Y., 1967).

[138] *Rules and Regulations of the Society for Political Inquiries* (Philadelphia, 1787), 1, as quoted by Paul W. Connor, *Poor Richard's Politicks: Benjamin Franklin and His New American Order* (New York, 1965), 106.

SEVEN

Independence and Dependence:
The Psychology of the Colonial Relationship on the Eve of the American Revolution

JUST BEFORE the American Revolution, Michel-Guillaume Jean de Crèvecoeur, a native of Caen, who in his early twenties had come to Canada with the French army in the 1750s and had settled in New York following the British capture of Quebec in 1759, wrote for a European audience a long essay on the character of life in British North America. This essay, first published in London in 1782 as *Letters from an American Farmer* and republished in Paris in 1784 as *Lettres d'un cultivateur américain*, has been justly and widely acclaimed by modern scholars for its penetrating analysis of the emerging American character.

"The strong lineaments"—the salient features—of that character, Crèvecoeur reported, were industry, activity, an avid pursuit of self-interest and self-improvement, a proud sense of personal independence, a jealous regard for the protection of individual rights and property, a distrust of all authority, and indifference to organized religion. Crèvecoeur's list suggests the existence in late eighteenth-century British North America of what modern social theorists would regard as a highly modernized mentality that was in great measure free from traditional restraints and put primary emphasis upon individual autonomy and self-fulfillment.[1] An understanding of this emerging "American" mentality and of the conditions that underlay it is necessary for any adequate comprehension of the origins and character of

---

[1] J. Hector St. Jean de Crèvecouer, *Letters from an American Farmer* (New York, 1957), 42.

the resistance movement that culminated in 1776 in the American Revolution.

This mentality was the result of the interaction among three converging sets of circumstances: first, the character of the English colonizing impulse; second, conditions of life in British North America during the first 150 years of settlement; and third, the nature of British colonial administration.

From the beginning, the English colonizing impulse, always essentially material in its primary thrust, had been highly individualistic in character. With the exception of Puritan New England, which had been settled by men hoping to found a New Jerusalem, all of the Anglo-American colonies both in the West Indies and on the mainland had been founded for the central purpose of enriching the individuals who sponsored and settled them. From the rich sugar islands of Barbados, the Leeward Islands, and Jamaica in the West Indies north through the profitable rice and tobacco colonies of the Carolinas and the Chesapeake and the fertile grain and livestock provinces in the Delaware and Hudson River valleys, most of the capital and the energy requisite for settlement had been supplied by individuals bent upon improving the material conditions of the lives of themselves and their families. Even in the relatively stingy physical environment of New England, such motives existed side by side with the ambitious religious objectives of Puritan leaders. Frequently drawn from sectors of English life that had already been heavily involved in the bubbling market economy that, during the sixteenth and early seventeenth centuries, had rapidly spread from Italy to northern Europe, these individuals were, in all probability, already less bound by tradition, more autonomous, and more willing to take risks in the quest for gain and the good life.

This original character of the English colonizing impulse was, moreover, intensified by the physical conditions the colonists found and the social conditions they created in America. The vast, seemingly limitless space on the continent was an open invitation to individual activity and enterprise. Depopulation among the native Indians during the sixteenth and seventeenth centuries primarily as a result of their exposure to new European diseases meant that there were no longer any large concentrations of population and few powerful political nations capable of mounting sustained resistance.

With so much rich land so easily available, practically every able-bodied and competent person could expect to acquire land. Only in the sugar colonies was it possible to amass a fortune in any way equivalent to the more substantial fortunes of traditional European landed society. But tobacco, rice, grain, and naval stores as well as subsidiary activities in commerce and the law were the basis for the accumulation of considerable wealth, while even the less successful could expect with industry and care to acquire a freehold, livestock, a decent habitation, good clothes, and some measure of economic and personal independence—those indispensable attributes of a free man. Such comparatively abundant opportunity whetted the material aspirations of men at all levels of society, gave rise to a heady sense of what Professor John Higham has called "boundlessness,"[2] and stimulated through the competitive pursuit of wealth a new ethic of rampant individualism, social fluidity, and atomistic social freedom.

Widespread opportunity was also an essential precondition for the extraordinary economic and demographic growth that characterized the British mainland colonies during the eighteenth century. The latter was perhaps unparalleled in the history of the world up to that time: between 1700 and 1770 the population of the mainland colonies increased from just under 200,000 to over 2 million—a rate of 30 to 40 percent per decade! Immigrants poured in not only from all parts of Britain and Ireland but also from Germany and, in smaller numbers, France (mostly Huguenots) and the Iberian Peninsula.

About a fifth of the total population in 1770 was slave and African in origin, forcibly brought to America to supply the labor necessary for their European purchasers to achieve greater profits. But the sense of optimism and individual opportunity that pervaded and shaped the mentality of the free segments of the population cannot perhaps be better illustrated than by the fact that three-fourths of its total growth during the eighteenth century was the result not of immigration but of natural increase. This strong sense of individual opportunity reached even into the niggardly physical environment of New England, where, at least in those urban and market-oriented areas whose economies were being increasingly integrated into the larger Atlantic economy during the early eighteenth century, the old religious and traditional corporate ideals of the Puritans gave way to the mentality of individual autonomy and initiative that had always been a distinctive feature of the rest of the colonies.

---

[2] John Higham, *From Boundlessness to Consolidation: The Transformation of American Culture, 1848–1860* (Ann Arbor, Mich., 1960).

The third factor that stimulated the rise of this "modern" mentality in America was the extraordinarily mild and benign administration of the metropolitan government. Within England, interest in colonies had always been primarily economic and only secondarily strategic, and this commercial orientation was evident in the laxity of metropolitan controls. Efforts were made from time to time to tighten controls in both the economic and the political areas. But, despite some notable successes in the economic realm, the British permitted their colonies far more economic latitude and vastly more self-government than any other colonizing power allowed to its overseas dominions during the early modern era. By 1760 all but the newest British colonies in America possessed virtually all of the conditions necessary for self-governing states. They had elective assemblies and other institutions of local government with broad powers over the internal affairs of the colonies and a large reservoir of political leaders drawn from authoritative and self-conscious local elites and experienced in providing effective and responsive government.

The style of political consciousness exhibited by these elites was commensurate with the general mentality attributed by Crèvecoeur to British Americans. American politics, said Crèvecoeur, was "country politics."[3] Like the country gentry who filled the back benches of the House of Commons in Westminster, American political leaders were fiercely independent. Deeply jealous of their power of self-government, they were wary of metropolitan political authority and aggressively protective of both local interests and the status and authority of their local legislatures. The tension between metropolitan authority and provincial self-government was everywhere manifest in the recurrent political battles between royal officials and local legislatures, battles in which royal officials often came out second best.

Yet, the autonomous mentality and the assertive tradition of self-government that had grown up in British America in response to these three sets of circumstances existed in an uneasy state of tension with more traditional models of personality and social behavior. For the colonists had come to America not only to improve their lives but also to re-create as closely as possible the society they had left behind in the Old World. That they had

---

[3] Crèvecouer, *Letters*, 42.

not entirely succeeded in this latter intention was apparent at every stage of colonial development. The relatively undifferentiated and simple agricultural societies that had grown up in America; the primitive character of colonial culture; the weakness of traditional institutions of social control such as the family, church, and community; the relative volatility of colonial economic and social life; even the highly autonomous and untraditional patterns of individual behavior—all of those and many other characteristics of colonial life served as visible and omnipresent measures of the extent of the colonists' failure to reproduce traditional European society in America. This failure created deep social and psychological insecurities, a major crisis of identity, that required a constant reference back to the one certain measure of achievement: the standards of the metropolis. The result was a deep psychological dependence upon Britain for social models.

This dependence was reinforced, moreover, by a continuing well of affection in the colonies for the parent state, an affection that was firmly rooted in ancient bonds of consanguinity, culture, traditions, and language; close ties of economic interest; the need for metropolitan military and naval protection; and, above all, a proud sense of being British, of belonging to a powerful European nation that permitted its citizens, as it was widely said by Britons and Europeans alike at the time, more liberty than any other nation on earth. The wish for autonomy and independence as so forcefully displayed in the mental character of British Americans was thus to some extent counterbalanced by an abiding dependence upon the parent culture. Unlike most more modern empires, the early modern British Empire was held together not by force but by these bonds of dependence and affection.

But this need for dependence and the associated—and massive—affection felt for Britain by the colonists was not so powerful as to bind the colonies to Britain under all conditions. In retrospect, in fact, it is clear that the affection was conditional and was based upon the expectation that the parent culture would be nurturant and protective toward its colonial offspring. What nurturance had come to mean to these autonomous and highly individualistic colonists can be briefly summarized: first, that the metropolitan government would not undermine in any serious way the colonists' self-esteem as defined by their capacity as individuals to act with a high degree of autonomy in the colonial environment; second, that it would interfere as little as possible with the colonists' ability to pursue whatever purposeful activity seemed to them to be in their best interests; third, that it would recognize the sanctity of local self-governing institutions on which they depended for the immediate protection of the property they had acquired as a result of that activity; and, fourth, that in its dealings with the colonies it would continue to manifest respect for all of those central imperatives of Anglo-American political culture that were thought by Britons everywhere to be essential for the preservation of liberty and property.

When British political leaders, increasingly aware of the growing economic and strategic importance of the colonies and fearful that the widespread powers of self-government enjoyed by the colonies might lead to colonial independence, sought to exert much tighter economic and political controls over the colonies following the close of the Seven Years' War in 1763 and thereby, from the point of view of the Americans, violated in crucial ways each of these four conditions, the Americans, not surprisingly, felt compelled to resist. To be so closely supervised by distant institutions over which they had no control was intolerable, not only because it seemed to threaten the property they and their ancestors had wrested from the wilderness and the liberty they had so jealously cultivated, but also because it appeared to be corrosive of the independence and autonomy that had come to define competence—and manliness—in British America.

American resistance to this new movement for tighter metropolitan controls was accompanied during the decade of altercation from 1765 to 1775 by two related impulses. First was a demand for greater colonial autonomy, with the several colonial legislatures having full jurisdiction under the king over the internal affairs of the separate colonies. Second was the desire to find a way to remain attached to Britain without threat of objectionable metropolitan intervention in their affairs. But the British political nation found these demands unacceptable because they challenged two of its most cherished beliefs: the old notion that the essential powers of sovereignty could not be divided and the post–1688 view that in the realm and dominions of Britain those powers were concentrated in an omnipotent king-in-Parliament assembled.

When in 1775 British leaders sought to enforce colonial obedience to metropolitan authority by force, the older continental colonies, freed from the need for metropolitan protection by the expulsion of the French and Spanish from eastern North America as a result of the Seven Years' War, withdrew their affections from Britain and opted for independence. Continued reliance upon Britain for defense against both neighboring colonies of rival European powers and hostile internal slave populations that ran as high as 90 percent of the inhabitants in some islands prevented the West Indian colonies from following suit, from breaking the psychology of dependence that had formerly tied all of the colonies to the parent state. For most British Americans on the continent, however, British use of force made it possible not only for them to break that psychology but also finally to learn, in the words of Thomas Paine, "the manly doctrine of reverencing themselves,"[4] to appreciate themselves and their societies for what they had become, and to accept the autonomous mentality described by Crèvecoeur as fully appropriate for a people living in the new condition of an independent America.

This essay was written for a special bicentennial issue of *Le Monde*, no. 9739 (May 17, 1976) and published on p. 18, cols. 1–6, under the title "De la resistance à la revolution" and again in June 1976 on p. 6, cols. 1–6 of a special supplement in English with the title "Dependence and Independence." It is reprinted from this special supplement with permission and minor changes and the addition of notes.

[4] Thomas Paine, "American Crisis," in *The Complete Writings of Thomas Paine*, ed. Philip S. Foner, 2 vols. (New York, 1945), 1:59.

EIGHT

Independence, Improvement, and Authority: *Toward a Framework for Understanding the Histories of the Southern Backcountry during the Era of the American Revolution*

T he *Southern Backcountry during the American Revolution*, the subtitle of the volume in which this essay first appeared, contains two large general conceptions: *southern backcountry* and *American Revolution*. As everybody understands, the first refers to that vast inland region stretching from the Potomac River south to Florida and from the fall line west to the Appalachian Mountains. But the term carries with it a cultural as well as a geographical connotation and strongly implies a basic socioeconomic, even an ideological, unity among the people who inhabited the area. The concept has a distinguished ancestry: as conventionally used, it coincides almost exactly with the southern portions of Frederick Jackson Turner's "Old West." Although it was divided into several parts, each of which was tied politically to one of the seaboard societies of the southern colonies, this area, according to Turner, was "a new continuous social and economic area, which cut across the artificial colonial boundary lines." More like Pennsylvania, an area from which it drew substantial numbers of settlers, than like the lowcountry South, this "new Pennsylvania," as Turner called it, existed in an uneasy relationship with older settled areas to the east and was defined primarily by its differences from those areas. To the extent that it was an extension of the older societies of the colonial South, it was, according to Turner, certainly a "new South," one that was altogether less dependent on slave labor, less devoted to a staple agriculture, and more self-sufficient and self-contained. It was not the first frontier in British America. But it was the British Americans' first frontier, and its very distance from the Old World combined with conditions of life on the frontier to make it the most purely American area up to that time. In terms of "its society, its institutions, and [its] mental attitudes," the southern backcountry, according to Turner, was a harbinger of what America was to become, and it was much more individualistic, egalitarian, democratic, and antagonistic to privilege, aristocracy, and religious and civil establishments than were the older, more European societies along the seaboard.[1]

Most later scholars have affirmed the essential socioeconomic and cultural unity of the southern backcountry and have continued to contrast it with the seaboard areas.[2] Indeed, according to Carl Bridenbaugh, the backcountry was, along with the Chesapeake and lowcountry South Carolina and Georgia, one of three distinctive "souths" at the time of the Revolution, though he followed Turner in linking the southern backcountry more closely to Pennsylvania than to the eastern Souths, referring to it as *"Greater Pennsylvania."* As in so many other respects, Bridenbaugh in this formulation anticipated one of the most powerful recent trends in early American historiography, the trend toward regionalization. As scholars have moved strongly away from political to social and economic history during the 1960s and 1970s, they have come to think of British America less as a congeries of separate colonies than as a group of socioeconomic regions. New England, the West Indies, the Chesapeake, the Middle Colonies, the Lower South— these have become the organizing categories, the overarching frames of reference, for much recent work. The underlying assumption behind this movement has been, of course, that distinctions revolving around the nature of socioeconomic life and not formal—in Turner's language, artificial— political designations constitute the most appropriate units of study within the broad culture area of colonial British America.[3]

Of course, this regionalization of colonial America has turned out to be but a preliminary stage in a second powerful historiographical trend that may be termed the deconstruction of early America. Especially during the past decade, the rapid proliferation of scholars working on early America

---

[1] Frederick Jackson Turner, *The Frontier in American History* (New York, 1947), 67–125. The quotations are from 68, 99–100.

[2] See, in particular, Carl Bridenbaugh, *Myths and Realities: Societies of the Colonial South* (Baton Rouge, La., 1952), 119–96; Jack M. Sosin, *The Revolutionary Frontier, 1763–1783* (New York, 1967), esp. 61–81, 161–92, 197–98, 207–10; and Rowland Berthoff, *An Unsettled People: Social Order and Disorder in American History* (New York, 1971), 81–134, 484–86.

[3] Bridenbaugh, *Myths and Realities*, 127. A powerful argument in behalf of this regional approach to early American history is to be found in part 2 of John J. McCusker and Russell R. Menard, *The Economy of British America, 1607–1789: Needs and Opportunities for Study* (Chapel Hill, N.C., 1985).

has produced a series of studies that have broken regions down into increasingly smaller temporal, spatial, and social units. With specific reference to the southern backcountry, Bridenbaugh also anticipated this development when he cautioned historians about the limitations of a broad regional characterization. Despite overall similarities in geographic, demographic, and economic conditions throughout the backcountry and despite a strong cultural similarity among various parts of the backcountry in comparison with the seaboard societies to which they were attached, the area "did not," Bridenbaugh insisted, "compose a uniform society." He called attention to the two important variables that distinguished one part of the backcountry from another. One was time of settlement and state of socioeconomic development; the other was the nature of political relationships with provincial and local governments in the east.[4]

If Bridenbaugh's cautions suggested the continuing relevance of political relations to backcountry behavior and development, the validity of his suggestion is dramatically underlined by the essays in *An Uncivil War: The Southern Backcountry during the American Revolution.* While its title strongly emphasizes the existence of a single grand socioeconomic unit, the southern backcountry, the essays demonstrate that, whatever similarities may have existed among them, there were at least five different backcountries in the South at the time of the American Revolution. Furthermore, as Richard R. Beeman has made explicit and as most of the authors imply, the nature of relations with the established seaboard political societies of which they were a part was an enormously important, probably the single most important, variable in distinguishing among these several backcountries and their distinctive histories.[5] Moreover, the logic of most of the essays and specific evidence in some of them strongly suggests that there was not just one Virginia and one South Carolina backcountry but several, distinguished one from another according to a great many variables, including ethnic composition and the nature of local leadership.[6] This suggestion underscores the

---

[4] Bridenbaugh, *Myths and Realities*, 122, 156–63.

[5] Richard R. Beeman, "The Political Response to Social Conflict in the Southern Backcountry: A Comparative View of Virginia and the Carolinas during the Revolution," in Hoffman, Tate, and Albert, *An Uncivil War: The Southern Backcountry during the American Revolution* (Charlottesville, Va., 1985), 213–39.

[6] In this regard, see especially Emory G. Evans, "Trouble in the Backcountry: Disaffection in Southwest Virginia during the American Revolution," ibid., 179–212; Jeffrey J. Crow, "Liberty Men and Loyalists: Disorder and Disaffection in the North Carolina Backcountry," ibid., 125–78; and Rachel N. Klein, "Frontier Planters and the American Revolution: The South Carolina Backcountry, 1775–1782," ibid., 37–69.

need for still further deconstruction into still smaller and smaller units of analysis if we are ever going to understand the rich complexity of either the southern backcountry during the late eighteenth century or its Revolutionary experience.

If the logic of scholarly inquiry into the social history of early America has pushed most scholars toward regional analysis and deconstruction, the study of the second general subject, the American Revolution, continues to suffer from a failure to achieve a consensus over precisely what perspective is most useful in understanding it. At least since the end of the last century, there have been two quite distinct and not always complementary approaches to the study of the Revolution. The first has seen the Revolution as a culmination of the colonial experience, as a contingent and highly problematic outcome of that experience. Hence, the classic questions for people writing on the American Revolution from this colonial approach have been why the Revolution happened at all and how it related to—that is, grew out of, reflected, altered, transformed, or rejected—the colonial experience. More particularly, they have wanted to know, not how the Revolution prefigured or contained early manifestations of later and as yet only vaguely defined socioeconomic and political developments or qualities that were characteristic of later United States history, but how it affected—that is, resolved, interacted with, or exacerbated—tensions already present in pre-Revolutionary America. Knowing where British-American society had been, they have been concerned to point out how the colonial experience informed the War for Independence, the creation and mobilization of the first independent political societies in the thirteen states and their respective localities, and the subsequent creation of a national political system and a national political society. For that reason, I think it is fair to say, they have generally tried to situate the Revolution in its contemporary context and tended to be far more impressed by the continuities than by the discontinuities between the colonial and Revolutionary periods. This is the perspective from which I have always tried to approach the American Revolution.[7]

By contrast, a second, national approach to the study of the Revolution has tended to look at it from the vantage point of later American developments. Knowing where the United States was going, those who have taken this approach have wanted to search the Revolutionary landscape for early indications of the democratic and egalitarian impulses and the sociopolitical divisions and conflicts that became so prominent in Jeffersonian and Jacksonian America. Relatively uninterested in relating the Revolutionary to the

---

[7] See Jack P. Greene, "The Social Origins of the American Revolution: An Evaluation and an Interpretation," *Political Science Quarterly* 88 (1973): 1–22.

colonial experience, they have emphasized both the discontinuities between the Revolutionary era and a supposedly much more rigidly structured and stable colonial past and the continuities between the Revolution and subsequent United States history. By applying to the Revolution terminology, concepts, categories, and units of analysis derived—and densely packed with layers of meanings—from later periods, this national approach has too often led in the direction of the sort of anachronistic results that are difficult to avoid when, in Marc Bloch's words, the "idol of origins," rather than the contemporary context, dictates the questions, concerns, and language we bring to the analysis of the past.[8]

Not all of the essays in *An Uncivil War* have entirely avoided the problems associated with this national perspective on the American Revolution. Nor, in focusing on their particular areas of investigation, have the authors much concerned themselves with some of the problems inherent in their essentially deconstructionist approach. While deconstruction is invariably enriching, all too often it is also confusing for it produces such an abundance of special cases as to make it difficult to comprehend the whole; it may even call into question the very existence of that whole. If we now know as a result of these nine chapters that there were several southern backcountries, each with its own peculiar Revolutionary experience, we are no longer so sure that those peculiar experiences had enough in common for it to make much sense for us to talk about the Revolutionary experience of the southern backcountry. To strengthen an as yet weak impulse toward still a third historiographical trend that, I hope, will gain momentum over the next few years, a trend

---

[8] Marc Bloch, *The Historian's Craft* (New York, 1959), 29–35. No doubt the transitional character of the Revolution has contributed to these divergent approaches. Like the era in which it occurred, the Revolution was both an early modern and a modern event, one that both looked backward to the re-creation of an earlier, golden era and forward to a new and better era. Not yet fully articulated, much less accepted, the idea of progress had not yet become the guiding assumption of revolutionaries that it would become during and after the French Revolution. See J. H. Elliott, "Revolution and Continuity in Early Modern Europe," *Past and Present*, no. 42 (1969): 35–56, and Jack P. Greene, "Paine, America, and the 'Modernization' of Political Consciousness," *Political Science Quarterly* 93 (1978): 73–92.

Historiographers have conventionally attributed this divergence in perspective to the sociopolitical perspectives of historians. My own feeling is that the point of view of intellectual mentors and the subject matter of initial research experiences are probably much more important.

A prime example of anachronistic language is the use of the terms *radical* and *conservative*. Neither acquired political connotations until the nineteenth century, the former in 1802 and the latter in 1830. Though some scholars of the Revolution have made a valiant effort to use these terms in a neutral way, they are laden with emotional connotations deriving from nineteenth- and twentieth-century western European and United States history.

that may be referred to as reconstruction, I would like in this essay, from the perspective of a colonial historian, to propose a general framework that may help us make sense of, or at least put into clearer perspective, the various histories of the southern backcountries during the American Revolution.

One place to begin is with the explicit contrast—present in most of the essays included in *An Uncivil War*—between backcountries and lowcountries. In general the authors follow Turner in making a sharp distinction between the loose frontier settlements in the backcountries and the "tradition-bound, stable" communities of the seaboard. The latter are said to have been characterized by "elaborately structured, hierarchical social systems" with authoritative institutional centers and "clearly defined hierarchies of power, prestige, and personal authority." Strong "lines of patronage and preferment . . . ran from the top down," and cohesive elites—"oligarchies" united by a common ideology, similar economic interests, close kinship ties, and a genteel life-style—presided over a deferential political order. In this order, the bulk of the white population, sharing with the elite a common fear of and separation from the large numbers of blacks in their midst, almost always deferred to their betters. By contrast, backcountry societies were composed of new, rapidly expanding, highly mobile, and ethnically and religiously diverse populations. They had weaker local traditions and commitments to place, less economic specialization and social differentiation, and inchoate or fragile institutions of authority. With ruling elites deficient in personal prestige, affluence, and gentility, political hierarchies in the several backcountries lacked clear definition, and politics there was less deferential and more egalitarian, democratic, contentious, and disorderly.[9]

[9] In addition to the essays in Hoffman, Tate, and Albert, *An Uncivil War*, see Richard R. Beeman, "Social Change and Cultural Conflict in Virginia: Lunenburg County, 1746 to 1774," *William and Mary Quarterly*, 3d ser., 35 (1978): 455–76; "Robert Munford and the Political Culture of Frontier Virginia," *Journal of American Studies* 12 (1978): 169–83; Beeman and Rhys Isaac, "Cultural Conflict and Social Change in the Revolutionary South: Lunenburg County, Virginia," *Journal of Southern History* 46 (1980): 525–50; A. Roger Ekirch, *"Poor Carolina": Politics and Society in Colonial North Carolina, 1729–1776* (Chapel Hill, N.C., 1981), 19–47, 161–202, 236–45, 266–79; Marvin L. Michael Kay and William S. Price, Jr., "'To Ride the Wood Mare': Road Building and Militia Service in Colonial North Carolina, 1740–1775," *North Carolina Historical Review* 57 (1980): 361–409; Richard Maxwell Brown, *The South Carolina Regulators* (Cambridge, Mass., 1963); Robert M. Weir, "'The Harmony We Were Famous For': An Interpretation of Pre-Revolutionary South Carolina Politics," *William and Mary Quarterly*, 3d ser., 26 (1969): 479–89; David R. Chestnutt, "'Greedy Party Work': The South Carolina Election of 1768," in Patricia U.

My contention is that this contrast has been considerably overdrawn. It rests upon both an overemphasis on the coherence and rigidity of older societies of the lowcountry and a misperception of the underlying nature and thrust of backcountry development and aspirations. Just as there were powerful continuities between the colonial and the Revolutionary eras, so there were fundamental continuities between the southern backcountries and the seaboard societies to which they were connected. Turner to the contrary notwithstanding, in several fundamental ways the southern backcountries were every bit as much a reflection of the older colonial British-American world as they were a prefigurement of the new American order.

Among recent literature, Robert D. Mitchell's impressive work on the Shenandoah Valley, the oldest and longest-settled of the southern backcountries, most fully anticipates this line of argument. It clearly reveals a strong tendency over time toward assimilation to seaboard norms. As the Shenandoah acquired better transportation facilities and more credit, as its population became more settled and less equal, as its elite became more affluent and more coherent, and as its institutions and social structure became more sharply articulated, it became more and more like the eastern Chesapeake. It moved from subsistence to a more specialized and commercial agriculture employing tenants and slaves, from ethnic spatial separation to ethnic mixing, and from relative isolation to much closer social and economic integration with the east. Similarly, in his work on Lunenburg County in Southside Virginia, Richard Beeman has noted a tendency over time toward a closer conformity to the colony's traditional political and social systems.[10]

If, with the increasing articulation of its socioeconomic and political structures, the oldest areas of the Virginia backcountry were thus becoming not less but more like the East, then the much-emphasized differences between backcountry and seaboard areas would seem to have been as much stadial as

Bonomi, ed., *Party and Political Opposition in Revolutionary America* (Tarrytown, N.Y., 1980), 70–86, 136–39; and Ronald Hoffman, "The 'Disaffected' in the Revolutionary South," in Alfred F. Young, ed., *The American Revolution: Explorations in the History of American Radicalism* (DeKalb, Ill., 1976), 273–316. The quotations are from Beeman, "Social Change and Cultural Conflict," 457, 468, 475.

[10] Robert D. Mitchell, "The Shenandoah Frontier," *Annals of the Association of American Geographers* 62 (1972): 461–86; "Content and Context: Tidewater Characteristics in the Early Shenandoah Valley," *Maryland Historian* 5 (1974): 79–92, and *Commercialism and Frontier: Perspectives on the Early Shenandoah Valley* (Charlottesville, Va., 1977); Beeman, "Social Change and Cultural Conflict," 463. See also Thomas Perkins Abernethy, *Three Virginia Frontiers* (Baton Rouge, La., 1940); Harry Roy Merrens, *Colonial North Carolina in the Eighteenth Century: A Study in Historical Geography* (Chapel Hill, N.C., 1964); and Daniel Thorp, "Wilkes County, North Carolina: The Articulation and Stabilization of a Late Eighteenth-Century Frontier Society" (seminar paper, Johns Hopkins University, 1978).

spatial phenomena, differences not in kind that would persist over time but in stages of development that would decline over time. At the time of the Revolution, this assimilative process was probably strongest in areas where the relationship with the East was most fully developed—in the lower Shenandoah Valley and in the oldest settled areas of the South Carolina backcountry—and weakest in Georgia, which, as all three chapters on Georgia in *An Uncivil War* strongly suggest, was, lowcountry and backcountry together, a wholly new society. But there is no reason to doubt that this assimilative process was at work throughout the southern backcountries and was supported and stimulated by shared values and aspirations. The remainder of this essay will explore the nature and emphasize the primacy of the two values alluded to in my title—independence and improvement. It will further explore the relationship between these values and the fragile authority structures that characterized the societies of colonial British America in the eighteenth century. Finally, it will speculate briefly about the profound ways in which these values may have affected the Revolutionary experiences of the southern backcountries.

Perhaps the most powerful drive in the British-American colonizing process from the seventeenth century through much of the nineteenth century, and from the eastern to the western coasts of North America, was the drive for personal independence. Quite simply, independence meant freedom from the will of others. It was the opposite of dependence, which was subordination or subjection to the discretion of others. Independence implied a sovereignty of self in all private and public relations, while dependence connoted the very opposite, the absolute "contrary of sovereignty." Indeed, the social categories independents and dependents historically had been the single most basic division in English social life. Among independent people there was a further distinction between those whose circumstances were merely "sufficient" and who therefore usually had to work with their hands and a much smaller group whose means were so substantial that they no longer needed to work with their hands and could therefore live like gentlemen. If independence did not require great affluence, it did imply, to quote Samuel Johnson's *Dictionary*, "a fortune . . . equal to the conveniences of life." Independence was also associated with competence, virility, and manhood and entitled people to respect from their inferiors, superiors, and themselves. Though it did not guarantee a man "plenary satisfaction," a modest independence did ensure that he and his family—his dependents—could live "at ease" rather than in anxiety, in contentment rather than want, in respectability rather than meanness, and, most importantly, in freedom from rather than thralldom to the dictates of others.[11]

In Britain the percentage of independents in the total male population was small. But in the American colonies the opportunity to acquire land or an independent trade was so widespread that the achievement of independence lay within the grasp of most able-bodied, active, and enterprising free men. The prospect for "a very comfortable and independent subsistence" held out by promotional writers, land developers, and governmental authorities acted as a powerful, perhaps the single most powerful, magnet in attracting settlers to new colonies and newly opening areas. Moreover, although the achievement of genuine affluence and a gentle status was confined to a very small number of people, as it had been in Britain, the comparatively widespread realization of independence by people whose beginnings were small, a realization achieved merely by the disciplined application of industry to the mastery of the soil, contributed to an equally broad diffusion of an expansive sense of self-worth through the independent, mostly landowning population in each new area of settlement.[12]

Even in America, however, the boundary line between independence and dependence was not so great that people who had once gained an independent status might not slip back into dependence. As Richard Beeman notes, "Only good fortune—or the avoidance of misfortune—separated the great mass of farmers from a return to dependence."[13] As well as pride in their own achievements and in their newly gained independence, the fear of a return to dependence was thus a powerful animating force among those who had only recently risen out of, or were not yet very far removed from, dependence. Among such people an intense jealousy and anxiety over the loss of recently gained or narrowly held independent status were probably never far below the surface of consciousness and could easily be activated. Certainly one reason why Americans from all sections appeared to be so tenacious of their liberty was that liberty was an essential attribute of their status as independent men.[14]

---

[11] The definitions in this and later paragraphs are derived from Samuel Johnson, *A Dictionary of the English Language*, 8th ed., 2 vols. (London, 1799). In stressing the importance to eighteenth-century Americans of the quest for personal independence, I emphatically do not, as the above paragraph makes clear, associate that quest with a drive for profit maximization.

[12] See, among many examples, the less familiar but extraordinarily thoughtful and full contemporory development of these themes in Samuel Williams, *The Natural and Civil History of Vermont*, 2 vols. (Walpole, N.H., 1794), 2:352–535. The quotation is from 354.

[13] Beeman, "Political Response to Social Conflict," 223.

[14] For citations to some of the many contemporary attributions of an unusually tenacious sense of liberty among colonial and Revolutionary Americans and a discussion of the social

The comparative ease of obtaining independence in the relatively open and new societies of colonial British America meant, of course, that failure to achieve or maintain an independent status bore a much greater social stigma than it did in contemporary Britain or continental Europe. Presumably such failure could correspondingly produce a much deeper sense of personal unworthiness. With no social excuse, the onus of failure fell directly and fully upon the failed individual. As Turner long ago emphasized, the presence of new places with new opportunities provided the failed with a new opportunity for redefinition. What part of the high mobility rates in the southern backcountry noted by several scholars was composed of failures is a subject that requires considerably more attention.[15] But much evidence presented in the essays published in *An Uncivil War* suggests that the surge of population into the southern backcountry during the last half of the eighteenth century contained not only the active and the enterprising, the character types conventionally associated with American frontiers, but also the failed. It indicates as well that the failed was a category comprised of two distinct, if also overlapping, groups: first, those in search of a new start in a new place as well as the individual redefinition that such a situation might make possible, and second, those who had either given up all hopes of success or rejected contemporary definitions of success in favor of a hand-to-mouth existence as hunters, vagabonds, or plunderers and thereby, in their own ways, sought to put themselves beyond dependence.[16]

Individuals came to the new societies of colonial British America not merely in quest of personal independence but also with the complementary hope of transforming those new societies into improved societies that could both guarantee the independence or, for the fortunate few, affluence they expected to achieve and enable them to enjoy the fruits of that independence or afflu-

---

meanings of *liberty* in the late eighteenth-century South, see Jack P. Greene, "'Slavery or Independence': Some Reflections on the Relationship among Liberty, Black Bondage, and Equality in Revolutionary South Carolina," *South Carolina Historical Magazine* 80 (1979): 193–214 [chap. 11 below].

[15] See Beeman and Isaac, "Cultural Conflict and Social Change," 544; Mitchell, *Commercialism and Frontier*, 45–58; Robert W. Ramsey, *Carolina Cradle: Settlement of the Northwest Carolina Frontier, 1747–1762* (Chapel Hill, N.C., 1964); Merrens, *Colonial North Carolina*, 53–81.

[16] The character and importance of independence and dependence in colonial and Revolutionary America are explored more fully in Jack P. Greene, *All Men Are Created Equal: Some Reflections on the Character of the American Revolution* (Oxford, 1976) [chap. 10 below].

ence to the fullest possible extent. Such demands and aspirations for improvement were nearly as prominent among settlers in new places as were those for independence and affluence. Ubiquitous in the economic writings of early modern Britain, the language of improvement referred primarily to schemes, devices, or projects through which the economic position of the nation might be advanced, the estates or fortunes of individuals might be bettered, or existing resources might be made more productive.[17] In the new societies of colonial British America, the term *improvement* carried similar connotations. Settlers sought to improve their situations by securing the necessary capital and labor to develop their lands and fortunes; towns that would provide them with local markets in which they could exchange the produce of their lands for finished goods; bounties that would encourage them to experiment with new crops; and roads, bridges, and ferries that would provide them with better access to wider markets and link them more closely to economic and administrative centers. To gain access to or to protect the broadly, though by no means equally, diffused benefits conferred by such improvements, men were even willing to perform or to permit their dependents to perform such burdensome obligations as road and militia service.[18]

In the new and relatively undeveloped societies of colonial British America, however, the term *improvement* also acquired a much wider meaning: it was used to describe a state of society that was far removed from the savagery associated with the native Indians. An improved society was one defined by a series of positive and negative juxtapositions. Not wild, barbaric, irregular, rustic, or crude, it was settled, cultivated, civilized, orderly, developed, and polite.[19] The model for an improved society in both colonial and Revolutionary America was emphatically not the egalitarian yeoman societies of the Old Northwest that were later glorified by Turner. The massive rustication of European life produced by the settlement of America had not, by the

---

[17] See especially Joan Thirsk, *Economic Policy and Projects: The Development of a Consumer Society in Early Modern England* (Oxford, 1978). Seventeenth-century English literature on improvement is analyzed from another perspective by Joyce Oldham Appleby, *Economic Thought and Ideology in Seventeenth-Century England* (Princeton, N.J., 1978).

[18] The pressure of such demands in the southern backcountries and how they affected development can be seen in Mitchell, *Commercialism and Frontier*, 133–240; Merrens, *Colonial North Carolina*, 85–172; Ekirch, *"Poor Carolina,"* 161–202; Brown, *South Carolina Regulators*, 13–37; and Kay and Price, *"'To Ride the Wood Mare.'"*

[19] Among earlier studies that have emphasized this dichotomy between the barbarous and the civilized are Roy Harvey Pearce, *The Savages of America: A Study of the Indian and the Idea of Civilization* (Baltimore, 1953), and Louis B. Wright, *Culture on the Moving Frontier* (Bloomington, Ind., 1955), 11–45.

time of the Revolution, yet led to the development of new, distinctly American, paradigms of the improved society. The celebration of a rural life by people like Robert Beverley, William Byrd of Westover, and other southern colonial writers earlier in the eighteenth century seems to have owed more to contemporary literary trends in Augustan England than to conditions in America and, unlike Jefferson's post-Revolutionary celebration of the virtues of rural life, served more as mock celebrations of, even apologies for, the still unimproved state of seaboard America.[20]

Before the American Revolution, settlers throughout the new societies of colonial British America seem to have aspired to the creation of a settled society on the distant model of the Old World and on the closer models of older-settled regions of colonial British America. During the last half of the eighteenth century, as during earlier phases of English colonization, the new societies of colonial British America, including those of the southern backcountry, saw the older societies to which they were attached not as negative but as positive points of reference. Insofar as those older societies were more improved, settled, orderly, and coherent, the newer societies in the West hoped to imitate them by themselves acquiring all those attributes of improvement. Re-creation, not innovation, was their aim. They aspired to a fully developed market society with credit, commercial agriculture, slavery, and a brisk circulation of money and goods. They wanted a more settled and hierarchical social structure with social distinctions ranging from the genteel down to the vulgar, a term that in contemporary usage meant simply "the common people." In particular, they wanted a social structure in which successful, independent, and affluent people would have the opportunity, in conformity with the long-standing traditions of Western civilization (and probably all other highly developed civilizations), to exploit dependent people, albeit they wanted, in imitation of seaboard America rather than of Britain, a ranked social order that would be based upon achievement and performance rather than upon ascription, legal privilege, or family charisma. They desired authoritative, if not very obtrusive, political institutions that could facilitate their socioeconomic and cultural development and would be pre-

---

[20] See Leo Marx, *The Machine in the Garden: Technology and the Pastoral Ideal in America* (New York, 1964), 75–114; Kenneth S. Lynn, *Mark Twain and Southwestern Humor* (Boston, 1959), 3–22; Richard Beale Davis, *Intellectual Life in the Colonial South, 1585–1763*, 3 vols. (Knoxville, Tenn., 1978), 1:84–91. Celebrations of the rural life in the literature of Augustan England are analyzed by Maren-Sofie Røstvig, *The Happy Man: Studies in the Metamorphoses of a Classical Ideal*, 2 vols. (New York, 1962–71), vol. 2; Maynard Mack, *The Garden and the City: Retirement and Politics in the Later Poetry of Pope, 1731–1743* (Toronto, 1969); and Raymond Williams, *The Country and the City* (New York, 1973), 1–68.

sided over by the "best [that is, the most successful] part of the community," men whose very success testified to their evident capacity for and legitimate claims to political leadership. They wanted vital traditional social institutions that would contribute to and stand as visible symbols of their improvement, including churches, schools, and towns. And they aspired to eventual political parity with older regions, a parity that would itself constitute recognition of their improved state.[21]

The concept of improvement thus enabled people in new colonial British-American societies to think of those societies in developmental terms. They assumed and hoped that the simplifications of traditional social forms that were so obvious during the first phases of settlement would sooner or later be followed by a process of social articulation. They also assumed that that process, in turn, would ultimately lead in the direction of an ever-greater assimilation to traditional paradigms derived from the socioeconomic and political order of older colonial societies on the seaboard. Indeed, despite the continuing tendency of many scholars to emphasize the egalitarianism of backcountry societies, no societies that put so much emphasis upon achievement and improvement, especially improvement in the way they defined it, could give a high priority or maintain an enduring commitment to egalitarianism, if that term in any way implies equality of social condition. In the early days of the southern backcountry such an equality of condition may very well have been a fact of life. But it was probably never a goal for more than a very few, not even the Separate Baptists. No less than their lowcountry predecessors, backcountry people showed no disposition to forgo exploitation of their fellowmen, no unwillingness to build their own independence and affluence at the cost of the dependence of other people, including white servants, laborers, and tenants as well as black slaves. Indeed, no less than in contemporary Europe, the status of independent men was defined to a significant degree by their capacity—their liberty—to have dependents and by the numbers of those dependents.

As long as the goals of achievement of independence and improvement

---

[21] Although in the case of the southern backcountries these aspirations for improvement may in the first instance have been articulated by those strategic, mostly elite segments of the population that have traditionally given definition to societies, my hypothesis is that they were widely diffused among the vast majority of independent men in the area. The quotation is from George R. Lamplugh, "'To Check and Discourage the Wicked and Designing': John Wereat and the Revolution in Georgia," *Georgia Historical Quarterly* 61 (1977): 304. For a general consideration of the power of English models in shaping early American social aspirations, see Jack P. Greene, "Search for Identity: An Interpretation of the Meaning of Selected Patterns of Social Response in Eighteenth-Century America," *Journal of Social History* 3 (1970): 189–220 [chap. 6 above].

continued to animate settlers, there could hardly be any rejection of class distinctions or any significant decline of "old hierarchic ideals" in favor of "a new egalitarianism."[22] The absence of legally privileged orders in the truncated societies of colonial British America certainly required some modifications in those older ideals, modifications that all but a tiny minority of Americans seem to have thought represented a distinct improvement upon their English inheritance. But if few people lamented the lack of a hereditary aristocracy in America, most contemporaries appreciated that the pursuit of happiness by people of ability and merit would, in the race of life—that metaphor of individual development that was so powerful among British-American social theorists during the late eighteenth century—invariably produce not equality but inequality.[23] Despite the subsequent idealization of equality in America life, few early Americans would have had it any other way. Like the continued presence of hunters and robbers among them, the persistence of an undifferentiated society was an unwelcome reminder of how far away they were from a fully improved social existence. The more settled, cultivated, slave-owning, commercial, urban, and differentiated they became, the more successful—that is, the more improved—these new societies were thought to be. The obvious differences between backcountries and low-countries in the 1760s and 1770s, differences that were largely a function of different stages in the colonizing process, have thus tended to obscure the existence in the backcountries of aspirations and expectations that were leading those societies strongly in the direction of the societies in the East. Only to the extent that they fell short of achieving those aspirations did those societies become an unintended forerunner or an early example of the democratic and egalitarian order of the New West idealized by Frederick Jackson Turner.[24]

---

[22] Rowland Berthoff and John M. Murrin, "Feudalism, Communalism, and the Yeoman Freeholder: The American Revolution Considered as a Social Accident," in Stephen G. Kurtz and James H. Huston, eds., *Essays on the American Revolution* (Chapel Hill, N.C., 1973), 281.

[23] See Williams, *History of Vermont* 2:374–76, 392–94, for a penetrating contemporary discussion of the limited nature of the American commitment to equality. More generally, see also Greene, *All Men Are Created Equal*, and "'Slavery or Independence,'" 205–13; and Isaac Kramnick, "Equal Opportunity and 'The Race of Life': Some Historical Reflections on Liberal Ideology," *Dissent* 28 (1981): 181–87.

[24] Among the essays included in Hoffman, Albert, and Tate, *An Uncivil War*, such aspirations are most evident in W. W. Abbot, "Lowcountry, Backcountry: A View of Georgia in the American Revolution," 321–32; A. Roger Ekirch, "Whig Authority and Public Order in Backcountry North Carolina, 1776–1783," 99–124; Harvey H. Jackson, "The Rise of the Western Members: Revolutionary Politics and the Georgia Backcountry," 276–320; and Klein, "Frontier Planters." But see also Mitchell, "Content and Context," 79–92; Ekirch,

Stressing the extent to which independent men in the southern backcountries aspired to re-create the social and political hierarchies of the East does not necessarily imply that those hierarchies were anywhere near as coherent, strong, and rigid as scholars have conventionally assumed. Certainly recent analysts have been correct in pointing out that colonial British-American seaboard societies were endeavoring to replicate and, to a growing extent, succeeding in assimilating to the "Old Society" of England as it has been defined, for example, by Harold J. Perkin.[25] In all probability, however, these scholars have considerably exaggerated the degree to which, even in long-settled areas such as tidewater Virginia and certainly in more recently developing places like lowcountry South Carolina, North Carolina, and Georgia, those aspirations for assimilation had by the 1750s and 1760s been achieved. In the process, perhaps, they have tended to confound aspiration for reality.

A conspicuous way in which the hierarchies of colonial British America fell short of assimilating to the metropolitan model was in their inability fully to solidify their authority. As here used, the concept *authority* must be carefully distinguished from power. In contemporary usage, power was a synonym for strength, force, and might. Although it was neutral term, it sometimes connoted an illegitimate exertion of strength for corrupt purposes: might as opposed to right. For this reason, among others, early modern British Americans, as Bernard Bailyn has shown, were extremely wary of power.[26] At the same time, however, they yearned for authority. Authority, which, as Sir William Temple noted in his late seventeenth-century tract on that subject, was "the foundation of all ease, safety, and order, in the Governments of the World," was a term that implied legitimacy and was associated with justice and right. Though power invariably "follow[ed] Authority in all Civil Bodies," authority, unlike power, was rooted not only in strength but, much more importantly, in respect, in "trust and opinion." It derived from popular regard, "strengthed and confirmed . . . by custom" and habit, for the "Wisdom . . . [and] Goodness" of the persons and insti-

"*Poor Carolina*," 161–202; and Rachel N. Klein, "Ordering the Backcountry: The South Carolina Regulation," *William and Mary Quarterly*, 3d ser., 38 (1981): 661–80.

[25] Harold J. Perkin, *The Origins of Modern English Society, 1780–1880* (London, 1969), 17–62. For a perceptive discussion of the extent to which tidewater Virginia conceived of itself in terms of the English model described by Perkin, see Rhys Isaac, *The Transformation of Virginia, 1740–1790* (Chapel Hill, N.C., 1982), 18–129.

[26] Bernard Bailyn, *The Ideological Origins of the American Revolution* (Cambridge, Mass., 1967), 66–93.

tutions to which it was accorded. Whereas power might compel people to submit to it, authority thus always commanded "the willing obedience of the people."[27]

That authority in the new societies of the southern backcountry was fragile seems to be widely accepted among scholars of all persuasions. Institutions were still weak and open to challenge, and local elites, as yet new and divided, had only tenuous claims to personal authority and little patronage or other utilitarian resources with which to attach the rest of the community to them. But the many open challenges to the authority of eastern elites both before and during the war raise the question of just how firm and entrenched authority was even within longer-settled localities. In North Carolina and Georgia, where elites had only modest wealth, were mostly new, were divided, and, in North Carolina, were also corrupt and irresponsible, the authority of existing political establishments—that is, the institutions and offices of government and the elites who presided over them—seems to have been little more secure than that of emerging elites in the backcountry. To be sure, where they were affluent, well established, and relatively cohesive, as in tidewater Virginia and lowcountry South Carolina, such establishments seem to have commanded considerable respect and exerted substantial influence. Where they had proved responsive to the interests, needs, and aspirations of new areas, had proved willing to devolve responsibility for local governance upon new local political units, had moved swiftly to incorporate those units fully into the existing political system, and had established strong personal, social, and economic links with the new areas, as in Virginia, these establishments were able, to a palpable degree, to extend their authority over the whole province.[28]

But not even the most respected, cohesive, and responsible of these older colonial political establishments seems to have been as secure in its authority as modern historical concepts such as *hierarchical society* and *deferential order* have come to imply. To understand the course and character of events in the southern backcountries during the Revolution, it is important to comprehend precisely how fragile the authority of these establishments actually was throughout colonial British America—in older as well as the new areas.

Characteristic of every colonial British-American society during the seventeenth and eighteenth centuries, with the possible exceptions of those

---

[27] Sir William Temple, "An Essay upon the Original and Nature of Government," *Miscellanea* (London, 1680), 55–59, 72–74, 82.

[28] See Bridenbaugh, *Myths and Realities*, 157–63; Beeman, "Political Response to Social Conflict"; Brown, *South Carolina Regulators*; Klein, "Ordering the Backcountry," 661–80; Ekirch, *"Poor Carolina,"* 161–202, 236–45; Abbot, "Lowcountry, Backcountry."

of the orthodox Puritan colonies of Massachusetts and Connecticut during their first two generations of settlement, the fragile nature of authority was evident in virtually every area of colonial life through the middle decades of the eighteenth century: in the successful challenges to religious establishments growing out of the Great Awakening;[29] in the massive popular uprisings against unresponsive or ineffective and corrupt political systems in several colonies;[30] in the difficulties governmental authorities had in containing these and other forms of civil strife, particularly those that occurred along disputed boundaries between political jurisdictions;[31] in the enervation of the militia, which, in the absence of effective constabularies, was the only significant source of coercive power available to civil officials and "the ultimate sanction of political authority" in colonial America; in the difficulties authorities experienced in trying to send the militia to places or on missions to which its members did not want to go;[32] in the laxity of law enforcement in many localities;[33] in the weakness of parental controls over

---

[29] See especially Richard L. Bushman, *From Puritan to Yankee: Character and the Social Order in Connecticut, 1690–1765* (Cambridge, Mass., 1967), 147–232; Isaac, *Transformation of Virginia*, 143–295.

[30] See Ekirch, *"Poor Carolina,"* 161–202; Richard Maxwell Brown, "Violence and the American Revolution," in Kurtz and Hutson, *Essays on the American Revolution*, 81–120, and *South Carolina Regulators*, 53–95; and John Crowley, "The Paxton Disturbance and Ideas of Order in Pennsylvania Politics," *Pennsylvania History* 37 (1970): 317–39.

[31] Sung Bok Kim, *Landlord and Tenant in Colonial New York: Manorial Society, 1664–1775* (Chapel Hill, N.C., 1978), 281–415; Thomas L. Purvis, *Proprietors, Patronage, and Paper Money: Legislative Politics in New Jersey, 1703–1776* (New Brunswick, N.J., 1986), 200–231; Frank W. Porter III, "From Backcountry to County: The Delayed Settlement of Western Maryland," *Maryland Historical Magazine* 70 (1975): 329–49.

[32] John Shy, "A New Look at Colonial Militia," *William and Mary Quarterly*, 3d ser., 20 (1963): 173–85, and "The American Revolution: The Military Conflict Considered as a Revolutionary War," in Kurtz and Hutson, *Essays on the American Revolution*, 149, 154; Clyde R. Ferguson, "Carolina and Georgia Patriot and Loyalist Militia in Action, 1778–1783," in Jeffrey J. Crow and Larry E. Tise, eds., *The Southern Experience in the American Revolution* (Chapel Hill, N.C., 1978), 174–99, and "Functions of the Partisan-Militia in the South during the American Revolution: An Interpretation," in W. Robert Higgins, ed., *The Revolutionary War in the South: Power, Conflict, and Leadership: Essays in Honor of John Richard Alden* (Durham, N.C., 1979), 239–58; Kay and Price, "'To Ride the Wood Mare,'" 384–85.

[33] See Douglas Greenberg, *Crime and Law Enforcement in the Colony of New York, 1691–1776* (Ithaca, N.Y., 1976), 154–236; Beeman, "Social Change and Cultural Conflict," 468; Gwenda Morgan, "The Hegemony of the Law: Richmond County, 1692–1776" (Ph.D. diss., Johns Hopkins University, 1980), 183–284; Michael Stephen Hindus, *Prison and Plantation: Crime, Justice, and Authority in Massachusetts and South Carolina, 1767–1878* (Chapel Hill, N.C., 1980), 1–84.

children;[34] in the insubordination of slaves toward their masters and overseers;[35] in the widespread fear, especially among less cohesive elites and in the uncertain times beginning with the Stamp Act crisis, of social revolt by the lower orders;[36] and, perhaps most of all, in the widespread lack of respect or deference of inferiors to their social betters and political officials, a lack of respect vividly expressed in the reference to the Continental Congress as "a passell of Rackoon Dogs."[37]

Historians have often regarded these and other examples of the tenuousness of authority in the older seaboard societies of colonial British America in the decades immediately before the American Revolution as evidence that those societies were suddenly coming apart, as formerly authoritative establishments came under challenge from new popular or "democratic" forces. But this interpretation is based upon a profound misunderstanding of the direction of social development in colonial British America. In the old Puritan colonies of Massachusetts and Connecticut authority was strong in the beginning and declined over time. In this as in many other respects, however, those colonies deviated sharply from British-American norms. Unlike the old Puritan societies, the rest of the British-American colonies moved

---

[34] See Philip J. Greven, Jr., *Four Generations: Population, Land, and Family in Colonial Andover, Massachusetts* (Ithaca, N.Y., 1970), 222–58; *The Protestant Temperament: Patterns of Child-Rearing, Religious Experience, and the Self in Early America* (New York, 1977), 21–61, 151–91, 265–331; Stephanie Grauman Wolf, *Urban Village: Population, Community, and Family Structure in Germantown, Pennsylvania, 1683–1800* (Princeton, N.J., 1976), 287–326; Daniel Blake Smith, *Inside the Great House: Planter Family Life in Eighteenth-Century Chesapeake Society* (Ithaca, N.Y., 1980), 25–54, 82–125; Michael Zuckerman, "Penmanship Exercises for Saucy Sons: Some Thoughts on the Colonial Southern Family" (Paper presented at the Sixtieth Annual Meeting of the Canadian Historical Association, Halifax, Nova Scotia, June 1981).

[35] Gerald W. Mullin, *Flight and Rebellion: Slave Resistance in Eighteenth-Century Virginia* (New York, 1972), 35–82; Morgan, "Hegemony of the Law," 136–82; Hindus, *Prison and Plantation*, 129–61; Daniel C. Littlefield, *Rice and Slaves: Ethnicity and the Slave Trade in Colonial South Carolina* (Baton Rouge, La., 1981), 115–73; Jeffrey J. Crow, "Slave Rebelliousness and Social Conflict in North Carolina, 1775 to 1802," *William and Mary Quarterly*, 3d ser., 37 (1980): 79–102.

[36] See Jack P. Greene, "Social Context and the Causal Pattern of the American Revolution: A Preliminary Consideration of New York, Virginia, and Massachusetts," in *La Rèvolution Amèricaine et L'Europe* (Paris, 1979), 55–63; Marvin L. Michael Kay, "The North Carolina Regulation, 1766–1776: A Class Conflict," in Young, *American Revolution*, 71–123; Kay and Lorin Lee Cary, "Class, Mobility, and Conflict in North Carolina on the Eve of the Revolution," in Crow and Tise, *Southern Experience*, 109–51.

[37] Crow, "Liberty Men and Loyalists," 150; Hoffman, "'Disaffected' in the Revolutionary South," 290–311.

not from order to disorder but from a state of profound unsettledness and uncertain and extremely weak authority to ever-greater social and political coherence. As a consequence of this development, provincial and local establishments, as well as the institutions and leaders of which those establishments were composed, had by the late colonial period acquired greater authority than they had ever had before. But that authority was still tenuous, and the many manifestations of its fragility listed above ought to be viewed as merely the most recent symptoms of a problem that had been endemic to these societies from their several beginnings.

The social sources of this continuing fragility of authority—often perceived as an absence of "all ideas [and habits] of subordination and dependence"—have never been explored in depth and can be only briefly considered here.[38] Throughout the first century and a half of English colonization in America, of course, independent Englishmen had taken jealous pride in their celebrated devotion to the preservation of the liberty that was thought to be the primary emblem of their status as independent men. In America this inherited regard for liberty and independence seems to have been extended significantly by the much broader diffusion of property and independence through the society as a whole. Simultaneously, in the southern colonies it appears to have been even further enhanced by the presence of so many permanent dependents in the persons of black slaves, who served as omnipresent reminders to independent men of precisely how valuable their independence was.[39] The very extent and depth of this jealousy of their independent status among the property holders of colonial British America thus seem to have served as a powerful preventive to their giving unreserved deference to people and institutions in authority. At the same time, truncated social structures with correspondingly narrower distances between elites and other independent men along with the newness and precariousness of elite status meant that not even the oldest and most-settled elites could command either the patronage or the respect accorded to their much more ancient and affluent counterparts in Britain. With few coercive resources at their disposal, political institutions suffered from a similar lack of regard.

Whatever the sources of the fragility of authority in colonial British America, the weakness of traditions and habits of subordination meant that

[38] The quotation is from Jack P. Greene, ed., "William Knox's Explanation for the American Revolution," *William and Mary Quarterly*, 3d ser., 30 (1973): 299.

[39] A fuller explanation of the relationship between slavery and the weakness of habits of subordination and deference among independent men may be found in Greene, "'Slavery or Independence,'" 193–214.

authority, wherever it was reasonably well established, most assuredly did not depend, as has so often been asserted, upon power, upon tight elite control "exercised on the basis of class prerogative or rightful privilege." If, Temple insisted, "Authority arising from opinion" resided "in those that govern, who are few," "Power arising from Strength" was "always in those that are governed, who are many." "The ground upon which all Government stands," the foundation for all genuine authority, was thus, according to Temple, "the consent of the people, or the greatest or strongest part of them." Temple's observations seem to apply with special force to the loose societies of colonial British America. With weak police powers and such a large proportion of independent men, their governments derived power almost entirely from "public opinion," from the consent and acquiescence of those constituent elements of political society who held residual power.[40]

Authority to govern in colonial British America thus rested, it cannot be emphasized too strongly, upon "a popular base," upon "the consent of ordinary property owners."[41] Not even among the most thoroughly entrenched elite groups did superior rank and the supposedly greater wisdom it carried with it seem to have been sufficient to command automatic deference from inferiors or to have enabled superiors to ignore, much less to go against, the wishes of the people. "Alienating the affections, losing the opinions, and crossing the interests of the people" were certain routes toward loss of authority. No doubt some elite figures, especially those new to or insecure in their status, presented themselves as proud, haughty, "hectoring [and] . . . domineering" tyrants and claimed political office on the basis of superior rank and social position.[42] But the usual approach of officials and representatives to their constituents seems to have been one that, to employ the language of the day, was characterized by affability, familiarity, complaisance, and condescension—*condescension* meaning at that time a departure "from the privileges of superiority by a *voluntary* submission," a willing descent "to equal terms with inferiors," a soothing "by familiarity." Deference of inferiors to superiors was thus most easily elicited by a corresponding deference of superiors to inferiors. "Influence with the People" in America, one

---

[40] Hoffman, "'Disaffected' in the Revolutionary South," 312; Temple, "Essay upon the Original and Nature of Government," 54, 84; Williams, *History of Vermont* 2:394.

[41] Jackson, "Rise of the Western Members," 319; Edmund S. Morgan, "Conflict and Consensus in the American Revolution," in Kurtz and Hutson, *Essays on the American Revolution*, 304.

[42] Temple, "Essay upon the Original and Nature of Government," 84–85; Crow, "Liberty Men and Loyalists," 139.

British official noted in the 1770s, could "only be obtained by following the humor or disposition of the People. To be the greatest was to be the servant of all. Withholding Grants or opposing Taxes . . . was the ready road to . . . favor, . . . as it flattered the People's pride by reducing those who assumed a higher rank than they, to become their dependents and supplicants." Such behavior, this official implied, not only "never failed" but was absolutely necessary "to attract [the people's] . . . regard and confidence."[43]

Indeed, from this perspective on the deferential systems of colonial British America, the preoccupation of the population with the pursuit of independence, affluence, and the improvements that would both guarantee and enhance their economic achievements suggests still another reason for the failure of the middle and lower orders of political society to play a more conspicuous role in political life. For the vast majority in those societies, the pursuit of happiness did not involve the pursuit of public office or even the active occupation of a public space. Although the sense of civic responsibility varied in strength from one political society to the next according to many different considerations, the primary concerns of most of these independent Americans were private rather than public. Their allegiances were to themselves rather than to their society. To quote one traveler, they were mostly "too much engaged in their respective occupations for the enticements" of public life.[44]

They or their ancestors had, in any case, left Britain or Europe not only to escape want and to gain independence but also, as contemporaries were fond of pointing out, to get away from excessive political intrusions into their private lives, intrusions in the form of high taxes, rapacious civil and religious establishments, obligations to military or naval service, and war. While they wanted enough government to secure peace and to maintain a just civil order, and this desire sometimes meant, as with the South and North Carolina Regulators, that they demanded more government than they had, they were usually, to quote one contemporary, in favor of just "so much government as will do justice, protect property, and defend the country."[45] As long as government performed these functions and did nothing to diminish their independence or to impede the improvement of their societies, Americans could be—and were—relatively indifferent to politics. Quite as

---

[43] Greene, "William Knox's Explanation," 300.

[44] François Alexandre Frédéric, duc de La Rochefoucauld-Liancourt, *Travels through the United States of North America*, 2 vols. (London, 1799), 2:679.

[45] See Brown, *South Carolina Regulators*, 38–111; Ekirch, *"Poor Carolina,"* 161–211, and "Whig Authority and Public Order"; Williams, *History of Vermont* 2:358, 424.

much as deference to superiors, then, indifference to public affairs would seem to have accounted for the widely noted depoliticization of most older colonial societies through the middle decades of the eighteenth century as well as for the political prominence of elites. A greater concern for other interests, private interests, and, in time, habit on the part of the constituency, thus lay behind the minimal levels of popular involvement in the political systems of late colonial British America, and elite predominance seems to have been as much or more the result of passive as of active endorsement. In societies where most men were absorbed by private concerns, elites governed by default—and without necessarily ever obtaining much authority, defined as public respect.

But the failure of the broader public to take a more active public role did not mean that it had lost its capacity to do so. In a society in which political institutions did not have a monopoly of force, where authority was fragile, and where traditions of subordination were not only weak but were deemed inappropriate for independent men, even long-standing habits of civil order and political inactivity could be rapidly transformed into public involvement characterized by widespread political mobilization, conflict, competition, and, ultimately, even open contempt for and active challenges to constituted authority. Such a transformation could be produced by any number of events or conditions that impinged upon the ability of individuals to pursue their traditionally private goals. These included the failure of existing institutions to provide a just order, to guarantee security of property, or to take routine measures designed to facilitate the socioeconomic or political interests of the population, including roads, new governmental units, courts, and schools. They also included fear of loss of the essential components of private welfare and independence through taxes, disorder, corruption, crime, murder, or military service and resentment against treatment that seemed to deny status and rewards thought appropriate to people in an independent and improved situation, including especially denial of the liberty and autonomy thought to pertain to that situation.

In a society with such a pronounced private orientation, public mobilization produced by these or other conditions and events could not, however, be easily sustained. Once the demands that had mobilized the polity had been secured and the people had once again been left at liberty, to borrow a contemporary cliché, to sit in safety and without fear under their own vines and fig trees enjoying the fruits of their labor—and that of their dependents—public concern with politics invariably receded, as it did following the Regulator movements in both Carolinas, and public life once again came to be dominated by elites.

An underlying assumption of this essay has been that prior social conditions determine much that happens in large-scale political events such as the American Revolution.[46] The argument has been that a fuller understanding of the aspirations for independence and improvement and of the fragility of authority in colonial British America, themselves all-important components of those prior conditions, can help put the sources and nature of conflict and other aspects of the Revolutionary experience of the southern backcountries into a clearer—and less anachronistic—focus.

A full comprehension of the strong orientation of the vast majority of the free population toward the pursuit and preservation of individual independence and their relative disinterest and lack of concern with government and public life makes it much easier to understand why the Revolution with its heavy demands presented so many problems for them. Even where society was already seriously divided and elites were the least cohesive and most insecure in their provincewide authority, as, to varying degrees, seems to have been the case in both Carolinas and Georgia, the challenge presented by the Coercive Acts and the initial stages of their military enforcement in 1774–76 could, as Gordon S. Wood and David Ammerman have shown, produce a contagion of "self-sacrifice and patriotism" that was surprisingly extensive, if by no means universal.[47] Like the Regulator movements in both Carolinas a few years before, this contagion seems even to have produced among those who were swept up in it a powerful and remarkably widely shared sense of group solidarity that in these profoundly private societies of militantly independent men may very well have appealed to and have been sustained by a deep, if in ordinary times usually sublimated, yearning for fraternity and communal dependence. But this early flush of public-spiritedness proved impossible to sustain among a population whose most basic drives were individual rather than collective, private rather than public. Wanting most of all to be left alone, they quickly found themselves confronted with many new and burdensome public intrusions into their private lives, including high taxes, military service, supply levies, demands for declarations of allegiance, and, eventually in many areas, military action.

---

[46] This point has been argued more fully in Greene, "Social Origins of the American Revolution," 1–22. See also Hoffman, "'Disaffected' in the Revolutionary South," 277.

[47] Gordon S. Wood, *The Creation of the American Republic, 1776–1787* (Chapel Hill, N.C., 1969), 413–25; David Ammerman, *In the Common Cause: American Response to the Coercive Acts of 1774* (Charlottesville, Va., 1974), 89–101.

All of these intrusions threatened both to undermine the order and security to which they aspired and to disrupt the progress they were making toward independence and improvement.[48]

In societies so strongly oriented toward private ends and with such weak authority structures, it is not at all surprising that people tended to pursue private, local, or regional interests at the expense of the larger public welfare wherever there was not a shared and broadly internalized consensus, a strong majority consensus, about precisely what constituted that larger public welfare. Where such a majority consensus existed, it could act as a powerful sanction—the sanction of opinion, the main ingredient in authority. Where it did not exist, however, those who sought to impose their definitions of the public welfare upon the rest of the population were unable to do so without the exertion of coercive resources that were considerably more powerful and dependable than those they had at their disposal. In modern societies consensual sanctions are usually achieved, or at least facilitated, through well-developed political infrastructures such as political parties. On the eve of the Revolution, however, none of the southern colonies had a well-developed party system that could serve as a colonywide organization to promote such a consensus, though in 1774–76 the committee system organized to resist the Coercive Acts began to serve that function.[49]

With a reasonably undivided, authoritative, and responsive central elite, with new economic opportunities presented by the war for people in the backcountry to increase their independence by supplying foodstuffs and other items for the army, and with a fair amount of sectional integration already established before the Revolution, the state government of Virginia was reasonably successful in achieving a consensus on the question of what constituted the public welfare, at least until a competing authority turned up with the invasion of the British army in 1780–81. Indeed, as Richard Beeman and Rhys Isaac have shown, this consensus about war aims in Virginia was strong enough to have a dampening effect upon long-standing and bitter internal contentions between Evangelicals and Anglicans.[50]

By contrast, where prior conditions were not especially conducive to the

---

[48] For similar assessments of the basically private orientations of the populace in the southern backcountries, see Ferguson, "Functions of the Partisan-Militia," 245; Hoffman, "'Disaffected' in the Revolutionary South," 278, 289, 300; Shy, "American Revolution," 147–52; Sosin, *Revolutionary Frontier*, 98.

[49] See Pauline Maier, "The Beginnings of American Republicanism, 1765–1776," in *The Development of Revolutionary Mentality* (Washington, D.C., 1972), 99–117.

[50] Mitchell, "Shenandoah Frontier," 478; Beeman and Isaac, "Cultural Conflict and Social Change," 536–37; Morgan, "Conflict and Consensus," 291.

realization of such a consensus, and this seems to have been the situation in both Carolinas and Georgia, the Revolution provided powerful new incentives for people at the center to try through concessions and patronage to build such a consensus, which, given the weakness of their coercive resources, was absolutely necessary to the extension of central authority to the peripheries. Where local leadership in the peripheries was still uncertain and had not coalesced into cohesive local or regionwide elites, as, again, was the case in both Carolinas and Georgia, such efforts risked failure because rivalries were so intense that concessions or patronage to one group could—and did—alienate other groups. Here the effort to achieve a statewide consensus produced instead much local disunity among leaders. When, as in the Carolinas and Georgia, local leadership was divided, the rest of the population, not surprisingly, also divided. The great uncertainties inherent in so radical a transition as that from colony to state, from dependence to independence, and the prior existence of significant distrust or resistance to people in power at the center further increased the potential for such divisions. In such situations, people, again unsurprisingly, seem to have chosen sides on the basis of which of the contending local leaders they were most closely attached to or which side seemed most likely to guarantee order, security, and independence.[51] In this context it may not make much sense to organize historical analyses around such traditional concepts as allegiance, loyalty, or even neutrality, concepts that imply a degree of certainty about and levels of long-term commitment to public positions that were uncommon in the developing societies of the southern backcountries.

Where internal divisions and a lack of majority consensus characterized the situation, as in both Carolinas and Georgia as well as in the areas of western Virginia described by Emory G. Evans, coercion through force was the only way for centers to maintain their authority, to suppress political dissent and resistance to legal authority, at least before the appearance of a sizable regular American army in 1779. The militia seems to have functioned reasonably well in this regard until the British army came, albeit in divided areas only through methods that produced a deepening of divisions and of resentments that would, at the first opportunity, send people scurrying to the British in the hope of settling old scores.[52]

---

[51] Ferguson, "Functions of the Partisan-Militia," 243; Klein, "Ordering the Backcountry," 679; Ekirch, *"Poor Carolina,"* 145, 171, 178, 212; James P. Whittenburg, "Planters, Merchants, and Lawyers: Social Change and the Origins of the North Carolina Regulation," *William and Mary Quarterly*, 3d ser., 34 (1977): 215–38; Klein, "Frontier Planters"; Jackson, "Rise of the Western Members."

[52] See Ferguson, "Carolina and Georgia Militia," 175–76, 191, 194, and "Functions of the Partisan-Militia," 240–43; Shy, "American Revolution," 145; Crow, "Liberty Men and Loy-

Notwithstanding the success of the militia in maintaining a semblance of central political power, authority remained fragile in all states during the Revolution and at the center as well as on the peripheries. This fragility contributed to a powerful chain of developments that led in dialectical fashion strongly in the direction of conflict and challenge to authority. Because authority was weak, people in authority were insecure. Because they were insecure, they were touchy about their authority and fearful that it would be challenged by competitors or would not be acknowledged by the rest of the population. Because of such fears and their justifiable doubts about the strength of their coercive resources, people in authority hesitated to exert their authority, a condition that, perhaps above all else, accounted for the looseness of sociopolitical controls over all of colonial British America during the late eighteenth century. Because authority was not consistently exerted and did not therefore consistently provide regular and predictable justice and protection, it was not especially respected. Because it was not respected, it was the more easily defied. When it was defied, those in authority tended to seek to establish it by overexerting it. Overexertion then invited overresistance in an escalating process that led to internecine strife, the breakdown of order, the loss or threat of loss of prosperity, independence, and life itself, and the subordination to a spirit of savagery of all aspirations for improvement.

Such a situation could be retrieved only by retreating to a pattern of minimal retribution, moderation, and accommodation, an eventuality that in a society with few coercive resources was merely a function of political wisdom and a recognition both that authority was fragile and that fragile authority had to be applied leniently if it was going to retain the respect of the public at large. Once elites had come to this recognition and begun acting upon it, and the end of the war made it no longer necessary for them to make heavy demands upon the public, they had little difficulty in retaining their authority.[53] As long as government facilitated, rather than impeded, the drives for

---

alists," and "Tory Plots and Anglican Loyalty: The Llewelyn Conspiracy of 1777," *North Carolina Historical Review* 55 (1978): 1–17; Abbot, "Lowcountry, Backcountry"; Edward J. Cashin, "'The Famous Colonel Wells': Factionalism in Revolutionary Georgia," *Georgia Historical Quarterly* 58 (1974): 137–56, and "'But Brothers, It Is Our Land We Are Talking About': Winners and Losers in the Georgia Backcountry," in Hoffman, Tate, and Albert, *An Uncivil War*, 240–75; Harvey H. Jackson, "Consensus and Conflict: Factional Politics in Revolutionary Georgia, 1774–1777," *Georgia Historical Quarterly* 59 (1975): 388–401; Evans, "Trouble in the Backcountry."

[53] See especially Robert M. Weir, "'The Violent Spirit,' the Reestablishment of Order, and the Continuity of Leadership in Post-Revolutionary South Carolina," in Hoffman, Tate, and Albert, *An Uncivil War*, 70–98; Klein, "Frontier Planters."

individual independence and social improvement that were so powerfully evident in and constituted the primary goals of all the new societies of colonial and Revolutionary British America, constituents were content to pursue those drives and, with their customary indifference to politics, to leave matters of governance to those few largely elite or would-be elite figures who aspired to a public role. If democracy implies a "leveling tendency in political life," the Revolution had clearly failed to make Americans "addicted to democracy."[54]

This was not a lesson American leaders learned only as a result of the Revolution. It was something they had known—and practiced—for a long time, albeit some political societies had done so much more adroitly and successfully than others. But if older and successful elites like those in tidewater Virginia had managed to build their authority upon an acute awareness of its fragility, the Revolution certainly contributed to reinforce that awareness and to bring it home even more powerfully to their newer counterparts in the Carolinas and Georgia. Given the fragility of authority of the political establishment all over colonial British America and their awareness of that fragility, what needs to be explained, then, is not why the Revolution produced contention and conflict. That could hardly have been avoided. The wonder is that those establishments had the nerve to undertake revolution in the first place. In any effort to explain that wonder, considerable emphasis needs to be given to the deeply rooted aspirations for independence and improvement and the ways they contributed to and interacted with the fragile authority structures that characterized colonial British America, including especially newly settled areas like the southern backcountries, before and during the Revolution.

This essay was written for delivery in Washington, D.C., on Mar. 19, 1982, as the closing address for a conference on "An Uncivil War: The Southern Backcountry during the American Revolution," sponsored by the United States Capitol Historical Society and the Institute of Early American History and Culture in Williamsburg. It is reprinted with permission and minor changes from Ronald Hoffman, Thad W. Tate, and Peter J. Albert, eds., *An Uncivil War: The Southern Backcountry during the American Revolution* (Charlottesville: University Press of Virginia, 1985), 3–46. An abbreviated version of this essay was presented as a lecture at the University of Alaska-Anchorage on Apr. 26, 1983, and as a paper at a conference on "The United States Frontier: Early America and Present Day Alaska" at the University of Alaska-Fairbanks on Apr. 27, 1983.

[54] Sosin, *Revolutionary Frontier*, 170–71; Hoffman, "'Disaffected' in the Revolutionary South," 290.

NINE

The Concept of Virtue in Late Colonial British America

A S SHORT A TIME as twenty years ago, the analysis of the political and constitutional cultures of early America still turned around a series of familiar concepts. Liberty, Rights, Consent, Representation, Rule of Law, Sovereignty, Separation of Powers, Equality, Property, Happiness—these were the terms of analysis within which historians and political scientists had long framed their discussions of the foundations of the American political system. During the intervening period, however, the concept of *virtue*, previously accorded almost no emphasis, has both acquired a place among the familiar concepts of early American political life and come to dominate much of the discussion of the ideological and cultural foundations of American political and constitutional development, and not just during the Revolutionary era but throughout much of the nineteenth century and beyond. After a short discussion of the historiography of this development, this chapter will focus mainly on the ways colonial Americans employed the term *virtue* and related concepts during the half century before 1763 and will explore briefly some of the implications of those uses for our understanding of the era of the American Revolution and the establishment of an American nation.

By stressing the extent to which Revolutionary Americans believed that no republic could "'be supported without *Virtue*,'" Gordon S. Wood first called our attention to the significance of virtue in revolutionary thought in 1969 in *The Creation of the American Republic, 1776–1787*. By the term "public virtue,'" Wood wrote, the eighteenth century meant the "willingness of the individual to sacrifice his private interests for the good of the community," and "this concept of public spirit," this "sacrifice of individual interests to the greater good of the whole," which was also sometimes referred to as "patriotism or love of country," he suggested in one of the book's most important theses, "formed the essence of republicanism and comprehended for Americans the idealistic goal of their Revolution." Precisely because it was "so divorced from the realities of American society" and "so contrary to the previous century of American experience," specifically because it called for such a profound "alteration in the very behavior of the people," Wood argued, this goal gave the Revolution a "socially radical character" that "alone was enough to make the Revolution one of the great utopian movements of American history."[1]

Over the next several years, J. G. A. Pocock profoundly enriched our comprehension of the importance of the concept of virtue in early modern political thought on both sides of the Atlantic, and our present understanding of the concept principally derives from his extensive commentaries. In numerous essays and in his magisterial and influential book, *The Machiavellian Moment: Florentine Political Thought and the Atlantic Republican Tradition*, published in 1975, Pocock emphasized the degree to which early eighteenth-century British political discourse was "dominated to the point of obsessiveness by concepts of virtue, patriotism, and corruption"[2] and tracked those concepts from antiquity through the civic humanist tradition as it emerged in Renaissance Italy in the writings of the Florentines Niccolò Machiavelli, Francesco Guicciardini, and Donato Giannoti and the Venetian Gasparo Contarini to late seventeenth-century English republican writers, including John Milton, Algernon Sidney, Henry Nevile, and, most important of all, James Harrington.

Following the Glorious Revolution, Pocock and other writers showed, three distinctive groups of "neo-Harringtonian" writers carried this tradition into the eighteenth century. These included, first and most directly, the radical commonwealth writers earlier discussed by Caroline Robbins, including Robert Molesworth, John Toland, Andrew Fletcher of Saltoun,

---

[1] Gordon S. Wood, *The Creation of the American Republic, 1776–1787* (Chapel Hill, N.C., 1969), 53–54, 68.

[2] See, principally, J. G. A. Pocock, *Politics, Language, and Time: Essays on Political Thought and History* (New York, 1971); *The Machiavellian Moment: Florentine Political Thought in the Atlantic Republican Tradition* (Princeton, N.J., 1975); and *Virtue, Commerce, and History* (Cambridge, 1985). The quotation is from J. G. A. Pocock, "Virtue and Commerce in the Eighteenth Century," *Journal of Interdisciplinary History* 3 (1972): 127.

Walter Moyle, and John Trenchard and Thomas Gordon.[3] Second were a succession of radical Whig historians, in particular Sir Bulstrode White-locke, Bishop Gilbert Burnett, the French Huguenot exile Paul de Rapin-Thoyras, William Guthrie, and James Ralph. A third group, analyzed at length by Isaac Kramnick, were several Tory critics of the new Whig polit-ical and commercial order: Henry St. John, Viscount Bolingbroke, Jonathan Swift, Alexander Pope, John Gay, James Thomson, and George Lord Lyt-telton.[4]

As Pocock has explained, these writers all analyzed the public world in terms of two discrete and opposing patterns of political and social relations, which they referred to as virtue and corruption. In the virtuous state, the only sort of state in which men could attain genuine liberty, citizenship was the highest form of active life, and *civic virtue*, a new term introduced by Pocock and defined as public-spirited and patriotic participation in a self-governing political community in pursuit of the common good, was the primary goal of citizenship and the only legitimate mode of self-fulfillment by citizens.

If civic participation was an essential qualification for the achievement of civic virtue, so was absolute individual independence. For, these opposition writers believed, virtue was attainable only by men of independent property, preferably in land, whose independent holdings permitted them to cultivate the intensely autonomous behavior that alone could preserve the polity in a stable and uncorrupted state. The institutional device through which these independent citizens exercised their autonomous wills in pursuit of civic virtue and the common good was the balanced constitution, or mixed gov-ernment. The necessary characteristic of such a government was that the constituent elements of the polity—usually defined as the one, the few, and the many (in early modern Britain, king, Lords, and Commons)—shared power in such a way that each was at once independent of the others and incapable of governing without their consent. Only by maintaining a strict balance, the primary obligation of all independent and virtuous citizens, could the polity be preserved in a perpetual stasis that would provide its citizens with full liberty, defined as the right of the citizen to participate—to pursue virtue—in the public realm.

The continuing viability of the virtuous polity thus depended, Pocock

---

[3] Caroline Robbins, *The Eighteenth-Century Commonwealthman: Studies in the Transmission, Development, and Circumstances of English Liberal Thought from the Restoration of Charles II until the War with the Thirteen Colonies* (Cambridge, Mass., 1959).

[4] Isaac Kramnick, *Bolingbroke and His Circle: The Politics of Nostalgia in the Age of Walpole* (Cambridge, Mass., 1968).

writes, on the "moral health of the civic individual," which in turn was a function of "his independence from governmental superiors, the precondition of his ability to concern himself with the public good, the *res publica*, or commonweal," while "the moral quality which only propertied independence could confer, and which became almost indistinguishable from property itself, was known as 'virtue,'" the "name" that also was "most tellingly used for balance, health, and civic personality."[5]

By contrast, in a corrupt state each of the three constituent components of the polity—usually the one or, as it was commonly denoted in British politics, the court or administration—sought through the calculated distribution of places and pensions among the members of the other two branches to extend its influence over them and thereby both to destroy their political independence and make its own power absolute. Whereas a virtuous polity was presided over by proud independent citizens who gloried in their capacity to defend the state with a citizen militia, a corrupt polity was dominated by dependent clients, professional men of government and commerce who were too addicted to the pursuit of private interests, too effete, and too lacking in moral fiber to defend themselves and so had to rely on a standing army. Whereas a virtuous state was distinguished by its rulers' patriotism and concern with the public welfare, unfettered self-government, and a balanced constitution, a corrupt state was characterized by the selfish pursuit of private interest and power by the dominant group, arbitrary and tyrannical rule, and an unbalanced constitution.

To adherents of this "country" ideology, early eighteenth-century Britain seemed to be beset by a number of menacing trends. While the rapid emergence of a market economy over the previous century and the consequent spread of luxury threatened to undermine the independence and destroy the potential for virtue among the British citizenry, the expansion of the standing army during the quarter century of war following the Glorious Revolution of 1688 and the various developments associated with the financial revolution of the 1690s, including the growing importance of new financial institutions like the Bank of England, the proliferation of joint-stock companies, the spread of the projecting spirit, and the mounting national debt, provided the court with vast new resources and opportunities with which to corrupt the constitution that had only recently been restored by the Revolutionary Settlement.

In the writings of such people, the standing army, "Placemen, Pensioners, National Debt, Excise, and High Taxation" were thus, in Pocock's words,

---

[5] Pocock, *Virtue, Commerce, and History*, 66–67; "Virtue and Commerce in the Eighteenth Century," 121.

all "part of a hydra-headed monster called Court Influence or Ministerial Corruption."[6] To prevent the polity from succumbing to that corruption, opposition writers stressed the utility of institutional devices such as rotation in office and frequent elections and emphasized the need both for a periodic return to the first principles on which the polity had been founded and for virtuous independent men to maintain a constant vigil against all efforts to aggrandize power on the part of the court.

For many of these writers, Pocock has shown, the critical variable determining whether a polity would remain virtuous or degenerate into corruption was the relationship among property, personality, and governmental authority. In their view, a self-governing agrarian society presided over by independent freeholders was far more likely to succeed in preserving its virtue than was a commercial one. By encouraging men to prefer their own interest to that of the public and by slowly leading them into an addiction to luxury, magnificence, and vice—in short, by rendering them incapable of virtue and thereby making them susceptible to the lures of the court—a commercial society, these writers believed, was much more prone to sink into corruption and tyranny.

Hence, they praised mediocrity of fortune, condemned excessive riches, and were deeply suspicious of any commercial developments the effects of which were not kept thoroughly in check by the vigorous efforts of the independent agrarian sector of society. For once the degeneration process had begun, these writers argued in drawing out the implications of the history of republican Rome, it was virtually impossible to arrest. For this reason, country ideologists were enormously skeptical of change, almost invariably thinking of it as moving only in one direction—toward corruption and destruction of liberty and civic virtue within the polity.

The pattern of thought elaborated by Pocock and others thus conceived of the health of political society as revolving around a series of antitheses. Defined as "the passion for pursuing the public good," virtue stood in opposition not just to corruption, but also to commerce, at least in its less savory manifestations in the persons of "the rentier, officer, placeman, pensioner, and (lowest of all in the scale of humanity) stock-jobber or speculator in public funds"; to interest, thought of as the private weal of individuals and groups; and to passion, conceived as "the pursuits of private and particular goods."[7]

Although the concept of virtue used by the neo-Harringtonians was in

---

[6] J. G. A. Pocock, "Machiavelli, Harrington, and English Political Ideologies in the Eighteenth Century," *William and Mary Quarterly*, 3d ser., 22 (1965): 563.

[7] Pocock, *Machiavellian Moment*, 471–72, 483; "Virtue and Commerce in the Eighteenth Century," 120.

part hierarchical and derived from the citizen's "membership in one of a hierarchy of orders who respected and deferred to one another," it was primarily, according to Pocock, thought to be a function of "civic independence" rooted in landed property and therefore necessarily resting on "an agrarian base."[8] Thus, in contrast to Wood, who stressed the individual moral roots of virtue and the extent to which "public virtue . . . was primarily the consequence of men's individual private virtues,"[9] Pocock emphasized its "material foundations" in landed property.[10]

More important, perhaps, Pocock also stressed the degree to which virtue in civic humanist thought was not leisured and passive but "dynamic, civic, and participatory." By his consistent use of the adjective *civic* preceding the word *virtue*, he deliberately endeavored to underline the extent to which the eighteenth-century concept of virtue was informed by a notion of the "*vita activa* and a *vivere civile*" that implied "an image of the human personality" that was not simply "intensely autonomous" but also "intensely participatory."[11] As Isaac Kramnick has pointed out, the revisionism inspired and sponsored by Pocock thus emphasized a view of man "as a political being whose realization of self occurs only through participation in public life, through active citizenship in the republic."[12]

That exponents of the civic humanist tradition as expounded by Pocock did not have a monopoly on the definition of virtue has been suggested by several scholars. Thus, Norman Fiering, John P. Diggins, Ruth Bloch, and James Kloppenburg have all called attention to the Protestant origins of American ideas about virtue, while both Fiering and Kloppenburg have also emphasized the importance of a liberal, Lockean notion of virtue as self-mastery.[13]

Yet, the enormous explanatory utility that has been accorded to the concept of virtue by early American historians in recent decades has been largely

---

[8] Pocock, *Virtue, Commerce, and History*, 70; "Virtue and Commerce in the Eighteenth Century," 133.

[9] Wood, *Creation of the American Republic*, 69.

[10] Pocock, *Machiavellian Moment*, 485.

[11] Pocock, "Virtue and Commerce in the Eighteenth Century," 134.

[12] Isaac Kramnick, "Republican Revisionism Revisited," *American Historical Review* 87 (1982): 630–31.

[13] Norman S. Fiering, "Franklin and the Way to Virtue," *American Quarterly* 30 (1978): 199–223; John P. Diggins, *The Lost Soul of American Politics: Virtue, Self-Interest, and the Foundations of Liberalism* (New York, 1984); Ruth Bloch, *Visionary Republic: Millennial Themes in American Thought, 1756–1800* (Cambridge, 1985), 5, 109; James T. Kloppenberg, "The Virtues of Liberalism: Christianity, Republicanism, and Ethics in Early American Political Discourse," *Journal of American History* 74 (1987): 11–12, 16.

stimulated by Pocock's own sustained and compelling elaboration of the complicated set of political and social ideas associated with the country ideologists. The consequence has been little short of a paradigm shift in early modern Anglo-American historical studies. "What we used to think of as the Age of Reason," Pocock announced in 1985, "may just as well be called the Age of Virtue; or rather, what used to appear as an age of Augustan serenity now appears an age of bitter and confused debate over the relations between reason, virtue, and passion."[14]

However prevalent the political culture of virtue as propounded by Britain's country ideologists may have been in early eighteenth-century Britain and in Revolutionary America, we know very little indeed about how and in what ways colonial British Americans may have received and employed it. From Clinton Rossiter's discussion of the British sources of American political ideas in the early 1950s,[15] we know that already by the 1720s most of the more significant works written in this tradition were widely available in the colonies and often cited by colonial writers. Rather astonishingly, however, astonishing in view of the emphasis given it in American Revolutionary studies, no scholar has investigated this subject in any detail for the period before the mid–1760s. In the absence of such an investigation and on the basis of Bernard Bailyn's comprehensive study of the role of country ideology in American political thought between 1764 and 1776 and his more casual—and far less cogent—analysis of the use of those ideas in colonial American political cultures during the earlier eighteenth century,[16] many scholars seem simply to have assumed that the political ideology of virtue was both widely manifest in the colonies and that its shape, emphasis, and degree of determinative import were roughly the same there as they were in Britain. They have, in other words, uncritically assumed that Pocock's analysis of Britain fully applies to the many British political subcultures in the colonies.

Not just political ideology but political development in general are subjects that have been relatively little studied during the resurgence of interest

---

[14] Pocock, *Virtue, Commerce, and History*, 66–67.

[15] Clinton Rossiter, *Seedtime of the Republic: The Origin of the American Tradition of Political Liberty* (New York, 1953).

[16] Bernard Bailyn, *The Ideological Origins of the American Revolution* (Cambridge, Mass., 1967); *The Origins of American Politics* (New York, 1968).

in early American history over the past three or four decades. From what we already know about these subjects, however, and from what we have more recently learned from a wide assortment of specialized studies on the social situation of the colonies, these assumptions would seem, on the surface, to be highly problematic.

Political, economic, and social conditions in the still crude and developing societies of colonial British America simply seem to have been too different from the complex polity of metropolitan Britain to have permitted the country ideology as described by Pocock and others even to have been transferred "intact, completely formed, as far back as the 1730's," as Bailyn has suggested, much less to have rapidly "acquired in the mid-eighteenth-century colonies an importance in public life that they did not have, and never would have, in England itself."[17]

For instance, none of the issues that stimulated and sustained the ideology of virtue in Britain were present to any significant degree in the colonies. Throughout the years when the country ideology was at its apogee in Britain, from 1710 until the mid–1750s, no colony had a standing army. Provincial taxes—and debts—were low. Colonial treasuries sanctioned no pensions and provided governors with scant unappropriated funds that could be employed for purposes of corruption. Few governors had more than a handful of offices, and not many of them very lucrative, with which to create a body of clients and supporters in the legislatures and thereby threaten the balance of the constitution. The small size of provincial bureaucracies makes it almost ludicrous even to think of them as administrations, much less as courts.

Indeed, for most colonies at most times, the central issues of politics diverged significantly from those in contemporary Britain. As Richard L. Bushman has shown in the case of Massachusetts, a palpable concern with administrative "corruption" focused not, as in Britain, on the potential subversion of the constitution by the executive but on simple peculation and the unauthorized expropriation of public funds for private uses.[18] In a similar departure from the metropolitan model, anxieties about the health and balance of the constitution were most common not among the "country" majorities in the legislatures but among the small circle of "court" adherents who were seeking to stem the aggressive efforts of the legislatures to thwart executive attempts to enforce the crown's continuing claims for extensive pre-

---

[17] Bailyn, *Origins of American Politics*, x.

[18] Richard Bushman, "Corruption and Power in Provincial America," in *The Development of a Revolutionary Mentality* (Washington, D.C., 1972), 63–91.

rogative powers in the colonies. Those claims, moreover, produced the sorts of fears that had animated seventeenth-century whig opponents of the Stuarts rather than those that were characteristic of eighteenth-century country ideologists.[19]

Differences extended beyond these issues into the very conditions of public life. In provincial societies in which the scope for public activity was narrow, offices were few, and officers mostly unpaid, volunteer, part-time, and discontinuous, the attractions of the public realm must have paled before the opportunities to build families, fortunes, or estates in the private sphere.[20] Notwithstanding some limited experiments with public banks amd loan offices as devices to raise money quickly or obtain a circulating medium of exchange in several colonies, the colonies presented scant opportunities for stockjobbers and speculators in public funds, while the widespread distribution of independent freeholds and the extensive demand for artisanal and other kinds of labor meant that there was as yet but limited scope for rentiers. Finally, in these relatively undifferentiated and unspecialized societies, every one of which had always had a strong commercial orientation and a keen appreciation of their social and cultural deficiencies vis-à-vis the parent culture, one would expect to find little antagonism to commerce, not very sharp distinctions between landed and commercial interests, and considerably more receptivity to change.

If the divergent issues and conditions of social and political life encourage a high degree of skepticism about the assumption that the ideology of virtue had the same meaning in the colonies that it had in Britain, a preliminary survey of the pamphlet and sermon literature between 1720 and 1765 strongly suggests that that skepticism is warranted. What this survey reveals, in fact, is precisely what one would expect in an extended political and cultural entity like the early modern British Empire: namely, that use of the discourse of the center in the several separate peripheries of the empire was highly selective and that that selectivity was a function of the relevance of aspects of that discourse to changing local needs and preoccupations.

---

[19] Jack P. Greene, "Political Mimesis: A Consideration of the Historical and Cultural Roots of Legislative Behavior in the British Colonies in the Eighteenth Century," *American Historical Review* 65 (1969): 337–67.

[20] Jack P. Greene, *Pursuits of Happiness: The Social Development of Early Modern British Colonies and the Formation of American Culture* (Chapel Hill, N.C., 1988).

An examination of the use of the term *virtue* in colonial American publications reveals extensive discussion of virtue*s* and almost no concern with virtue as an all-encompassing political abstraction of the kind limned by Pocock. Indeed, the most systematic and fullest discussion of the concept of virtue published in colonial America, a work entitled *Ethices Elementa. Or the First Principles of Moral Philosophy*, published in Boston in 1746 and written by Samuel Johnson, the New England Anglican minister who in the 1750s became the first rector of King's College in New York, was, as the title implies, a work not in political but moral philosophy. In this volume Johnson defined virtue as individual ethical behavior or moral rectitude. "*Virtue*," he declared, "consists in that Integrity, Firmness and Stablity of the Soul, whereby we do honestly and stedfastly persist in Spite of all Temptations to the contrary, in the Love and Practice of *Moral Good*, and the Hatred and Forebearance of *Moral Evil.—Vice*," he added, "is the contrary."[21]

In his discussion Johnson distinguished among three kinds of virtue. "*Human Virtue*" was the obligation of each individual "to behave sutably to that rational and immortal Nature which GOD had" provided him, "*divine Virtue*" was the duty to behave suitably toward God, and "*social Virtue*, or Virtue due to Society" consisted of the obligation "to behave sutably toward such a System of Beings as" were those who composed the society to which one belonged so that he might "be happy in them, and they in" him.[22] Although many contemporary ministers shared Johnson's concern with identifying the divine virtues, in the context of my investigation into the secular uses of the concept of virtue, his definitions of the human and social virtues are of most interest to us here and warrant recounting in some detail.

In his discussion of the "*human Virtues*," or "the *Duties* which we owe to *our selves*," Johnson identified seven separate virtues and their opposites. "*Moral Wisdom* or *Prudence*" stood "in Opposition to *Indiscretion* and *Incogitancy*"; "*Humility*, to "*Pride, Haughtiness, and Self-Sufficiency*"; "*Moderation*," to "all *ungoverned Lusts and Passions*"; "*Temperance* or *Sobriety* and *Chastity*," to "all *Intemperance* and *Debauchery*"; "*Meekness, Patience* and *Fortitude*," to "*Wrath, Hatred, Impatience* and *Pusillanimity*"; "*Contentment* and *Industry*," to "*Discontent, Envy* and *Idleness*"; and "*Care of the Soul*," to "the excessive *Love* to the *World* and the *Body*."[23]

---

[21] Samuel Johnson, *Ethices Elementa: or The First Principles of Moral Philosophy* (Boston, 1746), 9–10.

[22] Ibid., 46.

[23] Ibid., 47–50.

Johnson's consideration of the *"social Virtues,"* or "the *Duties* that we owe to our *Neighbours,* i.e., to *Mankind* in general, and our *Relatives* in particular," similarly identified seven virtues. *"Benevolence* and *publick Virtue,"* stood "in Opposition to *Selfishness* and *Malevolence";* *"Innocence* and *Inoffensiveness,"* to *"Injuriousness* and *Mischievousness";* *"Justice,* which" comprehended *"Exemplariness, Equity, Truth and Faithfulness,"* to "all Instances of *Injustice,"* including *"Tempting* to Sin, *Murder, Maiming, Oppression, Stealth, Robbery, Adultery, Fornication, Lying, Defamation, Cheating* and all *Deceitfulness";* *"Charity,* which" comprehended *"Candour, Affability, Hospitality, Mercy, Tenderness* and *Beneficence,"* to "all Instances of *Uncharitableness,"* such as *"Censoriousness, Moroseness, Envy, Cruelty, Ill-nature,* and *Hardheartedness";* *"Liberality, Generosity,* and *Magnificence,"* to *"Covetousness* and *Niggardliness,* or a *grudging narrow* and *contracted Spirit";* *"Quietness, Peaceableness, Friendliness* and *Forgiveness,"* to *"Ambition, Contention, Unfriendliness,* and *Irreconcilableness";* and *"Honour, Submission* and *Obedience"* in regard to "all Things lawful and honest," to "all Instances of *Turbulence, Faction* and *Rebellion."*[24]

Johnson's treatment was more extensive and comprehensive but not significantly different from what seems to have been the predominant colonial conception of virtue. His view of individual virtue as the product of the successful cultivation of a congeries of particular moral virtues was common in colonial British-American writing. When governors and judges called upon legislatures or grand juries to take measures to *"encourage* Religion and vertue,"[25] when ministers in funeral sermons or obituary writers in newspapers praised the deceased for "many Virtues, without the Alloy of a single Vice,"[26] when ministers in election and other public sermons identified good rulers as men possessed "of real and inward Vertue,"[27] and when authors of political, economic, and religious tracts advocated measures calculated to promote or restore "the *Vertue* and good *Morals"* of the people,[28] they were all subscribing, with Johnson, to a conception of virtue as individual moral integrity or uprightness as represented by the achievement of a series of personal or social virtues. Although many of the specific virtues they recommended had, in the words of the Pennsylvania official and savant James

[24] Ibid., 54–58.

[25] William Gooch, *A Charge to the Grand Jury* (Williamsburg, Va., 1730), 2.

[26] Benjamin Franklin, Obituary of James Logan, Nov. 7, 1751, *The Papers of Benjamin Franklin,* ed. Leonard W. Labaree et al., 27 vols. to date (New Haven, 1959—), 4:207–8.

[27] Samuel Fiske, *The Character of the Candidates* (Boston, 1731), 9–10.

[28] *Some Reasons and Arguments Offered to the Good People of Boston* (Boston, 1719), 2.

Logan, "ever since the . . . Times of the old Gallant Greeks and Romans adorn'd the most accomplished Heroes whether given us in Romance or History, Poetry or Prose, or in any other manner whatsoever,"[29] these virtues were also heavily Christian in their roots.

Throughout these discussions, writers, usually explicitly and, if not, almost always implicitly, associated individual virtue with "self-dominion."[30] To achieve virtue, the young Benjamin Franklin told the readers of the *American Weekly Mercury* in February 1729, a man had "to govern his Passions; in spite of temptation to be just in his Dealings, to be Temperate in his Pleasures, to support himself with Fortitude under his Misfortunes, [and] to behave with Prudence in all Affairs and in every Circumstance of Life."[31] Unless men wanted to risk losing "all Power and Authority over" their own "Spirits" and be "tossed to and fro by every Wind of Passion, and . . . enslaved to wild Desires, excessive Hopes, impotent Joys, and groundless Griefs," the Reverend William Stith told the Virginia legislature in 1752, he had to learn "to govern" his "Passions and command" his "Appetites."[32] "A true *Discipline* of the HEART and MANNERS," "*public Virtue*," Provost William Smith advised the student body at the College of Philadelphia in 1758, consisted of the individual's "Dominion of" his "own Passions, and" the "bring[ing of] every Movement of the Soul under Subjection, to *Conscience, Reason*, and *Religion*."[33]

The result neither of grace, as Jonathan Edwards and perhaps some other evangelicals believed,[34] nor of the "supposed instinctive love of virtue, and the impulses of the moral sense,"[35] as some of the Scottish commonsense philosophers thought, virtue thus required "a Self-denying Spirit,"[36] in Samuel Johnson's words, the active, "free and vigorous" employment of "Self-Exertion and Self-Determination" to bring the "Will, Affections, Ap-

---

[29] James Logan, *A More Just Vindication of the Honourable Sir William Keith* [Philadelphia, 1726], 4.

[30] William Livingston, *A Funeral Eulogium on the Reverend Mr. Aaron Burr* (New York, 1757), 11.

[31] Franklin, "The Busy-Body," no. 3, Feb. 18, 1729, in *Franklin Papers* 1:118–21.

[32] William Stith, *The Sinfulness and Pernicious Nature of Gaming* (Williamsburg, Va., 1752), 20.

[33] William Smith, *A Charge Delivered May 17, 1757* (Philadelaphia), 4–5.

[34] Fiering, "Franklin and the Way to Virtue," 222.

[35] Ezra Stiles, *A Discourse on the Christian Union* (Boston, 1761), 13.

[36] Samuel Whittelsey, *A Public Spirit Described and Recommended* (New London, Conn., 1731), 15.

petites and Passions" under "discipline" and regulation "according to [the dictates of] Reason and Truth."[37] To this "mighty struggle,"[38] Franklin observed in his Father Abraham letter in 1758, nothing contributed more "than a daily strict SELF-Examination."[39] In this emphasis upon the relationship between virtue and self-mastery, colonial British-American writers followed not only traditional Protestant teachings but also the prescriptions of John Locke, who, in *Some Thoughts on Education*, laid it down as "the great Principle and Foundation of all Vertue" that a man be "able to *deny himself* his own Desires, cross his own Inclinations, and purely follow what Reason directs as best, tho' the Appetite lean the other way."[40]

This "noncivic personal"[41] conception of virtue with its stress upon the responsibility of the individual for the active mastery over the self was appropriate for a society without established hierarchies in which such a large proportion of the free male adult population had managed to improve—and empower—themselves through their own active exertions. The widespread achievement of independence among the free population meant both that they were at once fiercely jealous of their independence and contemptuous of those who never managed to escape dependency. "To be dependent on the capricious Will of a Mortal," declared the Presbyterian minister Samuel Davies in 1762, was "a wretched State of Indigence, Servility and Anxiety"[42] inappropriate for any man capable of the conquest of his passions.

By freeing "a Man from those Temptations which attend a State of Poverty," a "Clear Estate and Independency of Fortune"[43] might make the quest for virtue easier, but the very extent of the independent and autonomous segment of the population probably explains why, in contrast to British country ideologists, free colonial British Americans seem to have put less emphasis on the material than on the moral foundations of virtue. On the western side of the Atlantic, at least, virtue seems to have been thought to be a

---

[37] Johnson, *Ethices Elementa*, 23–24, 34, 47.

[38] Samuel Johnson, "Raphael, or The Genius of the English America. A Rhapsody," post–1765, in *Samuel Johnson: His Career and Writings*, ed. Herbert W. Schneider, 4 vols. (New York, 1929), 2:540.

[39] Franklin, A Letter from Father Abraham, [Aug. 1758], in *Franklin Papers* 8:125–30.

[40] As quoted in Fiering, "Franklin and the Way to Virtue," 211.

[41] Isaac Kramnick, "The 'Great National Discussion': The Discourse of Politics in 1787," *William and Mary Quarterly*, 3d ser., 45 (1988): 21–22.

[42] Samuel Davies, *Religion and Public Spirit: A Valedictory Address* (Portsmouth, N.H., 1762), 11.

[43] *A Letter to the Inhabitants of the Province of the Massachusetts-Bay* (Boston, 1751), 5.

function more of individual moral exertion than of the possession of landed property.

Indeed, among the relatively undifferentiated and unspecialized societies of colonial British America, the concept of virtue seems never to have been socially or occupationally specific. With the individual responsible for his own moral behavior, virtue could be encouraged by, but had no necessary connection to, birth, education, social status, occupation, or fortune. Not "Bare power, wealth, and honour" but a man's active willingness to "make and embrace all opportunities of [being and] *doing good*" was the measure of a man's *"moral virtue."*[44] Nor, also in contrast to British country ideologists, was virtue particularly associated with land or agrarian wealth. Clergymen and social commentators often praised merchants, lawyers, and public officials for their "virtue."[45] Any person who was master of himself, even a landless artisan whose trade afforded "him honest Subsistence with Independence" from the control or will of other people, was capable of virtue.[46]

For societies, like those of the colonies, where there had always been a heavy emphasis on the pursuit of prosperity and "worldly happiness,"[47] few people saw much of a dichotomy between virtue and commerce. Although they knew that "a Trade" could "be gainful . . . to [particular] Merchants, which yet may prove ruinous to their Country"[48] and that some mercenary usurers might even seek to oppress "their Neighbours, by . . . exacting [excessive] Interest" and then "taking their Lands at half value,"[49] they also

---

[44] Ebenezer Pemberton, *A True Servant of His Generation Characterized* (Boston, 1712), 206–7, 209; Charles Chauncey, *Civil Magistrates Must Be Just, Ruling in the Fear of God* (Boston, 1747), 24–25; Fiske, *Character*, 45.

[45] Franklin, Obituary of Andrew Hamilton, July 30, 1741, in *Franklin Papers* 2:327–28; William Livingston et al., *The Independent Reflector*, ed. Milton M. Klein (Cambridge, Mass., 1963), 299; Jack P. Greene, "A Mirror of Virtue for a Declining Land: John Camm's Funeral Sermon for William Nelson," in J. A. Leo Lemay, ed., *Essays in Early Virginia Literature Honoring Richard Beale Davis* (New York, 1977), 189–201; Thomas Prince, *A Sermon at the Publick Lecture in Boston* (Boston, 1730), 11, 33; Roger Price, *A Funeral Sermon, Occasioned by the Much Lamented Death of John Jekyll, Esq.* ([Boston], 1733), 7, 16–17; Benjamin Colman, *The Peaceful End of a Perfect and Upright Life* (Boston, 1736), 11–12; John Lovell, *A Funeral Oration* (Boston, 1743), 6–9, 14.

[46] Franklin to Peter Timothy, Nov. 3, 1772, *Franklin Papers* 19:362. Colonial definitions of *independence* and the relationship between independence, virtue, and the suffrage are discussed in Jack P. Greene, *All Men Are Created Equal: Some Reflections on the Character of the American Revolution* (Oxford, 1976) [chap. 10 below].

[47] *Money the Sinews of Trade* (Boston, 1731), 10.

[48] *A Vindication of the Remarks of One in the Country* (Boston, 1720), 13.

[49] John Colman, *The Distressed State of the Town of Boston Once More Considered* (Boston, 1720), 2.

knew "that no Country" could "flourish without . . . Trade"[50] and that commerce was "absolutely necessary for the good of Humane Societies."[51] Decrying the fact that trade had been so "frequently treated with Contempt" and "Trading Men . . . even to this Day, excluded from the Privileges of gentlemen" in "some arbitrary Countries," Sir William Keith, onetime governor of Pennsylvania, emphasized what few contemporary colonials would have denied: that trade was essential "to enliven and circulate the vital Juices of the Body Politic."[52]

"Temporal Commerce and Trade," declared one economic analyst in Boston in 1721, were "as necessary for the Conveniency, Comfort and Outward Profit of Man, whilst he holds his Tenure on Earth, as Civil Alliance and Cohabitation." A society without commerce, he declared, might be satisfactory for "a People, who (to indulge themselves in great Idleness & Sloath,) Dwell[ed] in the Clefts of the Valleys, in the Caves of the Earth, and in the Rocks, and" dug "*Juniper Roots* for their Meat, or" could "live upon *Acorns*: But," he contended, it was "not at all agreable with a Wise and Busling People, that would spend their Life, to the height of Religion, and right Reason."[53] Indeed, wrote the author of an elaborate tract in praise of commerce in 1731, commerce often actually operated to draw "a People out of an Idle habit." By "encouraging Industry, Virtue, &c.," he observed, trade could "do more to reduce a People to a habit of Prudence and Industry than is possible to be effected by Whip or Hunger or by all the penal Laws that can be Invented for the Suppressing of Idleness."[54] That the "*Vertue* and good *Morals*" of a country was incompatible with its "*Outward* flourishing"[55] was a proposition few colonial British Americans would have found compelling. To the considerable extent that colonial British Americans already by the early eighteenth century regarded commerce and other forms of productive economic activity as a spur to virtuous behavior, they anticipated the late eighteenth-century Anglo-American association, described by Isaac Kram-

---

[50] Amicus Patriae, *Proposals for Traffick and Commerce, of Foreign Trade in New-Jersey* ([New York], 1718), 6.

[51] *An Addition to the Present Melancholy Circumstances of the Province Considered* (Boston, 1719), in Andrew McFarland Davis, ed., *Colonial Currency Reprints, 1682–1751*, 4 vols. (New York, 1964), 1:370–72.

[52] Sir William Keith, *The History of the British Plantations in America* (London, 1738), 5–6.

[53] *A Word of Comfort to a Melancholy Country* (Boston, 1721), 4.

[54] Amicus Reipublicae, *Trade and Commerce Inculcated in a Discourse* (Boston, 1731), 5–6.

[55] *Some Reasons and Arguments*, 2.

nick, of virtue not just with personal character but with "self-centered economic productivity."[56]

By the same reasoning, virtue and interest could be—and sometimes were—seen to be not only compatible but mutually reinforcive. So long as a man contained "himself within the limits of moderation," so long as his activities were not "inconsistent with the *Good* of the *Publick*," some writers believed, it was "surely innocent for a man to . . . Consult & Prosecute his own temporal Interest," his "private and personal" good. Because, as Samuel Johnson suggested in his *Ethices Elementa*, "the Law of *Self-Love* or *Self-Esteem*" laid men "under a Necessity of valuing our selves and our own *Interest*, and of seeking and pursuing our own *Preservation* and *Well-being* or Happiness," they were understandably "desirous of each other's Esteem and Good-Will" and therefore concerned to do what they knew would be "pleasing and advantageous to each other, so that self and social Good must not be considered as at all interfering, but as being intirely coincident, and subservient to each other."[57] Thus operating in such a socially benign way, self-interest could scarcely be interpreted as being usually inimical to virtue.

If colonial British Americans regarded both commerce and interest as compatible with virtue, the same was not true with the rising tide of corruption they saw all about them from the 1730s on. On some particular occasions and in some specific circumstances, one can find writers worrying about the sorts of political corruption that alarmed contemporary British country ideologists. Although perceptive observers recognized that no American governor possessed the resources ever to tempt any assembly to "enter into any Measure with a Governor to increase his Power to the Prejudice of the People,"[58] some commentators fretted about the "Corruption of a House of Representatives" through "a prudent Application of Posts and Pensions."[59] But the sort of corruption that primarily worried colonial commentators was not political but social and moral corruption.

From South Carolina to Massachusetts throughout much of the period from the early 1730s until the very eve of the American Revolution, writer

---

[56] Kramnick, "The 'Great National Discussion,'" 21–22.

[57] Whittelsey, *A Public Spirit*, 4–5, 9; Johnson, *Ethices Elementa*, 11–12.

[58] *To the Free-Holders of the Province of Pennsylvania* [Philadelphia, 1742], 4; Cadwallader Colden, "Observations on the Balance of Power in Government," n.d., in *The Letters and Papers of Cadwallader Colden*, 10 vols. (New York, 1918–37), 9:254.

[59] *O Liberty, Thou Goddess Heavenly Bright* [New York, 1732], 2. See also *The Deplorable State of New England by Reason of a Covetous and Treacherous Governour* (Boston, 1720), 21–22, and *A Letter to the Freeholders and Qualified Voters* (Boston, 1749), 8.

after writer deplored the moral degeneration of the several societies of colonial British America. With Judge Benjamin Whitaker of South Carolina,
they lamented the "Luxury and Excess, which within a few Years last past,
has pour'd in upon us like a Torrent" and "greatly contributed to enervate
and soften our Minds, and to sink us, into Indolence and Inactivity."[60] With
William Stith in Virginia, they professed alarm at the decline of "the ancient
British Virtue . . . among us" and denounced "the Demon, or rather Le-
gion, of Avarice [that] has gone forth and possessed the Nation" as well as
the predominance of "the Love of Money [that] has spread itself like a
devouring Flame."[61]

With the Reverend Charles Chauncey of Massachusetts, they complained
about the people's "laying out so much of the fruits of their labour" in an
"extravagant . . . manner of living."[62] With the Reverend Noah Hobart of
Connecticut, they were offended by "the Growth of Injustice and Profaneness, Idleness and Extravagance, Intemperance and Uncleanness."[63] With
the Reverend Nathaniel Potter, also of Massachusetts, they disdained the
"greedy Depradations . . . made upon" the moral health of the people "by
the Vices of Luxury and Extravagance" and "the studied Gratifications of
sensual Appetites" that "weaken[ed], debase[d] and impaire[d] Men's Reason and Understanding."[64]

Everywhere in colonial British America, commentator after commentator
complained, a flood of social vices was engulfing the population and pre-
venting many people from achieving that discipline, self-restraint, and moderation that had long served as the moral foundation for societies in the Old
World and were crucial supports for the individual rights and liberties—
including the right to pursue, accumulate, and be protected in the possession
of private property—that the colonists thought of as the principal badges of
their Englishness and their most valuable inheritance from the metropolis.
If the national vice of Virginia was gaming along with the attendant
"Crimes" of "Sharping, Robbing, Luxury, Drinking, Rioting, Lewdness,
[and] Duelling,"[65] the *"Immoralities"* of New England included intemper-

---

[60] [Benjamin Whitaker], *The Chief Justice's Charge to the Grand Jury* (Charleston, S.C.,
1741), 10.

[61] William Stith, *A Sermon Preached before the General Assembly* (Williamsburg, Va., 1746),
32–34.

[62] Charles Chauncey, *Civil Magistrates*, 62.

[63] Noah Hobart, *Civil Government the Foundation of Social Happiness* (New London, Conn.,
1751), 39.

[64] Nathaniel Potter, *A Discourse on Jeremiah 8th, 20th* (Boston, 1758), 12.

[65] Stith, *Sinfulness and Pernicious Nature of Gaming*, 24–25.

ance and uncleanness, oppression and injustice, lying and speaking falsely, pride and luxury, slander and calumny, and rudeness and ungovernableness in children.[66] Summoning their readers "to return to our former Frugality, Temperance and moderate Enjoyments,"[67] authors warned that "national Corruption" would "certainly bring with it national Ruin" and denied that there could "be any real Happiness, either publick or private, without Virtue."[68]

What these writers were denouncing were some of the many corrosive effects of prosperity and the consumer revolution upon the existing moral order. As Provost William Smith of Pennsylvania noted in 1759, they feared that plenty had given rise to luxury, and "Luxury [had] introduced a fatal corruption of every good and virtuous principle."[69] Unlike political corruption, which, according to the prescriptions of the country ideology, could be eliminated by a return to the original principles and balance of the constitution, such widespread social and moral corruption could only be remedied by a fundamental moral reformation within the colonial populations. If any of the colonies was going to recover "the Character of a well moraliz'd People,"[70] individuals would have to regain control over their "ungoverned lusts and passions."[71] "The Recovery of a national Virtue and Goodness," in Nathaniel Potter's words, thus heavily depended "upon the Amendment of [the individual virtue of] its particular Members."[72]

If, in all these many ways, the predominant concept of virtue in colonial British America before the mid–1760s differed profoundly from that articulated by the country ideologists, the preoccupation of so many colonial writers with promoting a more vital sense of the common good comes closer to resembling the civic definition of virtue emphasized by Pocock. The reader will recall that Samuel Johnson privileged the idea of benevolence or *"publick Virtue"* by placing it first on his list of social virtues.[73] Such

---

[66] Andrew Eliot, *An Evil and Adulterous Generation* (Boston, 1753), 16–20.

[67] Whitaker, *Chief Justice's Charge*, 10.

[68] Stith, *Sermon Preached before the General Assembly*, 32–34.

[69] William Smith, *Discourses on Several Public Occasions during the War in America* (London, 1759), 77.

[70] James Horrocks, *Upon the Peace* (Williamsburg, Va., 1763), 9–10.

[71] Johnson, "Raphael," in *Samuel Johnson* 2:540.

[72] Potter, *Discourse*, 27.

[73] Johnson, *Ethices Elementa*, 55.

a priority was fairly conventional. "Public Spirit, or in other Words, the Love of Country," declared the Anglican minister James Sterling to the Maryland legislature in 1755, was "the Sovereign of social Virtues,"[74] the "most conducive," said an anonymous writer in 1751, "to the Good of Society."[75]

Few themes were more prominent in the public literature of the colonies than the emphasis upon public spirit or, as it was often called after about 1750, patriotism. Citing both biblical and classical examples, colonial writers, in sermons, economic and educational tracts, and political pamphlets, praised individuals for their "manifest exertions of *Public Spirit*"[76] and extolled the beneficial effects of patriotism or a public spirit, which they defined as "a thorough disinterestedness in the procuring of" a "country's welfare."[77] Pointing out that "*Rome, Greece*, &c. flourished by Men of Great and Noble Spirits"[78] and contending that it was "the *will* of God that every man's private interest be subordinated to the good of the whole; that no man act as if born only for himself; but that all make the *publick* prosperity their *great view*,"[79] they condemned a "Private Spirit"[80] "narrow Notions, meerly local Views, and mean-spirited Images";[81] told electors that a "public spirit" was "one of the best Qualifications for any eminent Post or Station in the Government"; and called upon leaders when in office to consult "not . . . their own private Interest or Advantage, but . . . the Good of the Community, the Safety and Happiness of the whole Body Politic."[82] Politicians reponded to these appeals by promising that they would "intirely seek the Good and Well-fare of my Dear Native Country, ever rejecting and Contemning all Private Views and Interests, more especially when in Competition with the Publick Good."[83]

---

[74] James Sterling, *A Sermon Preached before His Excellency the Governor of Maryland and Both Houses of Assembly* (Annapolis, 1755), 20.

[75] *Private Vertue and Public Spirit Display'd* (Boston, 1751), 3.

[76] Lovell, *Funeral Oration*, 6–9.

[77] Thomas Pollen, *The Principal Marks of True Patriotism* (Newport, R.I., 1758), 3.

[78] *Some Proposals to Benefit the Province* (Boston, 1721) in Davis, *Colonial Currency Reprints*, 2:105.

[79] Pemberton, *True Servant*, 219.

[80] *Some Proposals to Benefit the Province*, in Davis, *Colonial Currency Reprints*, 2:106.

[81] Sterling, *Sermon*, 47.

[82] William Balch, *A Publick Spirit* (Boston, 1749), 21–22, 25.

[83] Elisha Cooke, *Just and Seasonable Vindication* (Boston, 1720), 17.

But, in contrast to British country ideologists, colonial writers recommended public spirit less as a hedge against the corrupting influences of an aggressive executive than as an antidote to two other seemingly pernicious tendencies: the widespread neglect of public life in the pursuit of private happiness and the intense factionalism that from time to time characterized the public life of some colonies. They were primarily concerned to condemn what they saw as the rising tendency of almost "every individual . . . to consider himself distinctly and apart from the Community of which he is a member."[84] When, as seemed to be the case in the colonies for much of their existence, men insisted upon "look[ing] on themselves as so many Individuals, distinct from the Public,"[85] when "every man's tho'ts" were "taken up" by considerations of "how he shall advance his own private Interest,"[86] when men permitted "Family Affection and private Friendship" to "engross" their "Hearts," they could scarcely avoid becoming "insensible of the general Welfare"[87] and permitting these "private Pursuits" to take precedence, with the result that the public interest "was always neglected."[88] Contrasting the patriot with the "Partisan,"[89] they denounced the spirit of factionalism and party, which engaged "particular Persons, in Opposition to the publick Interest,"[90] as "the very reverse" of "true public spirit."[91] Insofar as they thus saw egocentric and factional behavior as corruption, colonial British Americans were, in effect, using that term not just in the limited sense of political corruption associated with the British country ideologists but in a much broader sense to mean any form of self- or group-centered behavior that favored personal or group concerns over the larger weal of the public.

Indeed, as used by most colonial writers, the ideal of public spirit was by no means the precise equivalent of the civic humanist concept of civic virtue, albeit it was informed by many of the same imperatives. They did not regard patriotism as synonymous with *Virtue*, considered as an abstract and expan-

---

[84] Andrew Fletcher, *Vincit Amor Patriae* [New York, 1732], 1.

[85] *Industry and Frugality Proposed as the Surest Way to Make Us a Rich and Flourishing People* (Boston, 1753), 4.

[86] *Money the Sinews of Trade*, 11.

[87] Livingston, *Independent Reflector*, 216.

[88] *Industry and Frugality Proposed*, 4.

[89] "The Planter," no. 7, *American Magazine* 1 (1757–58): 325.

[90] *O Liberty*, 3.

[91] James Sterling, *Zeal against the Enemies of Our Country Pathetically Recommended* (Annapolis, 1755), 7–8.

sive political conception, but, variously, as "one of the master virtues,"[92] a "great Virtue,"[93] "as one of the noblest Virtues that ever inhabited the human Breast,"[94] as "that first-rate Virtue."[95] As in Samuel Johnson's conception, public spirit was the first among the social virtues.

Although praise of patriotism often appeared in tandem with laments about its decline "as the ruling Principle of Action"[96] in colonial public life, the frequency of this theme from at least the beginning of the eighteenth century on suggests that public spirit had never been abundantly manifest at any time or at any place in colonial British America. When they had had less wealth and less leisure during the earlier decades of the history of the colonies, the colonists might, as later generations often supposed, have exhibited more virtue, but they never seem to have displayed large amounts of public spirit. A brief and highly speculative analysis of the reasons why this was so may contribute to our understanding of why colonial British Americans did not, before the era of the American Revolution, expropriate much of the British country ideologists' concept of virtue and why their own definition of virtue was far more noncivic, personal, Christian, and Lockean than civic and republican.

The answer to the question of why Americans were not more patriotic, I would suggest, may be found in two separate areas. The first is in the nature of the public realm, which was small in scope, unprofitable, volatile, and threatening. If "the Scene of public Action"[97] on the provincial stages of colonial British America provided scant stimulus for the pursuit of fame and even less scope for its achievement, the notorious parsimony of both legislatures and publics in the several colonies, the seemingly settled reluctance to "pay very large Taxes"[98] and the "accustomed," and oft-lamented, "parsimonious Disposition of the public Money,"[99] provided few material incentives to tempt men into public service. Offering but "small Profit,"[100]

---

[92] John Barnard, *The Throne Established by Righteousness* (Boston, 1734), in A. W. Plumstead, ed., *The Wall and the Garden: Selected Massachusetts Election Sermons* (Minneapolis, 1968), 270–71.

[93] Balch, *Publick Spirit*, 25.

[94] *Industry and Frugality Proposed*, 5.

[95] Livingston, *Independent Reflector*, 218.

[96] Ibid., 216.

[97] William Smith, *A General Idea of the College of Mirania* (New York, 1753), 17.

[98] *A Letter from a Gentleman in New-York, to His Friend in Brunswick* [New York, 1750], 1.

[99] *An Address to the Freeholders of New-Jersey, on the Subject of Public Salaries* (Philadelphia, 1763), 3.

[100] William Smith, *A Brief State of the Province of Pennsylvania* (London, 1756), 8.

executive offices, judgeships, and legislative seats invariably were so poorly rewarded that those who held them had to "draw their Subsistence, in great Part, from their private Estate."[101]

Moreover, the widespread "Contempt shewed to Authority"[102] throughout the colonies and the aggressively autonomous and volatile behavior that, if usually latent, was sometimes exhibited by their independent populations laid the potential public servant open to insult, ingratitude, and rejection, while the competitiveness of elections and the contentiousness of public life both forced them, sometimes at the expense of their independence, to court popularity with the electorate and placed them at risk to incur the "resentment of a malicious faction."[103] In colonial British America, no less than in Britain, tracts and sermons extolling stewardship and deference should be taken for what they were: prescriptions for what some people thought should be, not descriptions of what actually was.

Indeed, throughout the course of the early eighteenth century, there seems to have been a significant devaluation of the public realm in colonial British America. Inspired by the Roman poets, especially Horace, and extolling the "Happiness of country life" and "the virtuous character of the man who courts rural solitude,"[104] the arcadian and pastoral literature of Augustan Britain struck powerful resonances in the colonies, where it was widely reprinted and imitated. By celebrating "the Virtues of a private Life"[105] with its "withdrawn felicity"[106] in some retired "rural Seat" like the one where "courtly *Horace* sung,"[107] colonial writers could at once apologize for their rusticity and their remoteness from the center of British culture, assert the superiority of their own mostly rural situations, and justify their flight from the ignominy, the turbulence, the absence of challenge, and the lack of deference in colonial public life.

William Livingston's *Philosophic Solitude*, first published in 1747 and reprinted several times thereafter, was only the most elaborate and successful of many odes on the superiority of the "rural scene," where a man, disdain-

---

[101] *Address to the Freeholders of New-Jersey*, 6.

[102] Gooch, *Charge*, 2.

[103] Cadwallader Colden, draft of a letter from George Clinton to Henry Pelham, Aug. 15, 1748, in *Colden Papers* 8:354.

[104] Maren-Sofie Røstvig, *The Happy Man: Studies in the Metamorphoses of a Classical Ideal*, 2 vols. (Oslo, 1962–71), 2:245.

[105] Smith, *General Idea of the College of Mirania*, 51.

[106] Maynard Mack, *The Garden and the City: Retirement and Politics in the Later Poetry of Pope, 1731–1743* (Toronto, 1969), 212.

[107] William Livingston, *Philosophic Solitude: A Poem* (New York, 1747), 18–19.

ing to "Pant after fame, and rush to war's alarms," could, in "obscurity and retirement" and remote from "discord, party-rage, and strife,"

> . . . live retir'd, contented, and serene,
> Forgot, unknown, unenvied, and unseen.

Like Alexander Pope at Twickenham, the "virtuous recluse"[108] celebrated by Livingston and other colonial writers deliberately "shunn'd applause," "declin'd all the Dignities" of state, and enjoyed the pleasures of a retired country life, "sail[ing] serenely along the stream of life" while improving his estate, knowledge, and character amidst the company of his family, friends, and books.[109]

Instead of glorifying the public sphere in the manner of the country ideologists, many colonial British Americans thus celebrated the felicities—and the superiority—of private life. "Esteeming the Ease and Quiet of a retired Life of Beneficence, more eligible than all the Honours of a public Station,"[110] they vastly preferred, they alleged, "to glide through the World in a private Station."[111] Joseph Addison's play *Cato* was enormously popular in the colonies, and the verses from it that were most widely quoted were those in which Cato advised honest men

> . . . to retreat betimes
> To thy paternal seat, the Sabine field,
> Where the great Censor toil'd with his own hands,
> And all our frugal ancestors were blessed
> In humble virtues, and a rural life.
> There to live retired, pray for the peace of Rome,
> Content thyself to be obscurely good.
> *"When vice prevails, and impious men bear sway,"*
> The post of honor is a private station.[112]

Such arcadianism was especially appealing to independent landowners of still mostly rural Virginia. Directly evoking the Horatian tradition, Landon

---

[108] Mack, *Garden and the City*, 233.

[109] Livingston, *Philosophic Solitude*, i, ix, 13, 17, 19; Livingston, *Funeral Eulogium*, 8; Smith, *General Idea of the College of Mirania*, 51.

[110] Thomas Barnard, *A Sermon Preached before His Excellency* (Boston, 1763), 23–24.

[111] Davies, *Religion and Public Spirit*, 6.

[112] Frederick M. Litto, "Addison's *Cato* in the Colonies," *William and Mary Quarterly*, 3d ser., 23 (1966): 442.

Carter named his family seat Sabine Hall, and George Mason, who liked to think of himself as a Catonic figure, carefully cultivated the persona of "a man who spends most of his time in retirement, and has seldom meddled in public affairs; who enjoys a modest but independent fortune, and, content with the blessings of a private station, equally disregards the smiles and favors of [the populace and] the great."[113]

If the public realm was so uninviting as to cause even prominent men and potential leaders to wonder, with an anonymous writer in 1732, "*Why should we trouble our selves about Politics?*"[114] the private sphere, as the widespread appeal of the arcadian tradition testifies, provided, by contrast, a large and attractive field for successful endeavor. From the earliest days of settlement, as I have argued elsewhere,[115] the pursuit of individual happiness had been the primary shaping social value. No other imperative was so important in determining the character of early American society or in forming American culture. As much of the new social history has revealed, moreover, for the overwhelming majority of colonial British Americans, the pursuit of happiness had always resided in the private, rather than the public, realm. Except for the orthodox Puritan colonies in New England, where, at least during much of the first two generations, the corporate impulse was strong and the public sphere relatively large, every society in colonial British America, including New England after about 1700, exhibited a basically private orientation, a powerful underlying predisposition among the members of its free population to preoccupy themselves with the pursuit of personal and family independence and the social improvements that would guarantee and enhance their individual social and economic achievements, enrich their lives, and give them a sense of personal self-worth.

Because "the greatest part" of the free population of colonial British America was, as Samuel Johnson remarked, "so intent upon their own private good, their pleasures, profits and ambitious views,"[116] public life, for them, held little appeal. So long as a man was secure in the knowledge that "the fruits of his Labour" were "his own"[117] and that, if he wanted and

---

[113] Jack P. Greene, *Landon Carter: An Inquiry into the Personal Values and Social Imperatives of the Eighteenth-Century Virginia Gentry* (Charlottesville, Va., 1967); "Character, Persona, and Authority: A Study in Alternative Styles of Political Leadership in Revolutionary Virginia," in W. Robert Higgins, ed., *The Revolution in the South: Essays in Honor of John Richard Alden* (Durham, N.C., 1979), 3–42; Howard Mumford Jones, *The Pursuit of Happiness* (Cambridge, Mass., 1953), 9.

[114] Fletcher, *Vincit Amor Patriae*, 1.

[115] See Greene, *Pursuits of Happiness*.

[116] Johnson, "Raphael," in *Samuel Johnson* 2:545.

[117] *Salus Populi* [Boston, 1728?].

thought it necessary, he could actively partake "in that Liberty that sweetens Labour"[118] and provided the ultimate bulwark against his subjection to oppression or tyranny, he could happily remain "in his private Way and Station,"[119] wasting no energy on pursuit of the "Civil Distinctions of Life" and thinking that "he hath answered the Ends of his Creation" merely by improving "his own Fortune, and" advancing "the Interest of his Family and Relations." For a man, for societies, thus circumstanced, there seemed to be little need for "large Notions of Virtue, or generous Sentiments of the publick Good."[120]

For all but a few colonial British Americans, then, the pursuit of happiness did not involve the pursuit of public office or even the active occupation of a public space, much less the diligent cultivation of what has come to be known as civic virtue. There was simply too much scope for the pursuit of individual and family goals in the private sphere for most people to be much interested in having a public career. Although the intensity of civic responsibility differed from place to place and time to time during the colonial era, the primary concerns of most independent colonists were private rather than public. Their primary allegiances were to themselves and their families rather than to the larger social and political entities to which they belonged. To quote one observer, they were mostly "too engaged in their respective occupations for the enticements" of public life.[121]

They or their ancestors had, in any case, left Britain or Europe not only to escape want and to gain independence but also, as contemporaries were fond of pointing out, to get away from the excessive public intrusions into their private lives, intrusions in the form of high taxes, rapacious civil and religious establishments, obligations for military or naval service, and war. The most popular cultural image invoked by colonial Americans was the biblical image of the industrious husbandman who sat contentedly, safely, and without want under the shade of his own vine and fig tree presiding over—and luxuriating in—the development of his family and estate. In societies that put so much emphasis upon the private sphere no wonder that the imperatives of civic virtue fell on such fallow ground or that conceptions of virtue were primarily personal and noncivic.

---

[118] Samuel Cooper, *A Sermon Preached in Boston* (Boston, 1753), 28–29.

[119] Stith, *Sermon Preached before the General Assembly*, 30.

[120] Fletcher, *Vincit Amor Patriae*, 1.

[121] François Alexandre Frédéric, Duc de La Rochefoucauld-Liancourt, *Travels through the United States of North America*, 2 vols. (London, 1799), 1:679.

If the foregoing analysis is correct, then it immediately raises the questions of when and to what extent the republican conception of civic virtue became an important concept in American public life. Was it during the debates over the Grenville and Townshend measures in the 1760s? The crisis over independence in 1774–76? Or the transition to republicanism in 1776? Because the demands for the restoration of virtue extensively exhibited during the nonimportation agreements of the late 1760s still seemed primarily to represent an appeal for moral reformation rather than for civic participation,[122] my guess would be that the crucial place to look is in 1774–76. The events and developments of those years generated an extent and intensity of public activity at all levels of government that was unprecedented in colonial history. Not even the Seven Years' War had engaged so many people, so fully, and over such a wide geographic area. By enormously increasing both the risks for public activity and the scope for fame, those same developments, moreover, also raised the stakes in—and the attractiveness and dangers of—public life and thereby may have encouraged the emergence of an ethic, even an imperative, of participation. Finally, by stimulating an enhanced, perhaps even a new, awareness of previously only faintly glimpsed implications in republican thought, the adoption of republicanism may very well have been accompanied by an emphasis upon the civic dimensions of the concept of virtue.

Even if these speculations turn out to be correct, however, there is room to doubt how central—how widespread and deep—an emerging conception of civic virtue had been to the unfolding Revolutionary movement. Of all of the thirteen new republics created in 1776, only Virginia placed the goddess *Virtus* on the new state seal and claimed virtue "as the genius of the commonwealth." But the virtue to which Virginians aspired was not the participatory, civic virtue of classical republicanism espoused, according to Pocock, by early eighteenth-century country ideologists, but the public virtue of self-control and moral rectitude that was itself the product of the private virtue of the individuals who composed that public.[123] Such a meaning is far more congruent with earlier colonial uses, with Gordon Wood's early explication of the function of the concept of virtue during the Revolution, with Lance Banning's recent redefinition of the term for postindependence Amer-

---

[122] Edmund S. Morgan, "The Puritan Ethic and the Coming of the American Revolution," in Jack P. Greene, ed., *The Reinterpretation of the American Revolution* (New York, 1968), 235–45.

[123] Jack P. Greene, "'*Virtus et Libertas*': Political Culture, Social Change, and the Origins of the American Revolution, 1763–1766," in Jeffrey J. Crow and Larry E. Tise, eds., *The Southern Experience in the American Revolution* (Chapel Hill, N.C., 1978), 55–58.

ica,[124] and, according to Joyce Appleby, with Jeffersonian Republican uses in the 1790s.[125]

What the foregoing analysis suggests, in fact, is that, notwithstanding the recent emphasis given it by the Anglo-American historical community, the significance of the concept of civic virtue in early America may have been considerably inflated. Whether or not the eighteenth century ought to be described as an age of virtue, in colonial British America at least, and perhaps also in Revolutionary America, the kind of virtue about which people were mostly concerned, a kind that was thought to be essential for representative monarchical as well as republican regimes, seems to have been the private and public virtue of self and social moral regulation. Most immediately, that conception appears to have derived directly and very largely out of the Protestant tradition and the long-standing concerns of moral philosophy, and it was manifest not just in the civic humanist but also in the several other major political traditions upon which colonial British and republican Americans drew in actively shaping political cultures appropriate to their own local circumstances.

What concepts of virtue were predominant in both colonial British and Revolutionary America is a question that needs to be studied far more closely and subtly than has been possible in this broad preliminary essay. With regard to not just virtue but all major components of eighteenth-century American social and political languages, we cannot continue blithely to assume that terms carried the precisely same meanings in the colonies that they did in Britain. The literature of colonial political and social thought may be less ample and less accessible than that for the Revolutionary and post-Revolutionary eras. But it is much more voluminous than the sparse historical literature on the subject would seem to suggest, and questions about how language and ideas were used during the long era before 1765 are susceptible to empirical investigation. To ignore such subjects is to neglect the rich interplay among language, tradition, and experience that had been going on in colonial British America for a century and a half at the time of the American Revolution.

Such neglect, moreover, may also contribute to considerable misunderstanding about the timing, nature, and significance of conceptual and behavioral change in early America as well as about the limits and potentialities,

---

[124] Lance Banning, "Some Second Thoughts on Virtue and the Course of Revolutionary Thinking," in Terence Ball and J. G. A. Pocock, eds., *Conceptual Change and the Constitution* (Lawrence, Kan., 1988), 194–212.

[125] Joyce Oldham Appleby, *Capitalism and a New Social Order: The Republican Vision of the 1790s* (New York, 1984).

the scope and direction, of the Revolution itself. In a discipline preoccupied with change, insufficient attention to continuities is an occupational hazard. But what appear to be changes when seen from the perspective of British practice very well may appear to be continuities when viewed from the vantage point of colonial American usages. Only with a much more enhanced comprehension of linguistic and conceptual norms in the several polities of colonial British America will we be able to develop a more refined appreciation of both continuities and changes during the Revolutionary era.

This essay was originally written as a paper for the Sixteenth Lawrence Henry Gipson Symposium on "Political Virtue in the Eighteenth Century" held at Lehigh University on Mar. 6, 1990. The present version was given as my inaugural lecture at the University of California, Irvine on Mar. 13, 1991, and was presented at the Early American History Seminar of the Henry E. Huntington Library, San Marino, California, on Apr. 12, 1992. It is reprinted here with permission from Richard Matthews, ed., *Virtue and Interest in the Eighteenth Century* (Bethlehem: Lehigh University Press, 1993). Portions of the second section of this essay are derived from Jack P. Greene, *The Intellectual Heritage of the Constitutional Era* (Philadelphia, 1986), 31–39, while part of the fifth section is adapted from "Introduction: The Limits of the American Revolution," in Jack P. Greene, ed., *The American Revolution: Its Character and Limits* (New York, 1987), 7–8. I wish to thank Lance Banning for his perceptive reading of the earliest draft of this essay.

TEN

All Men Are Created Equal:
Some Reflections on the Character
of the American Revolution

The great bulk of those, who were the active instruments of carrying on the revolution, were self-made, industrious men. These who by their own exertions, had established or laid a foundation for establishing personal independence, *were most generally trusted, and most successfully employed in establishing that of their country.*
David Ramsay, *The History of the American Revolution* (1789)

OVER THE PAST two centuries, most serious students of the American Revolution have tended to emphasize its revolutionary, even transforming character. David Ramsay in the late eighteenth century and George Bancroft in the mid-nineteenth century interpreted it as a giant stride toward the achievement of civil freedom and political democracy, while, among later generations, scholars such as J. Franklin Jameson emphasized the extent to which it had brought about changes that to a significant degree moved American society in "the direction of a levelling democracy."[1] During the 1950s and 1960s, years in which political revolutions, many of them characterized by violent internal conflict and comprehensive efforts at social re-

---

[1] See Jack P. Greene, ed., *The Ambiguity of the American Revolution* (New York, 1968), 2–10. The quotation is from J. Franklin Jameson, *The American Revolution Considered as a Social Movement* (Princeton, N.J., 1926), 18. I wish to thank Willie Paul Adams, Stanley Coben, Martin Diamond, H. T. Dickinson, Charles Hyneman, Thad W. Tate, and Fred Weinstein for comments or suggestions.

form, became almost routine, the American Revolution suddenly began to appear as scarcely revolutionary at all, and many scholars, including Daniel J. Boorstin, Louis Hartz, and Hannah Arendt, stressed the socially conservative nature of the Revolution, its commitment to constitutionalism, and its preoccupation with order and stability.[2]

More recently, however, there has been a strong reversion to the earlier tendency to insist upon the Revolution's radical character. Thus, both Bernard Bailyn and Gordon S. Wood have stressed the radicalism of the spirit of '76, Bailyn emphasizing the radical reconception of politics that emerged from the previous decade of intense political debate and Wood the American belief that independence would usher in a new era of freedom and bliss not only for Americans but for the whole of mankind. Bailyn argues that a basic reconception of traditional notions about the "fundamentals of government and of society's relation to government" and, more especially, the defiance of traditional order and distrust of authority contained within that reconception affected the very "essentials" of American social organization and helped permanently to transform the nature of American life.[3] The confident expectation that separation from a degenerate Britain and the institution of republican government would purge America of its moral and social impurities and thereby alter the very character of the American people by transforming them into virtuous citizens who would eschew the vices and luxuries of the Old World in favor of the simple virtues, put aside all individual concerns to seek the common good, and reconstruct their societies so that the only meaningful social distinctions would be those arising from natural differences among men—the confident belief that these utopian aspirations could be achieved, Wood contends, gave the Revolution a "socially radical character."[4]

Both Bailyn and Wood recognize, of course, that the potential radicalism of the Revolution was sharply tempered by the devotion of the men of the Revolution to the protection of private property. Almost twenty years ago, Edmund S. Morgan showed the great extent to which human rights and property rights were intertwined in Revolutionary thought,[5] and Winthrop

---

[2] See, for further discussion, Jack P. Greene, *The Reappraisal of the American Revolution in Recent Historical Literature* (Washington, D.C., 1967).

[3] Bernard Bailyn, *The Ideological Origins of the American Revolution* (Cambridge, Mass., 1967), 230, 301–2.

[4] Gordon S. Wood, *The Creation of the American Republic, 1776–1787* (Chapel Hill, N.C., 1969), esp. 68.

[5] Edmund S. Morgan, *The Birth of the Republic, 1763–89* (Chicago, 1956).

D. Jordan has illustrated how that devotion operated as "a serious and enduring impediment to compulsory abolition" of chattel slavery.[6] What has been much less appreciated, and what, I would like to suggest here, served just as powerfully to limit the quality and extent of sociopolitical change during the Revolution was the deep and abiding commitment of the Revolutionary generation to political inequality.

Perhaps no single phrase from the Revolutionary era has had such continuing importance in American public life as the dictum "all men are created equal" in the Declaration of Independence.[7] For each generation, it has served as an imposing reminder of what Americans might achieve and as a standard against which they could measure how far they had to go. Just what it meant to its author, Thomas Jefferson, and his contemporaries has been a perennial subject for debate within the American historical community. What precisely could such a phrase have meant in a society so riddled by inequalities as early America?[8] For contemporaries, the meaning of the word *equal* was itself quite unequivocal. It meant, according to Dr. Samuel Johnson, being "upon the same terms," "not inferior or superior."[9] But how could such a definition be applied to all men? Perhaps it could be said that all men were equal in the sense that they were all mortal, that they all had to die,[10] or, with the Levellers and Real Whigs in Britain, that all men were equal

[6] Winthrop D. Jordan, *White over Black: American Attitudes toward the Negro, 1550–1812* (Chapel Hill, N.C., 1969), 350.

[7] The Declaration of Independence can be found in Jack P. Greene, ed., *Colonies to Nation, 1763–1789: A Documentary History of the American Revolution* (New York, 1975), 298–301.

[8] That the form of equality Jefferson and his colleagues had chiefly in mind was equality "between Americans and Englishmen as subjects of the same empire" has been persuasively argued by David S. Lovejoy, "'Rights Imply Equality': The Case against Admiralty Jurisdiction in America, 1764–1776," *William and Mary Quarterly*, 3d ser., 16 (1959): 459–84. This argument has been recently seconded by J. R. Pole, "Loyalists, Whigs, and the Idea of Equality," in Esmond Wright, ed., *A Tug of Loyalties: Anglo-American Relations, 1765–85* (London, 1975), 66–92. But the term obviously had far wider implications, the best discussions of which will be found in Wood, *Creation of the American Republic*, 70–75, and Willie Paul Adams, *Republikanische Verfassang und bürgerliche Freiheit: Die Verfassungen und politischen Ideen der amerikanischen Revolution* (Darmstadt and Newwied, 1973), 162–90.

[9] Samuel Johnson, *A Dictionary of the English Language*, 2 vols. (London, 1755).

[10] This seems to have been the implication of George Mason's comment in April 1775 that "we came equals into this world, and equals we shall go out of it," in his Remarks on Annual Elections of the Fairfax Independent Company in *The Papers of George Mason*, ed. Robert A. Rutland, 3 vols. (Chapel Hill, N.C., 1970), 1:229.

before God, that he had created them "spiritually equal" in "the sense that" he had endowed each of them with the capacity "of knowing the dictates of virtue and of conducting themselves in accordance with those dictates."[11]

What the phrase clearly could not mean was that all men were equal by nature. One man differed "by nature" from another, John Adams wrote, "almost as much as man from beast." "By the law of nature," he said, "all men are men, and not angels—men, and not lions—men, and not whales— men, and not eagles—that is, they are all of the same species; and this is the most that . . . equality of nature amounts to."[12] The ideas "that the whole human race is born equal, and that no man is naturally inferior," snorted Jonathan Boucher, the conservative Anglican cleric from Maryland, were "equally ill-founded and false both in their . . . premises and conclusions."[13] "If this subject is considered even for a moment," wrote Edward Christian, professor of law in Cambridge, in his revision of Sir William Blackstone's influential *Commentaries on the Laws of England*, "the very reverse will appear to be the truth": "that all men are by nature unequal. For though children come into the world equally helpless, yet in a few years, as soon as their bodies acquire vigour, and their minds and passions are expanded and developed, we percieve an infinite difference in their natural powers, capacities, and propensities; and this inequality is still further increased by the instruction they happen to receive."[14] "The Notion of Levelism," William Cooper, a Congregational clergyman, had told his Massachusetts listeners in 1740, "had little Foundation in Nature."[15] No one could successfully argue, said Noah Webster, the articulate exponent of a distinctively American language, that men had been "endowed by the Creator" with "equal force of

---

[11] See Sanford A. Lakoff, *Equality in Political Philosophy* (Cambridge, Mass., 1964), 62– 63; Caroline Robbins, *The Eighteenth-Century Commonwealthman: Studies in the Transmission, Development, and Circumstances of English Liberal Thought from the Restoration of Charles II until the War with the Thirteen Colonies* (Cambridge, Mass., 1959), 16.

[12] John Adams to Thomas Brand-Hollis, June 11, 1790, and to ——, Feb. 4, 1794, *The Works of John Adams*, ed. Charles Francis Adams, 10 vols. (Boston, 1856), 1:462, 9:570.

[13] Jonathan Boucher, Discourse 11, "On Civil Liberty, Passive Obedience, and Nonresistance," [1775], in *A View of the Causes and Consequences of the American Revolution* (London, 1797), 514–16.

[14] Sir William Blackstone, *Commentaries on the Laws of England*, 2 vols., 12th ed. (London, 1793), 1:407. On Blackstone's influence among Americans, see Gerald Stourzh, "William Blackstone: Teacher of Revolution," *Jahrbüch fur Amerikastudien* (Heidelberg, 1970), 184– 200.

[15] William Cooper, *The Honours of Christ Demanded of the Magistrate* (Boston, 1740), 6–7, as quoted by Cecelia M. Kenyon, "The Declaration of Independence," *Fundamental Testaments of the American Revolution* (Washington, D.C., 1973), 31.

constitution, or physical strength," or "intellectual powers."[16] "When we say, that all men are [created] equal," wrote the Pennsylvania lawyer and legal theorist James Wilson just after the Revolution, "we mean not to apply this equality to their virtues, their talents, their dispositions, or their acquirements. In all these respects, there is, and it is fit for the great purposes of society that there should be, great inequality among men."[17] "Even the most radical [American] republicans in 1776," Wood tells us, "admitted the inevitability," even the utility, "of . . . natural distinctions: weak and strong, wise and foolish," and a host of others.[18]

Nor could a case be made for equality of social condition. Americans might not have had anywhere near the same extremes of wealth and poverty or the hereditary privileges and exclusions that characterized most Old World societies. "At present," said Eudoxus in the *Pennsylvania Packet* in April 1776, "there seems to be one order of people among us": there was no "set of *Barons* [who] have from time *immemorial*, claimed *prerogatives* utterly incompatible with *common liberty*."[19] But if, in comparison with Europeans, Americans still lived "so near to the state of original equality," as Dr. Joseph Warren of Boston boasted in 1766,[20] they clearly did not, as Benjamin Rush pointed out in 1777, enjoy a state of "perfect equality, and an equal distribution of property . . . among the inhabitants."[21] In "a new country" such as America, said the Vermont historian Samuel Williams in 1794, "the nearest equality will take place, that can ever subsist among men. . . . But nothing ever did, or ever can produce an equality of power, capacity, and advantages, in the social or in any other state of man. By making men very unequal in their powers and capacities, nature has effectually prevented this."[22] "Superior degrees of industry and capacity," declared an anonymous writer in the *Pennsylvania Journal* in 1777, had inevitably "in-

---

[16] Noah Webster, "That Intelligence and Virtue Are the Basis of a Republican Government," in *A Collection of Papers on Political, Literary, and Moral Subjects* (Philadelphia, 1837), 269–74. My attention was called to this reference by Charles Hyneman.

[17] James Wilson, "Lectures on Law," in *The Works of James Wilson*, ed. Robert Green McCloskey, 2 vols. (Cambridge, Mass., 1967), 1:240.

[18] Wood, *Creation of the American Republic*, 72.

[19] *Pennsylvania Packet* (Philadelphia), Apr. 22, 1776.

[20] Joseph Warren to Edmund Dana, Mar. 19, 1776, in Richard Frothingham, *The Life and Times of Joseph Warren* (Boston, 1865), 20–21, as quoted by Adams, *Republikanische Verfassung*, 168.

[21] Benjamin Rush, "Observations upon the Present Government of Pennsylvania . . . ," 1777, in Greene, *Colonies to Nation*, 359.

[22] Samuel Williams, *The Natural and Civil History of Vermont*, 2 vols. (Walpole, N.H., 1794), 2:328–29.

troduced inequality of property among us, and these have introduced . . . distinctions of rank . . . as certain and general as the artificial distinction of men in Europe."[23] "If 'Equality is the soul of a republic,'" asked the New Hampshire historian Jeremy Belknap in 1784, "Where, then, is our soul? Do not our . . . practical principles . . . all tend to inequality? . . . Where shall we look for an equal division of property? Not in the five southern States, where every white man is the lordly tyrant of an hundred slaves. Not in the great trading towns and cities, where cash in funds yields 13 or 16 per cent, and in trade much more." Not even among the "yeomanry of New England," who were "as mean and selfish as any other people, and have as strong a lurch for territory as merchants have for cash." Not "all the systems of metaphysics and bills of rights in the world," Belknap concluded, could "prevent one man from being stronger, or wiser, or richer than another." The "strong [would] always subdue the weak, the wise circumvent the ignorant, the 'borrower be servant to the lender.'" There would always be, in America as well as everywhere else, "a superiority and an inferiority."[24] Three years later, John Adams made the same point far more succinctly in his rhetorical question: "Was there, or will there ever be, a nation, whose individuals were all equal, in natural and acquired qualities, in virtues, talents and riches?"[25]

A stronger case can be made that when Americans spoke of equality they were talking about equality of opportunity, claiming, as the Reverend Francis Alison told his Presbyterian congregation in the 1760s, the equal right of all men "to reap the benefit of honest industry."[26] But this kind of opportunity, as Wood has pointed out, "implied social differences and distinctions."[27] In James Harrington's aphorism, "INDUSTRY of all things is the most accumulative, and accumulation of all things hates leveling";[28] and, as John Adams declared, Americans were perhaps "more Avaricious [that is, more accumulative] than any other Nation that ever existed the Carthagini-

[23] *Pennsylvania Journal*, May 28, 1777, as quoted by Adams, *Republikanische Verfassung*, 162.

[24] Jeremy Belknap to Ebenezer Hazard, Mar. 3, 1784, in *Belknap Papers*, Massachusetts Historical Society, Collections, 5th ser., 2 (Boston, 1877), 312–15.

[25] John Adams, *Defence of the Constitutions*, in *Works of Adams* 4:391–92.

[26] Francis Alison, "Of the Rights of the Supreme Power and the Methods of Acquiring it," 1760s, Alison Sermons, folder 5, no. vi, Presbyterian Historical Society, Philadelphia, as quoted by J. R. Pole, *Political Representation in England and the Origins of the American Republic* (London, 1966), 269.

[27] Wood, *Creation of the American Republic*, 70.

[28] James Harrington, "A System of Politics," in *The Oceana and Other Works of James Harrington* (London, 1977), 471.

ans and Dutch not excepted. The *Alieni appetens sui profusus* reigns in this nation as a Body more than any other I have ever seen."[29] Americans, said a South Carolinian on the eve of the Revolution, were in "one continued Race: in which everyone is endeavouring to distance all behind him; and to overtake or pass by, all before him; everyone is flying from his inferiors in Pursuit of his Superiors, who fly from him, with an equal Alacrity."[30] As Samuel Williams testified in 1794, Americans "all see that nature has made them very unequal in respect to their original powers, capacities, and talents," and they "become united . . . in availing themselves of the benefits, which are designed, and may be derived from the inequality, which nature . . . established."[31] Americans, in other words, agreed to employ any advantages that nature or chance had bestowed upon them in the race for social inequality, and that agreement, Williams suggested, acted as a powerful— could it have been the single most powerful?—social cement. There was, after all, obviously no point in treating those "inequalities which *necessarily* [and naturally] spring up among us [as] . . . disadvantages."[32]

Equality of opportunity thus meant to the Revolutionary generation the preservation of the individual's equal right to acquire as much as he could, to achieve the best life possible within the limits of his ability, means, and circumstances. Every man was to have an equal opportunity to become less equal. As J. R. Pole has remarked, a society based upon such a belief, like Harrington's ideal commonwealth *Oceana*, "could not only tolerate great economic inequalities, but require[d] them as a safeguard for propertied interests."[33] Radical republicans in Pennsylvania might propose—unsuccessfully—in 1776 to include a clause in the state constitution declaring "That an enormous Proportion of Property vested in a few Individuals is dangerous to the Rights, and destructive of the Common Happiness of Mankind; and therefore every free State hath a Right by its Laws to discourage the Possession of such Property."[34] But with property beyond the reach of few able-bodied and enterprising free men in what one contemporary observer, referring to the whole Anglo-American world, called this "Age of Reten-

---

[29] John Adams to Benjamin Rush, Apr. 4, 1790, in Alexander Biddle, ed., *Old Family Letters* (Philadelphia, 1892), 56–57.

[30] *South Carolina Gazette* (Charleston), Mar. 1, 1773, as quoted by Carl Bridenbaugh, *Myths and Realities: Societies of the Colonial South* (Baton Rouge, La., 1952), 115.

[31] Williams, *History of Vermont* 2:330.

[32] Jeremy Belknap to Ebenezer Hazard, Mar. 3, 1784, *Belknap Papers* 2:315.

[33] Pole, *Political Representation*, 9.

[34] *An Essay of a Declaration of Rights* (Philadelphia, 1776), as quoted by Eric Foner, *Tom Paine and Revolutionary America* (New York, 1976), 133.

tion,"[35] the kind of resentment and suspicion of the wealthy that underlay such a proposal could neither run deep nor exhibit much staying power. However egalitarian their society might appear to be to outsiders, Americans had always, as Benjamin Franklin had underscored for his British readers in the late 1750s in defending the New England colonies against charges that they were infused with "*a levelling spirit*," taken as great pains as the British to ensure the security of property.[36] Americans, said the English radical John Thelwall, had "too much veneration for property" and were too fond of "respecting mankind in proportion to their property" ever to be social levelers.[37]

Thus, although the Revolution generated a widespread examination of the social ramifications of the general concept of equality and even converted a few to the ideal of equality as social leveling—an ideal that has often resurfaced in American political life during times of economic and social distress over the past two centuries—the commitment to equality of opportunity and the admiration, suggested by the previously quoted remarks of Thelwall, for those people who had successfully taken advantage of that opportunity perforce meant that equality could not be widely regarded in America as implying "the equalization of property, or the invasion of personal rights of possession." For Americans, as for members of the Manchester Constitutional Society in 1792, "the EQUALITY to be contended for" was emphatically not "an *equality of wealth and possessions*."[38]

"True liberty," Edward Christian told Americans, "results from making every higher degree accessible to those who are in a lower, if virtue and talents are there found to deserve advancement." "The son of the lowest peasant" ought to be able to "rise by his merit and abilities to the head of the church, law, army, navy, and every department of state. The doctrine, that all men are, or ought, to be equal, is little less contrary to nature, and destructive of their happiness, than the invention of Procrustes, who attempted to make men equal by stretching the limbs of some, and lopping off those of others."[39]

Equality of opportunity thus was "not directly conceived of by Americans in 1776 . . . as a social levelling."[40] Of course, equality of opportunity

[35] *State of the British and French Colonies in North America* (London, 1755), 67.

[36] Benjamin Franklin to *London Chronicle*, May 9, 1759, *The Papers of Benjamin Franklin*, ed. Leonard W. Labaree et al., 27 vols., to date (New Haven, 1959—), 8:341–42.

[37] As quoted by Foner, *Tom Paine*, 230.

[38] As quoted ibid., 226–27.

[39] Blackstone, *Commentaries*, 12th ed., 1:408.

[40] Wood, *Creation of the American Republic*, 70.

required that no legal impediments be placed in the way of individuals, and the American hostility to the special legal, economic, social, and political privileges and exemptions that sustained the legally privileged orders of Europe was revealed in the constitutional prohibitions of monopolies, titles of nobility, and hereditary honors adopted by several states. Such privileges, said the Maryland constitution of 1776, were "contrary to the spirit of a free government, and the principles of commerce"[41] because, as the Massachusetts constitution of 1780 said, "No man, nor corporation, or association of men have any other title to obtain advantages, or particular and exclusive privileges, distinct from those of the community, than what arises from the consideration of services rendered to the public."[42] It was to be hoped, said a Virginian in 1776, that there would be no "subordination *besides* that which arises from the differences of capacity, disposition, and virtue."[43] Social, economic, and political distinctions were to be "fairly earned," the legitimate fruits of superior industry, talent, and virtue.[44] Political office, social status, economic benefits—all were to be equally accessible.

But accessible to whom? To answer this question one must examine still another—and much more prevalent—meaning applied to the concept of equality by the men of the Revolution—the idea that all men were "equal in respect to their rights; or rather that nature has given to them a common and an equal right to liberty, to property, and to safety; to justice, government, laws, religion, and freedom."[45] But the problem with this meaning of equality, as Edward Christian condescendingly pointed out, was that it was "an insignificant self-evident truth, which no one ever denied," and which amounted "to nothing more than to the identical proposition, that all men have equal rights to their rights; for when different men have perfect and absolute rights to unequal things, they are certainly equal with regard to the perfection of their rights, or the justice that is due to their respective claims."

---

[41] Francis Newton Thorpe, ed., *The Federal and State Constitutions, Colonial Charters, and Other Organic Laws*, 7 vols. (Washington, D. C., 1909), 3:1690.

[42] Ibid., 1890.

[43] Democratitus, "Loose Thoughts on Government," June 7, 1776, in Peter Force, ed., *American Archives* (Washington, D.C., 1837–53), 4th ser., 6:730–31.

[44] Wood, *Creation of the American Republic*, 70–73.

[45] Williams, *History of Vermont* 2:330. See also "The Essex Result," in Oscar and Mary Handlin, eds., *The Popular Sources of Political Authority: Documents on the Massachusetts Constitution of 1780* (Cambridge, Mass, 1966), 330; Wilson, "Lectures on Laws," in *Works of Wilson* 1:241; and Democratitus, "Loose Thoughts on Government," June 7, 1776, Force, *American Archives*, 4th ser., 6:730–31.

This, Christian argued, "is the only sense in which equality can be applied to mankind. In the most perfect republic," he emphasized, "unequal industry and virtues of men must necessarily create unequal rights" and various categories of people must therefore "be eternally unequal, and have unequal rights."[46]

Richard Bland, the Virginia lawyer and antiquary, made much the same point in 1766 in attacking the Stamp Act when he wrote that *"rights* imply *equality*, in the instances to which they belong and must be treated without respect to the dignity of the persons concerned in them."[47] Bernard Bailyn has suggested that Bland's statement carried an "emphasis upon social equivalence."[48] But it does precisely the opposite: it stresses, with Christian, the equivalence only of those who were entitled to similar rights and the inequivalence of those people who were not "concerned in" those rights. Thus, all men were not entitled to "equal liberty and equal privileges" in political society but only those who possessed the right to such equality. What we need to know, then, in order to determine how far the American commitment to equal political rights extended, is precisely what groups were entitled to those rights. "A popular government," as one Pennsylvania writer put it, might hold out the promise of "equal liberty and equal privileges" to "its citizens"—but who were, and were not, deemed citizens?[49]

A citizen, Dr. Johnson tells us, was "a freeman" of the polity, "not a foreigner; not a slave," while a freeman was "one not a slave, not a vassal" who partook of the "rights, privileges, or immunities" of the polity. As the most basic right in Anglo-American society, the right to vote—"in other words," said Dr. Johnson, "the rights of a citizen"—may be taken as the essential index to citizenship, to full membership in the polity, and to the legitimate claim to equal political rights.[50] An anaylsis of earlier English and colonial practices with regard to the suffrage, as well as of contemporary thought and the franchise provisions adopted by the new state governments during the Revolutionary era, should, therefore, provide us with a clear

---

[46] Blackstone, *Commentaries*, 12th ed., 1:407.

[47] Richard Bland, *An Inquiry into the Rights of the British Colonies* (Williamsburg, Va., 1766), in Greene, *Colonies to Nation*, 91.

[48] Bailyn, *Ideological Origins*, 307.

[49] As quoted by Wood, *Creation of the Republic*, 401.

[50] Johnson, *Dictionary*; Johnson quotes Sir Walter Raleigh: "All inhabitants within these walls are not properly *citizens*, but only such as are called freemen." See also Thomas Jefferson to Edmund Pendleton, Aug. 26, 1776, in *The Papers of Thomas Jefferson*, ed. Julian P. Boyd et al., 21 vols. to date (Princeton, 1950—), 1:504.

sense of how limited the American commitment to equal political rights actually was during the Revolutionary era and of the logic that lay behind those limitations.

Theoretically, as is well known, the English franchise was tied closely to the ownership of land. For the counties the basis of the franchise was a statute of 1430 which limited the suffrage to men who "shall have freehold to the value of forty shillings by the year within the county"[51] which was clear of all charges and deductions, except parliamentary and parochial taxes. Subsequent statutes prohibited voting by minors and perjurors. A freehold was usually land, but certain medieval incorporeal hereditaments such as annuities and rents issuing out of a freehold estate and life-tenure offices in the church, states, and courts could also be "freeholds which gave the franchise." But the county franchise excluded all but real property owners, and "it did not include all landowners—copyholders and tenants for terms of years were excluded."[52] Borough franchises varied enormously. Property either in the form of taxable possessions or in membership in the borough corporation was required in just over half of the boroughs, although in some of these the payment of scot—local taxes—and bearing of lot—the obligation to fill local offices—were sufficient to make adult males eligible to vote. The remaining boroughs—nearly 47 percent of the total—were freemen boroughs in which the franchise often extended beyond the "economically independent" adults to include "a large majority of all [male] householders" and even, in a few cases, all adult males. In the pot-walloper boroughs every male adult who had a hearth of his own to boil a pot on was eligible.[53]

As Richard L. Bushman and Derek Hirst have recently argued, there was a significant movement within the political nation under the early Stuarts to extend the franchise in both counties and boroughs. On the theory that a larger electorate would be more difficult to corrupt, the House of Commons, in decisions on disputed elections after 1604, had consistently found in favor of a broader franchise. The forty-shilling freehold qualification for the coun-

---

[51] Blackstone, *Commentaries*, 6th ed. (London, 1774), 1:172.

[52] Sir William Holdsworth, *A History of English Law*, 13 vols. (London, 1922–66), 10:554–57. Copyholders were explicitly excluded by 10 Anne c. 23 and 31 George II c. 14 (John Cannon, *Parliamentary Reform, 1640–1832* [Cambridge, 1973], 87n).

[53] Holdsworth, *History of English Law* 10:559–69, Pole, *Political Representation*, 400; Cannon, *Parliamentary Reform*, 29; Derek Hirst, *The Representative of the People?: Voters and Voting in England under the Early Stuarts* (Cambridge, 1975), 22, 90–105.

ties, Hirst has shown, "was by no means a rigorous or even particularly meaningful requirement" before the Civil War, and "politicians both locally and in the House of Commons displayed great readiness to allow more and more people in to vote in the towns."[54] However, sobered by "the glimpse of anarchy" they had received during the 1640s and 1650s and fearful of their position, the upper classes after 1647 moved steadily to restrict the political nation. Indeed, under Cromwell the property qualifications actually became far more severe, an act of 1653 restricting the county franchise to "all and every person and persons seized or possessed to his own use of any estates, real or personal, to the value of £200 [sterling]." Although these requirements were not continued after the Restoration, the movement persisted "towards the elimination of the unqualified, and a tighter control of those who were left, whose numbers were [in any case] being [slowly] diminished by economic and political change." At no time during the next century was there a serious attempt to extend the franchise. After 1688, John Cannon has found, the House of Commons tended increasingly "to find in favor of the narrow franchise—that is for corporations against the commonality and for scot and lot payers against the inhabitants at large."[55]

As many scholars—from Albert E. McKinley in 1905 to Chilton Williamson and J. R. Pole in the 1960s—have revealed, property requirements for the suffrage were, after the first few decades of settlement, just as pervasive all over colonial America.[56] The metropolitan government preferred that the English county franchise requirements be implemented in the colonies, but the precise requirements differed from one colony to the next. Only seven colonies actually required voters to own freehold property. The requirements varied from a freehold of a specific worth (£40 to £50) to one of a specified number of acres (usually with a smaller amount of improved land) to one producing a certain amount of annual income (such as 40s. in the English fashion). In six colonies there were legal alternatives to a free-

---

[54] Richard L. Bushman, "English Franchise Reform in the Seventeenth Century," *Journal of British Studies* 3 (1963): 36–56; Hirst, *Representative of the People*, 7, 65, 81–82, 232–36.

[55] Pole, *Political Representation*, 7; Hirst, *Representative of the People*, 25; Cannon, *Parliamentary Reform*, 12, 17–19, 23–25, 33–34, 41–42; Bushman, "English Franchise Reform," 55–56.

[56] See, esp., Albert E. McKinley, *The Suffrage Franchise in the Thirteen English Colonies in America* (Philadelphia, 1905); Chilton Williamson, *American Suffrage: From Property to Democracy, 1760–1860* (Princeton, N.J., 1960); and Pole, *Political Representation*. See Bushman, "English Franchise Reform," 36–37, for a discussion of the liberal franchise in early Virginia. T. H. Breen, "Who Governs: The Town Franchise in Seventeenth-Century Massachusetts," *William and Mary Quarterly*, 3d ser., 27 (1970): 460–74, lists the many other works on and contributes to the animated discussion on the franchise in early Massachusetts.

hold possession in the form of "a property (real and/or personal) or a tax-paying qualification." The usual formula was the possession of a clear estate or net worth of from £40 to £50. South Carolina, alone, permitted men to vote simply on the basis of payment of an annual tax of 20 shillings. Finally, two colonies—New York and Virginia—extended English practice, by designating as freeholders tenants, though, significantly, only those "who held leases for an indefinite number of years."[57] These alternatives to a freehold franchise represent, in Pole's words, "some attempt to set up a standard applicable to local conditions"[58] and, more specifically, the growing importance of personal property and commercial wealth—as opposed to real property—in the market-oriented societies of colonial British America. Borough franchises were governed by special laws, but they invariably carried a property qualification.[59]

Part of the logic behind these property requirements for voting was spelled out with great clarity by the Virginia legislature when it prefaced a law of 1670 with the statement that the "laws of England grant a voice in such election only to such as by their estates real or personal have interest enough to tie them to the endeavours of the public good."[60] Just as it was widely assumed in English and colonial law that membership in a corporation should be restricted to those with a full legal share, so citizenship in a polity—as symbolized by the right to vote—should be limited to those with a permanent attachment in the form of property. The same idea lay behind the inclusion of a residence requirement (including generally a specific period of time of from six months to two years) in nine of the thirteen colonies.[61]

But the lack of sufficient property—of a significant "stake in society"—was not the only—or even, perhaps, the most important—criterion for exclusion from the franchise. In both Britain and the colonies, whole categories of people were denied the franchise whether or not they met prevailing property stipulations. The largest group, by far, were women. In Britain and the colonies women lost their legal personality when they married, or rather, their personalities were absorbed by their husbands, who thenceforth exercised absolute responsibility for and full authority over them and their

[57] Williamson, *American Suffrage*, 12–15.

[58] Pole, *Political Representation*, 47–48.

[59] Cortlandt F. Bishop, *History of Elections in the American Colonies* (New York, 1893), 86, 90; Williamson, *American Suffrage*, 14–18.

[60] W. W. Hening, ed., *The Statutes at Large*, 13 vols. (Richmond, etc., 1809–23), 2:280, as quoted by Pole, *Political Representation*, 138.

[61] Williamson, *American Suffrage*, 15.

property. If married women were thus deprived of the property requisite for citizenship, unmarried women, including widows who easily met these property requirements, were deprived of the franchise by deeply rooted and pervasive custom. Although a few such women may have voted from time to time, they were exceptions who proved the rule. So deep did the tradition of female exclusion run that only four colonies bothered to include specific exclusions in their franchise laws. A similar situation obtained with males who had not reached their majority, which was commonly set at the age of twenty-one. Many youths below that age did not yet own property, of course, and those who did were mostly orphans whose holdings were still under the control of guardians. A minority of the colonies—six—stipulated a minimum voting age (twenty-one), in all probability a reflection of the strength of customary prohibitions as in the case of women.[62]

Other categories of people who were denied the franchise in the colonies were nonnaturalized aliens and members of non-Protestant groups. In excluding aliens, the colonies were again following deeply rooted English practice which restricted the legal rights of aliens in a large number of areas. The same was true of Catholics and Jews but not (except for brief periods in a few colonies) of Protestant Dissenters, all three groups of which were excluded from voting in eighteenth-century England. Again, the force of metropolitan custom made it unnecessary for the colonies to adopt specific exclusionary clauses, and only one colony (Pennsylvania) explicitly barred aliens; five colonies barred Catholics; and four, Jews.[63]

The one instance of exclusion in the colonies for which there was not a clear precedent in Britain was that of freedmen of partial African or Amerindian descent. The colonies from Virginia south through Georgia either

---

[62] See Linda Grant De Pauw, "Land of the Unfree: Legal Limitations on Liberty in Pre-Revolutionary America," *Maryland Historical Magazine* 68 (1973): 355–68. The attitude toward women and children was set forth by Anthony Ashley Cooper, third earl of Shaftesbury: "every *pater-familias*, or housekeeper is a natural prince, and is invested with an absolute power over his family, and has, by necessary consequence, the votes of all his family, man, woman, and child, included in his" ("Some Observations concerning the regulating of Elections for Parliament . . . ," [1679], in J. Somers, *A Collection of Scarce and Valuable Tracts*, 2d ed., 13 vols. [London, 1812], 5: 401). See also [James Tyrrell], *Patriarcha Non Monarcha* (London, 1681), 83, 109, especially his remark that "the Fathers of Families . . . were really and indeed all the People that needed to have Votes; since Women, as being concluded by their Husbands, . . . and Children in their Fathers Families being under the notion of Servants, and without any Property . . . had no reason to have Votes," and Mary R. Beard, *Woman as a Force in History* (New York, 1947), 77–144, 95–204, for a discussion of the position of women in English common law theory and the reception of that theory in America.

[63] Williamson, *American Suffrage*, 15–16.

specifically denied the franchise to free Negroes, mulattoes, and Indians or pointedly limited it to "whites." In trying to attract freedmen to Georgia, the legislature of that colony in 1765 promised them "all the Rights, Privileges, Powers and Immunities whatsoever which any persons born of British parents" could have—except the essential badge of citizenship: the right to vote and hold office. From Maryland north, these groups, like women and minors, were apparently excluded by custom rather than by positive legal stipulations. Only Jamaica of all British colonies legally extended the suffrage to freedmen of African descent—either in individual cases through private bills or as a group for those who were at least three degrees removed from African ancestry—policies Winthrop D. Jordan correctly interprets as desperation measures to add to an increasingly numerically inferior white population by "whitening" a few people of color.[64]

Women, minors, aliens, Catholics, Jews, nonwhites—these were all categories of people that could not be excluded on the grounds of property requirements alone or by the stake-in-society argument. Like slaves, servants, short-term tenants, the poor and the indigent, and even sons over twenty-one still living with their parents or on their parents' land (in Rhode Island alone, apparently, the eldest son of a freeholder was allowed the vote),[65] most married women and most minors could be denied citizenship on these grounds, but for unmarried women and any other members of these groups who may have met the property requirements, the grounds for denial had to lie elsewhere.

What precisely these grounds were, and what, in fact, seems to have been the most fundamental consideration in defining the boundaries of citizenship, may be surmised from an analysis of British legal and political theorists of the seventeenth and eighteenth centuries. During the English Revolution, some Levellers, following out the logic of "several decades of intermittent agitation for a wider parliamentary franchise," argued for the extension of the franchise to "the poorest that lives."[66] But it was not the Levellers but

[64] Jordan, *White over Black*, 126–27, 169, 176.

[65] Williamson, *American Suffrage*, 15.

[66] C. B. MacPherson, *The Political Theory of Possessive Individualism* (Oxford, 1962), 107–59, has mounted a powerful argument that the Levellers meant to exclude servants, almstakers, and even wage laborers from the franchise. But later writers have shown that the Levellers did not have a monolithic position on the franchise and that some of them, notably John Lilburn, Thomas Rainborough, and John Wildman, seem to have been arguing for

Cromwell's commissary general, Henry Ireton, arguing against them at the Putney Debates, who stated what would thenceforth be the dominant position. There ought, Ireton contended, to be two tests for the suffrage: first, and most familiar, "a permanent fixed interest in this kingdom," by which he meant specifically "the persons in whom all the land lies, and those in corporations in whom all trading lies," and, second, and not merely correlatively, personal independence. "If there be anything at all that is the foundation of liberty," Ireton declared, "it is this, that those who shall choose the law-makers shall be men"—and this is the crucial clause—"freed from dependence upon others."[67] Not property per se, Ireton was saying, but the personal independence property conferred was the most essential component of liberty and the sine qua non of citizenship. John Locke subscribed to precisely the same view later in the century when he suggested that citizens—those who deserved to exercise full political rights—had to be in "a *State of perfect Freedom* to order their Actions, and dispose of their Possessions, and Persons as they think fit . . . without asking leave, or depending upon the Will of any other Man." By definition, men "subjected to the Will or Authority of any other Man" could not be full participants in civil society.[68]

Following the Putney Debates, few people of any political persuasion challenged this view during either the seventeenth or the eighteenth century. A few people casually advocated changes in the suffrage. Thus, Shaftesbury in the 1670s and David Hume in the 1740s called for an increase in property requirements to disfranchise the many people "amongst the electing crowd"—that "undistinguishing rabble," said Hume, who, because they were men of "a mean and abject fortune," could scarcely be expected to exercise an independent vote.[69] Some others favored enlarging the franchise.

---

universal adult male suffrage. See J. C. Davis, "The Levellers and Democracy," *Past and Present*, no. 40 (1968): 174–80; David E. Brewster and Roger Howell, Jr., "Reconsidering the Levellers: The Evidence of *The Moderate*," ibid., 46 (1970): 68–79; Keith Thomas, "The Levellers and the Franchise," in G. E. Aylmer, ed., *The Interregnum: The Quest for Settlement, 1646–1660* (London, 1972), 57–78; and Cannon, *Parliamentary Reform*, 7–10. The quotations are from Thomas, "The Levellers and the Franchise," 63, and John Lilburne, *The Charters of London; or The Second Part of London's Liberty in Chaines Discovered* (London, 1646), 4.

[67] "The Putney Debates," Oct. 29, 1647, in A. S. P. Woodhouse, ed., *Puritanism and Liberty* (London, 1938), 54, 78, 82.

[68] John Locke, *Two Treatises of Government*, ed. Peter Laslett (Cambridge, 1960), 287, 322.

[69] See Shaftesbury, "Some Observations . . . ," [1679] in Somers, *A Collection of Tracts*, 396–98, 400; David Hume, "Idea of a Perfect Commonwealth," *Political Discourses* (Edinburgh, 1752), 295, 300.

One anonymous writer thought it "Very Unreasonable that a Copyholder of 2 or 3 hundreds £ per Annum" or "a Merchant Or Other Monied Man worth 50, 40, 30, 20, or so Thousand £ . . . should be debarred Voteing" and "a Poore freeholder of 40 shillings a Year . . . Admitted."[70] Similarly, Robert Molesworth in 1723 suggested that it was absurd that a small free-hold "worth barely forty Shillings *per Annum*" should give "a Title to choose a Representative in Parliament; when a large and beneficial Lease for a Term of Years, sets the Lessee only upon the Foot of one of the *Nomine censi* among the *Romans*, who had no Suffrage, nor any part in the Government of the Commonwealth."[71] Regulus, writing in the *Political Register* in 1768, wanted to extend the vote to "every substantial *housekeeper* who paid a tax for eight windows," while James Burgh in 1774 argued that "every person who pays tax, ought to have a vote."[72] As C. B. MacPherson has demonstrated, even the most radical thinkers—the Levellers, after Putney, and James Har-rington—were, in contending for the extension of the suffrage to all free men, endorsing the conventional view that independence was the prerequi-site for citizenship by themselves excluding, in Maximilian Petty's words, "apprentices, or servants, or those that take alms": that is, all adult males who, because they "depend[ed] upon the will of other men and should be afraid to displease [them]" were obviously not fully free.[73] Not until John Wilkes in language redolent of some of the early Levellers hinted in 1776 that the "meanest mechanic, the poorest peasant and the day-labourer" should have "some share . . . in the power of making those laws, which deeply interest them, and to which they are expected to pay obedience" does anyone seem to have risen to challenge this orthodoxy.[74] On the eve of the American

---

[70] Marginalia in British Museum copy of [Daniel Defoe], *The Original Power of the Collec-tive Body of the People of England, Examined and Asserted* (London, 1702), 18–19.

[71] Robert Molesworth, *Some Considerations for the Promoting of Agriculture and Employing the Poor* (Dublin, 1723), 43–44.

[72] Regulus, "View of the Present State of Public Affairs," *Political Register* 2 (1768): 222, 225–26; James Burgh, *Political Disquisitions*, 3 vols. (London, 1774–75), 1:39.

[73] MacPherson, *Political Theory of Possessive Individualism*, 120–36, 181. See also Thomas, "Levellers and the Franchise," 66–77; Lakoff, *Equality in Political Philosophy*, 67–68; Har-rington, "Oceana" and "The Art of Law-giving," in *Works of Harrington*, 77, 409. On Harrington's emphasis upon the relationship between independence and citizenship, see J. G. A. Pocock, "Machiavelli, Harrington, and English Political Ideologies in the Eighteenth Century," *William and Mary Quarterly*, 3d ser., 22 (1965): 555–57, 566–67. The quotation is from "Putney Debates," Oct. 29, 1647, in Woodhouse, *Puritanism and Liberty*, 83.

[74] As quoted by Cannon, *Parliamentary Reform*, 67. Endorsements of the traditional assump-tions may be found in [Henry Neville], *Plato Redivivus: or, A Dialogue Concerning Govern-*

Revolution, "the commonly received doctrine," said James Burgh, the dissenting political tractarian whose *Political Disquisitions* enjoyed an enormous popularity in the American colonies, was "that persons in servitude to others, and those who receive alms, ought not to be admitted to vote for members of parliament, because it is supposed that their votes will be influenced by those, on whom they depend."[75]

Sir William Blackstone elaborated the assumptions underlying this emphasis upon personal independence more fully:

> The *true* reason of requiring any qualification, with regard to property, in voters, is to exclude such persons as are in so mean a situation that they are esteemed to have no will of their own. If these persons had votes, they would be tempted to dispose of them under some undue influence or other. This would give a great, an artful, or a wealthy man, a larger share in elections than is consistent with general liberty. If it were probable that every man would give his vote freely and without influence of any kind, then, upon the true theory and genuine principles of liberty, every member of the community, however poor, should have a vote in electing those delegates, to whose charge is committed the disposal of his property, his liberty, and his life. But, since that can hardly be expected in persons of indigent fortunes, or such as are under the immediate dominion of others, all popular states have been obliged to establish certain qualifications; whereby some, who are

ment, 2d ed. (London, 1681), 50–51; [Tyrrell], *Patriarcha Non Monarcha*, 83–84; Speech of Sir Robert Sawyer, Jan. 28, 1688/89, in Anchitell Grey, ed., *Debates of the House of Commons from the Year 1667 to the Year 1694*, 10 vols. (London, 1769), 8:21–22; Algernon Sidney, *Discourses Concerning Government* (London, 1698), 75, 423; [Defoe], *Original Power of the . . . People*, 18; *Political Register* 2 (1768): 222, 225–26; and Burgh, *Political Disquisitions* 1:36–39, 49. Many writers who discussed the related and much more widely canvassed issue of electoral redistribution failed even to mention franchise reform. See John Toland, *The Art of Governing* (London, 1701), 75–78; Robert Molesworth, Preface to Francis Hotman, *Franco-Gallia: or, An Account of the Ancient Free State of France* (London, 1721), xxiii–xxiv; and [John Trenchard and Thomas Gordon], *Cato's Letters: or, Essays on Liberty, Civil and Religious*, 3d ed., 4 vols. (London, 1733), 2:239–40. See also Robbins, *Commonwealthman*, 110.

[75] Burgh, *Political Disquisitions* 1:36–37. On Burgh's enthusiastic reception in America, see Oscar and Mary F. Handlin, "James Burgh and American Revolutionary Theory," Massachusetts Historical Society, *Proceedings* 73 (1961): 38–57. Seconding Burgh, Montesquieu reported in *The Spirit of the Laws*, trans. Thomas Nugent, 6th ed. (London, 1793), 115, that in England those who were "in so mean a situation, as to be deemed to have no will of their own" were excluded from "voting at the election of a representative."

suspected to have no will of their own, are excluded from voting, in order to set other individuals, whose wills may be supposed independent, more thoroughly upon a level with each other.[76]

Property, then, was an essential precondition for the suffrage not only or even primarily because it demonstrated a permanent attachment to the community but because it alone conveyed personal—as well as economic and political—independence. *Independence*, said Dr. Johnson, was "freedom; exemption from reliance or control"—the "state over which none [other] has power," while *independent* meant "not depending; not supported by any other; not relying on another; not controlled." By contrast, *dependence* was defined as "a thing or person at the disposal or discretion of another," the "state of being subordinate, or subject in some degree to the discretion of another"— "the contrary of sovereignty," while a *dependent* was "one who lives in subjection to or at the discretion of another."[77] Dependence, wrote James Wilson in 1774, was "very little else, but an obligation to conform to the will . . . of that superiour person . . . upon which the inferiour depends."[78] Such a condition, observed Samuel Williams, too often, like luxury, destroyed "the vigour and powers of men, and by constantly enfeebling the body and mind, seems to reduce them to a lower order of beings. . . . The mind . . . scarcely retains its rational powers; and becomes weak, languid, and incapable of manly exertions, or attainments. To a state thus degraded, effeminate, and unmanly," dependence could reduce men until they had little more than "the remains of a human form."[79] "Freedom," said Thomas Paine, the most radical republican in America, "is destroyed by dependence."[80] "Dependency," added Paine's anonymous associate Candidus in March 1776, "is slavery," and people who put themselves "*under [such] absolute dominion*," declared Cassandra, another supporter of Paine, a few weeks later, were,

---

[76] Blackstone, *Commentaries*, 6th ed., 1:171. For endorsements of this logic by Americans in 1774–76, see James Wilson, *Considerations on the Authority of Parliament*, Aug. 17, 1774, in *Works of Wilson* 2:725–26; Alexander Hamilton, *The Farmer Refuted*, [Feb. 23], 1774, in *The Papers of Alexander Hamilton*, ed. Harold C. Syrett and Jacob E. Cooke, 19 vols. (New York and London, 1961–73), 1:105–7; and John Adams to James Sullivan, May 26, 1776, *Works of Adams* 9:375–78.

[77] Johnson, *Dictionary*.

[78] Wilson, *Considerations*, Aug. 17, 1774, in *Works of Wilson* 2:741.

[79] Williams, *History of Vermont* 2:331.

[80] Thomas Paine, *Dissertations on Government: The Affairs of the Bank; and Paper Money* (Philadelphia, 1786), in *The Complete Writings of Thomas Paine*, ed. Philip S. Foner, 2 vols. (New York, 1947), 2:399.

like "All [other] *animals*," "entitled only to be *fleeced*." A government in
which such people participated, wrote James Burgh, could be nothing more
than "a ptochocracy (the reader will pardon a new word) or government of
beggars." Certainly, said James Wilson, it could only be "an insult upon the
independent [electors] . . . that their uninfluenced suffrages should be adul-
terated by" any person who was such "an ignorant slave, or insidious tool"
that he was "not at liberty to speak as [he] thought." "Freedom and dependency" were thus, wrote Candidus, "opposite and irreconcilable terms."[81]

Harrington had translated the distinction between dependence and independence into social and political terms a century earlier in a brief maxim
set down in "A System of Politics": "The man that cannot live upon his own,
must be a servant; but he that can live upon his own, may be a freeman."[82]
And only freemen, those independent "Freeholders in the Country" and artisans and traders in the towns, Algernon Sidney had declared, were "properly *Cives*, [full] Members of the Commonwealth, in distinction from these
who are only *Incolae*, or Inhabitants, Vilains, and such as being under their
Parents, and not yet *sui juris*."[83] Independence was thus a necessary component of the freedom requisite for citizenship as well as for political equality.
For only men who were free from subjection "to the Will or Authority of
any other Man" could function freely and effectively as citizens—what were
referred to in 1776 during the debates over the Virginia constitution as the
"constituent members of our society"—of the commonwealth.[84]

---

[81] Candidus, *Pennsylvania Gazette*, Mar. 6, 1776; Cassandra, *Pennsylvania Packet*, Apr. 8,
1776; Burgh, *Political Disquisitions* 1:50; Wilson, *Considerations*, Aug. 17, 1774, in *Works
of Wilson* 2:725.

[82] Harrington, "A System of Politics," *Works of Harrington*, 465.

[83] Sidney, *Discourses concerning Government*, 75, 423. For a similar distinction, see [Defoe],
Original Power of the . . . People, 18–19.

[84] Edmund Randolph, *History of Virginia*, ed. Arthur H. Shaffer (Charlottesville, Va.,
1970), 253. See also George Mason's definition of "the people" as "those constituent members
from whom authority originated," Remarks on Annual Elections for the Fairfax Independent
Co., Apr. 17–26, 1775, in *Papers of George Mason* 1:230. The phrase "constituent members," Randolph tells us, was explicitly understood to exclude slaves. Nor was such reasoning
limited to southern states. As a Massachusetts Antifederalist declared in 1788, men "in a state
of slavery" were "not capable of any property" and could not, therefore, "in the state, be
considered as any part of civil society, the chief end whereof, is the preservation of property."
Echoed a New Yorker of the same persuasion in the same year, "it has never been alleged that
those who are not free agents can . . . have anything to do in government." As quoted in
Howard A. Ohline, "Republicanism and Slavery: Origins of the Three-Fifths Clause in the
United States Constitution," *William and Mary Quarterly*, 3d ser., 28 (1971): 582–83. See
also Adams, *Republikanische Verfassung*, 186–87.

As Samuel Williams's strictures on dependence suggest, independence was, moreover, thought to be necessary not only for citizenship but for manhood. People who forfeited or relinquished their independence, from servants up to government placemen, explained Thomas Paine, lost both "their original character of a man and . . . the full share of freedom appertaining to that character," and they could "repossess" neither until they had regained their independence.[85] Only a man of independent standing, said an Oxford undergraduate in 1748, could be "afraid of *no one* or *no man*" and therefore be truly a man.[86] Given this powerful identification of manhood with independence, it is scarcely surprising that Dr. Johnson in his *Dictionary* included, among his definitions of the word *man*, the following meaning: a "Wealthy or independent person"[87]—an identification that at least raises the possibility that the key word in Jefferson's phrase "all men are created equal" may not have been *equal* but *men*, that he may have been saying not that all humans were equal but that those who could meet the full requirements for being a man—and, therefore, a citizen—were equal.

A powerful case can, therefore, be made that it was the insistence upon personal independence—"free will"—even more than the emphasis upon having a stake in—"a common interest with"—society that lay behind the exclusion of so many categories of people from the suffrage and citizenship in both early modern England and the American colonies.[88] What most categories of people who were deprived of citizenship had in common was their dependence upon the wills of others: wives were dependent upon their husbands, minors and sons still living at home upon their fathers, servants and slaves upon their masters, short-term tenants and renters upon their landlords, aliens upon their native countries, Catholics upon the church, soldiers and sailors upon their commanders, debtors upon their creditors, and the poor and insane upon the community. The exclusion of most categories can be explained in this way. But not all. Not unmarried women, nonwhites, or Jews who could meet the property requirements and therefore presumably had the requisite personal independence—a fact which makes their exclusion of more than uncommon interest even though together all three categories were numerically insignificant in the Anglo-American world of the eighteenth century.

---

[85] Paine, "A Serious Address to the People of Pennsylvania," *Pennsylvania Packet*, Dec. 1, 1778, in *Complete Writings* 2:287.

[86] W. R. Ward, *Georgian Oxford: University Politics in the Eighteenth Century* (Oxford, 1958), 170, as quoted by Pocock, "English Political Ideologies," 567.

[87] This meaning of *man* is the eleventh offered by Johnson.

[88] The quotations are from Randolph, *History of Virginia*, 256.

To understand why these groups were excluded, we have to push our inquiry slightly further to determine the full meaning of "civic competence" in that particular world.[89] When we do so, we discover that independence—exemption from all external control or support—was the most important but not the only criterion for civic competence. Independence was a necessary precondition for but not an inevitable guarantee of such competence. A requirement of nearly equal importance was virtue, or the voluntary observance of the recognized standards of right conduct: that is, mastery of self, freedom from internal subjection to one's own passions. "Through a Savageness of Temper, or . . . Pride, Envy or Jealousy, or any other baser Passion," many individual independent adult white males were actually slaves, not to another person but to their own "Ill-nature." Until their bondage to "the tyranny of [their own] evil lusts and passions" robbed them of their economic independence or reduced them to a life of crime, however, there was no way for them to be easily identified, no external and immediately recognizable criteria by which they could be clearly distinguished from the rest of society and deprived of a voice in civil affairs.[90] But the same was not true of several categories of people, who, it was widely assumed in both Britain and America, had such major "natural" or cultural disabilities that, no matter how independent they might be in their circumstances, they were incapable of self-control and therefore lacking in the capacity to attain the virtue and the competence necessary to be accorded full civil status in society.

The insane as well as criminals who by their actions had proven "vicious in life" obviously fell into this category;[91] so also did women, nonwhites (in the colonies), and Jews. The conventional attitude toward women was elaborated in 1681 by James Tyrrell, one of Locke's associates, when he wrote that "there never was any Government where all the promiscuous Rabble of Women and Children had Votes, as being not Capable of it."[92] Although a

---

[89] The phrase "civic competence" is borrowed from Pole, *Political Representation*, 47–48.

[90] The Monitor, "On Good Nature," *Virginia Gazette* (Williamsburg), Jan. 28, 1737; Phillips Payson, *On Virtues Essential for Self-Government* (Boston, 1780), in John Wingate Thornton, ed., *The Pulpit of the American Revolution*, 2d ed. (Boston, 1876), 329–30.

[91] Pole, *Political Representation*, 37–38; Benjamin Franklin, "Some Good Whig Principles," 1774, in *The Political Thought of Benjamin Franklin*, ed. Ralph Ketcham (Indianapolis, 1965), 280.

[92] [Tyrrell], *Patriarcha Non Monarcha*, 83. See also Theophilus Parsons, "The Essex Result," Apr. 29, 1778, in Handlin and Handlin, *Popular Sources of Political Authority*, 340–41, for the argument that "women what age soever they are of, are considered as not having a sufficient acquired discretion; not from a deficiency in . . . mental powers, but from the

few people insisted that "all men, white or black" were "free-born" and therefore entitled to civil rights,[93] a similar lack of capacity was widely attributed to nonwhites and used as an excuse for their exclusion from voting rights in the colonies. The very "Nature of Negroes," said Lieutenant Governor William Gooch of Virginia in 1736 in explaining why a Virginia statute of 1723 had disfranchised freedmen of African descent, made it impossible to give them citizenship. They could never "be Accounted Equal" to "the Descendants of an Englishman" until, perhaps at some distant period, "time and Education has changed the Indication of their spurious Extraction, and made some Alteration in their Morals."[94] The specific rationale for the exclusion of Jews is less clear. The traditional identification of virtue with religious orthodoxy and the inherited stereotype of Jews as people who could not control a peculiarly strong passion of avarice—"where there is money to be got," said the duke of Bedford in 1753 during a House of Lords debate over whether privileges of naturalization for Jews in the colonies should be withdrawn, "there will be the greatest resort of that people"— were doubtless important considerations. But the conception of Jews as "a people cursed by God" and therefore obviously unworthy, as Thomas Potter, M.P. for St. Germans, put it in a debate over the same question in the House of Commons three weeks later, of having an "establishment in any country" also served to mark them off as still another category of people who were incapable of virtue and therefore not to be trusted with a full civic role.[95]

---

natural tenderness and delicacy of their minds, their refined mode of life, and various domestic duties" which "prevent that promiscuous intercourse with the world, which is necessary to qualify them for electors." See also the Return of Northampton, Mar. 2, 1789, ibid., 580.

[93] See James Otis, *Rights of the British Colonies Asserted and Proved* (Boston, 1764), in Bernard Bailyn, ed., *Pamphlets of the American Revolution 1750–1776* (Cambridge, Mass., 1965), 1:439; Return of Hardwick, June 1780, in Handlin and Handlin, *Popular Sources of Political Authority*, 830. See also Adams, *Republikanische Verfassung*, 181–86.

[94] William Gooch to Alured Popple, May 18, 1736, in Emory G. Evans, ed., "A Question of Complexion: Documents concerning the Negro and the Franchise in Eighteenth-Century Virginia," *Virginia Magazine of History and Biography* 71 (1963): 414. Montesquieu summarized and burlesqued conventional attitudes toward blacks in *Spirit of Laws*, 6th ed., 1:178–79.

[95] The quotations are from Leo F. Stock, ed., *Proceedings and Debates of the British Parliament respecting North America*, 5 vols. (Washington, D.C., 1924–41), 5:572, 576 (Nov. 15, Dec. 4, 1753). For an instance of similar attitudes toward political rights for Jews in the colonies, see "A Brother Chip," *Pennsylvania Gazette*, Sept. 27, 1770, in Charles H. Lincoln, *The Revolutionary Movement in Pennsylvania, 1760–1776* (Philadelphia, 1901), 81. See also

Citizens—truly "freemen"—had to be not only independent from all external control but also *"free* in the *inner man*; by being endowed with . . . firmness of mind in the cause of truth, against the terrors and the allurements of the world; and with such additional strength and vigour as enabled them more effectually to resist the natural violence of their lusts and passions." They had to be "Men of Reason . . . and not . . . incapable of [forming independent and objective judgements] . . . about Government." All categories of people who, like children, were still "in a State of Minority"[96] or, like Jews, nonwhites, women, criminals, and the insane, were scarcely ever "free from the dominion of vice" and "thus slaves to their lusts" could "never be free." As Gooch said of the free blacks and mulattoes in 1736, they clearly deserved, like all those other groups who depended upon the wills of other men, to be "as much excluded from being good and lawful Men, as Villains [*sic*] were of Old by the Laws of England."[97]

In a narrow sense, J. Franklin Jameson was correct in asserting fifty years ago that the Revolution "greatly altered" the "old colonial laws respecting the franchise." With some notable exceptions—such as Massachusetts, which actually increased property requirements by the constitution of 1780, and Virginia, which merely continued colonial stipulations—those requirements were either lowered or made more flexible. It may even be true, as Jameson argued, that this liberalization of the franchise actually meant that the phrase "We the people of the United States" in the Constitution of 1787 included "much larger" numbers than had a similar phrase in the Declaration of Independence in 1776.[98] But "the expansion of the suffrage," as Gordon S. Wood has remarked, "was in no way comparable to the enlargement of the number of representatives" or of elected officeholders generally.[99]

Thomas R. Perry, *Public Opinion, Propaganda, and Politics in Eighteenth-Century England: A Study of the Jewish Naturalization Act of 1753* (Cambridge, Mass., 1962), 13.

[96] Boucher, "On Civil Liberty," [1775], in *Causes and Consequences of the American Revolution*, 507; Phileleutheros, *An Address to the Freeholders and Inhabitants of the Province of the Massachusetts-Bay, in New-England* (Boston, [1751]), 8.

[97] *Benjamin Franklin's Autobiography*, ed. W. MacDonald (London, 1908), 85; Harmon Husband, Sermon, 1770, in William S. Powell, James K. Huhta, and Thomas J. Farnham, eds., *The Regulators in North Carolina: A Documentary History, 1759–1776* (Raleigh, N.C., 1971), 226; Gooch to Popple, May 18, 1736, in Evans, "A Question of Complexion," 415.

[98] Jameson, *American Revolution as a Social Movement*, 39–41.

[99] Wood, *Creation of the American Republic*, 167–69.

Vastly more important, the traditional logic of political exclusion remained essentially unchallenged. Every state retained some taxpaying or property qualification for the suffrage. Even Pennsylvania, whose innovative constitution of 1776 contained the most liberal franchise, stipulated that it should be restricted to "all free men having a sufficient evident common interest with, and attachment to the community." This stipulation might not require, in Edmund Pendleton's phrase, ownership "of fixed Permanent property," but it did necessitate possession of property in the form of some "profession, calling, trade or farm" and clearly excluded servants, paupers, and those on poor relief. The logic behind that requirement, as the Pennsylvania constitution spelled out, was the familiar notion that, in the absence of a freehold, some such calling, trade, or profession was necessary "to preserve" the citizen's "independence."[100]

The same logic was everywhere widely endorsed. The suffrage, that "darling privilege of *free* men," said James Wilson, "should certainly be extended as far as considerations of safety and order will possibly admit." But the "correct theory and true principles of liberty," he pointed out, required that it not be given to any person "whose circumstances" rendered "him necessarily dependent on the will of another."[101] "Such is the frailty of the human heart, that very few men who have no property, have any judgment of their own," declared John Adams a few weeks before Independence. "Generally speaking," he thought, even women, whom nature had "made . . . fittest for domestic cares," and children, who had "not judgment or will of their own," had "as good judgments, and as independent minds, as those men who are wholly destitute of property."[102] Although he did not agree that wealth alone was a sufficient guarantee of independence, Thomas Jefferson also believed that the only trustworthy voters were those who could "bid defiance to the means of corruption" and proposed to give every adult male who could not meet the property requirement a gift of a freehold in the hope that it would enable him to do just that.[103] Voting, echoed the North Carolina lawyer

---

[100] Thorpe, *Federal and State Constitutions* 5:3083–92; Edmund Pendleton to Thomas Jefferson, Aug. 10, 1776, *The Letters and Papers of Edmund Pendleton, 1734–1803*, ed. David John Mays, 2 vols. (Charlottesville, Va., 1967), 1:198. Those without "fixed Permanent property" Pendleton regarded as transients, and such "transient Inhabitants," as Franklin wrote in the margins of Josiah Tucker's *A Letter from a Merchant in London* . . . (London, 1766), were "not so connected with the Welfare of the State[,] which they may quit when they please, as to qualify them properly for such Privilege" (*Franklin Papers* 17:359).

[101] Wilson, "Lectures on Law," *Works of Wilson* 1:406–7, 411.

[102] Adams to James Sullivan, May 26, 1776, *Works of Adams* 9:376–77.

[103] Thomas Jefferson, *Notes on the State of Virginia*, ed. William Peden (Chapel Hill, N.C., 1955), 149. See also Kenyon, "Declaration of Independence," *Fundamental Testaments*, 39.

James Iredell, had to be restricted to those who "could be supposed exempt from influence." Otherwise, the "lowest and most ignorant of mankind must associate in this important business with those who it is to be presumed, from their property and other circumstances, are free from influence."[104] "Persons so abject as to have neither will nor sentiment of their own," said an anonymous Pennsylvania radical in April 1776, had to be deprived of the franchise,[105] and the town of Sutton, Massachusetts, thought that "poor, Shiftless, Spendthrifty men and inconsiderate youngsters that have no property" could be "cheap bought" and "ought not to have a full or equal Vote with those that had an Estate."[106] No less than during the colonial period or in contemporary Britain, being "*a free agent* in *a political view*," in the words of Alexander Hamilton, was a prerequisite for the right to vote and for citizenship in Revolutionary America.[107] Paraphrasing Blackstone, Theophilus Parsons, during the debate over the Massachusetts constitution of 1778, endorsed the principle in the Essex Result that "all the members of the state are qualified to make the election, unless they have not sufficient descretion [that is, virtue], or are so situated as to have no wills of their own [that is, independence]."[108]

The phrase "sufficient discretion" used by Parsons was a reiteration as well of the continuing commitment to the assumption that not just independence but the capacity for virtue and self-control was essential for citizenship. That this criterion had by no means been abandoned was indicated by the continued exclusion of women and free nonwhite property owners during and after the Revolution. This last group, which grew considerably in numbers as a result of manumissions and restrictions on slavery that occurred during the Revolution, was specifically denied the vote in all of the slave states except North Carolina and excluded from the polls by custom almost everywhere else. Indeed, as Winthrop D. Jordan has shown, black disabilities actually increased after the 1790s as a result of the allegedly "demonstrated" excesses and political incompetence of blacks during the Haitian Revolution—an event which, in the responses to it of Americans and Europeans alike, re-

---

[104] Iredell, "To the Inhabitants of Great Britain," September 1774, in *Life and Correspondence of James Iredell*, ed. Griffith J. McRee, 2 vols. (New York, 1857–58), 1:209–10.

[105] An Elector, *Pennsylvania Packet*, Apr. 29, 1776.

[106] Return of Sutton, May 18, 1778, in Robert J. Taylor, ed., *Massachusetts, Colony to Commonwealth: Documents on the Formation of Its Constitution* (Chapel Hill, N.C., 1961), 64–65.

[107] Hamilton, *Farmer Refuted*, [Feb. 23], 1774, in *Papers of Hamilton* 1:105.

[108] Essex Result, 1778, in Handlin and Handlin, *Popular Sources of Political Authority*, 340–41.

vealed more clearly than anything else perhaps the "limited" character of the so-called Age of Democratic Revolutions of the late eighteenth century. "Because a republic depended upon virtue and knowledge for its existence," Duncan J. MacLeod has recently observed, "it appeared foolhardy permanently to incorporate within it vice and ignorance."[109] Indeed, the only categories of people to gain citizenship during the Revolution were Catholics and Jews, who, in most places, were granted the suffrage through the abolition of religious tests for voting.[110]

The record of the states on the suffrage during the Revolution makes it clear that American revolutionaries were fighting quite as much for independence with a small *i* as for Independence with a large *I*—for the right to the privilege of all independent men to participate in governing themselves as well as for separation from Britain. Indeed, among the most powerful motives impelling them toward that separation was their resentment against Britain's seeming attempts to deny them this privilege and the implications of unworthiness that appeared to lie behind those attempts. The colonies, James Otis had said in 1764 in a tone of high indignation, "are well settled, not as the common people of *England* foolishly imagine, with a compound mongrel mixture of *English*, *Indian*, and *Negro*, but with freeborn *British white* subjects."[111] To accept subjection to a "British Parliament" which they had had no voice in choosing, wrote Alexander Hamilton in 1774 in one of many similar observations by Americans in the decade just before the Revolution, "the people in America, of *all* ranks and conditions, opulent as well as indigent . . . would be upon a less favourable footing, than that of the people of Britain, who," said Hamilton, quoting Blackstone, "are *in so mean a situation*, that they are supposed to have no will of their own."[112] To be thus linked with people of "servile dependence," with the outcasts, the rejected, and the scorned in Britain, was a blatant and unacceptable violation of some of the most precious components of the self-image of men who thought of

[109] Jordan, *White over Black*, 412–14; Duncan J. MacLeod, *Slavery, Race, and the American Revolution* (Cambridge, 1974), 79.

[110] Williamson, *American Suffrage*, 115. On the changing status of Jews during the Revolution, see Samuel Rezneck, *Unrecognized Patriots: The Jews in the American Revolution* (London, 1975), 5–11, 156–70.

[111] Otis, *Rights of the British Colonies*, in Bailyn, *Pamphlets of the American Revolution* 1:434.

[112] Hamilton, *Farmer Refuted*, [Feb. 23], 1774, in *Papers of Hamilton* 1:106–7.

themselves—and to function effectively in their societies needed to think of themselves—as individuals of independent competence and who associated passivity, servility, ignorance, and lack of discretion with those categories of people in their own societies—women, children, servants, and slaves—who had freedom from neither internal nor external control.[113] As Crèvecoeur pointed out in his famous *Letters from an American Farmer* in 1782, the great promise—perhaps the deepest meaning—of America was that even the outcasts of Europe—people whose circumstances had forever been those of misery, servility, and dependence—might in America finally "become men" and thereby "rank as citizens." The wide diffusion of property and the consequent ease of living "without the Vexation of Dependence" that underlay "this surprising metamorphosis," Crèveceour's remarks strongly suggest, only served to intensify the traditional stigma attached to those who failed to obtain "ease, and independence" at the same time that, for the many who actually had managed to achieve independence, they vastly increased the psychological need to preserve it along with the autonomy, mastery, self-control, and sense of manhood they had gained with it.[114] In sharp contrast to contemporary "dependents" in the Old World, American Revolutionaries, as Edmund S. Morgan has pointed out, "possessed two palpable sources of power": "most of them owned the land on which they lived, and a very large number of them owned guns. Land gave them economic and political power; and guns . . . gave them firepower."[115] More important, perhaps, these two forms of power combined to help give them a third: willpower, as defined by a proud and widespread sense of independent self that could only react with overwhelming revulsion to the status of passive dependence that seemed to be envisioned for them by the metropolitan government in the decades before the American Revolution.

As Morgan has also suggested, the specific kind of freedom the men of the American Revolution fought for was thus "not a gift to be conferred by

---

[113] On this point, see Fred Weinstein and Gerald M. Platt, *The Wish to Be Free: Society, Psyche, and Value Change* (Berkeley and Los Angeles, 1969), 46. See also Wilson, *Considerations*, in *Works of Wilson* 2:725–26. The quotation is from Michel-Guillaume Jean de Crèvecoeur, *Letters from an American Farmer*, 1782, in Jack P. Greene, ed., *Settlements to Society, 1607–1763: A Documentary History of Colonial America* (New York, 1975), 244.

[114] Crèvecoeur, *Letters from an American Farmer*, 1782, in Greene, *Settlements to Society*, 243; [Thomas Nairne], *A Letter from South Carolina* (London, 1710), 56; Williams, *History of Vermont* 2:328.

[115] Edmund S. Morgan, "Consensus and Continuity in the American Revolution," in Stephen G. Kurtz and James H. Hutson, eds., *Essays on the American Revolution* (Chapel Hill, N.C., 1973), 303.

governments" but "a freedom that sprang from the independence [and, I would add, virtue] of the individual."[116] Quite as much as the devotion to private property, the deep commitment to this conception of freedom and the concomitant revulsion against all forms of dependence—and all peoples who were dependent—meant that the spirit of '76 could not immediately generate a very sweeping movement in the direction of a more inclusive political society. For James Harrington and his early eighteenth-century followers, J. G. A. Pocock has suggested, the most important measure of a man's independence was his capacity to have dependents.[117] The same was true for free white males in America during the Revolutionary generation. No less than the nineteenth-century middle classes described by E. J. Hobsbawm, the independent men of the American Revolution defined themselves in terms of their "capacity to exercise power over people . . . and of not having direct power exercised over themselves."[118] Far, therefore, from being "perfectly clear that the principles for which Americans fought required the complete abolition of slavery," as Winthrop D. Jordan has argued, it can be contended from the perspective of the ideas and assumptions I have been describing here that those principles actually served to sustain an institution that merely functioned to preserve in an unfree status peoples who were thought to lack the independence and virtue requisite for freedom.[119] As one South Carolinian pointed out early in the nineteenth century, the "American Revolution was a *family quarrel among equals*" in which dependents and people of no discretion—like blacks—"had no concern."[120] Given the equation of manhood with independence and self-control in the thought of the men of the American Revolution, the phrase "all men are created equal" in the Declaration of Independence, like other elements in that document, built a case not for but "against equality in civil society,"[121] and the subsequent racist insight of John Taylor of Caroline that "mankind

---

[116] Edmund S. Morgan, "Slavery and Freedom: The American Paradox," *Journal of American History* 59 (1972): 7.

[117] Pocock, "English Political Ideology," 556, 566. On this point, see also the fascinating argument of Michael Paul Rogin, *Fathers and Children: Andrew Jackson and the Subjugation of the American Indian* (New York, 1975).

[118] E. J. Hobsbawm, "From Social History to the History of Society," *Daedalus* 100 (1971): 37.

[119] Jordan, *White over Black*, 342.

[120] [Frederick Dalcho], *Practical Considerations Founded on the Scriptures, Relative to the Slave Population of South-Carolina* (Charleston, S.C., 1823), 33n, as quoted by MacLeod, *Slavery, Race, and the American Revolution*, 28.

[121] See Robert Ginsberg, "Equality and Justice in the Declaration of Independence," *Journal of Social Philosophy* 6 (1975): 8.

did not include Negroes" was not so much "a major dilution" as an important amplification of that phrase. [122]

The men of the Revolution were primarily concerned not with equality but with liberation, and liberation required that independent men be able to make free use of any benefits, derived from either natural or "accidental and adventitious" distinctions, in their pursuit of economic and social inequality as expressed, in some important measure, by their capacity to have dependents. [123] For the time being, at least, America was to continue to be a place where people, to paraphrase John Milton, were

> If not equal all, yet free,
> Equally free; for social distinctions
> [Milton had said "orders and degrees"]
> Jar not with liberty, but well consist. [124]

The men of the Revolution firmly rejected all suggestions for the re-creation in America of the European system of privileged "orders and degrees." But their commitment to liberty, and the independence that was thought to be the essential badge of that liberty, meant that the only form of political equality they could firmly and widely endorse would be, in the words of one of them, "nothing more than an equality of rights"—for citizens. That commitment meant as well that many of the suggestions by people who sought during the Revolution to work out the apparent logic of Revolutionary rhetoric, suggestions for the abolition of chattel slavery and the extension of full civil rights to all categories of adults, including nonwhites and women, would neither automatically gain widespread public acceptance nor become integral components of the emerging "American Creed." [125]

The philosophy of civil rights championed by the American Revolutionaries was thus not, as so many have charged, betrayed but fulfilled by their failures to abolish slavery and adopt a more inclusive definition of citizen-

---

[122] MacLeod, *Slavery, Race, and the American Revolution*, 88, 130. The Reverend John Camm made this point explicit in 1765 when he asked Richard Bland what it meant, in Virginia, to say that "all *men* are *born* free." Did it mean, Camm asked, that Virginia "Negroes are not . . . *born slaves*, or that the said slaves are not men?" ([Camm], *Critical Remarks on a Letter Ascribed to Common Sense* [Williamsburg, Va., 1765], 19, as cited by Bailyn, *Ideological Origins*, 235–36).

[123] Salus Populi, Mar. 11, 1776, in Force, *American Archives*, 4th ser., 5:182–83.

[124] Milton, *Paradise Lost*, 6.5, line 790.

[125] Williams, *History of Vermont* 2:328–30. The term "American Creed" is borrowed from Gunnar Myrdal by MacLeod, *Slavery, Race, and the American Revolution*, 17, to refer to "the political philosophy of the Revolution."

ship. John Locke had himself carefully explained that when he wrote *"All Men by Nature are Equal"* he was not referring to "all sorts of *Equality*" but only to the *"equal Right* that every Man hath, *to his Natural Freedom*, without being subjected to the Will or Authority of any other Man" except by his own consent given either explicitly or implicitly.[126] That many people would either—through necessity or choice—bargain away that *"natural freedom"* or have insufficient discretion—and therefore power—to sustain it once they had entered into civil society was an empirical fact, in America as well as in Britain, and those who did thus either forfeit or lose their natural freedom thereby gave up any claim to equal political rights in civil society. The men of the American Revolution stretched their definition of who might be considered an independent and competent man as far as they could. Joel Barlow notwithstanding, they did not immediately endow "the word *people*" with "a Different meaning from what it" had "in Europe." They did not redefine *citizenship* to include "the whole community," to comprehend "every human creature."[127] Quite the contrary. They displayed little—and certainly no powerful or sustained—disposition to abandon the traditional British insistence upon personal independence and virtue as the criteria for all citizens.

That the insistence upon independence may have been far more important than the devotion to private property in setting such tight boundaries upon the American Revolution is suggested by the later American experience. During the past two centuries, the struggle for a more inclusive political society has been a central feature of American public life. Throughout, the American devotion to the sanctity of private property has remained strong; what has been gradually and continually changing—and expanding—is our conception of citizenship, of what categories of people should be admitted to those equal political rights won for themselves in 1776 by that small minority of the American population who by their own deeply held criteria merited public space and a vote in civil society.

---

[126] Locke, *Two Treatises*, 322.

[127] Joel Barlow, *Advise to the Priviledged Orders in the Several States of Europe*, 2d ed. (London, 1792), pt. 1, 33.

Early drafts of this essay were given as lectures at the Twenty-seventh Annual Pacific Northwest History Conference at Washington State University on Apr. 26, 1974; the University of Delaware's Bicentennial Lecture Series on "The Revolution and the Development of American Political and Social Institutions, 1776–1860," on Sept. 22, 1975; the Whig-Cliosophic Society's Bicentennial Lecture Series at Princeton University on Nov. 3, 1975; the University of Warwick in Coventry, England, on Jan. 22, 1976; and as a colloquium paper at the Woodrow Wilson Center for Scholars in Washington, D.C., on Apr. 28, 1975. The version reprinted here with permission with minor changes and corrections from *All*

Men Are Created Equal: Some Reflections on the Character of the American Revolution (Oxford: Clarendon Press, 1976) was my inaugural lecture as Harmsworth Professor of American History at the University of Oxford on Feb. 10, 1976. It was subsequently given as either lectures or seminars at University College, Dublin, on May 4, 1976; at the Bicentennial Conference at the University of Uppsala, Sweden, on May 31, 1976; at the Instituto Riva-Aguero of the Catholic University of Lima, Peru, on Sept. 1, 1976; at the Historical Institute of the University of Oslo on Oct. 11, 1976; at the conference on "America in 1976: Revolutionary or Counterrevolutionary?" at the University of Michigan-Flint on Oct. 14, 1976; and as the evening address at the 10th Annual Duquesne History Forum in Pittsburgh on Oct. 26, 1976.

—ELEVEN—

"Slavery or Independence":
Some Reflections on the Relationship among Liberty, Black Bondage, and Equality in Revolutionary South Carolina

"A LOVE OF FREEDOM," Edmund Burke declared to the House of Commons in his speech on conciliation on March 22, 1775, "is the predominating feature" in the "character of the Americans." "Stronger in the English colonies, probably, than in any other people of the earth," a "fierce spirit of liberty," he said, "marks and distinguishes the whole." But in the southern colonies, he asserted in an opinion widely shared by contemporaries on both sides of the Atlantic, this spirit was "still more high and haughty than in those to the northward."[1] Just a little over twelve years later, a delegate from one of these same southern colonies, long since become states, delivered the single most elaborate and passionate speech in celebration of American equality at the Federal Convention in Philadelphia. Equality, contended the South Carolina lawyer Charles Pinckney on June 25, 1787, with approval, was "the leading feature of the United States" and had to be the guiding principle in its future governance.[2]

Yet, these southern societies, especially South Carolina, were the very ones in which chattel slavery was most deeply entrenched and social inequality among the free population most pronounced. For men to be such violent advocates for their own liberties while they were simultaneously, as one northern cleric put it, "trampling on the sacred natural rights and privileges

---

[1] Edmund Burke, "Speech on Moving Resolutions for Conciliation with the Colonies," Mar. 22, 1775, in Thomas H. D. Mahoney, ed., *Selected Writings and Speeches on America* (Indianapolis, 1964), 131–32, 134, 137.

[2] Charles Pinckney, speech, June 25, 1787, in Max Farrand, ed., *The Records of the Federal Convention of 1787*, 4 vols. (Washington, D.C., 1911–37), 1:397–407.

of Africans," seemed to outsiders to be shamefully hypocritical.[3] "How is it that we hear the loudest yelps for liberty among the drivers of negroes?" trenchantly asked Dr. Samuel Johnson, the English critic and lexicographer who deplored Burke's lenient attitude toward the Americans, in an oft-quoted question.[4] How could members of a society like that of lowcountry South Carolina, one that appeared to visitors such as the Boston lawyer Josiah Quincy, Jr., in 1773, to be sharply "divided into opulent and lordly plant-ers, poor and spiritless peasants and vile slaves,"[5] possibly subscribe with any degree of sincerity to the pronouncement "all men are created equal" in the Declaration of Independence? Never systematically and thoroughly explored by modern scholars, these questions—the precise relationship among the commitment to liberty, chattel slavery, and the belief in equality—as they apply to Revolutionary South Carolina are the subject of this essay.[6]

For the eighteenth-century Anglophone world, the meaning of liberty was both clear and extensive. It meant, in a narrow constitutional sense, "exemp-tion from tyranny or inordinate government," but also, much more liberally, "*freedom*, as opposed to slavery" or "freedom, as opposed to necessity." "*Lib-erty*," said the philosopher John Locke, "is the power in any agent to do, or forbear, any particular action, according to the determination, or the thought of the mind, whereby either of them is preferred to the other."[7] Revolution-ary South Carolinians defined liberty in the same broad way. "By Liberty in general," declared the Presbyterian minister Hugh Alison in a sermon pub-lished in Charleston in 1769, "I understand [not just civil liberty but] the Right every man has to pursue the natural, reasonable and religious dictates of his own mind; to enjoy the fruits of his own labour, art and industry; to work for his own profit and pleasures, and not for others." In short, liberty

---

[3] [John Allen], *The Watchman's Alarm to Lord N—h* (Salem, Mass., 1774), 25–28, as quoted by Bernard Bailyn, *The Ideological Origins of the American Revolution* (Cambridge, Mass., 1967), 240.

[4] Samuel Johnson, *Taxation No Tyranny* (1775), in *Samuel Johnson: Political Writings*, ed. Donald J. Greene (New Haven, 1977), 454.

[5] "Journal of Josiah Quincy, Jr., 1773," ed. Mark A. DeWolfe Howe, Massachusetts His-torical Society, *Proceedings*, 49 (1916): 454–57.

[6] The notable exception is Edmund S. Morgan, who has explored the relationship between freedom and slavery in pre-Revolutionary Virginia. See his "Slavery and Freedom: The American Paradox," *Journal of American History* 59 (1972): 5–29, and *American Slavery, American Freedom: The Ordeal of Colonial Virginia* (New York, 1975), 376–87.

[7] Samuel Johnson, *Dictionary of the English Language*, 2 vols. (London, 1832), 2:45.

was "to live upon one's own terms," to have absolute disposal of one's "property, as may best contribute to the support, ease, and advantage of himself and his family," and to be possessed of *"an undoubted right to think and act for"* himself.[8]

This last aspect of liberty was especially important. "Free men," as the young William Henry Drayton defiantly announced in 1769 in refusing to be pressured into participating in the economic boycott against the Townshend Acts, had to "have free wills, in all cases, where the laws of our country do not restrain them." The right to exercise that will, to give an independent opinion, said a later opponent of Drayton, was "the immediate Inheritance of every Man born free." Supporting Drayton's position in 1769, the iconoclast William Wragg demonstrated just how much significance Revolutionary South Carolinians could attach to this right. "I would endure every thing," he declared, "rather than have the freedom of my will or understanding limited or restrained . . . by men not having authority." No man could be genuinely "at liberty" who did not have such personal independence, a concept every bit as hallowed as liberty in the lexicon of the eighteenth-century Anglophone world and one connoting an absolute exemption from any degree of subordination, support, or control by any other person. The distinguishing marks of a free man were thus that he was in no sense subject to "the disposal or discretion of another" and was in all things "governed [only] by himself, or by laws to which he has consented."[9]

Why Anglo-Americans had such an avid commitment to liberty and independence in this sweeping sense interested Burke in 1775, and he explained it in terms "of descent, of form of government, of religion in the northern provinces, of manners in the southern, of education, of the remoteness of situation from the first mover of government." David Ramsay, the noted South Carolina physician and historian, generally agreed. "Every thing in the colonies contributed to nourish a spirit of liberty and independence," he wrote in his *History of the Revolution of South-Carolina* in 1785:

> They were planted under the auspices of the English constitution in its purity and vigour. Many of their inhabitants had imbibed a large por-

---

[8] Hugh Alison, *Spiritual Liberty* (Charleston, S.C., 1769), 4; Robert M. Weir, ed., *The Letters of Freeman, etc.: Essays on the Nonimportation Movement in South Carolina Collected by William Henry Drayton* (Columbia, S.C., 1977), 18, 105.

[9] Weir, *Letters of Freeman*, 18, 27, 29–30; Johnson, *Taxation No Tyranny*, 427; A Back Settler, *Some Fugitive Thought on a Letter Signed Freeman* . . . (South Carolina, 1774), 3; Johnson, *Dictionary* 1:497, 767–69, 968–69.

tion of that spirit which brought one tyrant to the block, and expelled another from his dominions. They were communities of separate independent individuals, for the most part employed in cultivating a fruitful soil, and under no general influence, but of their own feelings and opinions; they were not led by powerful families, or by great officers in church or state. Luxury had made but very little progress among their contented unaspiring farmers. The large extent of territory gave each man an opportunity of fishing, fowling and hunting, without injury to his neighbour. Every inhabitant was or easily might be a freeholder. Settled on lands of his own, he was both farmer and landlord. Having no superior to whom he was obliged to look up, and producing all the necessaries of life from his own grounds, he soon became independent. His mind was equally free from all the restraints of superstition. No ecclesiastical establishments invaded the rights of conscience, or fettered the freeborn mind. At liberty to act and think, as his inclination prompted, he disdained the ideas of dependence and subjection.[10]

That all of these conditions had operated in precisely this way in South Carolina was, to Ramsay and others, entirely evident. For every one of the reasons that were present all over Anglophone America, Ramsay contended in his later *History of South-Carolina*, "the love of liberty had taken deep root in the minds of Carolinians long before it was called into action by the revolution." So strong, in fact, was this "spirit of liberty and independence" in South Carolina that almost alone it had "carried her sons honorably and triumphantly through" a war when they "had few or no local grievances to complain of, and might at any time have obtained good terms on submission to the mother country." Ever since the war, moreover, this same spirit had "taught them to resist all real and supposed attempts to invade their rights." Indeed, Ramsay was persuaded, the spirit of liberty and independence in South Carolina had since the Revolution been carried entirely too far, "especially . . . by the younger part of the community," who, as the Presbyterian minister Thomas Reese observed in 1788, seemed to have imbibed "the principles and spirit of freedom and independence with the milk of their mothers." "The high minded youths of Carolina," Ramsay thought, had de-

---

[10] Burke, "Speech on Conciliation," 131–37; David Ramsay, *History of the Revolution of South-Carolina*, 2 vols. (Trenton, N.J., 1785), 1:11, and An Oration, 1794, in "David Ramsay, 1749–1815: Selections from His Writings," ed. Robert L. Brunhouse, American Philosophical Society, *Transactions*, n.s., 55, pt. 4 (1965): 191.

veloped such "repugnance to subjection" that they found it extremely difficult to achieve that "temperate medium which as cheerfully submits to proper authority as it manfully opposes what is improper and degrading." To such a height had this "madness of independence" grown, Ramsay suggested, that it threatened the very bonds of society in South Carolina. Only in "an uncivilized State," Thomas Tudor Tucker, like Ramsay a physician, warned in 1784, did any man have an absolute "right to consider himself or his family independent of all the world."[11]

One of the central questions I wish to raise here is whether this apparently exaggerated sense of liberty and independence in Revolutionary South Carolina can be fully explained by the conditions cited by Ramsay as having been responsible for nourishing that sense all over Anglophone America? What I wish to suggest, in fact, is that it cannot and that, for a more comprehensive explanation, one has to look far more closely than has previously been done at the connection highlighted by the title of this essay: the relationship between independence and slavery.

When in 1776 in his charge to the grand jury *On the Rise of the American Empire* William Henry Drayton said that the choice facing Americans was "Slavery or Independence," he was reiterating what, as Bernard Bailyn pointed out almost fifteen years ago, had been a consistent theme in American protests against metropolitan efforts to tighten control over the colonies beginning with the revenue measures of George Grenville in 1764–65. To be required to pay taxes levied by the British Parliament without their consent, Americans claimed, put them in precisely the same position with regard to the metropolis as their slaves had in relation to them: they would be the "mere property" of Britain, which would thenceforth enjoy the absolute "disposal of their persons" and, of course, of their entire "substance and labour" as well. Once they had been driven "into servile submission," they would be in such an "abject and wretched" condition as to be, like all slaves, without "power of resistance," condemned "to groan and sweat under a slavish life," and an easy "Prey to the Ambition and Avarice, the Pride and Luxury of Masters, who will set no Bounds to their

---

[11] David Ramsay, *The History of South Carolina* . . . , 2 vols. (Charleston, S.C., 1809), 1:221–22, 2:384–86; Thomas Reese, *The Influence of Religion, in Civil Society* (Charleston, S.C., 1788), 78; Johnson, *Taxation No Tyranny*, 438; Philodemos [Thomas Tudor Tucker], *Conciliatory Hints . . . Submitted to the Consideration of the Citizens of the Commonwealth of South-Carolina* (Charleston, S.C., 1784), 13.

Lust; and in Order to keep Us in abject Slavery, will *rule Us with a Rod of Iron.*"[12]

That this was exactly what the metropolitan government had in mind seemed over the following decade to be more and more clear to South Carolinians, as well as to other Americans. Though, as the anonymous poet Rusticus asserted in a Charleston publication in 1770, Americans were "the Sons, not Slaves of Briton born," who, William Henry Drayton later added, were "equally with the people of England, entitled to those liberties which are emphatically termed the unalienable liberties of an Englishman," the metropolitan government, bristled the radical merchant Christopher Gadsden in 1769, had "rarely failed since the last peace [in 1763] (as if it had been one of the secret articles of that hopeful treaty) to put in practice every means, that arbitrary, diabolical cunning, clothed with power, could devise, to reduce us to the most miserable and abject subjection." Repeatedly, the Charleston lawyer John Mackenzie told South Carolinians in the same year, they had been "refused every right, which distinguishes you from galley slaves, . . . insulted—bullied—treated like emasculated eunuchs." Subsequently, in 1773, the tea commissioners, just like the "STAMP-MASTERS" in the previous decade, complained Scaevola in the *South Carolina Gazette*, were merely vile instruments "to force the loathsome pills of slavery and oppression down the throats of free, independent . . . people." By 1774–76 a large proportion of politically relevant South Carolinians seem to have agreed with William Henry Drayton that it was "as clear as the Sun at Noon" that the "whole System of British Policy respecting America since the year 1763" had been calculated "to compel America to bow the Neck to Slavery." Every metropolitan action that contained the merest hint of "subjection of any kind," reported Alexander Hewatt, the loyalist historian of the colony, "was called slavery." Even after the British had given up the struggle, one anonymous South Carolinian believed that they still regarded South Carolinians as "revolted slaves," while what Thomas Tudor Tucker called "the language of slavery" continued to inform the perceptions of South Carolinians of their own internal political debates.[13]

---

[12] William Henry Drayton, *A Charge, on the Rise of the American Empire* . . . (Charleston, S.C., 1776), 5, 8; *A Sermon Preached on the Anniversary Meeting of the Planter's Society* (Charleston, S.C., 1769), 12; John Jacob Zubly, *An Humble Inquiry into the Nature of the Dependency of the American Colonies upon the Parliament of Great-Britain* ([Charleston, S.C.], 1769), 12; Weir, *Letters of Freeman*, 5, 20; *South Carolina Gazette* (Charleston), Mar. 16, 1769.

[13] Rusticus, *Liberty: A Poem* (Charleston, S.C., 1770), 19; Alexander Hewatt, *An Historical Account of the Rise and Progress of the Colonies of South Carolina and Georgia*, 2 vols. (London, 1779), 2:328; *A Few Salutary Hints* . . . (Charleston, S.C., 1786), 13; Weir, *Letters of*

As Bailyn has persuasively shown, such references to slavery were not simple hyperbole: "'Slavery' was a central concept in eighteenth-century political discourse," one that referred "to a specific political condition" in which the vast majority of citizens held their rights and property entirely at the will of the government.[14] Far from being an abstraction, this condition of political slavery was in fact, early modern Anglo-Americans believed on both sides of the Atlantic and both before and after the American Revolution, characteristic of virtually all of the Earth's inhabitants. Almost everywhere, the South Carolina judge Aedanus Burke wrote in 1783, tyranny had been able to establish "her favourite principle, that mankind were destined by nature for slavery, and to be hewers of wood and drawers of water for *one* or a *few*." In all parts of the "old world," David Ramsay agreed, a few of the inhabitants "are exalted to be more than men, but the greater bulk of the people, bowed down under the galling yoke of oppression, are in a state of dependence which debases human nature. In the benighted regions of Asia, and Africa," Ramsay said, "ignorance and despotism frown over the unhappy land. The lower classes are treated like beasts of burden, and transferred without ceremony from one master to another." "The great mass of mankind," echoed Thomas Tudor Tucker "had, in all times, been held in a state of servitude, . . . their mental faculties had been stifled by oppression, and the fruits of their bodily labours seized on, to satisfy the rapacious luxury of their rulers."[15]

Britain and Anglo-America alone, it was widely believed before the Revolution, still provided a refuge for liberty. As its restriction to the British world so dramatically revealed, however, liberty was a tender plant that, even in Britain, was in constant danger of being rooted up and killed by the malign forces of power and luxury. For over a century before the Revolution, opposition writers in Britain had fretted that evil ministers and corrupt courtiers would eat away at British liberty until, as an anonymous writer in the London *Public Ledger* put it in a piece reprinted in the *South Carolina Gazette*, they had turned Britain "from . . . a nation possessed of legal Freedom, which has been the envy and Admiration of the world," into a country of "the veriest Slaves that ever groaned beneath the rod of Tyranny." And,

Freeman, 23, 61, 64; William Henry Drayton, *A Letter from Freeman of South-Carolina to the Deputies of North America* (Charleston, S.C., 1774), 29–30; [Tucker], *Conciliatory Hints*, 10; *South Carolina Gazette*, Nov. 30, 1767, Aug. 23, 1770, Nov. 15, 1773, Apr. 4, June 20, Sept. 26, Oct. 31, 1774; Bailyn, *Ideological Origins*, 232–46.

[14] Bailyn, *Ideological Origins*, 232–34.

[15] Aedanus Burke, *An Address to the Freemen of South Carolina* . . . (Philadelphia, 1783), 28; Ramsay, An Oration, 1794, in "David Ramsay," 193; Thomas Tudor Tucker, *An Oration Delivered in St. Michael's Church* . . . (Charleston, S.C., 1795), 4.

as John Mackenzie warned his fellow South Carolinians in 1769, "when liberty is once lost, it is almost as difficult to [be] recovered, as life when once extinguished."[16]

"As the absolute political evil," slavery was thus by common political convention the polar opposite of liberty. Whereas liberty meant "to live upon one's own terms" and "to work for" one's "own profit and pleasure, and not for others," slavery meant "to live at the mere mercy and caprice of another" and to drudge for those who "live[d] in idleness, and would riot in luxury, rapine and oppression." Liberty, declared Hugh Alison in 1769, held out "the most attractive charms, adorned with the pleasant fruits of peace, plenty, science, virtue and happiness," while slavery, in all "its native horror and deformity, black with ignorance, wickedness and misery," offered only "a continual state of uncertainty and wretchedness; often an apprehension of violence; often the lingering dread of a premature death." Such powerlessness, as Aedanus Burke subsequently emphasized, quickly degraded "men in their own opinion" of themselves, and once impressed with their own "conscious inferiority" they soon manifested those "timid, cringing habits" that announced that they were "fit tools for the ambitious designs, and arbitrary dispositions of haughty aspiring superiors." So "habituated to Slavery" did some men become, wrote Thomas Tudor Tucker, in seconding Burke, that they "no longer" had even "the presumption to imagine themselves created for any other purpose, than to be subservient" to the will of their masters. They learned to be "patient of the Yoke, and" could not "be roused to throw it off." "Blind to their own Claims and Interest," they could scarcely be persuaded that they were "of the same Class of Beings" or were "made of the same Materials" as freemen.[17]

When men became thus "incapable either to think, or judge, or act for themselves," announced the Presbyterian pastor Thomas Reese in 1788, they were suitable only for slavery, and it was "necessary, perhaps best for them, to have a master." To be in such a condition was, as the merchant and reluctant slave trader Henry Laurens wrote in 1767, to be "the most miserable of all Men, doom'd to Labour in the Planting & Watering, without hopes of reaping the Harvest" and with no control over the direction of one's own life. Obviously, "any one, who bore [even] the resemblance of man" would "be ashamed of the character" of a slave. No wonder that "in most heroick souls, the love of liberty" was "superiour to the love of life." As one anonymous essayist exclaimed in the *South Carolina Gazette* in June 1774, "not to

---

[16] Weir, *Letters of Freeman*, 25; *South Carolina Gazette*, Sept. 26, 1774.

[17] Bailyn, *Ideological Origins*, 132; Alison, *Spiritual Liberty*, 4–6; Burke, *An Address to the Freemen*, 8–9, 11; Johnson, *Dictionary* 2:653; [Tucker], *Conciliatory Hints*, 5, 15.

be, *is better than* to be a *slave*." What autonomous freeman would not prefer death than to stoop so low as to suffer himself "to be driven to market, and sold like a stock of sheep"?[18]

When Americans expressed the fear that British measures would reduce them to slavery, they were undoubtedly, as Bailyn has argued, echoing the anxieties of several generations of metropolitan opposition writers who feared for the durability of liberty in Britain. But the "language of slavery" as expressed by South Carolinians strongly suggests that at least in South Carolina, a place where "the general topics of conversation," according to one visitor, were very largely "of negroes," and probably in all colonies with huge numbers of black slaves, that language was powerfully informed by local perceptions of the nature of chattel slavery.[19] So many of the phrases quoted above—"mere property," condemned "to groan and sweat," ruled *"with a Rod of Iron,"* "emasculated eunuchs," forced to "bow the Neck," "hewers of wood and drawers of water for *one* or a *few*," "bowed down under the galling yoke," "treated like beasts of burden," "transferred without ceremony from one master to another," the "fruits of their bodily labours seized on" to "satisfy the rapacious luxury of their rulers," living "at the mere mercy and caprice of another," "black with ignorance, wickedness and misery," impressed with their own "conscious inferiority," characterized by "timid, cringing habits," "patient of the yoke," not "of the same Class of Beings" as freemen—these and other phrases employed to depict the terrors of political slavery were virtually interchangeable with those employed by South Carolinians or visitors to describe actual conditions of chattel slavery in South Carolina.

Slavery might have been "ten fold worse . . . in the West Indies." South Carolinians might, as Alexander Hewatt and other observers indicated, have "treat[ed] their slaves with as much, and perhaps more tenderness, than those of any [other] British colony where slavery exists." But they were still slaves. "Entirely at the mercy" of and forced to "yield absolute obedience" to their masters, they had to "drudge on without any prospect of reaping for themselves" and were "obliged to devote their lives, their limbs, their will, and every vital exertion to swell the wealth of masters." In this "state of perpetual humiliation," they acquired such "cowardly ideas" that some whites

---

[18] Reese, *Influence of Religion*, 83; Henry Laurens to Jonathan Bryan, Sept. 4, 1767, *The Papers of Henry Laurens*, ed. Philip M. Hamer et al., 12 vols. to date (Columbia, S.C., 1968—), 5: 289; Alison, *Spiritual Liberty*, 4; Weir, *Letters of Freeman*, 22, 38; *South Carolina Gazette*, Nov. 15, 1770, Nov. 29, 1773, June 3, July 4, 1774.

[19] "Journal of Josiah Quincy, Jr.," 450, 456; [Tucker], *Conciliatory Hints*, 10.

came to regard them as "beings of an inferior rank . . . little exalted above brute creatures."[20]

If whites were so inured to slavery that, as one contemporary observer wrote, "they neither see, hear, nor feel the woes of their poor slaves, from whose painful labours all their wealth proceeds," these linguistic similarities might have represented nothing more than a subliminal awareness of an identification between political slavery and chattel slavery. But it is not necessary to rely on linguistic parallels to show that for South Carolinians such an identification was conscious and explicit. "Whatever we may think of ourselves," wrote Christopher Gadsden in the *South Carolina Gazette* in June 1769, "we are as real SLAVES as those we are permitted to command, and differ only in degree: for what is a slave," he asked, "but one that is at the will of his master, and has no property of his own, but on the most precarious tenure." Those too timorous to resist enslavement by Britain, advised an anonymous writer in the same newspaper seventeen months later, "should go and entreat some negro to change states with you. Don't fear that you will change for the worse. His situation is greatly superior to yours. He has but one master; you have thousands: Should he be robbed, oppressed, or illused, by an Overseer or Driver; he may come in person, and lay his grievances before his owner, who can have no interest in suffering him to be illused. Can you do so, when you are injured by your [British] Drivers," this writer asked? "I leave it to you my Countrymen," said "A Carolinian" in the *Gazette* in June 1774, "whether we *are* not put upon a worse Footing than our Slaves."[21]

A comprehension of the very great extent to which South Carolinians made an explicit connection between political slavery and chattel slavery is an essential first step toward constructing an answer to the question of Dr. Johnson, quoted at the beginning of this essay, "How is it that we hear the loudest yelps for liberty among the drivers of negroes?" My argument is that it was precisely their intimate familiarity with chattel slavery that made

---

[20] Henry Laurens to John Laurens, Aug. 4, 1776, in Jack P. Greene, ed., *Colonies to Nation, 1763–1789: A Documentary History of the American Revolution* (New York, 1967), 396–97; *On the Threshold of Liberty: Journal of a Frenchman's Tour of the American Colonies in 1777*, trans. Edward D. Seeber (Bloomington, Ind., 1959), 14; Hewatt, *History of South-Carolina* 2:94–97, 101; Ramsay, *History of South Carolina* 2:92; J. Hector St. John De Crèvecoeur, *Letters from an American Farmer* (New York, 1912), 161; John Laurens to Henry Laurens, Feb. 2, 1778, *The Army Correspondence of Colonel John Laurens in the Years 1777–8* (New York, 1847), 116.

[21] Crèvecoeur, *Letters from an American Farmer*, 160; *South Carolina Gazette*, June 22, 1769, Nov. 15, 1770, June 22, 1774.

South Carolinians, and other southern and West Indian colonists, so sensitive to any challenges to their own liberty as free men—and for at least two reasons.

First, the institution of chattel slavery, which David Ramsay once referred to as "our local weakness," rendered South Carolina, in Christopher Gadsden's words, "a very weak Province." "Their Number so much exceeding [that of] the Whites," the slaves, as all white South Carolinians were aware, were "very dangerous Domestics" who posed an omnipresent threat of "domestic insurrections" and greatly limited the colony's capacity to resist the bonds its inhabitants thought the metropolis was forging for them. "We find in our case according to the general perceptible workings of Providence where the crime most commonly . . . draws a similar and suitable punishment," Gadsden wrote William Samuel Johnson in 1766, "that slavery begets slavery." The truth of this observation had already been demonstrated for Gadsden by the impotent responses of Jamaica and other British West Indian colonies to the Grenville revenue measures, and, he and other South Carolina opponents of Britain's menacing measures believed, it behooved people who, like the South Carolinians, were similarly exposed by the presence of such a powerful domestic enemy to take a militant stand against any threat to their liberty before that threat had become so formidable that they had, like their slaves, lost all "power of resistance."[22]

But their awareness of how vulnerable the large number of black slaves made South Carolina to metropolitan attacks upon the liberty of its inhabitants was not the only or even the primary reason why they yelped so loudly for liberty. Much more important, I would suggest, was their acute sensitivity, a sensitivity dramatically reinforced by daily experience, to the horrors and degradation of chattel slavery in South Carolina. Edmund Burke appreciated as much in 1775 when he attributed the peculiarly intense spirit of liberty in Virginia and the Carolinas to their "vast multitude of slaves." "Where this is the case in any part of the world," said Burke in persuasively

---

[22] Civis [David Ramsay], *An Address to the Freeman of South-Carolina, on the Subject of the Federal Constitution* (Charleston, S.C., 1788), 3; George Milligen-Johnston, *A Short Description of the Province of South-Carolina* (London, 1770), 25–26; Christopher Gadsden to William Samuel Johnson, Apr. 16, 1766, to Samuel Adams, May 23, 1774, *The Writings of Christopher Gadsden, 1746–1805*, ed. Richard Walsh (Columbia, S.C., 1968), 72, 93; *Constitution for South Carolina* ([Charleston, S.C.], 1776), 2; "Journal of Josiah Quincy, Jr.," 456–57. David Ramsay suggested still another sense in which slavery affected the free population adversely in his *History of the Revolution of South Carolina* 2:122: "The mischievous effects of negro-slavery were, at this time [of the British invasion], abundantly apparent. Several who had lived in ease and affluence from the produce of their lands, cultivated by the labour of slaves, had not fortitude enough to dare to be poor."

underlining the most salient feature of the intimate connection between liberty and slavery in Revolutionary America, "those who are free are by far the most proud and jealous of their freedom. Freedom is to them," Burke continued,

> not only an enjoyment but a kind of rank and privilege. Not seeing that freedom, as in countries where it is a common blessing and as broad and general as the air, may be united with much abject toil, with great misery, with all the exterior of servitude, liberty looks among them like something that is more noble and liberal. I do not mean, sir, to commend the superior morality of this sentiment, which has at least as much pride as virtue in it, but I cannot alter the nature of man. The fact is so, and these people of the southern colonies are much more strongly attached to liberty, than those to the northward. Such were all the ancient commonwealths; such were our Gothic ancestors; such in our days were the Poles; and such will be all masters of slaves, who are not slaves themselves. In such a people, the haughtiness of domination combines with the spirit of freedom, fortifies it, and renders it invincible.

So far from being inconsistent or incongruous with liberty, then, as Dr. Johnson's question implied, slavery, Burke appreciated, acted as its most powerful reinforcement—among free men.[23]

Nor did Revolutionary South Carolinians fail to appreciate the vibrant dialectic between chattel slavery and liberty, as two political essayists of the mid–1790s, lawyers Timothy Ford and Henry William DeSaussure, made abundantly clear during the famous debate over whether the overrepresentation of the lowcountry was a threat to the liberty of the upcountry. Both argued that it was not. Liberty, declared Ford, "is a principle which naturally and spontaneously contrasts with slavery. In no country on earth can the line of distinction ever be marked so boldly as in the lowcountry. Here there is a standing subject of comparison, which must be ever perfect and ever obvious. The instant a citizen is oppressed *below par* . . . in point of freedom," indicated Ford, "he approaches to the condition of his own slave, his spirit is at once aroused, and he necessarily recoils into his former standing. The constant example of slavery," Ford declaimed in language that could scarcely be more explicit, "stimulates a free man to avoid being confounded with the blacks; and seeing that in every instance of depression he is brought nearer to a par with them, his efforts must invariably force him

---

[23] Burke, "Speech on Conciliation," 134–35.

towards an opposite point. In the country where personal freedom, and the principles of equality, were carried to the greatest extent ever known," concluded Ford in referring to ancient Sparta, "domestic slavery was the most common, and under the least restraint." DeSaussure made much the same point when he insisted that "where inequality of property prevails, the citizens are more jealous and watchful of their liberties from that very circumstance. In relation to the government of the United States, this remark is certainly true; for the southern states, where such an inequality exists, are the most jealous." South Carolina, like "North Carolina and Virginia, particularly the latter," had been widely "celebrated as states extremely attached to liberty," and, DeSaussure pointed out, seconding Ford and expanding upon the point made twenty years earlier by Burke, "it has been remarked of the ancient free states of Greece, that their knowledge of the horrors of domestic slavery, which prevailed among them, rendered them more fiercely jealous of their liberties than any other people of the world." Dr. Johnson to the contrary notwithstanding, Ford and DeSaussure strongly argued, "domestic slavery, so far from being inconsistent, has, in fact, a tendency to stimulate and perpetuate the spirit of liberty."[24]

If free white South Carolinians gloried in their intense commitment to liberty during the Revolutionary era, they also took conscious pride in the equality of American life. The "people of the United States," Charles Pinckney approvingly told the delegates to the Federal Convention in Philadelphia in June 1787, were "more equal in their circumstances than the people of any other Country," while David Ramsay, in the following year, expressed pleasure that the new country abounded "with free men all of one rank, where property is equally diffused."[25] If, however, South Carolinians approved of the equality of American society, how could they reconcile their celebration of equality, meaning "not inferior or superior," with the institu-

[24] Americanus [Timothy Ford], *The Constitutionalist: or, An Inquiry How Far It Is Expedient and Proper to Alter the Constitution of South Carolina* (Charleston, S.C., 1794), 39–40; Phocion [Henry William DeSaussure], *Letters of the Questions of the Justice and Expediency of Going into Alterations of the Representation in the Legislature of South Carolina* (Charleston, S.C., 1795), 9, 18.

[25] [Ramsay], *An Address to the Freemen*, 11; Johnson, *Dictionary* 1:636; Jonathan Elliot, ed., *The Debates in the Several State Conventions on the Adoption of the Federal Constitution*, 5 vols. (Philadelphia, 1896), 4:123; Charles Pinckney, speech, June 25, 1787, in Farrand, *Records of the Federal Convention* 1:397–407.

tion of chattel slavery, which systematically kept at least a third of South Carolina's inhabitants in a state of perpetual inequality?

This was a question that had worried them throughout the Revolutionary era. During the debates with Britain in the 1760s and 1770s, South Carolinians had repeatedly claimed that they "were born to freedom, equally with" Britons in the home islands and were entitled to all of the same rights. As local critics pointed out, however, this position was fraught with danger for a slave society like South Carolina. Were such "Principles adopted, and every genuine Right of Liberty which is established in *England* made attainable in *America*," observed "A Back Settler" in an anonymous pamphlet published in 1774, "it would complete the Ruin of many *American* Provinces, as well as the *West-India* islands. A general Manumission of Negroes is a Doctrine badly calculated for the Meridian of either *America* or the Islands; yet it is one of those *original* Rights, the Exercise of which all human Forms immediately enjoy, by setting a Foot on that happy Territory [in Great Britain] where Slavery is forbidden to perch."[26]

Nor was "A Back Settler" the only one to express an awareness of this problem. When in June 1788 Charles Cotesworth Pinckney sought to explain to critics of the proposed Federal Constitution why he and other delegates at Philadelphia had not incorporated a bill of rights, he offered as one reason which "weighed particularly with the members for this state" the fact that "such bills generally begin with declaring that all men are by nature born free. Now, we should make that declaration with a very bad grace," he added, "when a large part of our property consists in men who are actually born slaves." Significantly, none of South Carolina's three late eighteenth-century constitutions contained any such declaration, and when in 1795 Henry William DeSaussure sought to counter Robert Goodloe Harper's assertion that "equality is the natural condition of man" during the pamphlet war over the inequity of representation in the legislature, he reminded Harper—and other South Carolinians—that "such is the state of society in South Carolina, that if this principle, which is the foundation of all others, was adopted and reduced to practice, it would instantly free the unfortunate slaves, who form two-fifths of the whole people, and are the only cultivators of the soil in the low country."[27]

---

[26] Weir, *Letters of Freeman*, 46–47; Back Settler, *Some Fugitive Thoughts*, 25.

[27] Elliot, *Debates in the Several State Conventions* 4:316; Elmer D. Johnson and Kathleen Lewis Sloan, comps., *South Carolina: A Documentary Profile of the Palmetto State* (Columbia, S.C., 1971), 179–81, 195–99, 232–37; [DeSaussure], *Letters on the Questions of the Justice and Expediency*, 8.

In denying civil equality to slaves, of course, South Carolina was by no means unique. As I have pointed out elsewhere,[28] every state, not only slave states, pointedly limited full civil rights to *"free Citizens,"* the "word free," as David Ramsay explained, having been specifically "introduced to exclude slaves." But the qualifying adjective was scarcely necessary in either South Carolina or the other states, for, in the English tradition, every state routinely denied full rights of citizenship to all dependents and "people without discretion," including servants, women, children, the unpropertied, and those "fit for *Bedlam."* From a long line of English theorists, from Henry Ireton in the mid-seventeenth century to Sir William Blackstone in the mid-eighteenth century, Americans had learned that those who lived "in subjection [to], or at the discretion" of others, those who had "no will of their own," had to be excluded from the full "privileges and immunities" of citizens because they lacked the requisite personal independence to ensure that they would be free—and equal—agents in the political process.[29]

In Revolutionary America, quite as much as in Georgian Britain, there were thus two distinct categories of people: free, independent adult males, who were full citizens, and the rest of the people, mostly dependents, who were merely "inhabitants or residents." And, as David Ramsay emphasized, there was "a great difference between" the two. Consisting of "any person living within a country or state," inhabitants had "no farther connection with the state in which" they resided "than such as" gave them "security for" their "person[s] and property, agreeably to fixed laws, without any participation in its government," while citizens had "a right of voting at elections, and many other privileges."[30]

But South Carolina excluded not just slaves but all blacks from citizenship, specifically confining the "rights of *election* and *representation*" to "free white men" of twenty-one or older, a limitation that makes clear that it was not just their status as dependents but their presumed disabilities as men that debarred slaves from citizenship. To be sure, as "A Back Settler" wrote in 1774, and the choice of language is significant, blacks did have "human

---

[28] Jack P. Greene, *All Men Are Created Equal: Some Reflections on the Character of the American Revolution* (Oxford, 1976) [chap. 10 above].

[29] David Ramsay, *Observations on the Division of the House of Representatives of the United States* (New York, 1789), 4; Weir, *Letters of Freeman,* 59; Johnson, *Dictionary* 1:497; Greene, *All Men Are Created Equal,* 17–23.

[30] Burke, *Address to the Freemen of South Carolina,* 32; David Ramsay, *A Dissertation on the Manner of Acquiring the Character and Privileges of a Citizen of the United States* (n.p., 1789), 3–4.

Forms." But many white South Carolinians, as Alexander Hewatt pointed out in a remark quoted earlier, were prepared to argue that blacks were "beings of an inferior rank, and [but] little exalted above brute creatures." Even local champions of emancipation such as John Laurens admitted that blacks would have to be raised on "the scale of being" before they could assume a status fully equal to that of whites. In South Carolina, then, all blacks, slave and free, as Ramsay remarked, were "inhabitants, but not citizens." They were not citizens, I would submit, because white South Carolinians of the Revolutionary generation, like their descendants in the following century, were persuaded that they were something less than full men and had, therefore, no claim for inclusion in the clause "all men are created equal" in the Declaration of Independence. That declaration had, after all, been the pronouncement of free, independent men in a revolution that, as a later South Carolinian pointed out, "was a *family quarrel among equals*" in which "the negroes [naturally] had no concern."[31]

When South Carolinians announced that "every man in this country . . . has a right to think and act as he pleases," they were thus obviously not including blacks in the category *man*. But even among the "free white inhabitants" there were, as Josiah Quincy, Jr., noted in the remarks quoted at the opening of this essay, such great social and economic inequalities as forcefully to raise the question of precisely what Revolutionary South Carolinians meant when they joined other Americans in subscribing to the assertion "all men are created equal" and in celebrating the equality of the new American nation. One thing they could have meant was merely that all men were equally mortal. As Timothy Ford observed in 1794, "every man came into the world equally naked and helpless and all returned to a state of perfect equality in the grave." Another was that all men, as the dissenting minister William Tennent set down in a dictum later incorporated into the South Carolina constitution, had "a full and undiminished freedom in the exercise of" their "own judgment, in all religious matters." But the form of equality South Carolinians seem to have valued most highly during the era of the

---

[31] Burke, *Address to the Freemen of South Carolina*, 32; Johnson and Sloan, *South Carolina*, 179–81, 195–99, 232–37; Back Settler, *Some Fugitive Thoughts*, 25; Hewatt, *History of South-Carolina* 2:101; Ramsay, *Dissertation on the Manner*, 3; William Henry Drayton, *Speech . . . upon the Articles of Confederation* (Charleston, S.C., 1778), 35; John Laurens to Henry Laurens, Feb. 2, 1778, *Army Correspondence*, 116; Greene, *All Men Are Created Equal*, 41.

American Revolution was what they referred to as civil equality, which was of course confined to citizens.[32]

For South Carolinians, as for most Americans, civil equality had two related meanings. First, it meant that there were "no privileged orders," that no man had "any privilege above his fellow-citizens," who were all "equally subject to the laws" with "the vote of any one elector" going "as far as that of any other." "We may congratulate ourselves in living under the blessings of a mild and equal government, which knows no distinctions but those of merits or talents," rhapsodized Charles Pinckney in the South Carolina ratifying convention in 1788, "under a government whose honors and offices are equally open to the exertions of all her citizens, and which adopts virtue and worth for her own, wheresoever she can find them." "Among us," added David Ramsay, "no one can exercise any authority by virtue of birth. All start equal in the race of life. No man is born a legislator."[33]

In another, closely connected but more general sense, civil equality meant that every citizen was "upon a footing of the most perfect equality with respect to every civil liberty." That is, as David Ramsay said in his Independence Day oration in 1794, "every citizen is perfectly free of the will of every other citizen, while all are equally subject to the laws. . . . We are not bound by any laws but those to which we have consented. . . . No man can be deprived of his life, liberty or property, but by the operation of laws, freely, fairly and by common consent previously enacted." At least among citizens, there should be no "unequal distribution of justice." In the same year as Ramsay's oration, lawyer Timothy Ford elaborated more fully upon the meaning of civil equality for South Carolinians. "To what . . . does the term equality relate," he asked in *The Constitutionalist*, one of three pamphlets published in response to Robert Goodloe Harper's call for equal representation for the upcountry. "I will answer in the words of the French Constitution; 'men are born and always continue free, and equal in respect to *their rights*.' Thus," Ford declared, "my personal liberty is equal to that of any other man; my life is *equally* sacred and inviolable; my bodily powers are *equally* my own; my power over my own actions is *equally* great and *equally* secured from external restraint; my will is *equally* free; what I acquire, be it greater or less, I have an *equal* right to possess, to use and to

---

[32] Weir, *Letters of Freeman*, 47; Drayton, *Speech*, 35; "Journal of Josiah Quincy, Jr.," 454–55; [Ford], *Constitutionalist*, 5; William Tennent III, *Mr. Tennent's Speech on the Dissenting Petition* . . . (Charleston, S.C., 1777), 15.

[33] Ramsay, *History of South Carolina* 2:132; [Tucker], *Conciliatory Hints*, 12; Elliot, *Debates in the Several State Conventions* 4:323; Ramsay, An Oration, 1794, in "David Ramsay," 192; Johnson, *Dictionary* 1:975.

enjoy. I have an *equal* claim upon the protection of the laws; an *equal* right to serve my country; and an *equal* claim to be exempted from service."[34]

South Carolinians disagreed over the extent to which their state had actually achieved this "fine, plain, level state of civil equality," some men fearing with Aedanus Burke and Robert Goodloe Harper that the "unequal distribution of property" and representation in favor of the lowcountry was causing it to run rapidly "into an aristocracy." But, although some men like Charles Pinckney praised that "mediocrity of fortune" that was so "unfavorable to the rapid distinction of ranks" all over the United States, there was widespread agreement that *"equality of conditions"* was emphatically not a legitimate social objective of republican government, at least not in South Carolina.[35] Again, Timothy Ford provided the fullest and most eloquent testimony. "In the endowment of natural gifts and faculties," he explained, in *The Constitutionalist*,

nature has instituted almost every gradation, from the confines of inferior animals to the state of superior creation. Her views in the *human condition* are evidently to inequality. Why hath she made one man strong, another weak; one nimble and alert, another heavy and inactive; one industrious and another slothful? Why hath she dropped scarcely a solitary spark of her celestial fire into one mind, and beamed into another the richest and most copious effulgence? Why are some men bold and others timid; some sagacious and others dull; some successful and others unfortunate?

Delivering mankind out of her hands so differently and unequally endowed in these respects, can it for a moment be imagined that nature ever intended they should be equal in their circumstances? If she did she stands fairly convicted of instituting means which must of necessity frustrate her own ends; of making war upon her own purposes. If nature then has not only made men unequal at first, but has put them into a situation in which the fruits of that inequality must be constantly accumulating; if in all the combinations into which men have been thrown in the world, it has ever been preserved, the unavoidable conclusion is, that inequality [—not equality—] is one of nature's laws.

[34] [Tucker], *Conciliatory Hints*, 9, 12; Ramsay, An Oration, 1794, in "David Ramsay," 192; [Ford], *Constitutionalist*, 35–36.

[35] Burke, *Address to the Freemen of South Carolina*, 14, and *Considerations on the Society, or Order of Cincinnati* . . . (Charleston, S.C., 1783), 10–11, 25–27, 30–32; Charles Pinckney, speech, June 25, 1787, in Farrand, *Records of the Federal Convention* 1:397–407; Elliot, *Debates in the Several State Conventions* 4:323; Appius [Robert Goodloe Harper], *An Address to the People of South Carolina* . . . (Charleston, S.C., 1794), 17, 20, 30, 36.

Ford did not deny that nature had "created all men free and equal *in their rights*." But he was absolutely persuaded that "*equality of rights*" in no sense required "*equality of condition*." "The former is so far from implying the latter," he contended, "that it is the true parent of the very reverse." "By the very principles of the social compact," society guaranteed "to each what each acquires; and in so doing must necessarily guarantee *inequality of condition*." "In a word," concluded Ford, "equality of *condition* is inconsistent with the laws of nature, not derivable from the rights of man, and not to be found in any of the institutions of civil society. It is as absurd to look for it, or to attempt to force the human condition to it, as *equality of happiness*."[36]

When South Carolinians expressed pride in the "principles of liberty and equality" that "pervade[d] the constitution and laws of the state," they were thus referring largely to "*equality of rights*" and most assuredly not to "*equality of condition*." "By equality is to be understood, equality of civil rights, and not of condition," declared Thomas Tudor Tucker in an oration, also in answer to Harper, delivered at St. Michael's Church in 1795, "for, the latter could never be produced, but by the total destruction of the former, and could only have place in a state of barbarism and wretchedness. Equality of rights necessarily produces inequality of possessions; because, by the laws of nature and of equality, every man has a right to use his faculties, in an honest way, and the fruits of his labour are his own. But, some men may have more strength than others, some more industry, and some more ingenuity, than others; and, according to these, and many other circumstances, the products of their labour must be various, and their property must become unequal." Even Harper agreed that "'*equality of conditions*' cannot be preserved in society." What separated him, on the one hand, and Ford and Tucker, on the other, was that the latter were persuaded that inequality of condition was not only inevitable but desirable. "So far from being an evil," Tucker declared, "this inequality . . . is absolutely necessary to the well being of society; it is the cement that binds together the various employments of life, and forms the whole into a beautiful system of mutual dependencies. The rights of property," both Ford and Tucker emphasized, "must be sacred, and must be protected; otherwise, there could be no exertion of either ingenuity or industry, and, consequently, nothing but extreme poverty, misery and brutal ignorance."[37]

In their critiques of the notion of equality of condition, Ford and Tucker

---

[36] [Ford], *Constitutionalist*, 7–9, 30–36.

[37] Tucker, *Oration*, 20–21; [Harper], *Address to the People of South Carolina*, iii; Ramsay, *History of South Carolina* 2:142.

revealed just how strongly South Carolina conceptions of equality had been shaped by a prior and much more pervasive and absolute commitment to liberty. No form of equality that in any way restricted a citizen's liberty, as Tucker phrased it, "to use his faculties, in an honest way," to acquire whatever property he possibly could, could have received much support from a people that took such "warm and animating pride" in their own liberty. Indeed, in rejecting all ideas of equality of condition, Ford and Tucker were merely reaffirming a strong commitment to what, from its very beginning, had perhaps been the deepest meaning of South Carolina for its free, white inhabitants—the promise of a "sure road to competency & independence" for the "frugal & industrious." "From the first settlement in this country," wrote David Ramsay, the "facility of procuring landed property . . . gave every citizen an opportunity of becoming an independent freeholder." "Industrious people" in South Carolina, Alexander Hewatt agreed, "though exposed to more trouble and hardship for a few years," had far "better opportunities than in Europe for advancing to an easy and independent state." "Every industrious man," said Dr. Lionel Chalmers, could "find employment and receive high wages for his labour; so that with economy, he has a prospect of acquiring a tolerable fortune, in a space of sixteen or twenty years," including "plantations and slaves in the country." Once "upon his plantation," moreover, a man could set "himself down, and being both landlord and farmer, immediately" find "himself an independent man. Having his capital in lands and negroes around him, he can [then] manage and improve them as he thinks fit. He soon obtains plenty of the necessaries of life from his plantation; nor need he want any of its conveniences and luxuries." No country, said Christopher Gadsden, had "more openings . . . for adventurous men, of greater credit than capitals, to make a fortune by."[38]

Such prospects of "Affluence, Plenty and Independence" not only spurred men to industry but, as many contemporaries noted, unleashed an "ambitious . . . grasping after . . . wealth." In such an atmosphere, even "the *best* of men" were easily induced "to take every Step of aggrandizing their Fortunes" so that, for many people, as one acerbic social critic contended in the *South Carolina Gazette* in March 1773, "their whole Lives" were but "one

---

[38] Tucker, *Oration*, 20–21; Burke, *Consideration on the Society*, 10–11; Charles Pinckney, speech, June 25, 1787, in Farrand, *Records of the Federal Convention* 1:397–407; David Ramsay, "An Oration on the Advantages of American Independence," 1778, and An Oration, 1794, in "David Ramsay," 187–88, 191; Hewatt, *History of South Carolina* 2:130–134; Weir, *Letters of Freeman*, 78; [Christopher Gadsden], *A Few Observations on Some Late Public Transactions* . . . (Charleston, S.C., 1797), 24; Lionel Chalmers, *An Account of the Weather and Diseases of South-Carolina* (London, 1776), 30.

continued Race; in which every one is endeavouring to distance all behind him, and to overtake, or pass by, all before him; every one is flying from his Inferiors in Pursuit of his Superiors, who fly from him with equal Alacrity." Thus, this writer argued,

> every Tradesman is a Merchant, every Merchant is a Gentleman, and every Gentleman one of the Noblesse. We are a Country of Gentry, *Populous generosorum*: We have no such Thing as a common People among us: Between Vanity and Fashion, the Species is utterly destroyed. The Sons of our lowest Mechanics are sent to the Colleges of Philadelphia, England, or Scotland, and there acquire, with their Learning, the laudable Ambition of Becoming Gentle-Folkes, despite their paternal Occupations, and we are all solicitous for the more honourable Employment of Doctors, Lawyers, and Parsons; whilst the pretty little Misses at Home are exercised in no Professions at all, except those of Music and Dancing, which . . . make them very agreeable Companions, but will render them very expensive Wives.[39]

With such a mentalité, stimulated for most of the last half of the eighteenth century by a boom economy, freemen could scarcely have tolerated in the name of equality any diminution of their liberty to employ whatever natural or adventitious advantages they might have possessed in the race for profits and the status that derived from having "a stately Slave stand on every Perch of" an "extensive Plantation." To have done so would have constituted an unacceptable abridgment of that very independence that was the single most important quality that distinguished a free man from a slave.[40]

"Slavery or Independence"? The question was not a new one that had been suddenly posed for white South Carolinians by the conflict with Britain and the experience of the American Revolution. Rather, it was one that the very composition of their social system, specifically, the institution of chattel slavery, had powerfully thrust upon them at least three-quarters of a century before the Revolution and that would continue to demand their attention until that institution was finally abolished at the end of the American Civil War. What this essay has tried to show is that the symbiotic relationship

---

[39] Milligen-Johnston, *Short Description*, 87; Reese, *Influence of Religion*, 25; Back Settler, *Some Fugitive Thoughts*, 34; *South Carolina Gazette*, Mar. 1, 1773.

[40] Back Settler, *Some Fugitive Thoughts*, 34.

between slavery and independence in their daily lives was an important shaping influence in their political responses, both to British measures between 1763 and 1776 and to their own internal contentions in subsequent decades, and in their application and conceptions of the Revolutionary ideas of liberty, slavery, and equality.

This essay was written for presentation as the annual address before the South Carolina Historical Society in Charleston on Feb. 24, 1979. It has been reprinted in Kermit L. Hall, ed., *The Law of American Slavery* (New York, 1988) and Paul Finkelman, ed., *Slavery, Revolutionary America, and the New Nation* (New York, 1989), 191–214. It is reprinted here with permission and minor corrections from *South Carolina Historical Magazine* 80 (1979): 193–214.

—TWELVE—

A Fortuitous Convergence:
Culture, Circumstance, and Contingency in the Emergence of the American Nation

THOUGH THERE have been a few dissenters, most historians have agreed upon two propositions about the emergence of American nationalism. First, in contrast to the situation in most later new nations emerging from a colonial to an independent status, nationalism was a result, not a cause, of America's war for "national liberation" in 1775–83. Indeed, perhaps the central outcomes of the American Revolution, as S. N. Eisenstadt has remarked, were "the reconstruction of the boundaries of the new political community and [the] generation of the symbols of . . . national . . . identity."[1] Second, as Yehoshua Arieli has emphasized, "American nationalism rested on assumptions fundamentally different from those of [most] other nations." Unlike those of most Europeans, the national identity of Americans was "not based on stressing the common historical experience of primordial groups" or upon ethnic, religious, and cultural homogeneity, "the primary conditions for the consciousness of national unity and community" in most other political societies. Rather, Arieli argues compellingly, it "was based from the outset on the acceptance of the 'American way of life,' on the acceptance of a system of social and political institutions and the norms and values embodied in them." In contrast to other nations, the American nation, he explains, thus "established its identity in a pattern of political and social organization and in the benefits and powers deriving from its territory and its state. Citizenship was the only criterion which made the individual a member of the

---

[1] S. N. Eisenstadt, *Revolution and the Transformation of Societies: A Comparative Study of Civilizations* (New York, 1978), 241–42.

national community: and national loyalty meant loyalty to the Constitution. The formative force of American national unity has been, then, the idea of citizenship; through this concept the integration of states and society into a nation has been achieved."[2]

This essay represents a preliminary exploration of two quite speculative propositions. First, it argues that, far from being inevitable, the appearance of the American nation along with its peculiar variant of nationalism during the American Revolution was, in fact, highly problematic, the result of a fortuitous and short-range social and cultural convergence among Britain's North American colonies. Second, it suggests that the pace and direction of social development among those colonies was such that an American nation could not have emerged either much earlier or much later.

Perhaps the best way to begin discussion of this subject is to place in evidence two quotations. The first is by Benjamin Franklin and is taken from a pamphlet written in 1760, just a decade and a half before the Declaration of Independence. Britain, wrote Franklin, had

> already fourteen separate governments on the maritime coast of the continent, and if we extend our settlements shall probably have as many more behind them on the inland side. Those we now have, are not only under different governors, but have different forms of government, different laws, different interests, and some of them different religious persuasions and different manners. Their jealousy of each other is so great that however necessary an union of the colonies has long been, for their common defence and security against their enemies, and how sensible soever each colony has been of that necessity, yet they have never been able to effect such an union among themselves, nor even to agree in requesting the mother country to establish it for them.[3]

---

[2] Yehoshua Arieli, *Individualism and Nationalism in American Ideology* (Cambridge, 1964), 19, 24, 33; S. N. Eisenstadt in "Symposium: America Facing the Future," *The American Experience in Historical Perspective* (Ramat Gan, Israel, 1979), 300.

[3] Benjamin Franklin, *The Interest of Great Britain Considered* (London, 1760), in *The Papers of Benjamin Franklin*, ed. Leonard W. Labaree et al., 27 vols. to date (New Haven, 1959—), 9:90.

The second quotation is by Thomas Paine and dates from 1776 on the very eve of the first tentative formation of an American nation. "It might be difficult, if not impossible, to form the continent into one government half a century hence," Paine warned Americans in *Common Sense* in imploring them not to "let slip the opportunity" for forming a national union: "The vast variety of interests, occasioned by an increase of trade and population, would create confusion. Colony would be against colony. Each being able would scorn each other's assistance: and while the proud and foolish gloried in their little distinctions, the wise would lament that the union had not been formed before."[4]

Franklin's emphasis upon the differences and jealousies among the colonies was not without foundation. Indeed, if one looks closely at the two major centers of English settlement on the North American continent during the first half of the seventeenth century, at the tobacco colonies of the Chesapeake and the Puritan colonies of New England, it would be difficult to imagine how any two areas composed almost entirely of Englishmen could have been any more different. About the only characteristics they had in common were their ethnic homogeneity, their ruralness, and, after the first few years, an abundant local food supply. In almost every other respect, they were diametric opposites.

Within a decade after the settlement of Virginia in 1607, the Chesapeake societies were oriented toward the production of a single staple crop—tobacco—for the metropolitan market, and the high profits for this product quickly made the reckless and single-minded pursuit of individual gain the central animating impulse and the chief social determinant of a region that also included Maryland to the north after 1634 and the northern portions of Carolina to the south beginning in the 1660s. In quest of wealth that would take them back to the civilized comforts they had left behind in England, men greedily took high risks, dispersed themselves over the land, and engaged in ruthless exploitation of labor. This highly exploitative, labor-intensive, dispersed, transient, and secular market-oriented society was composed very heavily of landless single men, most of them English bond servants. With few families, the structure of its households more closely resembled those in nineteenth-century mining boomtowns than in contemporary rural England. With a high death rate and a low birth rate, population increased very slowly and largely through immigration. The differential success rates characteristic of staple economies meant that wealth was concentrated in a relatively few hands and levels of social differentiation,

---

[4] Thomas Paine, *Common Sense* (Philadelphia, 1776), in *The Complete Writings of Thomas Paine*, ed. Philip S. Foner, 2 vols. (New York, 1945), 1:36.

based almost entirely upon wealth, were high. At the same time, the fragility of life and fortune and the lack of clear connection between wealth and the traditional attributes of leadership as they were understood by Englishmen in the home islands meant that political and social authority was weak, impermanent, and open to challenge and that the potential for social discord was great. The last thing that seemed to interest these early Virginians, a later observer remarked, was the building of "a Country for posterity."[5]

By sharp contrast, the Puritan colonies of New England had been settled by families in a single massive migration concentrated in the 1630s and motivated very largely by the desire to escape the religious impurity of Albion and to establish a city upon a hill, a true religious commonwealth that would serve as a model for the Christian world. Highly religious, with pronounced communal impulses, the inhabitants settled in nuclear households and in small villages organized around the church, villages that from the very beginning were conceived of as permanent. With no profitable staple, they engaged primarily in mixed subsistence agriculture and built societies that were far more egalitarian in terms of the distribution of wealth than those to the south. With a benign disease environment and a balanced sex ratio, mortality was low, fecundity high, and demographic growth rapid, primarily the result of natural increase. With a large number of visible leaders who obviously had all the attributes of sociopolitical authority among the initial immigrants and a high degree of cooperation between secular and clerical leaders, lines of authority were clear and the potential for contention and discord was low.[6]

At least on the surface, these strong social divergencies among the English colonies seemed to increase over time as the Chesapeake colonies acquired a strong biracial character with the transition from European servant to African slave labor between 1680 and 1730 and with the establishment of two new—and also distinctive—nodes of settlement during the last decades of the seventeenth century. The so-called Middle Colonies, consisting of New York, conquered from the Dutch in 1664, New Jersey, Delaware, and Pennsylvania, settled by the English between 1664 and 1681, were characterized

---

[5] See Edmund S. Morgan, *American Slavery, American Freedom: The Ordeal of Colonial Virginia* (New York, 1975), and Thad W. Tate and David L. Ammerman, eds., *The Chesapeake in the Seventeenth Century: Essays on Anglo-American Society* (Chapel Hill, N.C., 1979). The quotation is from John Hammond, *Leah and Rachel* (London, 1656), in Clayton C. Hall, ed., *Narratives of Early Maryland, 1633–1684* (New York, 1910), 286.

[6] For summaries of the conclusions of recent literature on colonial New England, see John M. Murrin, "Review Essay," *History and Theory* 11 (1972): 226–75, and Jack P. Greene, "Autonomy and Stability: New England and the British Colonial Experience in Early Modern America," *Journal of Social History* 7 (1974): 171–94.

by profound ethnic, religious, and social diversity, rapid change, and, at least through their first decades of English control, high levels of public contention.[7] The other node, stretching out from Charleston on the South Carolina coast north into North Carolina and south into coastal Georgia, was similarly diverse. With rice, naval stores, and eventually indigo as enormously profitable staples, these colonies, at least at their center, were even more materialistic and far more slave and African than the Chesapeake. Many parishes in lowcountry South Carolina had a black-white ratio ranging from 7 to 1 to 9 to 1 and looked far more like the West Indian colonies of Barbados and Jamaica than any colonies to the north.[8]

Nor was Franklin's assessment of the effects of this extraordinary diversity among Britain's continental colonies peculiar to him. Quite the contrary, virtually every commentator on both sides of the Atlantic in the decades just before the Revolution was far more impressed with the differences than with the similarities among the colonies. They were, moreover, entirely persuaded that those many differences made any form of union impossible. The validity of this conclusion seemed to be dramatically underscored by the fate of the Albany Plan of Union in 1754. This proposal for a limited defensive confederation against the French was not ratified by a single colony.

Even worse, several colonies had shown very little concern for the welfare of their neighbors during the Seven Years' War. When their assistance had "been demanded or implored by any of their distressed neighbours and fellow subjects," charged the metropolitan economist Malachy Postlewayt in 1757, some colonies had "scandalously affected delays" and "by an inactive stupidity or indolence, appeared insensible to their distressed situation, and regardless of the common danger, because they felt not the immediate effect of it."[9] "Being in a state of separation, and each acting solely for its own interest, without regard to the welfare or safety of the rest," an anonymous author had warned two years earlier, "naturally begat jealousies, envyings,

---

[7] See Patricia U. Bonomi, "The Middle Colonies: Embryo of the New Political Order," in Alden T. Vaughan and George A. Billias, eds., *Perspectives on Early American History: Essays in Honor of Richard B. Morris* (New York, 1973), 63–92, and Douglas Greenberg, "The Middle Colonies in Recent American Historiography," *William and Mary Quarterly*, 3d ser., 36 (1979): 396–427.

[8] See Peter H. Wood, *Black Majority: Negroes in Colonial South Carolina from 1670 through the Stono Rebellion* (New York, 1974), and Converse D. Clowse, *Economic Beginnings in Colonial South Carolina, 1670–1730* (Columbia, S.C., 1971).

[9] Malachy Postlethwayt, *Britain's Commercial Interest Explained and Improved*, 2 vols. (London, 1757), in Jack P. Greene, ed., *Great Britain and the American Colonies, 1606–1763* (New York, 1970), 298.

animosities, and even a disposition to do one another mischief rather than good."[10] "We are all jealous of each other," admitted Henry Frankland from Boston in September 1757.[11] "'Tis well known," declared Franklin, that the colonies "all love[d Britain] much more than they love one another,"[12] which was scarcely surprising in view of the obvious fact that they were more "directly connected with their Mother Country" than "with each other."[13]

How, contemporaries seem mostly to have thought, could it have been otherwise? "The different manner in which they are settled, the different modes under which they live, the different forms of charters, grants, and frames of government they possess, the various principles of repulsion, . . . the different interests which they actuate, the religious interests by which they are actuated, the rivalship and jealousies which arise from hence, and the impracticability, if not the impossibility of reconciling and accommodating these incompatible ideas and claims," explained Thomas Pownall in 1764 in language redolent of that expressed by Franklin four years earlier, all these differences, said Pownall, would "forever" keep the colonies "disconnected and independent of each other."[14] The colonies, said another writer, were a mere "rope of sand," the individual strands of which were all too "peculiarly attached to their respective constitutions of Government," forms of society, and interests ever "to relish a union with one another."[15]

So deep were the differences and animosities among the colonies thought to run that they became an important element in the calculations of both metropolitan officials and American resistance leaders during the controversies that preceded the American Revolution. "The mutual jealousies amongst the several Colonies," Lord Morton assured Chancellor Hardwicke in the early 1760s, "would always keep them in a state of dependence,"[16] and metropolitan strategy in the Coercive Acts, the measures that played such a crucial role in stimulating the final crisis that led to war in 1775 and the

---

[10] *State of the British and French Colonies in North America* (London, 1755), 54.

[11] Henry Frankland to Thomas Pelham, Sept. 1, 1757, Additional Manuscripts 33087, f. 353, British Library, London.

[12] Franklin, *Interest of Great Britain Considered*, in *Franklin Papers* 9:90.

[13] "Some Thoughts on the Settlement and Government of Our Colonies in North America," Mar. 10, 1763, Add. Mss. (Liverpool Papers) 38335, ff. 74–77, British Library.

[14] Thomas Pownall, *The Administration of the Colonies* (London, 1764), in Greene, *Great Britain and the American Colonies*, 306.

[15] "Some Thoughts on the Settlement and Government of Our Colonies," 74–77.

[16] As quoted by Sir Lewis Namier, *England in the Age of the American Revolution* (London, 1963), 276.

American decision for independence in 1776, was based upon the supposition that colonial opposition could easily be defused by a policy of divide and rule, a policy the British continued to pursue throughout the nine years of war that followed.

Nor before 1774 were many American leaders very sanguine about their capacity even to offer a united resistance, much less to weld themselves together into a single political society. Many people feared that the colonies' own notorious disunion would lead to nothing more than, in the words of John Dickinson, the famous Pennsylvania farmer, "a multitude of Commonwealths, Crimes and Calamities—centuries of mutual Jealousies, Hatreds, Wars and Devastations, till at last the exhausted Provinces shall sink into Slavery under the yoke of some fortunate conqueror."[17] The dread of such a highly predictable outcome was certainly one of the more important deterrents to colonial revolt during the first stages of the controversy with Britain.

What all these assessments missed entirely was the very great extent to which during the century after 1660 the colonies were becoming not less but more alike. This process can be seen in the gradual diminution of the sharp divergencies that had initially distinguished Virginia from New England. The slow improvement of health conditions in Virginia during the seventeenth century had led by the first decades of the eighteenth century to a balance of sex ratios and a more typically European family structure. Similarly, as tobacco profits settled down to less spectacular if somewhat steadier levels, expectations among the successful of returning to England all but disappeared, the commitment to Virginia became stronger, settlement became more compact and expansion more measured, and the devotion to staple production was less exclusive. Concomitantly, social, religious, and political institutions acquired more vigor, society became far more stable, and the communal impulse was much more evident, as Virginia society cohered around an emergent and authoritative socioeconomic elite, members of which exhibited all of the traditional attributes of social leadership as they strove successfully to assimilate themselves to the powerful cultural model of the English gentry. The new sense of coherence and community which was so strikingly manifest in Virginia after 1725 was, perhaps ironically, actually intensified among the free white population by the pressures toward

---

[17] Dickinson to William Pitt, Dec. 21, 1765, in Chatham Papers, PRO 30/8/97, Public Record Office, London.

racial solidarity created by the transition to a heavily African slave labor force on the plantations.[18]

At the same time, in New England, the deterioration of health conditions brought mortality to levels by the mid-eighteenth century not too much lower than those in Virginia, while a variety of other developments pushed the region closer to patterns of behavior and values toward which Virginians were moving. Thus, impressive population growth, the consequent dispersion of people out from the original village centers to individual farms, an increasing differentiation of society and complexity of kinship networks, a growing diversity in many aspects of town life, the acceleration of the economy as a result of rapid internal population growth and the increasing integration of the New England economy into the larger Atlantic economy, the slow attenuation of the social and religious synthesis of the founders, a growing demand for and exhibition of autonomy among the sons of each successive generation, more individualism and more conflict within the public life of the towns, and a marked rise in geographical mobility—all of these developments weakened the bonds of community and pushed New England in the direction of greater individualism, personal autonomy, and social fluidity.[19]

Not just the Chesapeake and New England colonies but the other continental colonies as well were moving closer together in their configuration of socioeconomic and political life, the Carolinas and New York moving in the same direction as Virginia, and Pennsylvania, which also began with a strong corporate and religious impulse, in the same direction as New England, only at a vastly more accelerated rate. Envision a hypothetical continuum running between the two poles of pure individualism and tight communalism at three different times—1660, 1713, and 1763—with each colonial area plotted along the line according to its dominant patterns of behavior and values. What such a continuum would show, I submit, would be a steady convergence toward the center with, to take only the major continental colonies as examples, Virginia, South Carolina, and New York moving from individualism toward community and Massachusetts and Pennsylvania moving from

---

[18] See Tate and Ammerman, *Chesapeake in the Seventeenth Century*, 206–96; Morgan, *American Slavery, American Freedom*, 131–211, 195–362; and Jack P. Greene, "Society, Ideology, and Politics: An Analysis of the Political Culture of Mid-Eighteenth-Century Virginia," in Richard M. Jellison, ed., *Society, Freedom, and Conscience: The Coming of the Revolution in Virginia, Massachusetts, and New York* (New York, 1976), 14–76, 191–200.

[19] See, especially, Murrin, "Review Essay," 240–75; Greene, "Autonomy and Stability," 187–93; Richard L. Bushman, *From Puritan to Yankee: Character and the Social Order in Connecticut, 1690–1765* (Cambridge, Mass., 1967).

community toward individualism until by the last half of the eighteenth century the differences among the colonies were less than they had ever been before.

New England was still more religious and had much lower levels of wealth concentration than the colonies to the south, while Virginia and South Carolina with their legions of slaves were certainly more strongly oriented toward acquisitiveness and more exploitative. But not even the presence of so many slaves in the southern colonies, certainly the most conspicuous difference between them and New England, was yet a crucial distinguishing feature among the colonies. Though the ratio of black slaves to the free population decreased steadily from the most southern to the most northern colonies, slavery as late as 1770 was still an expanding, not a contracting, institution in every one of the colonies that revolted except New Hampshire; and New York, Rhode Island, Pennsylvania, and New Jersey all had populations with a higher proportion of slaves than had the Chesapeake colonies as late as 1700 to 1720.[20]

The explanation for this growing convergence is to be found, I would argue, in two overlapping processes that were simultaneously at work in all the colonies. For purposes of analysis, they may be designated, rather crudely, as processes of Americanization and Anglicization. Distance from the metropolis, the looseness of British controls, the (relatively) easy availability of land and other exploitable resources, and incorporation into the larger metropolitan economy and, increasingly, into the broad Atlantic trading system stretching from West Africa to the West Indies in the south and North America to western Europe in the north—all of these conditions combined to produce levels of prosperity sufficient to support societies that were everywhere becoming more and more pluralistic, complex, differentiated, and developed. They also worked to stimulate the high levels of individual activity and expansiveness that underlay the remarkable economic and demographic growth that characterized all of the North American colonies through the middle decades of the eighteenth century. These developments and the conditions that lay behind them also seem to have led to the development of "more autonomous personality types" that were impatient with authority and jealous of the personal independence that was the chief defining quality of their status as fully competent men.[21]

---

[20] Population figures may be found in *Historical Statistics of the United States, Colonial Times to 1957* (Washington, D.C., 1960), 756.

[21] See Edwin G. Burrows and Michael Wallace, "The American Revolution: The Ideology and Psychology of National Liberation," *Perspectives in American History* 6 (1972): 287–88.

This "fierce spirit of liberty" and deep antiauthoritarianism were frequently said by Americans and outsiders alike to be, as Edmund Burke
declared to the House of Commons in his speech on conciliation on March
22, 1775, "the predominating feature" in the "character of the Americans."[22]
"'Tis the Nature of" this "People to do all in their Power to pull down every
legal Authority," lamented the earl of Loudoun, commander-in-chief of the
British military forces in the colonies during the early stages of the Seven
Years' War; "there is no Law prevailing at present here, that I have met
with, but the Rule every Man pleases to lay down to himself." "Every Man,"
he complained, insisted upon "follow[ing] the dictates of his own Will without Controul."[23] "Our People," the Massachusetts legislature had observed a
year earlier in drawing an implicit contrast between them and Englishmen,
"were *not calculated* to be confined in Garrison or kept in any particular
Service; they soon grow troublesome & uneasy by reflecting upon their Folly
in bringing themselves into a State of Subjection when they might have
continued free and independent."[24]

Throughout the free segments of the British-American population, from
one region to the next and from the cradle to the grave, visitor after visitor
reported, people seemed to exhibit very little respect for authority. "A love
of freedom," Burke believed, was "stronger in the English colonies, probably, than in any other people of the earth,"[25] "No people in the world,"
echoed the Pennsylvania lawyer Joseph Galloway, "have higher notions of
liberty."[26] And this pervasive and deeply engraved commitment to personal
freedom and independence, said Samuel Williams, whose *History of Vermont*, published during the last decade of the eighteenth century, constitutes
one of the first systematic analyses of the components of the emerging American society, "had been the constant product and effect, of the state of society
in the British colonies" for "a century and a half," and, he should have

---

[22] Edmund Burke, "Speech on Moving Resolutions for Conciliation with the Colonies,"
Mar. 22, 1775, in *Edmund Burke: Selected Writings and Speeches on America*, ed. Thomas H.
D. Mahoney (Indianapolis, 1964), 131–32.

[23] Earl of Loudoun to Earl of Halifax, Dec. 26, 1756, and to Thomas Pownall, Nov. 17,
1757, Loudoun Papers 2416C, 4853, Henry E. Huntington Library, San Marino, Calif.

[24] "A Representation of the Case of His Majesty's Province of Massachusetts Bay," 1755, in
Add. Mss. 33029, ff. 206–9, British Library, as quoted in Lawrence Henry Gipson, *The
British Empire before the American Revolution*, 15 vols. (Caldwell, Idaho, and New York,
1936–72), 9:43.

[25] Burke, "Speech on Conciliation," 131–32.

[26] As quoted by Max Savelle, "Nationalism and Other Loyalties in the American Revolution," *American Historical Review* 67 (1962): 910.

added, of the social, economic, and physical forces that produced that society.[27]

If, as Williams observed, a "similarity of situation and conditions" had gradually pushed the colonies toward a similitude of society and values, more specifically, toward "that natural, easy, independent situation, and spirit, in which the body of the [free] people were found, when the American war came on," still a second major influence—growing anglicization—was important in helping to erode differences among the colonies.[28] Partly, this development was the result of deliberate efforts by metropolitan authorities to bring the colonies under closer control, including the gradual conversion of the vast majority of the colonies into royal provinces directly under the supervision of the crown; the imposition of a common political system, at least at the provincial level, upon those colonies; strong pressures upon the five remaining private colonies to assimilate to that system; and the largely successful attempt, beginning in the 1650s, to subordinate the economies of the colonies to that of the metropolis. These efforts led both to the establishment of a common pattern of political institutions among the colonies and to an ever more intense involvement between metropolis and colonies in both the political and economic spheres. This growing involvement, together with an increasing volume of contacts among individuals and the improved communications that accompanied them, drew the colonists ever closer into the ambit of British life during the eighteenth century, provided them with easier and more direct access to English, Irish, and, increasingly, Scottish ideas and models of behavior, and tied them ever more closely to metropolitan culture.

As the ties with the metropolis thus tightened, the pull of metropolitan culture increased, and the standards of the metropolis more and more came to be the primary model for colonial behavior, the one certain measure of cultural achievement for these provincial societies at the outermost peripheries of the British world. Throughout the colonies, and especially among the emergent elites, there was a self-conscious effort to anglicize colonial life through the deliberate imitation of metropolitan institutions, values, and culture. Thus, before the mid–1770s British Americans thought of themselves primarily as Britons, albeit Britons overseas, and, contrary to the dominant opinion among earlier historians, colonial comparisons of the colonies with Britain did not usually come out in favor of the colonies. Quite the contrary. The central cultural impulse among the colonists was not to

---

[27] Samuel Williams, *The Natural and Civil History of Vermont*, 2 vols. (Walpole, N.H., 1794), 2:431.

[28] Ibid., 429–30.

identify and find ways to express and to celebrate what was distinctively American about themselves but, insofar as possible, to eliminate those distinctions so that they might—with more credibility—think of themselves—and be thought of by people in Britain itself—as demonstrably British.[29] In no person better illustrated than in the quintessential provincial and, down to 1774, British patriot Benjamin Franklin, this impulse was supported by the "objective disparity between British power and colonial power" in the cultural as well as the economic, political, and military realms and revealed "a deep sense of comparative weakness and inferiority" among the colonists.[30]

Not simply their shared commitment to their own personal independence and, if with considerably more ambivalence, to the social configurations that had been produced by the common circumstances in which they found themselves in America, then, but their incorporation into the larger Anglophone world was an essential component of colonial self-esteem: for the colonists before 1775 a positive sense of identity was dependent upon their ability to identify themselves as "free Englishmen, inheriting the liberties," rights, and culture of all British subjects. These powerful mimetic impulses and the "feeling of a community of values" and identity between Britain and the colonies to which they contributed and on which they rested had by the middle decades of the eighteenth century "all but obliterated" any "sense of separation and distinctiveness" that the colonists, especially New Englanders, might have had earlier in the colonial period.[31]

Evidence of this change is widespread. There was not "a single true *New England* Man, in the whole Province," reported the Reverend John Barnard in 1734 from Massachusetts, the colony that had been most skeptical and most resistant to the benefits of metropolitan imperialism, cultural as well as economic and political, during the seventeenth century, "but what readily subscribes" to the belief that "that form of Civil Government is best for us, which we are under, I mean the *British Constitution*."[32] "The inhabitants of the colonies," wrote an anonymous American in 1755 in one of many such

---

[29] A fuller discussion of this subject may be found in Jack P. Greene, "Search for Identity: An Interpretation of the Meaning of Selected Patterns of Social Response in Eighteenth-Century America," *Journal of Social History* 3 (1970): 189–224 [chap. 6 above]. The contrary view is succinctly stated in Savelle, "Nationalism and Other Loyalties," 904.

[30] See Jack P. Greene, "The Alienation of Benjamin Franklin—British American," *Journal of the Royal Society of Arts* 124 (1976): 52–73. The quotations are from Burrows and Wallace, "American Revolution," 274.

[31] Arieli, *Individualism and Nationalism*, 45–49.

[32] John Barnard, *The Throne Established by Righteousness* (Boston, 1734), as quoted by Paul A. Varg, "The Advent of Nationalism, 1758–1776," *American Quarterly* 16 (1964): 172.

observations, "do not think themselves aliens, or the less a-kin to those of *Great Britain*, because separated by a vast ocean, and dwelling in a distant part of the globe: they insist that they are branches of the same *British* tree, tho' transplanted in a different soil; that they have not forfeited their *British* rights by that removal, because they removed with consent of the government, and sincerely acknowledge themselves to be subjects of the same King." They believed, he said,

> that they daily extend the power and dominion of *Great Britain*, by extending their settlements and commerce; . . . That their industry is employ'd not more for their own than their brethren's advantage, who are enriched by their labour and the valuable produce of their several colonies: that for this reason, they think themselves intitled both to [the] . . . love and assistance [of those at home], which it is not less their interest than it is their duty, as brethren, to afford them; that in short, they speak the same language, and are of the same religion with them; so that they ought not be thought presumptuous, if they consider themselves upon an equal footing with [Englishmen at home or be] . . . treated the worse, because they will be *Englishmen*.[33]

Britain and the colonies, the colonists insisted, were united by similarities in manners, "religion, liberty, laws, affections, relations, language and commerce."[34]

Given this widespread identification with Britain and the British, it is scarcely surprising that, far from being exponents of American nationalism, the colonists exhibited "an intense personal affection, even reverence, for" British "leaders, institutions, and culture" and the most profound feelings of British nationalism.[35] Nor were these feelings at any time more intense than in the 1760s during the wake of the Seven Years' War. That so much of that war had been fought in the colonies, that the metropolitan government had made such a substantial and expensive effort to defend the colonies, and that the colonies had themselves—for the very first time—made, as they were persuaded, an important contribution to such a great national cause increased the immediacy and the strength of colonial ties with Britain, produced a surge of British patriotism among the colonists, and created among them heightened expectations for a larger and more equivalent role within the empire. Such a status, after all, was only appropriate for colonial societies

---

[33] *State of the British and French Colonies*, 63–64.

[34] John Dickinson, as quoted by Savelle, "Nationalism and Other Loyalties," 908.

[35] Burrows and Wallace, "American Revolution," 275–76.

which, as they had become progressively more pluralistic, complex, and differentiated, had not only come to appear more British but, through their conscious cultivation of metropolitan culture, had actually come to be more British.[36]

As each of the colonies had during the century previous to the American Revolution become both more American and more British, as they increasingly assimilated to a common American social and behavioral pattern and to British cultural models, they became more and more alike, and this growing convergence, to reiterate the suggestion made at the beginning of this essay, was a necessary precondition for either the American Revolution or the emergence of an American nation and an American nationality. As the late David Potter has reminded us, however, social and "cultural similarities alone will not provide a basis of affinity between groups." Nationalism and similar collective loyalties, he argues, have to rest on "two psychological bases": the "feeling of a common culture and the feeling of common interest." "Of the two," he posits, "the concept of culture is, no doubt, of greater weight," but it cannot have its full effect without a mutual awareness of common interests.[37]

In the American case, it must be said that a prior awareness of a common interest was necessary even for a clear and full recognition of the existence of a common culture. As several scholars have argued, the emergence during the middle decades of the eighteenth century of intercolonial trading patterns and communications networks, an interlocking elite, closer interurban ties, and common participation between 1739 and 1763 in two wars against the neighboring colonies of foreign metropolitan powers resulted in the colonies' becoming increasingly more interested in one another and perhaps even in the development of some nascent sense of American community. This development was in turn stimulated to some degree by the metropolitan penchant, especially evident during the intercolonial wars, for treating the continental colonies as a unit and describing them under the common rubric *American*.[38] Perhaps the most important point that can be

---

[36] Max Savelle, *Seeds of Liberty: The Genesis of the American Mind* (New York, 1948), 553–87, and "Nationalism and Other Loyalties," 901–23; Varg, "Advent of Nationalism," 160–81; Greene, "Search for Identity."

[37] David M. Potter, "The Historians' Use of Nationalism and Vice Versa," *American Historical Review* 67 (1962): 935, 949.

[38] See Albert Harkness, Jr., "Americanism and Jenkins' Ear," *Mississippi Valley Historical Review* 37 (1950): 61–90; Richard L. Merritt, *Symbols of American Community, 1735–1775*

made about the Albany Plan of Union in the early 1750s, in fact, a point that seems not to have been appreciated by anybody at the time, was not that it was universally rejected but that it had been proposed and adopted by a conference of leaders in the first place, for its mere initiation manifested at least a rudimentary consciousness of the existence of some bases for an "American" union.

But Americans did not fully understand nor attach any special importance to the many—and growing—commonalities among them—as opposed to the similarities that linked them all to Britain—until the metropolis vividly impressed upon them that they had a common interest by challenging their pretensions to an equal status with Britons at home in a series of new, restrictive measures between 1763 and 1776. In pointing out the seemingly vast differences among the colonies and stressing the extent to which those differences made united action improbable, Franklin had warned metropolitans in 1760, in words echoed both by himself and many later observers, that a "grevious tyranny and oppression" might very well drive them to unite,[39] and during the 1760s, many colonists had pointed out, in the words of Richard Henry Lee of Virginia, that the colonists' attachment to Britain could be preserved "on no other terms . . . than by a free intercourse and equal participation of good offices, liberty and free constitution of government."[40] But Lee's point was appreciated in Britain virtually by Burke alone when he pointed out that America's affection for Britain had always been conditional upon its continuing ability to carry "the mark of a free people in all" its "internal concerns" and to retain at least "the image of the British constitution."[41]

Britain's insistence upon treating the colonies as separate and unequal in the 1760s and 1770s was thus the contingent development that, in Arieli's words, provided the "point of observation and comparison from which" the colonists could finally come to appreciate the many unities among them.[42] Increasingly during those years, they came to comprehend that, given exist-

(New Haven, 1966); Michael Kraus, *Intercolonial Aspects of American Culture on the Eve of the Revolution, with Special Reference to the Northern Towns* (New York, 1928); and Carl Bridenbaugh, *Cities in Revolt: Urban Life in America, 1743–1776* (New York, 1955).

[39] Franklin, *Interest of Great Britain Considered*, in *Franklin Papers* 9:90.

[40] Richard Henry Lee to Arthur Lee, July 4, 1765, in *Letters of Richard Henry Lee*, ed. James C. Ballagh, 2 vols. (New York, 1912–14), 1:11. See also, among many expressions of similar beliefs, Robert M. Calhoon, "William Smith Jr.'s Alternative to the American Revolution," *William and Mary Quarterly*, 3d ser., 22 (1965): 117.

[41] Edmund Burke, "Speech on American Taxation," Apr. 19, 1774, in *Edmund Burke*, 79.

[42] Arieli, *Individualism and Nationalism*, 45.

ing attitudes among those in power in Britain, membership in the British Empire did not mean, for them, the equality as freeborn Englishmen to which they had so long aspired. Rather, it meant an inferior status equivalent, in the bitter words of Alexander Hamilton in 1774, only to that of those unworthy people in Britain who were *"in so mean a situation"* that they were "supposed to have no will of their own" and, according to Blackstone, therefore deserved no role in governing themselves.[43] As the colonists slowly came to this comprehension they gradually began to lose their British nationalism and to develop, as grounds for asserting their own worthiness against their metropolitan antagonists, an awareness of the common histories of the colonies as asylums for the oppressed and places where unfortunates could make new beginnings and of the many social and cultural similarities among them. Only then did they begin to acquire some sense of their possible "future power and imperial greatness" as a separate American people.[44]

Yet, along with other deterrents, the intensity of British nationalism, the fear of their own disunity, and their mutual suspicions of each other were so powerful that it required a total newcomer to America, Thomas Paine, to make their own commonalities and potential fully cognizable to them. For, far more than anyone else, it was Paine, in America for only thirteen months, who finally undermined most of those beliefs that had sustained British nationalism among the colonists even in the face of what they took to be a long chain of oppressive and tyrannical actions against them. Paine shattered those beliefs in *Common Sense* in early 1776 by persuading the colonists that their connection with Britain was not essential to their prosperity and safety, that the British constitution was far from the most perfect political contrivance in the history of man, and that monarchy was neither a legitimate institution nor necessary for the preservation of liberty.

Even more important for the history of the emergence of American nationalism, Paine not only destroyed those cherished misconceptions that had long caused so many Americans, as he put it, to "think better of the European world than it deserves," he also, as he later told the Abbé Raynal, taught Americans "the manly doctrine of reverencing themselves." He did so by showing them that so many of the features of American society for which they had traditionally been so apologetic and which were among their most important commonalities—its simplicity, its newness, its rusticity, its inno-

---

[43] Alexander Hamilton, *The Farmer Refuted*, [Feb. 23], 1774, in *The Papers of Alexander Hamilton*, ed. Harold C. Syrett and Jacob E. Cooke, 19 vols. (New York and London, 1961–73), 1:106–7.

[44] Arieli, *Individualism and Nationalism*, 67–68.

cence, its very size—were not deficiencies but advantages that, once separation had been achieved from Britain, would serve as a basis for the creation of a political society that would be an example for the rest of the world. By thus universalizing their struggle, Paine, in this powerful, self-legitimating, and exhilarating vision, held out to Americans both a new sense of worth and a place of the first importance in the unfolding course of human history.[45]

Neither Paine's articulation of the social and cultural unities among the colonies nor his flattering vision of America's universal meaning could, however, immediately produce a powerful, subsuming national consciousness of the kind usually connoted by the word *nationalism*. "Begun by necessity, [and] cemented by oppression and common danger," the Revolution had, in any case, initially been undertaken by groups in the name of the premises of the metropolis and for the purpose not of forming a new nation but, as the Virginia Convention of August 1774 phrased it, of securing the "Peace, and the good Order of Government within this ancient Colony." Historians have frequently cited Patrick Henry's famous declaration at the First Continental Congress in the fall of 1774 that the "distinctions between Virginians, Pennsylvanians, New Yorkers, and New Englanders, are no more. I am not a Virginian, but an American." But it would be at least two further generations before most Americans, including Henry, would give first priority to American, as opposed to their own state or regional, loyalties.[46]

As John Shy has argued, the actual course of the War of Independence and more especially the behavior of the British army and the widespread popular participation in the war contributed to a kind of "hothouse nationalism, whose strengths and weaknesses would baffle observers for decades."[47] Similarly, the Revolution itself provided Americans with an instant common past. But levels of distrust remained high and the commitment to the American nation weak throughout the war and the immediate postwar period. Southerners continued to be suspicious of New Englanders, New Englanders of southerners, and both of New Yorkers and Pennsylvanians. Moreover, the several states continued to think of themselves as independent sovereign-

---

[45] Paine, *Common Sense*, and Paine "To Mr. Secretary Dundas," June 6, 1792, in *Complete Writings of Paine* 1:21, 2:452. For an elaboration of this argument, see Jack P. Greene, "Paine, America, and the 'Modernization' of Political Consciousness," *Political Science Quarterly* 93 (1978): 73–92.

[46] Eisenstadt, *Revolution and the Transformation of Societies*, 242. The quotations in this paragraph are taken from Savelle, "Nationalism and Other Loyalties," 906, 918–19.

[47] John Shy, "The American Revolution: The Military Conflict Considered as a Revolutionary War," in Stephen G. Kurz and James H. Hutson, eds., *Essays on the American Revolution* (Chapel Hill, N.C., 1973), 155.

ties, and the first national government, the Articles of Confederation, was nothing more than a league of independent states that was emphatically "not inspired by a clear concept of nationality." Not until the establishment of the present federal government in 1787–88 was a framework established suitable for providing a context for the emergence of a genuinely *American* nationalism.[48]

Arieli has analyzed this development over the following century with cogency and in detail. In the process, he has shown what a peculiar form of nationalism it was. In contrast to most other variants of nationalism it was defined exclusively by "patterns of social and political values" rather than by "natural or historic factors of national unity and cohesion" and was conceived of more as loyalty to a system which permitted the maximum assertion of individualism than as allegiance to some transcendent metaphysical entity. Built, as Arieli argues, "upon the language and concepts of natural-rights philosophy," the emerging American national consciousness was also, as Samuel Williams so profoundly appreciated, founded upon, and profoundly affected by, the "state of [American] society." "*Paine*, and other writers upon American politics, met with such amazing success," observed Williams, "not because they taught the people principles, which they did not before understand; but because they [the writers] placed the principles which they had learned of them [the people], in a very clear and striking light, on a most critical and important occasion." Paine and other political writers, Williams insisted, had learned their principles not just from European writers but "from the state of society in America," which had "produced, preserved, and kept alive" that extraordinary and almost universal commitment to liberty defined by the insistence of individuals upon being dependent "upon no beings or precautions under heaven, but themselves." Far from being an abstraction, Williams insisted, liberty, perhaps the central component of the emerging American nationalism, was in America a "living principle" that was firmly rooted in social circumstance.[49]

The process by which Americans began to think of themselves as "a people" thus did not become visibly manifest until the mid–1760s, was still in a primitive stage of development between 1775 and 1787, and would not be fully elaborated for at least another fifty years. From the perspective of the

---

[48] Arieli, *Individualism and Nationalism*, 32–33, 41, 81.

[49] Ibid., 25, 29; Williams, *Natural and Civil History of Vermont* 2:372–73, 433; Potter, "Historians' Use of Nationalism," 929.

pre-Revolutionary controversy with Britain and the Revolution itself, however, it had finally become clear to Americans, as Washington said in his Farewell Address in 1796, that "with *slight* shades of difference," they had "the same religion, manners, habits and political principles." These fundamental similarities were the result, I have argued here, of a powerful social and cultural convergence during the century before the American Revolution. As Washington went on to suggest, that convergence had been of crucial importance in enabling Americans to fight and "triumph together" in "a common cause" and, against a variety of "common dangers" and sufferings, to gain the "independence and liberty" they then enjoyed.[50]

Whether these many similarities would continue to operate so favorably in behalf of the American nation, whether they were so permanent, so fundamental, and so decisive, as Washington implied, is a question that brings us back to Thomas Paine and to the quotation I offered at the beginning of this essay. "The vast variety of interests" and growing distinctions, Paine predicted in 1776, would make it "difficult, if not impossible, to form the continent into one government half a century hence."[51] Already by the 1790s, such divergencies were beginning to become unmistakably manifest, especially between the northern commitment to abolition and the southern devotion to the preservation of a slave labor system. In an oration on March 5, 1776, Peter Thatcher, a Boston lawyer, had told his audience that America had to face a dilemma as to whether "the rising empire of America" should "be an empire of slaves *or* of freemen."[52] The particular choice he had in mind, of course, was the one between political slavery under Britain or political freedom with independence. But the dilemma he posed for America was not actually resolved by the Revolution, and, it slowly became clear following the gradual evaporation of abolitionist sentiment in the Upper South after 1785, the "rising empire of America" would be an empire of slaves and freemen.

Over the first seventy years of the new republic, the South's continuing commitment to a slave labor system resulted in a growing divergence between its patterns of social organization and values and those of the increasingly urban and industrialized societies of the North. In their obvious "hierarchy, the cult of chivalry—the unmatched civilization, the folk society, the rural character of life, the clan values rather than the commercial values," the southern states, as Potter has argued, seemed to have acquired a

---

[50] As quoted by Arieli, *Individualism and Nationalism*, 27.

[51] Paine, *Common Sense*, in *Complete Writings of Paine* 1:36.

[52] The quotation from Peter Thatcher is from Savelle, "Nationalism and Other Loyalties," 919.

"*distinctiveness* of a deeply significant kind," one that was less and less congruent with the social character and orientation of the states to the north.[53] Some scholars have argued vigorously, of course, that the United States by the middle of the nineteenth century actually comprised two separate cultures, one northern and one southern.[54] But one does not have to subscribe to this extreme conception of the problem to recognize that by 1860 the divergencies between the northern and the southern states were perhaps as great as they had ever been and certainly greater than they had been at any time since the beginning of the eighteenth century.

These great and growing divergencies, which produced increasingly strident demands, in the North, for the reconstruction of southern society in the image of that of the North, and, in the South, for the dissolution of the American nation, strongly suggest that Paine may have been correct and that it might indeed have been impossible for Americans to unite in revolution and form an American nation a mere thirty to forty years later. They also suggest that the Revolution and the creation of a federal union, developments we now take for granted, were the results of a fortuitous combination of two related phenomena. On the one hand, a powerful social and cultural convergence had by the mid-eighteenth century made the several British-American political societies of North America more alike than they had ever been before or would be again before the destruction of slavery in the southern states as a result of the Civil War. On the other hand, the quarrel with the metropolis produced among those societies that powerful sense of a commonality of culture and interests that did in fact lead to revolution and the formation of the American nation during the last quarter of the eighteenth century.

This essay was written for delivery as the Ben Eliezar Annual Lecture in the History of Nationalism and National Liberation Movements at the Hebrew University of Jerusalem on June 29, 1979. It was also given as a lecture at St. John's College, Collegeville, Minn., on Nov. 16, 1981; the annual Washington's Birthday Convocation at Washington College, Chestertown, Md., on Feb. 20, 1982; as a Wentworth Lecture at the University of Florida on Oct. 4, 1982; in the Department of American Studies at Doshisha University in Kyoto, Japan, on July 7, 1987, and at the Faculty of Law at the University of Hokkaido in Sapporo, Japan, on July 22, 1987. It is reprinted with permission and minor changes from *Religion, Ideology, and Nationalism in Europe and America: Essays Presented in Honor of Yehoshua Arieli* (Jerusalem: Historical Society of Israel and the Zalman Shazar Center for Jewish History, 1986), 243–62.

[53] Potter, "Historians' Use of Nationalism," 943.

[54] For a compelling argument for the continuing similarities between North and South, see Carl N. Degler, *Place over Time: The Continuity of Southern Distinctiveness* (Baton Rouge, La., 1977), 67–97.

—THIRTEEN—

The Pursuit of Happiness, the Private Realm, and the Movement for a Stronger National Government

FROM THE EARLIEST DAYS of settlement of the English-American colonies, the pursuit of happiness has almost certainly been the primary shaping social value. No imperative has been so important in determining the character of American society or in forming American culture. For the overwhelming majority of Americans, moreover, the pursuit of happiness has always resided in the private rather than the public realm. Notwithstanding this basic fact of American life, historians have until quite recently concentrated most of their attention upon events and developments in the public realm. A sweeping revolution in historical studies over the past twenty years has, however, taken historians out of the halls of government and into the busy and variegated scenes of private activity that have traditionally comprised the essence of American life.

One of the most important things this scholarly revolution is uncovering is the basically private orientation of American society, a powerful underlying predisposition among the free populations of seventeenth- and eighteenth-century America to preoccupy themselves with the pursuit of personal and family independence and the social improvements that would guarantee and enhance their individual economic achievements, enrich their lives, and give them a sense of personal self-worth. For all but a few Americans, the pursuit of happiness did not involve the pursuit of public office or even the active occupation of a public space. There was simply too much private space for most people to be much interested in having a public space. Although the intensity of civic responsibility differed from place to place and time to time during the colonial era, the primary concerns of most independent Americans were private rather than public. Their allegiances were to themselves and their families rather than to the larger social entities to which they belonged. To quote one observer, they were mostly "too engaged in their respective occupations for the enticements" of public life.[1]

They or their ancestors had, in any case, left Britain or Europe not only to escape want and to gain independence but also, as contemporaries were fond of pointing out, to get away from excessive public intrusions into their private lives, intrusions in the form of high taxes, rapacious civil and religious establishments, obligations to military or naval service, and war. The most popular cultural image invoked by early Americans was that of the biblical husbandman who sat contentedly under the shade of his own vine and fig tree presiding over—and basking in—the development of his family and estate.

The new emphasis upon the private orientation of early American society has at least implicitly raised the question of how it affected public life and public institutions. Or, more to the point, how it was reflected in the new federal framework created in 1787 and 1788. For the founding fathers almost all recognized the wisdom of that classic early modern political truism, that all government was founded on opinion, by which they meant that no government could long survive that did not have the support of the people it served.

Throughout the colonial period, the private orientation of American society had meant that in most places and at most times the public realm had been small. With only a tiny bureaucracy and no police, a localized judicial system that rarely met more than fifteen to thirty days in any given year, and legislatures that in peacetime were rarely in session for more than a month in any given year, government was small, intermittent, and inexpensive. Except during wartime, taxes were low, and the only public activities that engaged most men were infrequent militia or jury service and somewhat more frequent participation in vital public works such as building and repairing of bridges and roads. With little coercive power—and very little presence—government in America was consensual and depended for its energy upon the force of community opinion, which was the sum of individual opinion.

Government in early America was thus largely a device, in the traditional sense, for maintaining orderly relations among people and protecting them from their own and others' human frailties. Even more important, it was an agency for the protection of one's individual property in land, goods, and person, one's property in person including the right of striving, of pursuing

---

[1] François Alexandre Frédéric, duc de La Rochefoucauld-Liancourt, *Travels through the United States of North America*, 2 vols. (London, 1799), 2:679.

(as well as protecting) one's interests, of seeking to alter one's place on the scale of economic well-being and social status. While they wanted enough government to secure peace and to maintain a just and open civil order, they were usually, to quote one contemporary, in favor of just "so much government as will do justice, protect property, and defend the country."[2]

The critical point about the implicit conception of political society that underlay this pattern of governance is that it assigned to political society no more authority over the individual and to the individual no more obligation to political society than was absolutely necessary to make sure that all free individuals had approximately the same scope for private activity. Political society was thus regulative as it was in the traditional societies of Europe. But it was also facilitative in at least two senses. First, it acted to "enlarge" the private realm by overseeing and stimulating those public improvements that would provide people with an ever larger field for the pursuit of happiness, for the realization of their individual potentials. Second, it encouraged individuals to pursue their own goals without forcing them to be much concerned with the social well-being of the community as a whole.

The American Revolution represented a radical challenge to these enduring and already quite ancient arrangements and to the traditional division of emphasis between the private and the public spheres. The demands of war both raised taxes and significantly increased the range of public demands upon individuals, while the imperatives of the new republicanism and the absence of a strong controlling central power encouraged the state governments to involve themselves in a variety of new activities. The result was a dramatic growth of government, especially at the state level, an enlargement of the public realm that represented a massive—and thitherto unprecedented—intrusion of the public into the private realm. Never before in the history of British America had the public realm made such heavy demands upon the citizenry.

At the conclusion of the War for Independence, people expected a return to the old order, a restoration of the old system whereby, in the vast majority of areas, the private realm took precedence over the public. Like George Washington, they had for nine long years looked forward to their return to those domestic and private pursuits that had traditionally engaged most of their attention, and the energy with which they threw themselves into those pursuits in the immediate postwar years was evident in the rapid recovery of the United States from many of the effects of the war. "It is wonderful,"

---

[2] Samuel Williams, *The Natural and Civil History of Vermont*, 2 vols. (Walpole, N.H., 1794), 2:358, 424.

Washington wrote to a French correspondent less than three years after the war, "to see how soon the ravages of war are repaired. Houses are rebuilt, fields enclosed, stocks of cattle which were destroyed are replaced, and many a desolated territory assumes again the cheerful appearance of cultivation. In many places the vestiges of conflagration and ruin are hardly to be traced. The arts of peace, such as clearing rivers, building bridges, and establishing conveniences for travelling &c. are assiduously promoted."[3]

As Washington's emphasis upon clearing rivers and building bridges suggests, nothing seemed more vital to the recovery and more important to the future development of Americans than commerce. Trade, they clearly understood, had been the basis for the extraordinary economic and demographic growth and social and cultural development that had characterized colonial British America for the century before Independence. Although a few devout republicans condemned commerce in traditional terms as the seed of "luxury, effeminacy, and corruption," most Americans agreed with Washington both that such evils were "counterbalanced by the convenience and wealth" generated by commerce and that "the spirit of Trade which pervades these States" was already too deeply engraved upon American life ever to "be restrained."[4]

They looked to internal commerce to bind the new union together and to connect the old states with the new and already burgeoning sections of the West. They looked to foreign commerce as the key to prosperity and growth. The United States might be the world's best "poor man's Country, but," as one contemporary observed, "without . . . an Opportunity of exporting our produce it cannot flourish."[5] Commerce, indeed, many leading Americans believed, including even a pragmatic realist like Washington, could be expected not only to bring wealth and unity to their new country but, in time, to transform the world and perhaps even human nature itself. "I cannot avoid reflecting with pleasure on the probable influence that commerce may hereafter have on human manners and society in general," Washington wrote Lafayette in August 1785. On the occasion of such reflections, he continued, "I consider how mankind may be connected like one great family in fraternal ties. I indulge a fond, perhaps an enthusiastic idea, that as the world is evidently much less barbarous than it has been, its melioration must still be

---

[3] George Washington to Chevalier de La Luzerne, Aug. 1, 1786, *The Writings of George Washington*, ed. John C. Fitzpatrick, 39 vols. (Washington, D.C., 1931–44), 28:500–501.

[4] Washington to James Warren, Oct. 7, 1785, ibid., 290–91.

[5] Caleb Wallace to James Madison, July 12, 1785, *The Papers of James Madison*, ed. William T. Hutchinson et al., 17 vols. (Chicago and Charlottesville, Va., 1962–91), 8:321.

progressive; that nations are becoming more humanized in their policy, that the subjects of ambition and causes for hostility are daily diminishing, and, in fine, that the period is not very remote, when the benefits of a liberal and free commerce will, pretty generally, succeed to the devestations and horrors of war."[6]

To produce such beneficial effects, however, commerce had to be free from unnatural restraints and to operate within an environment in which the public faith was inviolable and money and property were secure, and in this connection Americans of the 1780s faced three problems. First were the restrictions imposed on their trade by other countries, especially Britain. Second were the restrictions and contradictory measures imposed on trade by the several states. Third was the impotence of the national government to do anything about either of the first two problems. Historians have traditionally focused upon the first problem. But the second was in many respects every bit as worrisome to people who advocated strengthening the national government. With the end of the war, the state legislatures showed few signs of wanting to relinquish the enormous powers they had acquired during the war or to diminish the scope of their activities, and during the 1780s the advocates of a more energetic union increasingly came to believe that the unrestrained power of the states over trade was productive of discord among the states, inimical both to the Union and to the private welfare of the people in general, and oppressive to many key minority groups, especially creditors, within the states. At the same time, the states' extensive control over trade and other aspects of economic life, including money and credit, had left American society vulnerable to the uncertain influences of "local politics and self-interested views," which invariably, as Washington once complained to David Humphreys, "obtrude[d] themselves into every measure of public utility."[7]

The result, as Washington put it, was "that property was [not] well secured, faith and justice [were not] well preserved," government was unstable, and public confidence was low and falling, all developments that, in his view, were detrimental to commerce and to the individual interests and welfare—the private potentialities—of the citizenry at large. "In a Country like this where equal liberty is enjoyed, where every man may reap his own harvest, where proper attention will afford him much more than is necessary for his own consumption, and where there is so ample a field for every mercantile and mechanical exertion," Washington wrote a correspondent in

---

[6] Washington to Marquis de Lafayette, Aug. 15, 1785, *Writings of Washington* 28:520–21.

[7] Washington to David Humphreys, July 25, 1785, ibid., 204.

the spring of 1788 while the new constitution was still in process of ratification, the absence of "money . . . to answer the . . . necessary commercial circulation" could only be interpreted as a certain indication that there was "something amiss in the ruling political power" that, in the interest of restoring public confidence, required "a steady, regulating and energetic hand to correct and control."[8]

James Madison agreed. "Much indeed is it to be wished," he wrote to James Monroe in August 1785, "that no regulations of trade, that is to say, no restrictions or imposts whatever, were necessary. A perfect freedom," he declared, "is the System which would be my choice." But, he continued, "If it be necessary to regulate trade at all, it surely is necessary to lodge the power, where trade can be regulated with effect [and where such regulations cannot be fettered by the cramped and local views of state politicians], and," Madison added, "experience has confirmed what reason foresaw, that it can never be so regulated by the States acting in their separate capacities. They can no more exercise this power separately [or responsibly], than they could separately carry on war, or separately form treaties of alliance or Commerce."[9]

The American people, proponents of a stronger central government thus came to believe, had to be freed from the intrusive and obstructive interventions of the majorities in the state legislatures before commerce could achieve its full potential as a bountiful arena for the free exertion of individual talents and resources, before the private realm in general and economic life in particular could once again become, as they had been for many decades before the Revolution, the central domain for the realization of individual human potential, the pursuit of happiness, in American society.

Historians have traditionally interpreted the Constitution as a movement for stronger government, and to an important degree it was. But it is also necessary to call attention to the very significant extent to which, in seeking a stronger national government, the men who wrote and supported the Constitution were also endeavoring to reduce the power of the states and thereby, in Joyce Appleby's words, "to constrict [an important section of] the public sphere they could not control and expand the private realm they occupied as undifferentiated individuals." In so doing, they constructed a political system that was far more compatible with the basic predispositions of the American people than had been the Revolutionary state governments, a system that helped, at least in the short run, to set men free from the intrusions of the

---

[8] Washington to John Armstrong, April 25, 1788, ibid., 29:467.

[9] Madison to James Monroe, Aug. 7, 1785, *Madison Papers* 8:333–34.

public realm and to enable them "to pursue happiness by choosing their own goals" in the private sphere.[10] In so doing, they also helped to reinforce the hope that through commerce, commerce facilitated by government and pursued for the private happiness of individuals, "population and wealth," in Washington's words, "would flow to us, from every part of the Globe, and, with a due sense of the blessings, make us the happiest people upon earth."[11]

These remarks were presented at a session on "The Constitution: Commerce and 'The Pursuit of Happiness'" sponsored by Project '87 at Mount Vernon, Virginia, on Apr. 2, 1985. They are reprinted with permission and minor corrections and the addition of footnotes from *'this Constitution*, no. 8 (1985): 40–42.

[10] Joyce Appleby, "An Economic Interpretation of the Constitution of the United States" (Paper presented at the conference on "The Creation of the American Constitution," Philadelphia, Oct. 19, 1984).

[11] Washington to John Armstrong, April 25, 1788, *Writings of Washington* 29:467.

—FOURTEEN—

"An Instructive Monitor":
Experience and the Fabrication of the Federal Constitution

F ROM THE PERSPECTIVE of the constitutional history of the modern era, the achievement of the fifty-five men who came together in Philadelphia during the late spring and summer of 1787 to fabricate the Federal Constitution seems little short of remarkable, an achievement that may perhaps even be deserving to be called the "Miracle at Philadelphia," the title of both Catherine Drinker Bowen's evocative narrative of the Convention of twenty years ago and an excellent exhibit now at the First Bank of the United States by the Friends of National Independence Historical Park.[1] Certainly, contemporary supporters and opponents of the Constitution were fully aware of what the Massachusetts delegate Elbridge Gerry referred to in the Convention as the "novelty and difficulty of the experiment."[2] "The novelty of the undertaking immediately strikes us," its principal architect James Madison admitted in *Federalist* no. 37,[3] while Patrick Henry, one of its most vociferous adversaries, denounced it as a "perilous innovation," "an entire alteration of government," a hodgepodge of "novelties" that, taken together, comprised a government that was "so new, it wants a name."[4]

Yet, historians and informed lay Americans have long understood that,

---

[1] Catherine Drinker Bowen, *Miracle at Philadelphia: The Story of the Constitutional Convention, May to September 1787* (New York, 1967).

[2] Elbridge Gerry, speech, June 5, 1787, in *Notes of Debates in the Federal Convention of 1787 Reported by James Madison*, ed. Adrienne Koch (Athens, Ohio, 1966), 69.

[3] James Madison, in *The Federalist*, ed. Jacob E. Cooke (Middletown, Conn., 1961), no. 37, 233.

[4] Patrick Henry, speech, in Jonathan Elliot, ed., *The Debates in the Several State Conventions, on the Adoption of the Federal Constitution*, 4 vols. (Washington, D.C., 1836), 3:55–56.

however extraordinary and inventive an achievement it represented at the time and still appears to be two hundred years later, the Federal Constitution was far less novel than contemporaries liked to suppose and was both deeply rooted in the socioeconomic, political, and intellectual context out of which it came and far less the product of a miracle than of hard work, a penetrating application of intellect and expertise, and considerable political compromise. Especially during the century since the celebration of the centennial of the Constitution in 1887, historians have developed a relatively sophisticated comprehension of the complex forces that lay behind and informed the formation and content of that document. For the better part of fifty years after Charles A. Beard published his seminal work *An Economic History of the Constitution* in 1913, they focused very heavily upon the economic and sectional divisions that both shaped the struggle over the Constitution and informed the document itself.[5] More recently, historians have stressed two additional and related aspects of the battle over the Constitution: first, the broader social and political tensions underlying that battle,[6] and, second, the extent to which it was rooted in and reflective of ideological traditions that had been inherited from Britain and Europe and were subsequently modified to meet conditions in Revolutionary America.[7]

As a consequence of this emphasis, many of the complex aspects of the specific social context of the struggle over the Constitution, what the South Carolina delegate Charles Pinckney called "the situation of our people,"[8] are

---

[5] Charles A. Beard, *An Economic Interpretation of the Constitution* (New York, 1913); Merrill Jensen, *The Articles of Confederation* (Madison, Wis., 1940), and *The New Nation: A History of the United States during the Confederation, 1781–1789* (New York, 1950); Robert E. Brown, *Charles Beard and the Constitution* (Princeton, N.J., 1956); and Forrest McDonald, *We the People: The Economic Origins of the Constitution* (Chicago, 1958).

[6] Lee Benson, *Turner and Beard: American Historical Writing Reconsidered* (Glencoe, Ill., 1960); Jackson Turner Main, *The Antifederalists: Critics of the Constitution, 1781–1788* (Chapel Hill, N.C., 1961), and *Political Parties before the Constitution* (Chapel Hill, N.C., 1973); and Forrest McDonald, *E Pluribus Unum: The Formation of the American Republic, 1776–1790* (Boston, 1965).

[7] See, especially, Gordon S. Wood, *The Creation of the American Republic, 1776–1787* (Chapel Hill, N.C., 1969); Gerald Stourzh, *Alexander Hamilton and the Idea of Republican Government* (Stanford, Calif., 1970); J. G. A. Pocock, *The Machiavellian Moment: Florentine Political Thought and the Atlantic Tradition* (Princeton, N.J., 1975); Joyce Appleby, *Capitalism and a New Social Order: The Republican Vision of the 1790s* (New York, 1984); Morton White, *The Philosophy of the American Revolution* (New York, 1978); Forrest McDonald, *Novus Ordo Seculorum: The Intellectual Origins of the Constitution* (Lawrence, Kans., 1985); Jack P. Greene, *The Intellectual Heritage of the Constitutional Era: The Delegates' Library* (Philadelphia, 1986).

[8] Charles Pinckney, speech, June 25, 1787, in Madison, *Notes of Debates*, 183.

now beginning to be fairly well understood. Similarly, we now have a much broader appreciation of the deep learning displayed by many of the framers along with their indebtedness to inherited traditions of thought and their extensive use of certain celebrated works, including especially those of Montesquieu, Blackstone, and Hume. But an acute awareness of social context and solid grounding in the broad intellectual heritage of Britain and Europe were not the only ingredients that informed the calculations of the men who contrived and contended over the Constitution in the late 1780s.[9] Not surprisingly among elite figures in that age of self-conscious enlightenment, they frequently appealed, as many intellectual historians have emphasized, not just to circumstances and learned authorities but also to reason. Defined by Dr. Samuel Johnson in his *Dictionary* as the deliberative power by which people deduced "one proposition from another" or proceeded "from premises to consequences" in the effort to achieve logical and coherent perceptions of situations and problems, reason was thought of as both consistent with common sense and incompatible with passion and prejudice. Thus, with Alexander Hamilton, late eighteenth-century Americans often recommended their views as conformable "to the dictates of reason and good sense."[10]

What has perhaps tended to be somewhat underemphasized and what certainly was no less important than social context, learning, and reason in shaping action and thought in the Constitutional era was what learned men of the age referred to as experience. In the speeches in the debates both at the Convention and in the state ratifying conventions and in the polemical writings of the period, perhaps no term was more ubiquitous than experience. "No word," Douglass Adair pointed out in a brilliant article twenty years ago, "was used more often [in the Convention debates]; time after time 'experience' was appealed to as the clinching argument."[11] Invoking experience, the principals in the debate over the Constitution urged their audiences to consult or look to experience in support of their positions. Using a broad assortment of active verbs, they declared that what they called the "concurring testimony of experience," "unequivocal experience," or "in-

---

[9] See, in addition to the items cited in note 7, Donald S. Lutz, "The Relative Influence of European Thinkers on Late Eighteenth-Century American Political Thought," *American Political Science Review* 78 (1984): 189–97, and David Lundberg and Henry F. May, "The Enlightened Reader in America," *American Quarterly* 28 (1976): 262–93.

[10] Hamilton, *Federalist* no. 70, 474.

[11] Douglass G. Adair, "Experience Must Be Our Only Guide: History, Democratic Theory, and the United States Constitution," in Jack P. Greene, ed., *The Reinterpretation of the American Revolution* (New York, 1968), 399.

dubitible experience" either did—or did not—"fully" or "emphatically" prove, overrule, sanction, corroborate, teach, evince, confirm, deny, qualify, admonish, enforce, point out, produce, determine, warn against, show, satisfy, illustrate, instruct, urge, guide, inform, exemplify, ascertain, attest, convince, provide models for, or present lessons about whatever point they were trying to make.[12]

Experience, they asserted, was "the best of all tests,"[13] "the parent of wisdom,"[14] "the least fallible guide of human opinions,"[15] "the guide that ought always to be followed whenever it can be found,"[16] the "best oracle of wisdom."[17] "Experience," declared John Dickinson, "must be our only guide. Reason may mislead us."[18] "Theoretic reasoning," agreed Madison, "must [always] be qualified by the lessons of practice," that is, experience.[19] All speculation had to yield, said Hamilton, "to the natural and experienced course of human affairs."[20] Warning against "curious speculations," Melancton Smith urged his fellow delegates to the New York ratifying convention "to adopt a system, whose principles have been sanctioned by experience."[21] "Experience," echoed James Duane in the same gathering, "ought to have more influence on our conduct, than all the speculation and elaborate reasonings of the ablest men."[22] Experience, said the Maryland delegate Daniel Carroll, simply "overruled all other calculations."[23] "Where its responses are unequivocal," agreed Madison, "they ought to be conclusive and sacred."[24]

This widespread and laudatory use of the concept of *experience* raises two important questions: first, what did the framers and their contemporaries mean when they used the term, and, second, what were some of the more important conclusions they drew from experience.

---

[12] Madison, *Notes of Debates*, and *Federalist*, passim.

[13] George Mason, speech, June 4, 1787, in Madison, *Notes of Debates*, 64.

[14] Hamilton, *Federalist* no. 72, 490.

[15] Ibid., no. 6, 32.

[16] Madison, ibid., no. 52, 355.

[17] Hamilton, ibid., no. 15, 96.

[18] John Dickinson, speech, Aug. 13, 1787, in Madison, *Notes of Debates*, 447.

[19] Madison, *Federalist* no. 43, 293.

[20] Hamilton, ibid., no. 25, 162.

[21] Melancton Smith, speech, in *The Debates and Proceedings of the Convention of the State of New-York* (New York, 1805), 35.

[22] James Duane, speech, ibid., 110.

[23] Daniel Carroll, speech, Aug. 22, 1787, in Madison, *Notes of Debates*, 511.

[24] Madison, *Federalist* no. 20, 128.

When his colleagues elected George Washington to chair the Convention, he reminded them "of the novelty of the scene of business in which he was to act, lamented his want of better qualifications, and claimed the indulgence of the House towards the involuntary errors which his inexperience might occasion."[25] Four days later, in placing the Virginia Plan before the Convention, Washington's younger colleague Edmund Randolph expressed his "regret, that it should fall to him, rather than [to] those, who were of longer standing in life and political experience to open the great subject of their mission."[26] Washington and Randolph respectively used the terms *inexperience* and *experience* on these occasions to mean personal knowledge acquired by an individual during his lifetime.

If Washington and Randolph each felt a keen sense of his lack of experience in the particular role in which he found himself, however, the collective personal experience in public life of the delegates was enormously impressive. With Benjamin Franklin the oldest at 81 and New Jersey delegate Jonathan Dayton the youngest at 27, the mean age of the delegates was 43.5 years. Notwithstanding the relative youthfulness of many members of the group, however, the delegates had a combined record of public service in provincial and continental offices of well over 750 years! The mean was 13.6 years, and 11 was the median number of years. These figures do not include service in local government. Forty-nine—all but six of the fifty-five delegates—had served in one or the other and in some cases both branches of their colonial and state legislatures, six had been governors of states, and at least seven had taken a prominent part in the state judicial systems. Almost half—49 percent—were lawyers, who routinely in their private occupations came in contact with the public world many days every year. Twenty-two had taken an active role with the army during the War for Independence, and forty-three, just over 80 percent, had served at least one year in the Continental Congress, the mean term in Congress being 4.1 and the median 4 years. All together, they had served a total of 175 years in that body.[27]

[25] George Washington, speech, May 25, 1787, in Madison, *Notes of Debates*, 24.

[26] Edmund Randolph, speech, May 29, 1787, ibid., 28.

[27] The figures on age and numbers of lawyers are taken from Richard D. Brown, "The Founding Fathers of 1776 and 1787: A Collective View," *William and Mary Quarterly*, 3d ser., 33 (1976): 467, 469. The other statements in this paragraph have been computed from the data in *Biographical Directory of the American Congress, 1774–1971* (Washington, D.C., 1971), and the *DAB*.

If, as John Jay remarked in *Federalist* no. 2, the First Continental Congress back in 1774 had been "composed of many wise and experienced men" and "if the people at large had reason to" place their confidence "in the men of that Congress, few of whom had then been fully tried or [were] generally known" outside the boundaries of their own colonies, the public had even more reason to trust the judgement of the members of the Convention. For, as Jay explained, it was "well known that some of the most distinguished members of that Congress, who have been since tried and justly approved for patriotism and abilities, and who have grown old in acquiring political information, were also members of this Convention and carried into it their accumulated knowledge and experience."[28] "The respectability of this convention," a respectability deriving out of the extensive service and experience of its members, predicted Madison correctly on the floor of the Convention, would in itself "give weight to their recommendation[s]."[29]

As Douglass Adair pointed out in the article referred to earlier, however, the founders used the concept of experience not simply to mean individual "political wisdom gained by participation" in public life but also in a second and much broader sense to mean "the political wisdom gained by studying past events,"[30] what Hamilton referred to in *Federalist* no. 6 as "the accumulated experience of the ages."[31] This is the sense in which Madison employed the word when he told the delegates that they had "the experience of other nations before them."[32] Very often in the literature surrounding the Constitution, the terms *history* and *experience* were employed interchangeably. Thus, when Madison claimed in the Convention that his observations on the tendency of majorities to violate the rights of minorities were "verified by the Histories of every Country antient & modern"[33] and when Melancton Smith announced in the New York ratifying convention that he could illustrate his argument that a large number of representatives was unnecessary to retain the confidence of the public "by a variety of historical examples, both ancient and modern,"[34] they were using "history" synonymously with experience.

Of the several histories available to the founding generation, that of Great

---

[28] Jay, *Federalist* no. 2, 11–12.

[29] Madison, speech, June 12, 1787, in Madison, *Notes of Debates*, 107.

[30] Adair, "Experience Must Be Our Only Guide," 400.

[31] Hamilton, *Federalist* no. 6, 28.

[32] Madison, speech, June 26, 1787, in Madison, *Notes of Debates*, 193.

[33] Madison, speech, June 6, 1787, ibid., 76–77.

[34] Melancton Smith, speech, in *Debates and Proceedings of New-York*, 37.

Britain, as John Jay remarked in *Federalist* no. 5, was the "one with which we are in general the best acquainted," and he agreed with Madison that it presented "to mankind . . . many political lessons, both of the monitory and exemplary kind," "useful lessons" that enabled Americans, as Jay put it, to "profit by" the British "experience without paying the price which it cost them."[35] But they also referred often to the history of confederated republics, from both the ancient world, including the Achaean League, the Amphyctyonic Confederacies, and the Lycean Confederacy, and the modern world, including especially the Swiss, German, and Dutch confederacies. For the supporters of the Constitution and a more energetic central government, "all the examples of other confederacies . . . fully illustrated" the "same tendency of the parts to encroach upon the whole" and "prove[d] the greater tendency in such systems to anarchy than to tyranny; to a disobedience of the members than to usurpations of the federal head."[36]

By contrast, opponents of the Constitution cited the same histories to make the well-known Antifederalist point that, in George Mason's words, "there never was a government, over a very extensive country, without destroying the liberties of the people: history also, supported by the opinions of the best writers," Mason added, "shews us that monarchy may suit a large territory, and despotic . . . governments ever so extensive a country: but that popular governments can only exist in small territories."[37]

If this extensive use of experience as a synonym for history helps to establish Adair's point that the founders' "conscious and deliberate use of history and theory" played an important part in their deliberations, he certainly overstated his case when he argued that when the founders used the word *experience*, they referred, "more often than not, to the precepts of history" conceived of as the wisdom of the ages as transmitted to America from Europe.[38] Indeed, for every person who, like Dickinson, extolled "the singular & admirable mechanism of the English Constitution" and recommended the "long experience" of Britain as a guide,[39] there were many more who, with the South Carolina delegate Pierce Butler, decried the tendency to be "always following the British Constitution when the reason of it did not apply."[40] In direct answer to Dickinson, Butler's colleague John Rutledge traced many

---

[35] Jay, *Federalist* no. 5, 105; Madison, ibid., no. 56, 382.

[36] Speeches, June 19, 21, in Madison, *Notes of Debates*, 142–43, 164–65.

[37] George Mason, speech, in Elliot, *Debates* 3:60.

[38] Adair, "Experience Must Be Our Only Guide," 398–400.

[39] Dickinson, speech, Aug. 13, 1787, in Madison, *Notes of Debates*, 447.

[40] Pierce Butler, speech, June 13, 1787, ibid., 113.

of the defects of the state constitutions "to a blind adherence to the British model,"[41] while James Wilson insisted that "the British Model . . . was inapplicable to the situation of this Country; the extent of which was so great, and the manners so republican, that nothing but a great confederated republic would do for it."[42] "When applied to our situation which was extremely different," said Elbridge Gerry in seconding Wilson, "maxims taken from the British constitution were often fallacious."[43] In Edmund Randolph's words, the Convention had absolutely "no motive to be governed by the British Governm[en]t as our prototype."[44]

But it was not just the British experience that was of marginal relevance to the United States. "We have unwisely considered ourselves as the inhabitants of an old instead of a new country," lamented Charles Pinckney in asserting that the American situation was entirely "distinct from either the people of Greece or Rome, or of any State we are acquainted with among [either] the antients" or the moderns.[45] For five weeks, complained Roger Sherman of Connecticut on June 28, "we have gone back to ancient history for models of Government, and examined the different forms of those Republics which having been formed with the seeds of their own dissolution now no longer exist. And we have viewed Modern States all round Europe, but find none of the Constitutions [and little of their experience] suitable to our Circumstances."[46] There was little point, Edmund Randolph told the Virginia ratifying convention, in wasting time "with . . . historical references, which have no kind of analogy to the points under our consideration."[47]

What appears to have been far more relevant to most delegates to the Convention and probably also to most supporters of the Constitution in the state ratifying conventions was what Dickinson had dismissed as "the short experience of 11 years" that Americans had had in trying to govern themselves.[48] In their fear of a distant central power and their advocacy of local autonomy, Antifederalists showed a distinct preference for emphasizing the experience of the pre-Revolutionary years when the colonies were faced by

[41] John Rutledge, speech, Aug. 13, 1787, ibid., 448–49.

[42] James Wilson, speeches, June 1, 7, 1787, ibid., 47, 85.

[43] Gerry, speech, May 31, 1787, ibid., 41.

[44] Randolph, speech, June 1, 1787, ibid., 46.

[45] Charles Pinckney, speech, June 25, 1787, ibid., 184–85.

[46] Roger Sherman, speech, June 28, 1787, ibid., 209.

[47] Randolph, speech, in Elliot, *Debates* 3:94.

[48] Dickinson, speech, Aug. 13, 1787, in Madison, *Notes of Debates*, 447.

an aggressive centralizing power in Britain.[49] By contrast, Federalists were far more impressed by the American experience with republican government in the years after 1776.

As the delegates acknowledged over and over again in Convention debates, their experience with republican government had contributed to help make the framers of the Constitution acutely aware of the political limits within which they worked. Perhaps even more than their predecessors during the colonial period, they understood the force of that hallowed early modern political maxim that "All government . . . depend[ed] . . . in a great degree on opinion."[50] "No government," said James Wilson, "could subsist without the confidence of the people."[51] "If the Gov[ernmen]t is to be lasting," declared George Mason, it had to "be founded in the confidence & affections of the people, and must be so constructed to obtain these."[52]

More specifically, experience had taught them that no government could obtain the confidence of the American public that was not "organized in the republican form,"[53] that did not guarantee the sanctity of the existing states, that was too expensive, or that went beyond the minimal functions of securing respect abroad and maintaining "happiness & security" at home.[54] "The industrious habits of the people of the present day, absorbed in the [private] pursuit of gain, and devoted to the improvements of agriculture and commerce," Alexander Hamilton noted, were "incompatible" with a large public realm or an expensive government.[55] People could expect no more from government, averred Charles Pinckney, than to be "capable of extending to its citizens all the blessings of civil & religious liberty—capable of making them happy at home" in the private realm.[56]

But their "own experience" with independent republican government beginning in 1776 had not only underlined for American political leaders the popular limits of political action; it had also revealed a wide variety of perplexing problems.[57] "Experience had evinced" a want of energy in the cen-

---

[49] See on this point the excellent article by Frederick R. Black, "The American Revolution as 'Yardstick' in the Debates on the Constitution, 1787–1788," American Philosophical Society, *Proceedings* 117 (1973): 162–85.

[50] Melancton Smith, speech, *Debates and Proceedings of New-York*, 36.

[51] Wilson, speech, May 31, 1987, in Madison, *Notes of Debate*, 41.

[52] Mason, speech, Aug. 29, 1787, ibid., 549.

[53] Madison, June 12, 1987, ibid., 111.

[54] Charles Pinckney, speech, June 25, 1987, ibid., 185.

[55] Hamilton, *Federalist* no. 8, 47.

[56] Charles Pinckney, speech, June 25, 1987, in Madison, *Notes of Debates*, 185.

[57] Wilson, speech, June 20, 1787, ibid., 162.

tral government, an absence of "an effectual control in the whole over its parts," and "a constant tendency in the States to encroach on the federal authority; to violate national Treaties; [and] to infringe the rights & interests of each other."[58] Within the states, moreover, "experience had proved a tendency in our governments to throw all power into the Legislative vortex,"[59] where "the mischievous influence of demagogues" and a palpable lack of regard for minority rights and interests produced a "multiplicity of laws" characterized by their "mutability," "injustice," and "impotence."[60] To "check the precipitation, changeableness, and excesses" of the state legislatures,[61] to "protect the people ag[ain]st those speculating Legislatures which" at that very moment were "plundering them throughout the U[nited] States,"[62] experience told them, required a two-house legislature and a strong executive.

The hope of remedying these and many other "evils" they had "experienced" after 1776 inspired the framers to attempt a bold new experiment in framing an extended republic of a kind never before attempted, and they cautiously hoped that what they had contrived might be less flawed than they suspected. If, however, in the process of making their great contribution to the "science of politics,"[63] the founders had "paid a decent regard to the opinions of former times and other nations," they also, as Madison said in *Federalist* no. 14, had never "suffered a blind veneration for antiquity, for custom, or for names, to overrule the suggestions of their own good sense, the knowledge of their own situation, and the lessons of their own experience."[64] Their own collective experience with republican government, Madison thus suggested, almost certainly correctly, was the most important of the several empirical foundations of the Constitution.

This essay was written for delivery at a symposium on "The Genius of the United States Constitution" held as part of the annual meeting of the American Philosophical Society in Philadelphia on Apr. 24, 1987. It is reprinted with permission and a few corrections from American Philosophical Society, *Proceedings* 121 (1987): 298–307.

[58] Madison, speech, June 7, 1787, and Wilson, speech, June 8, 1987, ibid., 88, 91.

[59] Madison, speech, July 17, 1987, ibid., 312.

[60] Madison, speech, June 19, 1787, and Randolph, speech, Aug. 13, 1787, ibid., 145, 443.

[61] Gouverneur Morris, speech, July 2, 1987, ibid., 233.

[62] John Francis Mercer, speech, Aug. 14, 1987, ibid., 451.

[63] Hamilton, *Federalist* no. 9, 51.

[64] Madison, *Federalist* no. 14, 88.

Fifteen

The Constitution of 1787 and the Question of Southern Distinctiveness

HISTORIANS of the southern colonies and states during the seventeenth and eighteenth centuries can only welcome the devotion of several annual meetings of a major symposium on southern history to the origins of the South in the colonial and early national periods. Historians of the South, it seems to an outsider such as myself, have concentrated largely upon only a few major themes: the character and institutions of the Old South at the pinnacle—or the nadir—of its development between 1830 and 1860; the South's gallant but unsuccessful defense of its way of life during the Civil War and, for the South, the humiliating aftermath of that war; the intermittent and difficult efforts thereafter to build a New South in the image of the North; and the continuing burden of the region's past upon its present.

As a result of their efforts, the defining characteristics of the Old South, the central features that, despite significant regional variations, bound the southern states together as a single sociocultural unit and formed the basis for the articulation of a distinctive and regionwide sectional identity, are well known. These include plantation agriculture, a racially prescribed system of slave labor, high levels of property and wealth concentration among an agricultural elite, an unsystematic pattern of land occupation, weak commercial infrastructures, high levels of economic growth combined with low levels of economic development, and dominance of political institutions by a family-conscious and increasingly exclusive elite. These highly visible social features were combined with a distinctive mentality that was anticapitalistic, if not "feudal"; deeply committed to an agrarian way of life; uninterested, if not actually hostile, to economic and technological innovation;

self-consciously traditional and backward-looking in its cultivation of civility and other European upper-class values and in its suspicion of change; defensive about its continuing commitment to slavery in an era when that institution was being abandoned by most of the rest of the civilized world; acutely aware of its minority position within the American political union; and vigorously assertive of states rights against the authority of the national government.

The relative disinterest of students of the Old South in the history of the region before the 1820s and 1830s has contributed to considerable confusion over several important questions. Of particular importance are the highly general questions of whether this cluster of characteristics that seem for the mid-nineteenth century to define the South as a coherent and distinctive segment of American culture had always been present among the several societies that subsequently came to compose the South, and, if not, when and why those characteristics appeared.

In specific relation to the subject of this symposium, these general questions can be refined into several more precise ones: to what extent was there an entity we can call the South, a First South, the antecedent of the Old South, at the time of the fabrication of the Federal Constitution in 1787–88? To what extent was that entity already a distinctive—even a deviant—component of the emerging American cultural order? To what extent did leaders of the "southern" states manifest an awareness of the existence either of such an entity or of the common features that composed it? To what extent did such an awareness shape their actions in 1787–88? Some preliminary answers to these questions, all of which are implicit in the title of this symposium, are necessary before the role of the southern states in the constitutional era can be fully appreciated.

That there was a broad sociocultural fault line separating the southern colonies from the northern colonies and that there were significant behavorial and characterological differences between inhabitants of the two regions was already widely asserted by contemporaries during the era of the American Revolution. Thomas Jefferson's brief commentary on these differences to the marquis de Chastellux in 1785 is well known. North of Pennsylvania, Jefferson observed, people were "cool, sober, laborious, independent, jealous of their own liberties, and just to those of others, interested, chicaning, and superstitious and hypocritical in their religion." From Maryland south, by contrast, people were "fiery, voluptuary, indolent, unsteady, zealous for their own liberties, but trampling on those of others, generous, candid, and without attachment or pretentions to any religion but that of the heart."[1]

But others anticipated Jefferson's remarks with even fuller analyses of this phenomenon. One of the most impressive of these was by the London Quaker philanthropist Dr. John Fothergill, who summed up a century and a half of impressions among informed London opinion in his *Considerations relative to the North American Colonies*, a pamphlet pleading for the repeal of the Stamp Act published in London in 1765. Cautioning his readers not to identify "the Inhabitants of *North America*" with those of the "*West-India* Islands," he noted that the "*British* Inhabitants of *North America*" were "of two Sorts; those who live[d] in the northern Part of the Continent, and those who inhabit[ed] the Southern. *Nova Scotia, New England* and its Dependencies, *New York*, the *Jerseys* and *Pensilvania*," he wrote, "belong[ed] to the former Division: *Maryland* may be divided between both; *Virginia*, the *Carolinas* and *Georgia*, are the other Part."

What accounted for these two broad behavioral groupings, according to Fothergill, were contrasting physical environments and configurations of socioeconomic life. "The Inhabitants of the northern Part," Fothergill wrote, "live like our lower *English* Farmers; they plough, sow, reap, and vend different Kinds of Grain, as the Land they occupy and the Climate permits; Maize, Wheat, Barley, Oats, Pease, and the like rural Produce. They raise Cattle, Hogs, and other Domestick Animals for Use and Sale; also Hemp, Flax, [and] Naval Stores . . . . Their Summers are hot, their Winters severe, and their Lives are passed with the like Labour and Toil . . . as the little Farmers in *England*." A few people, also as in England, went into trade and, "aided by Capacity and Industry," thereby raised themselves "above the Level." Even though they could obtain land cheaply, marry young, and, in most cases, count on at least a modest inheritance, however, most people had to be satisfied with acquiring little more than was "sufficient to maintain their Families just above Want." If they could "afford to have an *English* Utensil, or *English* Cloathing," they considered themselves "rich."

By contrast, the inhabitants of the southern North American colonies "approach[ed much] nearer to the *West Indians*." Their lands were "capable of producing Riches of another Nature; Tobacco," that "pleasing Intoxication of many Nations," was produced in "*Maryland* and *Virginia*, chiefly by the Labour of Negroes. Rice" was "the Product of the *Carolinas*, a happy Succedaneum for Bread; [and] the proper, the most suitable Support of hot Countries," which was "likewise . . . raised, cultivated, [and] dress'd by the

---

[1] As quoted by John Richard Alden, *The First South* (Baton Rouge, La., 1961), 17.

Labour of Negroes." "Properly cultivated," a few acres of the liberal soils of these southern North American colonies, like those in the West Indies, thus yielded crops that were far more salable and considerably superior in value to those produced on much larger plots in the North, and higher profits permitted the owners to purchase the black slaves whose heavy toils both exempted their owners from the obligation of "labour[ing] for themselves" and enabled them to become comparatively rich. "Surrounded in their Infancy with a numerous Retinue of" slaves, moreover, whites in this area became "habituated by Precept and Example, to Sensuality, Selfishness, and Despotism" and addicted to "Splendor, Dress, Shew, Equipage, [and] every thing that can create an Opinion of their Importance."

Whereas "the Northern People of *America*" thus had to "trust to their own Industry," "Southern Inhabitants" were "rich in Proportion to the Number of Slaves they possess[ed]." Whereas the northern colonies were populated mostly by "low and middling People" and had few or none who were "great or rich," the southern colonies had "few middling People, a very few" of whom were "considerable, [with all] the rest . . . below the middle Class in general." Whereas northerners were industrious, "contented with a little, [and excellent] Examples of Diligence and Frugality, the best Riches of a State," southerners were "too often the Reverse," enervated, given to "Idleness and Extravagance," unable to "be contented with Mediocrity," and lustful "to contrive every Means of Gratification."[2]

Fothergill's contention that southern North Americans and the southern colonies had more in common with West Indians and the West Indian colonies than with northern North Americans and the northern colonies presents an image of the southern continental colonies and their free inhabitants that is reasonably compatible with modern historical portraits of the Old South and its inhabitants. In all probability, however, the distinctions made by Fothergill were much more clearly understood in London than in any of the colonies. Despite a growing volume of contacts among the colonies through the middle decades of the eighteenth century, each colony still represented a discrete and largely self-contained political environment that was much more closely connected to London, and probably also even more familiar to informed observers in the metropolis, than it was to any of its immediate neighbors in America.

But the American Revolution abruptly changed this situation. Once united resistance had begun in the mid–1770s, close associations in the Continental Congresses and in the army brought large numbers of people from

---

[2] [John Fothergill], *Considerations relative to the North American Colonies* (London, 1765), 36–43.

all the colonies together in the common cause of resisting British policy and seeking to establish American independence. To an important degree, this process helped to impress many people with a strong sense of a commonality among the colonies, commonalities not just of interest in seeking these common goals but also in culture and orientation. Thus could Benjamin Rush credibly insist in congressional debate during the summer of 1776 that, whatever the continuing variety among the new American states, their interests, "Trade, Language, Customs, and Manners" were by no means "more divided than they are among . . . people in Britain."[3] But more intense and sustained contact also produced a heightened awareness of regional diversities in interests, cultural configurations, and character. Indeed, that contact no doubt helped in many instances to confirm long-building stereotypes and to intensify the suspicions and the distrust implicit in those stereotypes.

"The Characters of Gentlemen in the four New England Colonies," John Adams wrote to Joseph Hawley in November 1775, "differ from those in the others . . . as much as [in] several distinct Nations almost. Gentlemen, Men of Sense, or any Kind of Education in the other Colonies are much fewer in Proportion than in N[ew] England," Adams thought, expressing his customary sectional pride. "Gentlemen, in the other Colonies have large Plantations of slaves, and the common People among them are very ignorant and very poor. These Gentlemen are accustomed, habituated to higher Notions of themselves and the distinction between them and the common People, than We are." Ever the realist, Adams understood that it would be difficult to fabricate an American union and an American identity out of such discordant materials, and he stressed the improbability of ever bringing about any fundamental change in "the Character of a Colony, and that Temper and those Sentiments which its Inhabitants imbibed with their Mother[']s Milk, and which have grown with their Growth and strengthened with their Strength."[4]

More cautious delegates especially continued to doubt that any effective or lasting union among such heterogeneous components could ever turn out well. "Their different Forms of Government—Productions of Soil—and Views of Commerce, their different Religions—Tempers and private Interest—their Prejudices against, and Jealosies of, each other—all have, and ever will, from the Nature and Reason of things, conspire to create such a Diversity of Interests, Inclinations, and Decisions, that they never can

---

[3] Benjamin Rush's "Notes for a Speech in Congress," [Aug. 1, 1776], in Paul H. Smith et al., eds., *Letters of Delegates to Congress*, 18 vols. to date, (Washington, D.C., 1976—), 4:592, 599.

[4] John Adams to Joseph Hawley, Nov. 25, 1775, ibid., 2:385.

[long] unite together even for their own Protection," predicted Joseph Galloway. "In this Situation Controversies founded in Interest, Religion or Ambition, will soon embrue their Hands in the blood of each other."[5] Not just timid and future loyalists like Galloway but also ardent proponents of continental union like John Adams worried about the long-range prospects of a union of such apparently disparate parts. "I dread the Consequencies of this Disimilitude of Character" among the colonies, Adams wrote, "and without the Utmost Caution . . . and the most considerate Forbearance with one another and prudent Condescention . . . , they will certainly be fatal."[6]

Whether the American Union might split along sectional lines and what those sections might be were, however, questions about which there was a great variety of opinion. When John Dickinson worried in July 1776 about the eventual dissolution of the American Union, he drew the line not between the slave-powered staple economies of the South and the mixed agricultural and commercial economies of the North but between New England and the rest of the states.[7] West and south of the New York–New England border, in fact, distrust of New England was chronic and widespread throughout the revolutionary era and beyond. Indeed, very few people in the 1770s and 1780s seem to have thought in terms of a consolidated northern interest, and many carefully distinguished between the "Eastern," or four New England, states and the "Middle" states from New York south to and sometimes including Maryland and even Virginia. Alexander Hamilton expressed this increasingly conventional point of view in *Federalist* no. 13 when he predicted that any breakup of the Union would be followed by the establishment of three confederacies, one composed of the four northern or New England states, a second of the four middle states, and a third of the five southern states.[8]

Recent scholarship on the socioeconomic and cultural development of Britain's North American colonies during the early modern era has tended to confirm the accuracy and utility of this more complex and subtle sectional analysis. During the last two decades, scholars have analyzed the socioeconomic landscape of colonial British America more deeply and more extensively than ever before, and they have increasingly come to conceptualize that landscape in terms of several clearly distinguishable regions. On the basis of what has been essentially a functional analysis of emerging socio-

---

[5] Joseph Galloway to [Samuel Verplanck], Dec. 30, 1774, ibid., 1:288.

[6] Adams to Hawley, Nov. 25, 1775, ibid., 2:385–86.

[7] John Dickinson's "Notes for a Speech in Congress," July 1, 1776, ibid., 4:356.

[8] Alexander Hamilton, *Federalist* no. 13, in *The Federalist*, ed. Jacob E. Cooke (Middletown, Conn., 1961), 80.

economic configurations and cultural orientations in colonial British America, historians have charted the development of not three but five broad culture areas by the last half of the eighteenth century, two northern, two southern, and one western.

Identical with those defined by the Revolutionary generation themselves, the two northern are New England, composed of the four New England colonies, Nova Scotia, and, after 1775, Vermont, and the Middle Colonies, including New York, New Jersey, Pennsylvania, and Delaware. The two southern regions are the Chesapeake or Upper South, consisting of Virginia, Maryland, and the northern half of North Carolina, and the Lower South, composed of South Carolina, the southern half of North Carolina, Georgia, and, after 1763, East and West Florida. The western region is the New West, the broad arc of inland settlements stretching from western Pennsylvania south into Georgia and then, after 1770, west into Kentucky and Tennessee.

To be sure, the Chesapeake and the Lower South shared many important attributes. These included a strong commitment to plantation agriculture and black slavery, an economy oriented heavily toward agricultural and extractive exports, relatively high levels of wealth and property consolidation among the free population, a marked interest in economic and technological innovation, high levels of white immigration, and, at least in the older colonies of Virginia, Maryland, and South Carolina, stable political leadership. But there were also significant differences between these two regions. The Chesapeake had a much larger population with a substantially greater proportion of whites; lower per capita wealth among whites; a considerably more diverse agricultural and manufacturing economy; a large slave population whose vigorous natural growth was by the 1760s sufficient to make it unnecessary to import many new slaves; and a slave system in which most slaves lived under the direct management of white families, many on smaller units of production, and thus enjoyed relatively little autonomy and were strongly subjected to the assimilative pressures of white paternalism.

The Lower South, by contrast, had a smaller population with a much higher ratio of blacks to whites; a less diversified economy; a proportionately considerably greater commitment to plantation agriculture and a continuing high demand for slave imports; and a slave system in which blacks, consisting of a much higher percentage of native Africans, concentrated on larger units, and, mostly working by the task system with a minimum of white supervision, had considerably more autonomy in their daily lives and were able to preserve far more of their African heritage. To the west of both these areas and including a large proportion of North Carolina, the New West, with a much smaller concentration of slaves and only a limited involvement with plantation agriculture, still more resembled the mixed farming areas of the Middle Colonies and the fringe areas of the Chesapeake than it did the cultural core of either of the Upper or the Lower South.[9]

Perhaps because of this considerable diversity among the southern states as well as because, as H. James Henderson's studies of divisions in the Confederation Congress reveal, patterns of voting in the national arena very often cut across sectional lines,[10] not many people during these years seem in fact to have thought in terms of a distinctive "southern" interest that might have provided the basis for a political alliance among these several "southern" regions. When, in 1778, William Henry Drayton of South Carolina expressed alarm at the possibility that, according to the Articles of Confederation, the nine other states might drive through Congress "the most important transactions . . . contrary to the united opposition of Virginia, the two Carolinas and Georgia," he was one of the few who seems to have had an acute appreciation of the possibility that "the nature of the climate, soil and produce of the several states" would "naturally and unavoidably" give rise to a distinctive "northern and southern interest in many particulars."[11]

In the Philadelphia Convention itself and in the ratifying conventions that followed, delegates used a wide range of categories to describe the divergent interests within the United States, and these categories were almost invariably framed in terms of polar opposites. They talked in terms of large states vs. small states, commercial states vs. noncommercial (sometimes referred to as landed or agricultural) states,[12] carrying states vs. noncarrying (sometimes called productive) states,[13] and distant vs. central states.[14] John Rut-

---

[9] See Jack P. Greene, *Pursuits of Happiness: The Social Development of Early Modern British Colonies and the Formation of American Culture* (Chapel Hill, N.C., 1988), and Carl Bridenbaugh, *Myths and Realities: Societies of the Colonial South* (Baton Rouge, La., 1952).

[10] H. James Henderson, *Party Politics in the Continental Congress* (New York, 1974). See also Joseph L. Davis, *Sectionalism in American Politics, 1774–1787* (Madison, Wis., 1977).

[11] As quoted by Alden, *First South*, 51.

[12] Elbridge Gerry, speech, June 7, 1787, in *Notes on Debates in the Federal Convention of 1787 Reported by James Madison*, ed. Adrienne Koch (Athens, Ohio, 1966), 84; Alexander Hamilton, speech, June 18, 1787, ibid., 133; James Madison, speech, Aug. 29, 1787, ibid., 550.

[13] Hamilton, speech, June 18, 1787, ibid., 216; William Grayson, speeches, June 11, 26, 1788, in Jonathan Elliot, ed., *The Debates in the Several State Ratifying Conventions on the Adoption of the Federal Constitution*, 4 vols. (New York, 1968), 3:278, 616; Madison's speech, June 12, 1788, ibid., 312–13.

[14] William Patterson, speech, June 16, 1787, in Madison, *Notes of Debates*, 124; George Mason, speech, Aug. 10, 1787, ibid., 429; Grayson's speech, June 24, 1788, in Elliot, *Debates* 3:615.

ledge of South Carolina even anticipated a future division between Atlantic states and western states.[15] Within the Convention, however, the perception that the most important division among the states revolved around the distinction between the northern states and the southern states and that that division had been and would continue to be fundamental to national political life quickly acquired the status of a self-evident truth.

As was the case with so many other aspects of the Convention debates, James Madison was responsible for initially articulating this perception. Trying to allay the fears of delegates from the small states that a representational system based on population might both deprive the small states of their identity as states and leave them at the mercy of the large states, Madison on June 30 observed, in a oft-cited remark, "that the States were divided into different interests not by their differences of size, but by other circumstances; the most material of which resulted partly from climate, but principally from the effects of their having or not having slaves. These two causes," he explained, "concurred in forming the great division of interests in the U[nited] States. It did not lie between the large & small States: It lay between the Northern & Southern, and if any defensive power were necessary, it ought to be mutually given to these two interests." In an interesting aside that has not been much emphasized by historians, Madison went on to propose a bicameral legislative system in which one house would represent only the free population and the second both slaves and free people, an arrangement, he pointed out, that would give "the Southern Scale . . . the advantage in one House, and the Northern in the other."[16]

No other delegate seems to have picked up on this particular proposal, but Madison's analysis of "the great division of interests" obviously struck deep resonances among the delegates. If a few delegates explicitly lamented with Pennsylvania delegate Gouverneur Morris that an invidious "distinction had been set up & urged, between the No[rthern] and Southern States,"[17] several others reiterated Madison's views that, in the words of Rufus King of Massachusetts, the "difference of interests did not lie where it had hitherto been discussed between the great & small States; but between the Southern & Eastern"[18] and that the critical variable in accounting for that difference was the presence of large-scale racial slavery in the southern states, what George Mason referred to as that "peculiar species of property,

---

[15] John Rutledge, speech, July 11, 1787, in Madison, *Notes of Debates*, 270.

[16] Madison, speech, June 30, 1787, ibid., 224–25.

[17] Gouverneur Morris, speech, July 13, 1787, ibid., 285.

[18] Charles Pinckney, speech, July 2, 1787, ibid., 232; Rufus King and Jonathan Dayton, speeches, July 10, 1787, ibid., 261; Mason, speech, Aug. 16, 1787, ibid., 467.

over & above the other species of property common to all the States."[19]
Already by July 14, Madison could observe without fear of contradiction
that it "seemed now to be pretty well understood that the real difference of
interests [in the Union] lay . . . between the N[orthern] & South[er]n
States" and that the "institution of slavery & its consequences formed the line
of discrimination."[20]

There was considerably less agreement over where to draw the line be-
tween those two great interests. That Georgia, South Carolina, and North
Carolina fell within the southern interest while the four New England states,
New York, and New Jersey fell within the northern interest seemed clear,
albeit both New Jersey and New York still had significant numbers of slaves.
Where Pennsylvania, Delaware, Maryland, and Virginia belonged was far
less obvious. Madison and many others drew the line at the Maryland-
Pennsylvania border,[21] but Jonathan Dayton of New Jersey argued that
Pennsylvania was a swing state and included Delaware among the southern
states,[22] while Charles Cotesworth Pinckney of South Carolina found it necessary to insist that Virginia ought to be considered "a Southern State."[23]

Once it had been so widely articulated and sanctioned by solemn discussion in the Philadelphia Convention, the conception of the American Union
as a potentially fragile amalgam between distinctive northern and southern
interests could scarcely fail to inform discussions over the merits of the new
Constitution. Many leaders, perhaps those who were most deeply committed
to perpetuating the union that had guided the republic through a long and
successful war for independence, denounced the tendency to view national
political life in such terms, decried the climate of sectional jealousy and
suspicion that both supported and perpetuated that tendency, and stressed the
mutuality of interests between the productive states of the South and the
carrying states of the North, between states made strong by their large populations of free people and those rendered weak by their numerous slaves.
With Archibald Maclaine of the North Carolina ratifying convention, they
denied that "the interests of the states" were "so dissimilar" and argued that
the states were "all nearly alike, and inseparably connected."[24] Still others

---

[19] Mason, speech, July 11, 1787, ibid., 269.

[20] Madison, speech, July 14, 1787, ibid., 295.

[21] Ibid.

[22] Jonathan Dayton, speech, July 10, 1787, ibid., 261.

[23] C. C. Pinckney, speech, July 10, 1787, ibid., 261.

[24] Robert Barnwell, speech, Jan. 17, 1788, in Elliot, *Debates* 4:296–97; James Innes,
speech, June 25, 1788, ibid., 3:633; Archibald Maclaine, speech, July 28, 1788, ibid.,
4:151.

resisted the tendency to conflate complex regional differences "in soil, climate, customs, produce, and every thing" into two discrete and antagonistic interests and continued to think in terms of a tripartite division among the "Eastern, Southern, and . . . Middle States."[25]

Notwithstanding the efforts of such people, opinion leaders among both the pro- and anti-Constitution forces persisted in thinking in terms of a broad north-south split in the Union. In extensive discussions in the press, in correspondence, in legislative chambers, and in the ratifying conventions, people often referred to—and thereby gave credence and legitimacy to—the idea that, in the words of James Iredell of North Carolina, the Union was divided into "what is called the northern and southern interests."[26] Even when they admitted that the "pursuits, habits, and principles" of the "Eastern States" were "essentially different from those of [both] the Middle and Southern States," they often avowed, as did Charles Pinckney in the South Carolina ratifying convention, that, however great the differences between the eastern and middle states might be, they were by no means so "striking" as those between the two northern sections, on the one hand, and the southern, on the other. "Nature," said Pinckney, in elaborating what was rapidly becoming conventional wisdom, "has drawn as strong marks of distinction in the habits and manners of the people as she has in her climate and productions. The southern citizen beholds, with a kind of surprise, the simple manners of the east . . . while they, in their turn, seem concerned at what they term the extravagance and dissipation of their southern friends, and reprobate, as unpardonable moral and political evil, the dominion they hold over part of the human race."[27]

As Pinckney's remark reveals, while American political leaders during the struggle over the Constitution were coming to define national political life in terms of a broad north-south division, they were also defining that division mostly in terms of the extent and depth of the commitment to slavery. In Europe as well as in all parts of America during the 1780s, the conviction that slavery was a moral outrage and incompatible with civilized life was still relatively new and by no means commanded widespread acceptance in the public world. The great revolution in sentiment on this issue, perhaps the most profound and most astonishing revolution that occurred during the late eighteenth century, was yet at about midpoint in its development. As late as 1770, slavery was an expanding institution in all of Britain's continental American colonies except Nova Scotia, New Hampshire, and

---

[25] Timothy Bloodworth, speech, July 28, 1788, ibid., 4:135.

[26] James Iredell, speech, July 29, 1788, ibid., 186.

[27] Charles Pinckney's speech, May 14, 1788, ibid., 323–24.

Canada, and, as the New York lawyer John Jay subsequently remarked, "the great majority" of Americans manifested no hostility to slavery, "very few of them even" doubting "the propriety and rectitude of it."[28]

But the Revolution had put slavery on the road to extinction in all states in which it had limited economic utility. By the late 1780s only Delaware, New Jersey, and New York among the northern states still had large numbers of slaves,[29] and there was a growing feeling, even among many large slave-holders of the Upper South, that, as Maryland delegate Luther Martin suggested in the Philadelphia Convention, any encouragement of slavery "was inconsistent with the principles of the revolution and dishonorable to the American character."[30] For the first time in the national arena, debate over the appropriate formula for taxing and representing slaves and the abolition of the slave trade produced a vigorous and extensive exchange over the institution of slavery. Delegates from the Middle States and the Upper South, in particular Gouverneur Morris and George Mason, unequivocally denounced slavery and its social effects, Morris contrasting "the free regions of the Middle States, where a rich & noble cultivation marks the prosperity & happiness of the people, with the misery & poverty which overspread the barren wastes of V[irgini]a Mary[lan]d & the other States having slaves"[31] and Mason decrying the "pernicious" influence of slavery on arts, manufactures, and manners and predicting that it would in time "bring the judgment of heaven on" the "Country."[32] The states these men represented—Pennsylvania and Virginia—were also the most insistent upon putting an immediate end to the slave trade.

The defense of slavery in the Convention came entirely from delegates from the Lower South, with the South Carolinians taking the lead. Threatening to leave the Union if the slave trade was not permitted to continue for a limited time, they argued that, at least for the immediate future, South Carolina and Georgia could not "do without slaves." John Rutledge declared that "Religion & humanity had nothing to do with the question," while Charles Pinckney "cited the case of Greece and Rome & other antient States"

---

[28] John Jay to Granville Sharp, 1788, *The Correspondence and Public Papers of John Jay*, ed. Henry P. Jackson, 4 vols. (New York, 1890–93), 3:342, as quoted by William W. Freehling, "The Founding Fathers and Slavery," *American Historical Review* 77 (1972): 86.

[29] Arthur Zilversmit, *The First Emancipation: The Abolition of Slavery in the North* (Chicago, 1967); Donald L. Robinson, *Slavery in the Structure of American Politics, 1765–1820* (New York, 1971).

[30] Luther Martin, speech, Aug. 21, 1787, in Madison, *Notes of Debates*, 502.

[31] Gouverneur Morris, speech, Aug. 8, 1787, ibid., 411.

[32] Mason, speech, Aug. 22, 1787, ibid., 503–4.

as well as "the sanction given by France[,] England, Holland & other modern States" to support his argument that, so far from being "wrong," slavery was "justified by the example of all the world," "one half" of which "in all ages" had "been slaves."[33]

Notwithstanding the vow of secrecy that bound the Convention, echoes, even direct paraphrases, of these discussions could be heard in the ensuing debate over the Constitution. Rumors spread through the southern states that northerners wanted to do away with not merely the slave trade but slavery itself. "It is well known to have been the intention of the Eastern and Northern States to abolish slavery altogether when [they had it] in their power," Lachlan McIntosh of Georgia wrote to a correspondent in late 1787,[34] and in all of the southern ratifying conventions for which records of debate survive, in South Carolina, Virginia, and North Carolina, Antifederalists charged that adoption of the Constitution would lead eventually to the destruction of slavery. In South Carolina, Rawlins Lowndes expressed alarm that "Without negroes, this state would degenerate into one of the most contemptible in the Union" and vigorously defended slavery "on the principles of religion, humanity, and justice."[35] No one came forward with a positive defense of slavery in Virginia, but both Patrick Henry and George Mason were fearful that the national government would eventually act against slavery and argued that "prudence" forbade its abolition.[36]

To allay these fears, Federalists found themselves driven to assure their audiences, as they had done with reference to so many contested elements in the Constitution, that, as Madison put it, the "general government" had only delegated powers and that those powers did not include authority "to interpose with respect to the property in slaves now held by the states."[37] Thus, while acknowledging his agreement with Lowndes "that the nature of our climate, and the flat, swampy situation of our country, obliges us to cultivate our lands with negroes, and that without them South Carolina would soon be a desert waste," C. C. Pinckney insisted that the failure of the Constitution expressly to grant the national government power to emancipate slaves

---

[33] John Rutledge, speech, Aug. 21, 1787, ibid., 502; Charles Pinckney, speech, and C. C. Pinckney, speech, Aug. 22, 1787, ibid., 505.

[34] Lachlan McIntoch to John Wereat, Dec. 17, 1787, in Merrill Jensen et al., eds., *The Documentary History of the Ratification of the Constitution* (Madison, Wis., 1978—), 3:260–61.

[35] Rawlins Lowndes, speech, Jan. 16, 1788, in Elliot, *Debates* 4:272–73.

[36] Patrick Henry, speech, June 24, 1788, ibid., 3:590–91; Mason, speech, June 11, 1788, ibid., 270.

[37] Madison, speech, June 15, 1788, ibid., 453.

provided ample security that it would never do so.[38] At no point during the Philadelphia Convention, Edmund Randolph told the Virginia convention, had "the *Southern States, even South Carolina herself* . . . had *the smallest suspicion of an abolition of slavery*."[39]

If the debate over the Constitution contributed to the widespread articulation and circulation of an enhanced sense of potential tensions between the northern and the southern states, a heightened awareness of the controversial nature of slavery, and perhaps even a fuller comprehension among southerners of the cultural similarities that linked them together in opposition to the Middle and New England states, it did not witness the emergence of an all-subsuming southern identity. As David Potter has reminded us, recognition of social and "cultural similarities alone will not provide a basis of affinity between groups." Nationalism and similar collective loyalties have to rest on "*two* psychological bases": an awareness "of a common culture *and* the feeling of common interest." "Of the two," he posits, "the concept of culture is, no doubt, of greater weight," but it cannot have its full effect without a mutual awareness of common interests.[40]

That the southern states did not yet have an overriding sense of a common interest can be seen by the divisions among them over both the slave trade and slavery. Even if they could not see any way to abolish slavery, many Virginians, both among the delegation to the Philadelphia Convention and in the Virginia ratifying convention, condemned slavery and militantly opposed the slave trade. South Carolinians and Georgians, on the other hand, insisted on not closing the slave trade, candidly admitted the utility of slavery to the economy of the Lower South, and, in a few cases, even defended slavery in positive terms. In North Carolinia there were political leaders who subscribed to each of these views.[41]

In Philadelphia, even their common interest as staple-exporting states in keeping foreign trade open and unencumbered could not override disagreements among the southern states over the slave trade. Rather than forming a united front on issues involving commercial regulations, the Lower South

---

[38] C. C. Pinckney, speech, Jan. 17, 1788, ibid., 285–86.

[39] Edmund Randolph, speech, June 24, 1788, ibid., 598–99.

[40] David M. Potter, "The Historians' Use of Nationalism and Vice Versa," *American Historical Review* 67 (1962): 935, 949.

[41] See the speeches by James Galloway, July 26, 1788, and James Iredell, July 26, 1788, in Elliot, *Debates*, 4:100–101.

states aligned themselves with New England in a well-known bargain, opposed by the Upper South, by which the Lower South agreed to endow the federal government with authority to enact navigation laws while New Englanders consented not to empower it to close the slave trade for twenty years.[42]

Indeed, a close look at Forrest McDonald's table on voting compatibility among the states in the Federal Convention quickly reveals that the southern states demonstrated relatively little voting cohesion. North Carolina, South Carolina, and Georgia all voted together rather consistently (more than 65 percent of the time). Although Virginia voted often with North Carolina, it voted far more frequently with Pennsylvania and Massachusetts than it did with either Georgia or South Carolina. To the extent that there was a southern voting bloc, Maryland was not a part of it. Although Maryland sided with Virginia almost as often as it did with Delaware, it voted less with South Carolina than with any other state and less with North Carolina than with any of the other states except New York and South Carolina.[43] These findings have more recently been confirmed by Calvin H. Jillson and Cecil L. Eubanks in their illuminating analysis of voting patterns in the Convention. They depict a broad division not between northern states and southern states but between a liberal, expansive central core and a more parochial and locally oriented periphery. Though this pattern by no means held on all issues, it clearly placed Virginia closer to the Middle States, especially to Pennsylvania, than to the states of the Lower South.[44]

However much leaders of the southern states may have come to think of themselves as part of a broad southern, slaveholding interest during the Revolutionary era, many Virginians, as evidenced both by their voting behavior and by their explicit declarations, clearly regarded Virginia more as a "central" than as a southern state. George Washington was by no means the only prominent Virginian who referred to the Carolinas and Georgia as the "Southern states" and classified Virginia as one of "the middle states."[45] Not just because of its "central situation" geographically within the Union but also because of its size, wealth, and conspicuous leadership in most of the major events associated with the Revolution and foundation of the American

---

[42] Alden, *First South*, 90–98; Calvin C. Jillson and Cecil L. Eubanks, "The Political Structure of Constitution Making: The Federal Constitution of 1787," *American Journal of Political Science* 28 (1984): 452.

[43] Forrest McDonald, *We the People: The Economic Origins of the Constitution* (Chicago, 1958), 96.

[44] Jillson and Eubanks, "Political Structure of Constitution Making," 439–47.

[45] As quoted by Alden, *First South*, 9–10.

nation, Washington and others thought of Virginia as being "at the centre of the states." Well aware that Virginia was one of the "commanding" states of the Union and was admirably situated in terms of its location to preside over and reap large benefits from the westward and southwestward expansion of population into Kentucky, Tennessee, and the Ohio country, they automatically assumed that it would have a defining role in the new union and had no intention of permitting it to be shunted off into a marginal position.[46]

This was precisely the sort of leadership role Virginia had assumed at the Philadelphia Convention. George Washington was the unanimous choice of the delegates to preside; Edmund Randolph introduced the plan that formed the basis for early discussions; and James Madison contributed so heavily to the discussions that he has often been referred to as the father of the Constitution. A tally of Madison's notes reveals that Madison, George Mason, and Randolph were all among the ten most frequent participants in the debates, Madison being exceeded in this regard only by Gouverneur Morris, and Mason only by Morris, Madison, and James Wilson. Together, Virginia's seven delegates accounted for just over 19 percent of Convention interventions, just a fraction of a percentage point below the figure for Pennsylvania's eight delegates.

In 1787–88 Virginians had no reason to think that Virginia's contribution to the new union might be any less conspicuous, and in the short run, of course, they were correct. Supplying four of the first five presidents, the most prominent chief justice of the Supreme Court, and a large number of congressional leaders, Virginia did indeed play a key part in the formation of the federal union. Only after its rapid decline in prestige and power after 1815 had deprived Virginia of its central place did it slowly drift into a closer emotional association with the rest of the southern states and itself begin to become more self-consciously southern.[47]

To describe Virginia's role as central in 1787–88 is by no means to suggest that that of the other southern states was marginal. Georgia, which was scarcely more than a half-century old, and North Carolina still had relatively undeveloped and small leadership pools and played a less prominent part in

---

[46] William Grayson, speech, June 24, 1788, in Elliot, *Debates* 3:615; Francis Corbin, speech, ibid., 113. See also the article by Drew McCoy, "James Madison and Visions of American Nationality in the Confederation Period: A Regional Perspective," in Richard Beeman, Stephen Botein, and Edward C. Carter II, eds., *Beyond Confederation: Origins of the Constitution and American National Identity* (Chapel Hill, N.C., 1987), 234–36.

[47] Daniel P. Jordan, *Political Leadership in Jefferson's Virginia* (Charlottesville, Va., 1983); Norman K. Risjord, *The Old Republicans: Southern Conservatism in the Age of Jefferson* (New York, 1985).

the Convention. But the four delegates from South Carolina, the state with the highest per capita wealth in the Revolutionary generation, were far from invisible. Charles Pinckney ranked seventh among all delegates in terms of frequency of participation in the debates, while John Rutledge ranked twelth, Pierce Butler fourteenth, and C. C. Pinckney seventeenth. Only the delegates from the three largest states, Pennsylvania, Virginia, and Massachusetts, had more interventions, with the four South Carolina delegates accounting for 14 percent of the total, just a fraction less than the four Massachusetts delegates and well above Connecticut, whose delegates were responsible for just over 11 percent of interventions. Eighth on the list, Hugh Williamson was the only delegate from North Carolina to rank among the twenty-five most frequent participants. With 6 percent of the interventions, however, the North Carolina delegation slightly exceeded the contributions of those from Delaware and Maryland and was way ahead of those from New York, New Jersey, New Hampshire, and Georgia. At seventeenth, Luther Martin was the only Marylander to be in the top twenty participants, and no Georgian appeared in the top thirty.

In contrast to Virginia, the states of the Lower South neither played such a conspicuous part in the constitutional revolution of 1787–88 nor aspired to such a prominent role in the Union, but it is important to emphasize that they all were highly optimistic about their respective futures during the founding era. For several decades, South Carolina and Georgia had had the highest value of exports per capita of any states in the Union, and in recent decades only New Hampshire had matched those two states and North Carolina in terms of their rates of white population growth. Between 1750 and 1780 the white population of Georgia had increased more than seven times, that of North Carolina by 237 percent, and that of South Carolina by 232 percent. These figures are somewhat higher than those for New Hampshire at 224 percent and well ahead of any found for the same period in the other states to the north, among whom New York with 188 percent, Pennsylvania with 174 percent, and Virginia with 145 percent were the leaders. Over the same period, the slave populations, to some extent still a reflection of buying power, also rose rapidly, that of Georgia increasing almost twenty times, that of North Carolina by 360 percent and that of South Carolina by 149 percent, a figure just below Virginia's 154 percent.[48]

A substantial part of the astonishing white population growth among the Lower South states was, like that for Virginia, the result of immigration

---

[48] The data on exports and population may be found in *Historical Statistics of the United States, Colonial Times to 1980* (Washington, D.C., 1975), pt. 2, 1168–78.

IMPERATIVES, BEHAVIORS, AND IDENTITIES

from the northern states. Both because most "of the Northern States," as
Edward Rutledge of South Carolina declared during the debate over
whether to refer the Constitution to state ratifying conventions, "were already full of people," because "the migrations to the south were immense,"
and because the southern states all had "great quantity of lands still uncultivated," it seemed evident, as Pierce Butler announced in the Philadelphia
Convention, that the "people & strength of America" were "evidently bearing Southwardly & S[outh] westw[ar]dly" and that the southern states, including Virginia, would soon "predominate" over what one North Carolina
delegate referred to as the "small, pitiful states to the north." The rapid
growth of Kentucky and Tennessee in the late 1770s and 1780s seemed to
provide additional testimony for the legitimacy of these expectations. Within
a half century, predicted David Ramsay of South Carolina, the southern
states could scarcely fail to have "a great ascendency over the Eastern."[49]

In the final analysis, of course, all of the southern states acted in the
struggle over the Constitution in a way a majority of their leaders thought
best in terms of their interests and conceptions of their own goals and priorities not as a part of the South but as separate and mostly long-established
corporate entities, each with a long history and a clearly understood sense of
its own potentialities and weaknesses in the situation in which it then found
itself. "Each State like each individual," Connecticut delegate Roger Sherman told his colleagues in Philadelphia, "had its peculiar habits, usages and
manners, which constituted its happiness." In these early days of nationhood
and national community formation, loyalties to these state interests and identities still took precedence over sectional considerations.[50]

The tendency to think in terms of state or even national rather than sectional considerations was reinforced by mutual suspicions and hostilities
among states. Southerners were skeptical not only about northerners but
about each other. South Carolinians regarded Virginian attitudes on slavery
and the slave trade as "interested and inconsistent,"[51] C. C. Pinckney pointing out in the Philadelphia Convention that because Virginia had more slaves
than it needed it would actually "gain by stopping the importations" and

[49] John Rutledge, speech, Jan. 1, 1788, in Elliot, *Debates* 4:276–77; C. C. Pinckney,
speech, May 20, 1788, ibid., 335; Joseph M'Dowall, speech, July 28, 1788, ibid., 124;
James Iredell, speech, July 29, 1788, ibid., 186; Pierce Butler, speech, July 13, 1787, in
Madison, *Notes of Debates*, 286; Madison, speech, July 11, 1787, ibid., 274; Alden, *First
South*, 105–6.

[50] Roger Sherman, speech, June 20, 1787, in Madison, *Notes of Debates*, 161.

[51] C. C. Pinckney, speech, Jan. 17, 1788, in Elliot, *Debates* 4:285.

thereby raising the value of their surplus slaves.[52] Virginians looked askance at their weaker and less prominent southern neighbors, Patrick Henry describing North Carolina as "a *poor, despised place*" and William Grayson suggesting that South Carolinians still went abroad "mounted on alligators."[53]

If there was a growing awareness in the southern states during the late Revolutionary era of a broad southern interest and of the extent to which a strong commitment to slavery defined that interest, the southern states in 1787–88 did not yet constitute a cohesive sectional unit. The states of the Upper South, especially Virginia, had quite different attitudes toward slavery and the slave trade and a different conception of their relationship to the Union than did the states of the Lower South. Partly because antislavery sentiment was still relatively new and relatively limited, partly because the process of abolition had not yet even begun in the northern states of New York and New Jersey, and partly because northerners had not yet attacked slavery in the southern states, slavery was by no means as important either as a point of sectional differentiation or as a social and political issue as it would become after 1830 or even after 1820, and its potentially disruptive effects were by no means so clear as they would be by 1820.

Similarly, population growth among the southern states, the spread of slavery into Kentucky and Tennessee, and the expansiveness to which those developments gave rise inhibited the emergence of the idea that the southern slave interest might be a permanent minority interest within the Union. Nor had explicit sectional politics yet come into play in the national arena. New Englanders had not yet retreated into that "unbending Federalism that would later set" their region "at odds with the rest of the nation" and especially with southern Republicans.[54] The militantly agrarian minority of southern Republicans had not yet formulated their defensive states-rights and narrow-constructionist political position.[55]

Indeed, the prominence of the southern states in the major events of the

---

[52] C. C. Pinckney, speech, Aug. 22, 1788, in Madison, *Notes of Debates*, 505.

[53] Henry, speech, June 12, 1788, in Elliot, *Debates*, 3:314; Grayson, speech, June 11, 1788, ibid., 277.

[54] Joyce Appleby, "What Is Still American in the Political Philosophy of Thomas Jefferson?" *William and Mary Quarterly*, 3d ser., 39 (1982): 292.

[55] Risjord, *Old Republicans*.

Revolution as well as in the formation of the Federal Constitution and the establishment and early years of the American republic clearly reveals that their inhabitants had not yet come to be thought of by people from other areas or to think of themselves as distinctive or outside the central currents of American development. No less than residents of the states to the north, inhabitants of the Chesapeake and the Lower South believed that they were squarely within the republican tradition. Virginians especially had no trouble in defining themselves as being in the center of American political culture.

With the phased abolition of slavery in the British Empire and the spread of disdain for slavery throughout the northern areas of the United States after 1820, the southern states' continuing commitment to a slave labor system resulted in a growing divergence between their patterns of social organization and values and those of the increasingly urban and industrialized societies of the North. In their obvious "hierarchy, the cult of chivalry—the unmachined civilization, the folk society, the rural character of life, the clan values rather than the commercial values," the southern states, as Potter has argued, seemed to have acquired a *"distinctiveness* of a deeply significant kind," one that was both less and less congruent with the social character and orientation of the states to the north and out of step with the rest of the civilized world. Notwithstanding their economic origins, the southern states seemed to have developed "a climate that was uncongenial" to the capitalist spirit that still thrived in the North.[56]

From the perspective of these developments, the divergencies among the southern and northern states during the Revolutionary era would appear in retrospect by 1850 and 1861 to have been latently significant. From the immediate perspective of their common experience in mounting and carrying out a successful war for independent nationhood, however, their commonalities probably seemed much more impressive than their differences and gave credence to the widely held hope that all the states were part of "a common culture that transcended sectional differences." Few could have found incredible Washington's assertion in his Farewell Address in 1796 that "with slight shades of difference" Americans had "the same religion, manners, habits and political principles."[57] Insofar as it already existed, how-

---

[56] Potter, "Historians' Use of Nationalism," 943; C. Vann Woodward, "The Southern Ethic in a Puritan World," *William and Mary Quarterly*, 3d ser., 25 (1968): 343–70.

[57] Joseph F. Kett and Patricia A. McClung, "Book Culture in Post-Revolutionary Virginia," American Antiquarian Society, *Proceedings* 94, pt. 1 (1984): 136; Robert E. Shalhope, "Thomas Jefferson's Republicanism and Antebellum Southern Thought," *Journal of Southern History* 42 (1976): 529–56. The Washington quotation is from Yehoshua Arieli, *Individualism and Nationalism in American Ideology* (Cambridge, Mass., 1964), 27.

ever, southern distinctiveness did not appear to be of overriding importance to most members of the Revolutionary generation in either the northern or the southern states. The development of a powerful, self-conscious, slavery-conscious sectionalism lay ahead, primarily in the years after 1820.

This essay was presented as a lecture at the Porter L. Fortune Chancellor's Symposium on Southern History: The Constitutional Convention and Bill of Rights, 1787–1791, held at the University of Mississippi on Oct. 7, 1987. It is reprinted with permission and with substantial corrections from Robert J. Hawes, ed., *The South's Role in the Creation of the Bill of Rights* (Jackson: University of Mississippi Press, 1991), 19–31, 147–49.

America and the Creation of the Revolutionary Intellectual World of the Enlightenment

O NE HAS ONLY to read through some of the correspondence of the generation that created an independent American nation to appreciate the high levels of activity and energy, the exuberant spirit of empirical inquiry, and the expansive optimism that characterized the American intelligentsia during the half century after the Declaration of Independence. Along with a confident faith in a future limited only by the extent of man's ingenuity, these qualities of that generation's approach to life and to the world about them gave them a mentality that will seem to most of us strikingly modern. So similar indeed is the orientation of that generation to our own that it has been difficult for mid-twentieth-century people to appreciate how revolutionary it was within the context of the development of Western thought and culture. But this outlook was in fact something quite new, something quite uncharacteristic of earlier generations, and it constituted a fundamental transformation in the nature of human expectations about the world and about mankind, a transformation that, occurring during the late eighteenth century, was significantly accelerated by the specifically American developments of that time.

"Realistic yet hopeful, scientific but humanist, respectful but secular, trusting in institutions yet treating them as provisional, and looking to the day when all men [would be] . . . autonomous," the "inquisitive, liberating, intellectually adventurous frame of mind" exhibited by so many Americans of that time held out new hope for mankind. Confident that reason and science would lead them to an ever fuller understanding of the world, they believed that that understanding would permit people to become active agents in a wholesale reconstruction of their social environments and of the

social institutions that governed them. In this new world, passive acceptance
of authority would be replaced by an active spirit of free critical inquiry;
tradition and a respect for the past would give way to an orientation toward
the future; a social system characterized by hierarchy, ascription, dependence, and exploitation would yield to one emphasizing equality, merit, personal independence, human fraternity, and social benevolence; a human condition dominated by failure, frustration, despair, and misery would be
wiped away in favor of one characterized by opportunity, achievement, ful-
fillment, and happiness—a world of limits, in short, would be replaced by
one that knew no bounds.[1]

Borrowing a term from the times, cultural historians refer to this "great
revolution in man's thinking that came to dominate the Western world in the
eighteenth century" as the Enlightenment, and they have generally explained
it as a development that had its origins almost wholly within Europe. Thus,
Peter Gay, the most influential recent American student of the Enlightenment, has traced it to a series of largely internal European developments—
"the triumph of Newtonian science, striking improvements in industrial and
agricultural techniques, a widespread loss of religious fervor and a corresponding rise of 'reasonable' religion, an ever bolder play of the critical
spirit among the old mysteries of church and state which had for centuries
escaped criticism, [and] a new sense of confidence in man's power over his
worldly destiny." Although Gay and most other students of the Enlightenment have not denied that the creation of the American federal republic
between 1776 and 1788 both accelerated and was widely regarded as one of
the outstanding achievements of the Enlightenment, they seem generally to
agree that in formulating the ideas and expectations of the Enlightenment
the "American colonists [and colonies] had no part." Indeed, students of the
American phase of the Enlightenment, including Donald H. Meyer and
Henry F. May, have had no trouble in accepting the judgments of European
historians that the American Enlightenment was provincial and derivative,
that the "Americans were consumers, depending heavily, almost exclusively,
on borrowings from overseas," that American philosophers like Franklin,
Jefferson, Adams, and Madison were "apt and candid disciples" who "went
to school to a handful of European thinkers."[2]

In this chapter, I want not so much to challenge this view but to look in a

---

[1] Peter Gay, "The Enlightenment," in C. Vann Woodward, ed., *The Comparative Approach
to American History* (New York, 1968), 38; Donald H. Meyer, *The Democratic Enlightenment*
(New York, 1976), viii, xiii-xvii, xix.

[2] Gay, "Enlightenment," 34, 38, 40; Meyer, *Democratic Enlightenment*; Henry F. May, *The
Enlightenment in America* (New York, 1976).

frankly playful and highly speculative way at the American relationship to the intellectual transformation of the late eighteenth century from a somewhat different—and much longer—perspective. Specifically, I want here to explore the extent to which America first helped to inspire and then came to epitomize the transformation in the character of human expectations during the early modern era.

This is not a subject that has been widely canvassed. As J. H. Elliott has remarked, historians have mostly assumed that Europe's impact on the rest of the world, including America, was of much "greater interest and concern than the impact of the world on Europe." Not only, they agree, were other significant developments contemporary with the discovery and exploration of America—the revival of interest in antiquity associated with the Renaissance, the so-called educational and scientific revolutions, the Protestant Reformation, and the expansion of external trade both within Europe and between Europe and the Levant, Africa, America, and Asia—more important in helping to stimulate different modes of thought and mental outlooks in the early modern era. The discovery of America, several scholars have emphasized, appears to have "made relatively little impression on Europe" and, astonishing as it may now seem, to have "registered little impact on the values, beliefs, and traditions of the sixteenth and seventeenth centuries."[3] Notwithstanding these judgments, there are strong reasons to suspect that the role of America in contributing to stimulate changes in traditional mental outlooks from the early sixteenth century on has not yet been sufficiently appreciated.

[3] J. H. Elliott, *The Old World and the New, 1492–1650* (Cambridge, 1970), 2–3, 56–59; Margaret T. Hodgen, *Early Anthropology in the Sixteenth and Seventeenth Centuries* (Philadelphia, 1964), 113; Michael T. Ryan, "Assimilating New Worlds in the Sixteenth and Seventeenth Centuries," *Comparative Studies in Society and History* 23 (1981): 519. For similar views, see also G. V. Scammel, "The New Worlds and Europe in the Sixteenth Century," *Historical Journal* 12 (1969): 389–412, and *The World Encompassed: The First European Maritime Empires, c. 800–1650* (Berkeley and Los Angeles, 1981); and J. H. Elliott, "Renaissance Europe and America: A Blunted Impact?" in Fredi Chiapelli, ed., *First Images of America: The Impact of the New World on the Old*, 2 vols. (Berkeley and Los Angeles, 1976), 1:11–23. For contrary views, see Walter Prescott Webb, *The Great Frontier* (Austin, Texas, 1964); Ernest J. Burrus, "The Impact of New World Discovery upon European Thought of Man," in J. Robert Nelson, ed., *No Man Is Alien: Essays on the Unity of Mankind* (Leiden, 1971), 85–108; Arthur J. Slavin, "The American Principle from More to Locke," in Chiapelli, *First Images of America* 1:139–64; and William Brandon, *New Worlds for Old: Reports from the New World and Their Effect on the Development of Social Thought in Europe, 1500–1800* (Athens, Ohio, 1986).

As many scholars have pointed out, the New World of America was revealed to Europe not immediately upon discovery but only gradually over several centuries.[4] Within a quarter century after Columbus's first landing at San Salvador, however, Europeans understood two powerful truths about the land Columbus had encountered: first, that it was a genuinely new, that is, a previously unknown world, that was not, as Columbus initially hoped, part of the continent of Asia; and, second, that it was enormous. The newness of the New World was dramatically indicated by the hitherto unknown animals, plants, and peoples it contained and by the accounts of its peculiarities of climate and terrain, and these new aspects of the New World—in the words of the French philosopher Louis LeRoy, "new lands, new seas, new formes of men, manners, lawes, and customes; new diseases and new remedies; new waies of the Heavens, and of the Ocean, never before found out"—fired their imaginations and turned their attention more and more away from the Mediterranean and toward the Atlantic. But no aspect of the New World probably operated so powerfully in this regard as did its immense space. "The discovery of [such] a boundless country," declared Montaigne in the late 1570s, was indeed "worth[y of] consideration."[5]

As the awareness of the seeming boundlessness of America penetrated more deeply into European consciousness, America, in the words of the Dutch historian Henri Baudet, became a place "onto which all identification and interpretation, all dissatisfaction and desire, all nostalgia and idealism seeking expression could be projected." "In observing America," Elliott has noted, Europe "was, in the first instance, observing itself." Throughout the Middle Ages, Europeans had posited the existence of a place—for a time to the east but mostly to the west of Europe—without the corruptions and disadvantages of the Old World. The discovery of America intensified this "nostalgia for the Golden Age and the Lost Paradise" and aroused new hope for their discovery somewhere on the western edge of the Atlantic.[6]

---

[4] See, especially, Edmundo O'Gorman, *The Invention of America: An Inquiry into the Historical Nature of the New World and the Meaning of Its History* (Bloomington, Ind., 1961), and Hugh Honour, *The European Vision of America* (Cleveland, 1975), 2.

[5] Louis LeRoy, *Of the Interchangeable Course, or Variety of Things in the Whole World* (London, 1594), 127, as quoted by Ryan, "Assimilating New Worlds," 523; *The Essays of Montaigne*, trans. George B. Ives (Cambridge, Mass., 1925), 1:171.

[6] Henri Baudet, *Paradise on Earth: Some Thoughts on European Images of Non-European Man* (New Haven, 1965), 55; Elliott, "Renaissance Europe and America," 20; Loren Baritz, "The Idea of the West," *American Historical Review* 46 (1961): 617–40; Durand Echeverria, *Mirage in the West: A History of the French Image of American Society to 1815* (Princeton, N.J., 1957), vii. See also Harry Levin, *The Myth of the Golden Age in the Renaissance* (Bloomington, Ind., 1969).

Remarkably soon after its discovery, in fact, America became the locus for a variety of "imaginary . . . utopian constructions." Indeed, the very term *Utopia* was invented by Sir Thomas More in 1515–16 in his famous tract of that name. Although most students of More and of the utopian tradition put little emphasis upon it, More located Utopia in the Atlantic and used as his central literary device the experienced traveler just returned from the "unknown nations and countries" of the New World. As these facts and a close reading of his text also make clear, More was obviously inspired in this effort by the as yet unknown potential of the immense New World. Specifically, the discovery of America—in all its vastness—suggested to More the heady possibility of finding a place where all the problems of a decadent Europe either had been resolved or had not yet been permitted to develop. Nor did this close association between America and the utopian tradition end with More. From More through Jonathan Swift and beyond, utopian writers continued to associate America with the dream of a perfect society and to locate their fairylands, their New Atlantis, their City of the Sun in some distant place in the vicinity of America.[7]

But it is important to emphasize that all of these early utopias looked backward to Europe's "own ideal past" rather than forward into some wholly novel world of the future: invariably, their authors turned their imaginary "new worlds into very old ones."[8] As we have learned from modern anthropologists, "knowledge of other cultures and eras [invariably] depends on the cultures and eras doing the knowing."[9] Thus, as William Brandon has recently argued, the depiction in reports from the New World of America—

---

[7] Echeverria, *Mirage in the West*, viii; Frank E. and Fritzie P. Manuel, *Utopian Thought in the Western World* (Cambridge, Mass., 1979), 113; Sir Thomas More, "Utopia," in Henry Morley, ed., *Ideal Commonwealths* (London, 1901), 4; Bertrand de Jouvenal, "Utopia for Practical Purposes," in Frank E. Manuel, ed., *Utopias and Utopian Thought* (Boston, 1966), 219–20; Slavin, "American Principle," 146–47; Levin, *Myth of the Golden Age*, 92–93; Paul A. Jorgenson, "Shakespeare's Brave New World," in Chiapelli, *First Images of America* 1:85–86; Brandon, *New Worlds for Old*, 8–11. J. H. Hexter, *More's Utopia: The Biography of an Idea* (Princeton, N.J., 1952), the most extensive and penetrating discussion of More's tract, makes no mention of its relationship to the discovery of America.

[8] Several scholars have pointed out that Europe's traditional fixation on its own past had been intensified at the time of the discovery and exploration of America by its simultaneous recovery and glorification of antiquity and have emphasized the extent to which their conceptions of the New World were shaped by their new knowledge of the ancient world. See Scammel, "New Worlds and Europe," 393–96; Elliott, *Old World and the New*, 15–16; and Ryan, "Assimilating New Worlds," 526–34. See also Elliott, "Renaissance Europe and America," 20.

[9] See James A. Boon, "Comparative De-enlightenment: Paradox and Limits in the History of Ethnology," *Daedalus* 109 (1980): 89.

in contrast to Europe, Africa, and Asia—"as a land of liberty, where the earth like the air belonged to all in common and where wealth, like the water of a river, was shared by all; where there were none of the lawsuits engendered by the words Thine and Mine," may very well eventually have served as a principal stimulus for the development in early modern European thought of the entirely new—and modern—Enlightenment conception of liberty as equality and masterlessness.[10]

Yet, conventional preconceptions seem initially to have prevented all but a handful of European commentators from recommending the alleged liberty of the American Indians as a condition to be pursued by Europeans. For that reason, it is certainly incorrect to suggest that the discovery of America immediately enabled the European "to picture himself as a free agent in the deep and radical sense of possessing unlimited possibilities in his own being, and as living in a world made by him in his own image and to his own measure." Nevertheless, with its large unexplored areas and its many unfamiliar groups of people and cultures, America did provide the European with powerful additional impetus for the exertion of the critical spirit of Renaissance humanism and for posing basic questions about his own society and its organization, values, and customs, and it is in this context that the utopian tradition in early modern Europe must be understood.[11]

That tradition consisted of several types of utopias ranging from pastoral arcadias to perfect commonwealths to millennial kingdoms of God. Whatever their form, however, they all betrayed "deep dissatisfaction" with contemporary Europe and were intended, in More's words, as "patterns . . . for correcting the errors of these [European] nations among whom we live." Having, before the discovery of America, expressed this dissatisfaction in their "longing for a return to . . . the lost Christian paradise, or to the Golden Age of the ancients," Europeans now exchanged this desire for "a world remote in time" for one distant in space. Arcadia, Eden, the New Jerusalem, or the scientifically advanced and dominated Bensalem created by Francis Bacon, now could be plausibly located in America. In their good order, just government, supportive society, peaceful abundance, and absence of greed, vice, and private property, these happy social constructions, situated by their authors in the New World, served as the antithesis of the Old.[12]

---

[10] Brandon, *New Worlds for Old*, 15, 143, 151, 165.

[11] O'Gorman, *Invention of America*, 129–30; Elliott, *Old World and the New*, 26; Ryan, "Assimilating New Worlds," 520–21; Slavin, "American Principle," 146–47.

[12] Howard Mumford Jones, *O Strange New World: American Culture, the Formative Years* (New York, 1964), 14–21, 35–36; Elliott, *Old World and the New*, 25–26, and "Renaissance Europe and America," 20; Slavin, "American Principle," 146–47; J. C. Davis, *Utopia and*

Although Europeans continued to locate their utopias in the unknown wilds of America, the dream of finding a perfect society somewhere in the physical spaces of America gradually lost force during the century from 1550 to 1650. As America and Americans came to be better known and as no such utopias were discovered, people realized that America, to the extent that it was known, was not an unalloyed paradise to be contrasted with a European hell. Scholars have written much about the fascination of European scholars with the exotic productions of America and in particular with the noble savages who inhabited it, and this interest should by no means be minimized. The tendency to glorify the Indians by depicting them as strong-limbed Greeks who, though pagan and simple, lived free with little labor and without regard for private property in a blissful state of nature was widespread. But it existed in an uneasy state of tension with a still stronger impulse to emphasize what appeared to Europeans to be overwhelming evidence of European cultural superiority. Very few Europeans, in fact, seem to have been capable of appreciating the integrity and quality of Indian culture or not to have viewed America from a Europocentric perspective, and from that perspective the Indians, for all their supposed simple felicity, were neither Christian nor civilized but pagan and primitive, at most the equivalents of Europe's own early "rude inhabitants" before their conversion to Christianity and acquisition of civilized manners. Along with the relative ease of the European conquest, this perspective only helped to confirm Europeans in a deep sense of superiority and in the belief that Europe, for all its social and political warts, was, in the words of the late sixteenth-century English publicist Samuel Purchas, "the sole home of 'Arts and Inventions.'"[13]

the Ideal Society: A Study of English Utopian Writing, 1516–1700 (Cambridge, 1981), 20–23; Levin, Myth of the Golden Age, xv; More, "Utopia," 6; Francis Bacon, "New Atlantis," in Morley, Ideal Commonwealths; Tommaso Campanella, "The City of the Sun," ibid.; Frank E. Manuel, "Toward a Psychological History of Utopias," in Manuel, Utopias and Utopian Thought, 70–80; Baudet, Paradise on Earth, 32.

[13] Elliott, Old World and the New, 13–15, 26–27, 103, and "Renaissance Europe and America," 20; Jones, O Strange New World, 14–20; Antonello Gerbi, "The Earliest Accounts of the New World," in Chiappelli, First Images of America 1:39; Baudet, Paradise on Earth, 31; Charles L. Sanford, The Quest for Paradise: Europe and the American Moral Imagination (Urbana, Ill., 1961), 75; Samuel Purchas, in Purchas His Pilgrimes, ed. Galsgo, 1:249, as cited by Scammell, "New Worlds and Europe," 409. See also Anthony Pagden, The Fall of Natural Man: The American Indian and the Origins of Comparative Ethnology (Cambridge, 1982); Olive Patricia Dickason, The Myth of the Savage and the Beginnings of French Colonialism in the Americas (Edmonton, Alberta, 1984); Henry S. Bausum, "Edenic Images of the Western World: A Reappraisal," South Atlantic Quarterly 47 (1968): 672–87; and the various essays in Edward Dudley and Maximillian E. Novak, eds., The Wild Man Within: An Image

Indeed, it was not only their contact with America that contributed to this sense of superiority. Developments within Europe were also important. In particular, the new science and technology associated with the scientific revolution—the growing use of the experimental method, the increased use of quantification and mathematics as a scientific tool, and a burgeoning interest in technology—led to scientific advances and technological achievements, especially in printing, warfare, and navigation, that seemed from a European point of view not only to put Europe miles ahead of even the most technologically advanced peoples encountered in America but also actually to serve as instruments for extending the "cultural and political influence of . . . Europe over all other parts of the globe." Although some of its leading exponents, Francis Bacon, Johann Valentin Andrae, and Tommaso Campanella, revealed through their utopian tracts an impatience with the rate of scientific discovery, the new achievements in science would, they confidently believed, ultimately lead to the betterment of mankind and the improvement of society.[14]

This urge for improvement was also manifest in a contemporary rage for projects and projecting that swept England, the Netherlands, and France beginning in the middle of the sixteenth century. Projects were schemes to introduce or improve old manufactures, crops, agricultural techniques, transportation, internal and external markets, and employment. These schemes were mostly designed with the intention of enriching their authors; but, taken together, they also acted, especially in England, to enrich society as a whole and to enhance the sense that material conditions and the quality of peoples' lives even at the lowest rungs of society were gradually getting

---

in Western Thought from the Renaissance to Romanticism (Pittsburgh, 1972).

On a related theme, Ronald L. Meek, *Social Science and the Ignoble Savage* (Cambridge, 1976), analyzes the relationship between the perception of American Indians as living examples of a primitive state of society and the emergence of both a new interest in "natural" man among natural law theorists such as Grotious, Hobbes, Puffendorf, and Locke and, among eighteenth-century French and Scottish theorists, a new theory of the progressive development of society from rudeness to refinement "through four more or less distinct and consecutive stages, each corresponding to a different mode of subsistence, these stages being defined as hunting, pasturage, agriculture, and commerce" (2). This four-stage theory, which held "that societies of the European type had normally *started out as and developed from* societies of the American type" (40), of course also contributed to reinforce what Fulvio Papi has called "the presumptuous conceit of European civilization that in itself was realized the [highest development of the] nature of man," (Papi, *Antropologia e Civita nel Pensiero de Giordano Bruno* [Firenze, 1968], 200, as quoted by Brandon, *New Worlds for Old*, 153).

[14] See, in this connection, Allen G. Debus, *Man and Nature in the Renaissance* (Cambridge, 1978), 1, 6–7, 116–21, 134–41; Charles Webster, *The Great Instauration: Science, Medicine, and Reform, 1626–1660* (New York, 1976), 1–31.

more ample, if not necessarily better. The simultaneous expansion of commercial activity had much the same effect by stimulating and then catering to new levels of demand that ultimately seem to have brought levels of material prosperity in western Europe considerably higher than they had been earlier or than they were then among any of the native peoples of America.[15]

If the new science, many successful projects, and the expansion of commerce enhanced Europe's sense of superiority over America after 1500, America itself came increasingly to be seen not simply as an exotic new land inhabited by primitives but as a place to be acted upon by Europeans, a place that was chiefly important for the new opportunities it provided for the mass conversion of souls to Christianity or, more commonly, for the acquisition of individual wealth. As America was "invested with the main chance," it was, increasingly "divested of magic." For the new European exploiters of America, the Indians came to seem far less like noble savages and far more like the devil's children. What had initially seemed to be a paradise turned out to be a desert or a wilderness "haunted by demonic beings," infested with poisonous snakes and plants and vicious alligators, and subject to terrifying hurricanes and other inimical acts of nature. Indeed, in the conventional iconography of the time the allegorical figure of America was usually represented with an alligator which, as Hugh Honour has pointed out, quickly "acquire[d] a derogatory significance, especially when set beside Europe with her bull, Asia with her camel, and Africa with her lion."[16]

But it was not only the people, animals, plants, and natural phenomena that were native to America that gave it an ill fame but also the behavior of the Europeans who went there. In *Utopia*, More had worried whether "this discovery [of America], which was thought would prove so much to" the "advantage [of the discoverers, might] . . . by their imprudence become an occasion of much mischief to them." And that seemed to be precisely what had happened as, unable to control their lust for riches, the Spaniards had

---

[15] On the rage for projects and its effects, see Joan Thirsk, *Economic Policy and Projects: The Development of a Consumer Society in Early Modern Europe* (Oxford, 1978). The expansion of trade and its effects may be followed in D. C. Coleman, *The Economy of England, 1450–1750* (Oxford, 1977), 48–68, 131–50, and B. A. Holderness, *Pre-Industrial England: Economy and Society, 1500–1750* (London, 1976), 116–70, 197–220. See also Ralph Davis, *The Rise of the Atlantic Economies* (Ithaca, N.Y., 1973), and Neil McKendrick and John Brewer, *The Birth of a Consumer Society: The Commercialization of Eighteenth-Century England* (Bloomington, Ind., 1982).

[16] Baritz, "Idea of the West," 633; Levin, *Myth of the Golden Age*, 61; Jones, *O Strange New World*, 39–40, 57–61; Mircea Eliade, "Paradise and Utopia: Mythical Geography and Eschatology," in Manuel, *Utopias and Utopian Thought*, 265–68; Honour, *European Vision of America*, 8; Elliott, *Old World and the New*, 80–81.

themselves turned savage in their wholesale exploitation and destruction of entire nations of Indian peoples. Not all the demons infesting America were American. Outside the bounds of traditional restraints, Europeans in America had permitted their most primitive instincts to triumph in their avid quest for individual gain, heedless of all civilized conventions and of all social and human costs. As this black legend of Spanish cruelty circulated widely through Europe during the late sixteenth century, America came more and more to be viewed as a place of cultural regress, for natives and immigrants alike, a place that was almost wholly barren of culture and that was important chiefly for the riches it yielded in such abundance for the benefit of a Europe that was the exclusive seat of civilized life.[17]

But riches were not the only thing that America exported to Europe during the sixteenth and seventeenth centuries. In his important and recently translated book *The Civilizing Process*, Norbert Elias has shown how, coincidental with the discovery and early exploration of America, Europeans were showing an ever-greater concern for civility, a concern, he argues, that over the next three hundred years actually resulted in Europe's becoming more civilized.[18] Elias does not consider the possibility that the discovery of America might have had a role in this process. By providing Europeans with concrete examples of what they were not and did not want to become, however, greater and more extensive contacts with the so-called primitive peoples of America and elsewhere outside of Europe seem to have required them to define more explicitly standards of what was and what was not civilized and thereby to have functioned as a powerful stimulus to this civilizing process. For Europeans continued to exhibit a powerful awareness that, whatever the extent of their vaunted cultural superiority over peoples elsewhere, they themselves often displayed, even within Europe itself, many of the same base and primitive characteristics that they attributed to Indians and to Europeans living in America. Thus, the new science, as Keith Thomas has shown in the case of England, coexisted with powerful undercurrents of belief in magic, witchcraft, astrology, and other forms of superstition.[19]

Perhaps more important, the new economic and religious conditions of the sixteenth and seventeenth centuries seemed to produce many unsettling

---

[17] More, "Utopia," 6; Elliott, *Old World and the New*, 94–95; Jones, *O Strange New World*, 40–41; Hodgen, *Early Anthropology*, 361; Slavin, "American Principle," 146–47; Michael Kraus, *The Atlantic Civilization: Eighteenth-Century Origins* (Ithaca, N.Y., 1949), 309; Brandon, *New Worlds for Old*, 44.

[18] Norbert Elias, *The Civilizing Process: The History of Manners* (New York, 1978).

[19] See Keith Thomas, *Religion and the Decline of Magic* (New York, 1971).

side effects. The expansion of trade, the penetration of the market, the pro-liferation of joint-stock companies and the projecting spirit, the emergence of new and expanding forms of consumerism, and, toward the end of the seventeenth century, the development of a money economy complete with new financial institutions like the Bank of England and a mounting national debt undermined the traditional foundations of authority and stimulated new and extensively manifest forms of self-interested and egocentric economic, social, and political behavior. At the same time, the religious ferment asso-ciated with the Reformation, including especially the proliferation of a be-wildering variety of sects and religious opinions, led to heightened religious discord, both civil and international war, and the shattering of the old uni-tary ecclesiastical order. In combination, these economic and religious de-velopments evoked widespread anxieties that the Old World was rapidly degenerating into a social and moral chaos.

Animated by these fears and nostalgic for the old order, a long line of social critics of radically different persuasions in England called, during the century and a half from 1575 to 1725, for a return to an older, more static, and more coherent social and religious order and to the traditional values of hierarchy, stewardship, virtue, simplicity, thrift, moderation, and piety. This almost ubiquitous yearning for order, this pervasive persistence of con-ventional habits of thought, vividly indicates just how disquieting English-men found the steady acceleration of the pace of economic, social, and reli-gious change that began under the Tudors and the extreme difficulty they had in discovering a vocabulary and patterns of perception appropriate to the changing conditions in which they lived. Although a few people, includ-ing John Locke, Bernard Mandeville, and several less well known liberal economic writers tried to work out a rationale for the new socioeconomic order, the logic of that new order was by and large obscured by nostalgia, and most social commentary from the Puritans through Filmer and Har-rington to Bolingbroke and Swift betrayed a profound "desire for the re-newal of old values and structures, the hope of a radical *renovatio*," a "great instauration," that would once again restore coherence to the world.[20]

---

[20] See, in this connection, David Bevington, *Tudor Drama and Politics: A Critical Approach to Topical Meaning* (Cambridge, Mass., 1968); W. H. Greenleaf, *Order, Empiricism, and Politics: Two Traditions of English Political Thought, 1500–1700* (Oxford, 1964); Webster, *Great Instauration*, 1–31; William M. Lamont, *Godly Rule: Politics and Religion, 1603–1660* (London, 1969); Gordon J. Schochet, *Patriarchalism in Political Thought: The Authoritarian Family and Political Speculation and Attitudes Especially in Seventeenth-Century England* (New York, 1975); James Daly, *Sir Robert Filmer and English Political Thought* (Toronto, 1979); C. B. McPherson, *The Political Theory of Possessive Individualism* (Oxford, 1962); Slavin, "American Principle," 152–59; Joyce Oldham Appleby, *Economic Thought and Ideology in*

Nor were such impulses peculiar to England. A "traditional culture, suspicious of change and oriented to a mythic past, whose members fulfilled themselves in relationship to a divine reality outside time," early modern Europe was "a world that still sought its future in the past" and found it extremely difficult to come to terms with novelty. All of the great seventeenth-century upheavals in the Netherlands, France, Spain, and Italy were, like the English Revolution of the 1640s and unlike the democratic revolutions at the end of the eighteenth century, "dominated, by the idea, not of progress, but of a return to a golden age in the past." Still holding to a theory of history that saw the past as either a providential design or a recurring cycle of advances and declines, they aspired to renovation, not innovation.[21]

Disappointed in their efforts to recapture the world they had lost in England, some men in the seventeenth century, like More a century earlier, turned to America as a place in which their objectives might be accomplished. In contrast to More, however, they thought in terms not of finding a preexistent utopia but of founding one in the relatively "empty" spaces of North America. Some Spaniards, the Jesuits with their theocratic *reducciones* in Paraguay and Vasco de Quiroga with his communal religious villages in Santa Fe in New Spain, were already by the early seventeenth century striving to fashion utopias among groups of Indian peoples in America.[22]

But it was North America, which had a far smaller and, in most places, considerably less settled aboriginal population than Hispanic America, that seemed to offer the unlimited and, even more important, the as yet unoccupied and unorganized space in which a new society, free from the imperfections and restraints of the old, might be created. In dramatic contrast to the "civilized and filled space[s]" they had encountered in the Levant and the Orient, North America presented itself to Europeans as an immense, sparsely populated, and bounteous territory that was "open for experimen-

Seventeenth-Century England (Princeton, N.J., 1978); Isaac Kramnick, *Bolingbroke and His Circle: The Politics of Nostalgia in the Age of Walpole* (Cambridge, Mass., 1968); Eliade, "Paradise and Utopia," 261; Davis, *Utopia and the Ideal Society*, 86.

[21] Ryan, "Assimilating New Worlds," 523; Hodgen, *Early Anthropology*, 114; J. H. Elliott, "Revolution and Continuity in Early Modern Europe," *Past and Present*, no. 42 (1969): 43; Webster, *Great Instauration*, 1–31; Baudet, *Paradise on Earth*, 37–38; Levin, *Myth of the Golden Age*, 139–67; Robert Forster and Jack P. Greene, eds., *Preconditions of Revolution in Early Modern Europe* (Baltimore, 1970).

[22] Magnus Mörner, *The Political and Economic Activities of the Jesuits in the La Plata Region: The Hapsburg Era* (Stockholm, 1953); Silvio Zavala, "The American Utopia of the Sixteenth Century," *Huntington Library Quarterly* 10 (1947): 337–47, and *Sir Thomas More in New Spain* (London, 1955). See also, Scammel, "New Worlds and Europe," 397–98; Baudet, *Paradise on Earth*, 37; Levin, *Myths of the Golden Age*, 93.

tation." With "neither a history nor any political forms at all," it invited people to consider how in an as yet unarticulated space Old World institutions and socioeconomic, religious, and political arrangements might be modified to produce the best possible commonwealths. "In the beginning all the World was America," John Locke wrote in his *Second Treatise of Government*, and this conception of America as an unformed and "free space," a place still without the corruptions and "trammels of the Old World" and waiting to be the site of Europe's new beginning, inspired English colonial organizers with the dream of creating through conscious instrumental human action and planning a New Jerusalem or a New Eden. If an existing paradise of the kind imagined by Sir Thomas More was not to be found in America, Englishmen now hoped to design and construct one in the wide open spaces of America.[23]

Shakespeare set out the formula by which this dream could be realized in 1611 in *The Tempest*, which was inspired by an actual wreck in Bermuda of an English ship bound for the new colony of Virginia. In that play, it will be recalled, Prospero, employing his superior European knowledge and skill, managed in little more than a decade to bring a civilized order out of the natural chaos of a virgin and only lightly occupied wilderness, in the process transforming it into "an idyllic land of ease, peace, and plenty." Beginning with the founding of Virginia in 1607, virtually every one of the new English colonies on the mainland and in the Caribbean was to some extent animated by the hope of equaling Prospero's accomplishment. Over the succeeding century and a half, Anglo–North America seemed to offer a fertile soil for a large number of attempts to realize European dreams for the recovery of its own ideal past in a new carefully constructed society.[24]

Those attempts differed radically from one place to another. Puritan leaders in Massachusetts Bay and Connecticut hoped to establish the New Jerusalem in which, with God's help and their own considerable exertions, they would re-create the true church and live in Godly communion with one another in the millenial kingdom of God on Earth.[25] Lord Baltimore in

[23] Echeverria, *Mirage in the West*, viii; Slavin, "American Principle," 139–49; John Locke, *Two Treatises of Government*, ed. Peter Laslett (New York, 1963), 343; Jorgenson, "Shakespeare's Brave New World," 85–86; Levin, *Myth of the Golden Age*, 61; Baudet, *Paradise on Earth*, 37.

[24] Leo Marx, *The Machine in the Garden: Technology and the Pastoral Ideal in America* (New York, 1964), 43–69; Levin, *Myth of the Golden Age*, 93, 190.

[25] Baritz, "Idea of the West," 634–37; Webster, *Great Instauration*, 44–45; Avihu Zakai, "Exile and Kingdom: Reformation, Separation, and the Millennial Quest in the Formation of Massachusetts and Its Relations with England, 1628–1660" (Ph.D. diss., Johns Hopkins University, 1982).

Maryland and the duke of York in New York hoped to establish the sort of well-ordered feudal societies that had not existed in England for at least a century and a half. James Harrington's semiutopian tract *Oceana* inspired the early plans for organizing the new colony of Carolina in the 1670s, and those plans, along with contemporary ones for New Jersey, were at least partly the work of Sir Anthony Ashley Cooper, first earl of Shaftesbury, and his secretary John Locke. William Penn undertook a carefully planned holy experiment in Pennsylvania and Delaware in the 1680s, and fifty years later, in the 1730s, a group of humanitarian reformers established the new colony of Georgia as a model of social benevolence.[26] Despite their variety, all of these enterprises, no less than More's *Utopia*, exhibited a strong desire for the establishment of an ordered world, "an idealized version of old England," that would be without the problems and the anxieties of the metropolitan society.[27]

Of course, all of these efforts were failures. Indeed, with the exception of the Puritan experiment in New England which managed to perpetuate itself through the better part of two generations, their failures were almost immediate. In colony after colony, men discovered, to paraphrase a familiar aphorism, that you could take Englishmen out of England but you could not take England out of Englishmen, who did not lose their vices in the new soil of America. Yet, as John Murrin has pointed out, the "real significance" of the Anglo-American utopias lies not in their predictable failures but in the fact "that they were tried at all." For over a century, the unorganized space of North America had encouraged "some Englishmen to try out in practice" a great variety of religious, social, economic, and political ideas that could never have been attempted in the organized world of England itself.[28]

Notwithstanding their inability to realize or to sustain the utopian goals of their founders, moreover, all of the colonies—within a few decades in the case of the early ones and usually even sooner with most of the newer ones—did exceptionally well, and their economic, demographic, and territorial growth became the wonder not just of England but of all Europe. So rapid was their growth that they came to be known, in contrast to Old England and continental Europe, as lands of abundance and opportunity in which

---

[26] See the discussion of these early British-American social experiments in John M. Murrin, "Colonial Political Development," in Jack P. Greene and J. R. Pole, eds., *Colonial Anglo-America, 1607–1763* (Baltimore, 1983), 417–24.

[27] Marx, *Machine in the Garden*, 62.

[28] Murrin, "Colonial Political Development," 424. See also Lyman Tower Sargent, "Utopianism in Colonial America," *History of Political Thought* 4 (1983): 483–522.

men could enjoy plenty, independence, and freedom from the persecutions, the want, and the humiliating constraints of the crowded and constricted world from which they had come.[29]

Despite their spectacular and much envied growth, however, the Anglo-American colonies continued right down to the American Revolution to represent something of a disappointment, a disappointment not merely in terms of their inability to achieve their original utopian aspirations but also in terms of their failure to live up to or to achieve the standards of civilized development represented by Europe itself. As the creations of Europeans, these new settler societies in Anglo-America, created in the image of their creators, were "peculiarly the artefact of Europe, as Asia, Africa, and aboriginal America were not." For Europeans as well as for their descendants in America, that image was, moreover, as I emphasized earlier, the only legitimate image. European culture, the Mexican historian Edmundo O'Gorman has correctly argued, was never conceived of as one among many cultures but as "the only truly significant culture; European history was universal history. Europe became history's paradigm, and the European way of life [, whatever its defects,] came to be regarded [again, by Europeans and Euro-Americans,] as the supreme" standard by which the European societies in America were to be judged.

No less than the original native cultures, the new European colonies "could not be recognized and respected" in their own terms but could only expect to be considered complete when they had succeeded in transforming themselves into "a replica of the 'old' world." In colonies and metropolis alike, the primary hope, the central aspiration, was not that the colonial societies would come to terms with their environments but that, in the manner of Prospero and, a century later, Robinson Crusoe, they would master and reorder those environments along European lines until, as a result of a series of incremental improvements, they had slowly moved from primitive simplicity to higher—and more European—levels of cultural development. Indeed, in this colonial context, the term *improvement* was virtually interchangeable with *European, English,* or *metropolitan.*[30]

---

[29] See Richard Hofstadter, *America at 1750: A Social Portrait* (New York, 1971), 3–32; Kraus, *Atlantic Civilization,* 216–62; Jack P. Greene, "The American Colonies during the First Half of the Eighteenth Century," *Reviews in American History* 1 (1973): 69–75; Echeverria, *Mirage in the West,* vii-viii.

[30] O'Gorman, *Invention of America,* 135–40; Elliott, *Old World and the New,* 5, 50–51; Baudel, *Paradise on Earth,* 45; A. Bartlett Giamatti, "Primitivism and the Process of Civility in Spenser's *Faerie Queene,*" in Chiapelli, *First Images of America* 1:72–74; Marx, *Machine in the Garden,* 43–69; O. Mannoni, *Prospero and Caliban: The Psychology of Colonization* (New York, 1956); James Sutherland, "The Author of *Robinson Crusoe,*" and Ian Watt, "*Rob-

Of this exalted standard, Britain's Anglo-American colonies, however rapid and vigorous their growth throughout the first seven decades of the eighteenth century, fell considerably short. Many people on the Continent, including Voltaire and Montesquieu, and many more in Britain, admired the colonies for their prosperity, freedom, and pastoral simplicity. But the crude, simple, undifferentiated, rural, and provincial nature of these societies, most of which were in large part built on the cruel exploitation of black people through an unremitting system of racial slavery, and the impoverished and derivative character of their artistic and intellectual life were so striking as to suggest to some commentators, the most prominent of whom were the comte de Buffon and the Abbé Corneille de Pauw, that conditions in America were so unfavorable to life as to cause a marked physical, mental, and moral degeneration among the creole (native) descendants of the Europeans. The same unfavorable comparisons of colonial America with metropolitan European cultures underlay both a strong popular prejudice against and condescension toward the colonies in the Old World and a palpable sense of inferiority and dependence among the colonists themselves.[31]

Thus, in America, no less than in England, did the constraining inheritance of the past operate powerfully to prevent people from coming to terms with the present. The sense of openness and opportunity that had excited the founders of the colonies was to a very great extent counteracted by a strong countervailing force: an inability—common to Europeans and Americans alike—to define the present except in terms of the past. In this situation, the Anglo-American colonies came increasingly to be thought of not as new societies that would fulfill dreams people had been unable to realize in Europe but as a field for ambition and a place of opportunity for individuals and as valuable adjuncts to the economic and strategic power of Britain.[32]

Although it can be argued that throughout much of the early modern era the vast unexplored and unorganized spaces of America were of enormous

---

inson Crusoe, Individualism and the Novel," in Frank H. Ellis, ed., *Twentieth Century Interpretations of Robinson Crusoe: A Collection of Critical Essays* (Englewood Cliffs, N.J., 1969), 25–54.

[31] Echeverria, *Mirage in the West*, 3, 6, 14–19; Jack P. Greene, "Search for Identity: An Interpretation of Selected Patterns of Social Response in Eighteenth-Century America," *Journal of Social History* 3 (1970): 189–220 [chap. 6 above]; Henry Steele Commager, *The Empire of Reason: How Europe Imagined and America Realized the Enlightenment* (New York, 1977), 126–27; Meyer, *Democratic Enlightenment*, xx-xxi.

[32] See Kraus, *Atlantic Civilization*, 41–43; Hodgen, *Early Anthropology*, 189; Elliott, *Old World and the New*, 1, 102.

significance in helping to excite and to sustain Europe's dreams of making a new beginning for mankind, it cannot be suggested that in the early eighteenth century America provided much immediate inspiration for the Enlightenment. Indeed, when Enlightenment philosophers wanted to point to an example of an enlightened society, they turned to England itself, not to England's American colonies or to any other part of America, which remained largely "peripheral to Europe's experience of itself." But this situation changed radically after Britain's long, drawn-out, and intense quarrel with its American colonies beginning in 1765 had first focused attention upon them and then driven them to revolt and independent nationhood. As these Anglo-Americans first defiantly stood up for their rights and then sought to transform themselves into an extensive new republic with a government created by themselves on enlightened principles, exponents of the Enlightenment both in Britain and on the Continent examined the state of Anglo-American society more thoroughly and found it to be a close approximation, in many ways, an almost perfect demonstration, of their dream of a new order "in which men would escape from poverty, injustice, and corruption and dwell together in universal" prosperity, virtue, "liberty, equality, and fraternity."

Having long been valued for the gold, silver, sugar, tobacco, and rice that it sent back to enrich the Old World, America, specifically British North America as it was reorganized into the new United States, now came to be celebrated because it seemed to represent an "immediate [and working] application of most of the controversial social and political ideas [then] under discussion in Europe." As such, America suddenly became "an example to the world," in the words of Turgot, "the hope of the human race," "living, heartening proof that men had a capacity for growth, that reason and humanity could become governing rather than merely critical principles," and that, in the manner of Plato's *Republic*, philosophers of the kind who produced the Declaration of Independence, the new republican state constitutions, and the Federal Constitution of 1787 could become governors. "Who could not experience a thrill of pleasure," exclaimed the marquis du Chastellux ecstatically, "in thinking that an area of more than a hundred thousand square leagues is now being peopled under the auspices of liberty and reason, by men who," free from the corrupting vices and luxuries of the Old World and from the restraints of the dead hand of the past, made "equality the principle of their conduct and [simple] agriculture the principle of their economy?"[33]

---

[33] Kraus, *Atlantic Civilization*, 220; Echeverria, *Mirage in the West*, 3, 35, 38; Commager,

As the United States came to be celebrated as a "laboratory for Enlightenment ideas" and the "workshop for liberty" by Europeans, it acquired the respect not only of the outside world but also of its own people. For virtually the entire existence of the British-American colonies, their inhabitants had measured themselves against metropolitan England and found themselves wanting. Now in view of their heroic achievements during the last quarter of the eighteenth century, they learned, to paraphrase a contemporary remark of Thomas Paine, that they had long thought better of the European world than it deserved. No longer did Europe seem to be the center of the world. Now, instead of Americans going to school to Europe, Europe was going to school to America. As Americans thus came more and more, again in Paine's language, "to reverence themselves," Europe became, at least in the short run, the same sort of negative reference for them that they had earlier been for Europe, while those features of their society for which they had traditionally been so apologetic—its simplicity, its newness, its rusticity, its innocence, its very size and openness—suddenly came to be perceived not as deficiencies but as virtues, positive advantages that gave America a special place in the creation of a new, enlightened order.

Some enthusiasts even revived the slumbering millennial hopes of the early Puritan settlers and once again touted America as the New Jerusalem and Americans as the chosen people. More common was the simple depiction of America as a seat of civic republicanism imbued with the values of frugality, moderation, industry, and simplicity, the national home of peace, prosperity, justice, equality, freedom, and statesmanship, an entity whose great Revolutionary heroes, exemplified in Charles Willson Peale's Gallery of Great Men in his museum in Philadelphia, showed that America— simple, undifferentiated America—was not merely a place of abundance and liberty but a scene for heroic actions, a theater of fame. Given the glorious events of the 1770s and 1780s, who among Peale's contemporaries could doubt his optimistic and expansive prediction that in the future the Pennsylvania State House, now Independence Hall, would be "a building . . . more interesting in the history of the world, than any of the celebrated fabrics of Greece or Rome!"[34]

Empire of Reason, 11–12; Gay, "Enlightenment," 36–37, 40–42; Honour, *European Vision of America*, 9–10; Ryan, "Assimilating New Worlds," 537.

[34] Gay, "Enlightenment," 42; Meyer, *Democratic Enlightenment*, vii; Jack P. Greene, "Paine, America, and the 'Modernization' of Political Consciousness," *Political Science Quarterly* 93 (1978): 73–92; Samuel Williams, *The Natural and Civil History of Vermont*, 2 vols. (Walpole, N.H., 1794), 2:310; Daniel J. Boorstin, "The Myth of an American Enlightenment," in *America and the Image of Europe: Reflections on American Thought* (New York, 1960), 19;

If America's accomplishments during the Revolutionary era and the new appreciation of its social state helped, at least temporarily, to liberate it from its own sense of dependence and cultural inferiority, they also played a key role in enabling the whole Western world to free itself from the burden of the past by contributing to a transformation in social and political consciouness that was every bit as fundamental and far-reaching as that produced in the religious sphere by the Reformation of the sixteenth and seventeenth centuries. As a result of this transformation, people came to be not only receptive but eager for change, to be oriented toward the present and future rather than the past, to be confident of the efficacy of human reason operating on—and generalizing from—experience to shape that present and future, and to be committed to the revolutionary hopes that the world might be changed for the better, that man might be liberated from the tyranny of his ancient prejudices, that what had formerly been perceived as manifest disorder in the autonomous behavior of free people might actually comprise the basis for a new kind of order, and that criteria for membership in the political nation should be universalistic rather than prescriptively narrow. Henceforth, instead of searching for utopia in a remote corner of the world, instead of endeavoring to re-create some past golden age, men would create a wholly new world in the future—a world in which the inadequacies of past and present worlds would, as seemingly had already occurred in North America, at last be overcome.[35]

That America had had a significant role in this important transformation has been the central thesis of this essay. Initially, in the sixteenth and seventeenth centuries, America had served as a place on which people in the Old World could project their hopes for recovering a lost world that had been simpler, better ordered, more benign, and more virtuous. Eventually, British North America, reconstituted as the United States, became a concrete example that encouraged people to project their hopes for a better world into the future. No matter that the new American republic had to some degree deceived the Old World, that, to a major extent, the liberty, prosperity, and expansiveness

Commager, *Empire of Reason*, 63–65; James West Davidson, *The Logic of Millennial Thought: Eighteenth-Century New England* (New Haven, 1977), 213–97; Edgar P. Richardson, Brooke Hindle, and Lillian B. Miller, *Charles Willson Peale and His World* (New York, 1982), 60, 92, 183.

[35] Echeverria, *Mirage in the West*, 151–52; Elisabeth Hansot, *Perfection and Progress: Two Modes of Utopian Thought* (Cambridge, Mass., 1974), 95; Jouvenal, "Utopia for Practical Purposes," 220; Eliade, "Paradise and Utopia," 262–68.

it provided for so many of its free inhabitants had been and for another seventy-five years would continue to be purchased at the cost of keeping a large part of its population in chains, that American culture continued to be in so many respects crude, provincial, and derivative, or that Americans themselves turned out to be more devoted to the pursuit of material self-interest than to the cultivation of that republican virtue they had appeared to epitomize at various points during their Revolution. By seeming to provide a harbinger of the future progress to which mankind could aspire, America in the late eighteenth century had helped Europe finally to transcend its ancient obsession with the past and had nourished on both sides of the Atlantic the confident and widely diffused expectation that the future would become mankind's most valuable inheritance.

This chapter was originally written for delivery as a lecture on Nov. 16, 1982 at the National Portrait Gallery in Washington, D.C., in conjunction with the gallery's exhibit Charles Willson Peale and His World and was entitled "The Future as Inheritance: The Revolutionary World of Charles Willson Peale." Subsequent drafts were presented as lectures at Tulane University on Mar. 17, 1986; the Winston Churchill Historical Society, Churchill College, Cambridge, on May 9, 1986; the annual meeting of the Association Française d'Etudes Américaines in Paris, Oct. 3, 1986; the Department of English, University of Oporto in Oporto, Portugal, Jan. 23, 1987; a program to commemorate the 250th anniversary of the birth of Thomas Paine at the University of Minho in Braga, Portugal, on Jan. 26, 1987; and the Aston Magna Outreach Academy in Moorhead and Park Rapids, Minn., on Mar. 28 and 29, 1987. The present version was given on Mar. 12, 1987, at the National Defense University, Fort Lesley J. McNair, Washington, D.C., as part of the United States Army Lecture Series on the Bicentennial of the Constitution organized by the Center of Military History and again at the Department of American Studies, Nanzan University in Nagoya, Japan, on July 10, 1987. It is reprinted here with permission and minor corrections from John W. Elsberg, ed., *Papers on the Constitution* (Washington, D.C.: Center of Military History, Department of the Army, 1990), 73–94.

Index

Demographic development (*cont.*)
79; of South Carolina, 73, 85,
94–95
Denmark, 4
De Pauw, Abbé Corneille de, 363
Dependence, personal: as negative
cultural imperative, 188–90,
263–64; as social condition, 8,
11; definition of, 254; desire to
escape as motive for migration
to South Carolina, 101
Dependence on Britain, 174–80; effects of slavery upon, 60–61; effects of, on character of white
Barbadians, 60–61; of Barbados, 49–50, 60–63
Dependents: definition of, 254; desire
for among backcountry settlers,
192–93; excluded from franchise, 246–56; in Barbados, 31;
possession of, definition of independence, 264
DeSaussure, Henry William, 279,
280, 281
Deterrents to American Revolution,
305
Developmental expectations of backcountry settlers, 193
Developmental model, intellectual
sources of, 9–10
Dickinson, John, 61, 63, 168, 296,
320, 323, 332
Diet in Barbados, 19
Diggins, John P., 213
Disease environment. *See* Health conditions
Disenfranchised, categories of the,
248–50
Disenfranchisement, logic of,
250–59
Dissenters: excluded from franchise
in some colonies, 249; in South
Carolina, 94
Distinctions, natural, American belief
in, 239–40
Diversity, social, among colonies,
294–96, 331–32

Dominica, 17, 69
Douglas, David, 123
Douglas, James, sixteenth earl of
Morton, 295
Douglass, William, 131, 156
Drayton, John, 85–86
Drayton, William Henry, 270, 272,
273, 334
Drax, James, 21
Duane, James, 320
Duke, Henry, 46
Dunlop, William, 93
Dunn, Richard S., 71, 74
Dutch, 242; in New York, 293

Earthquake in New England in
1755, 154
Ease of life in South Carolina, 95–96
Eastern states as regional concept in
Revolutionary America, 332,
337
East Florida, 69, 115, 333
Ebenezer, Ga., 122, 128, 129
Economic development: of Barbados,
38, 44, 50, 77–78; of Georgia,
121–22, 138, 140; of Jamaica,
79–80; of Leeward Islands, 78–
79; of South Carolina, 74–75,
81–82, 94
Ecumene as type of cultural space, 6
Edict of Nantes, 105
Education: in Barbados, 52–53; his-
tory of early American, viii
Edwards, Jonathan, 219
Elias, Norbert, 9, 357
Elites: authority of, 200–201, 207;
fear of social revolt among, 197;
in Barbados, 31–34, 71; in Ja-
maica, 80–81
Elitism, as cultural imperative,
165–68
Elliott, J. H., 350
Ellis, Henry, 132, 135, 136, 139
Empowerment, 263–64
England, 4, 20, 31, 84, 95, 100,
160, 339, 355; as social model
for colonies, 159–71; gentry of

MARIA GREY
LIBRARY
W. L. I. H. E.

WITHDRAWN

30 0132306 7